DATE DUE

NATIONAL DEVELOPMENT AND THE WORLD SYSTEM

THE AUTHORS

John Boli-Bennett, *Stanford University*
Christopher Chase-Dunn, *Johns Hopkins University*
Jacques Delacroix, *Stanford University*
Yilmaz Esmer, *Boğaziçi University, Istanbul*
Jeanne Gobalet, *Stanford University*
Michael T. Hannan, *Stanford University*
John W. Meyer, *Stanford University*
François Nielsen, *University of Chicago*
Francisco O. Ramirez, *San Francisco State University*
Richard Rubinson, *Johns Hopkins University*
George Thomas, *Stanford University*
Jane Weiss, *University of Iowa*

NATIONAL DEVELOPMENT AND THE WORLD SYSTEM
Educational, Economic, and Political Change, 1950–1970

Edited by
JOHN W. MEYER
and
MICHAEL T. HANNAN

THE UNIVERSITY OF CHICAGO PRESS
Chicago and London

THE UNIVERSITY OF CHICAGO PRESS, CHICAGO 60637
THE UNIVERSITY OF CHICAGO PRESS, LTD., LONDON
© 1979 by The University of Chicago
All rights reserved. Published 1979
Printed in the United States of America
83 82 81 80 79   5 4 3 2 1

JOHN W. MEYER is professor of sociology, and
MICHAEL T. HANNAN is associate professor of sociology,
both at Stanford University.

Library of Congress Cataloging in Publication Data
        Main entry under title:

National development and the world system.

    Bibliography: p.
    Includes index.
    1. Education—Economic aspects. 2. Education
and state. I. Meyer, John W. II. Hannan,
Michael T.
LC65.N37   309.1′045   78-26986
ISBN 0-226-52136-2

Contents

Preface

In 1970 we began to meet with a small group of graduate students to try to do some quantitative studies in what might be called, broadly, macrosociology. The work group has functioned more or less continuously since; several generations of graduate students have cycled through and have left their mark on the project. This book reports on the work we have done.

The final product reflects only dimly our original interests and concerns. Meyer began with an interest in the effects of national political authority on the shape of educational enrollment pyramids. Hannan was intrigued with the idea of applying structural equation methods and ideas from ecology to the study of changes in national structures. However, the project took on a life of its own and moved in directions that we had not planned initially. Its evolution was influenced by a variety of factors. These include (1) rapid advancement of sophistication in macrosociology and in quantitative methods within sociology more generally; (2) the diverse interests each individual brought to the project; (3) increasing availability and accuracy of data on many nations; and (4) the flow of research findings within the project that challenged our intuition.

The main consequence of this evolution was a progressive broadening of the scope of the book. We began with rather specialized interests, perhaps developed with the tacit assumption that researchers with greater stature and resources were "minding the store"—using comparative data to test the main lines of argument in our field. We reluctantly came to the conclusion that this was not so. Time after time we would ask our students to track down the relevant comparative studies on fundamental issues, for example on the major cultural, structural, and political effects on economic development, and would learn that no genuinely longitudinal comparative studies had been done. If broad comparisons with quantitative data were to be made, perhaps we would have to do it. So with excessive public confidence and private uncertainity (not to say fear); we began to take on the broader task. Our problem became not the detailed investigation of a few narrow issues, but a general longitudinal assessment of the reciprocal effects of central features of social, political, cultural, and economic organization of nations.

As we discuss in chapter 1, even this problem broadened as the years passed. It has become clear to us and to many other comparative researchers that the evolution of national societies depends critically on the world system in which they are embedded, and which itself evolves. Sharp-eyed readers will no doubt detect differences in emphasis on such factors in the chapters that reflect different epochs of our project. Were we to begin afresh, we would have sought more systematically to link development at the national level with changes in the structure of the world system. Nonetheless, we believe that we have taken important first steps in the quantitative study of such coupled change processes.

The social organization of our project was somewhat unusual. Our student collaborators did not simply help us carry out a previously designed project. We compiled a common data base and made a commitment to use a common research design to study broad features of change in national societies. Students often worked on projects we had begun. But most of them also struck out in their own directions. A number of the chapters of this book began as dissertations and have been shaped by subsequent theory and research. As is clearly indicated in the authorship of chapters, much of our joint work represents the creative contributions of our student collaborators. We have not attempted to reconcile the many divergent orientations that have motivated sections of the work. We believe that this diversity, controlled to some extent by the common data and design, is an important feature of the project and of the book. It suggests something of the range of sociological ideas that may be applied to macrosocial change and of the feasibility of implementing such ideas in a concrete design.

We received help and encouragement from a number of sources. In addition to those students whose work is collected here, James Roth and Jean Tuttle Warren conducted dissertation research that helped shape the early development of the project. We also wish to acknowledge the encouragement of our more senior colleagues, both at Stanford and elsewhere. This encouragement came despite their concern that the available data would not support the type of enterprise we undertook.

Their reservations reflected several widely held views. First, accuracy of national data was widely suspect. More precisely, everyone knew of at least a few cases in which official statistics were completely misleading. We hoped that such errors (many of which have been corrected since the prevailing attitudes were formed), which loom large to students of a particular society, would have less impact on studies that use the full range of cross-national variation. In some measure this had earlier turned out to be the case in quantitative studies of data on individuals and organizations, about which similar doubts had been initially expressed. The second reservation concerned the prospect that properties of national social structure might turn out to be so highly correlated (perhaps around a "development factor") that analyses of separate effects would be impossible. A third and related doubt was that change in major features of national social structure might be so glacial that we would have no intertemporal variation with which to test effects. Finally, they recognized that data were not available for many cases in certain periods and for certain variables. But we learned that the machinery of international data collection and reporting had been operating long enough and well enough that these problems did not overwhelm our attempts. Clearly, we obtained enough measured variation over time and over nations to estimate and test a wide variety of hypotheses.

The major financial support for the project was a grant from the National Science Foundation (GS-32065). We also received support from a variety of other sources. These include two small grants from Stanford's Center for Research in International Studies, a seed-money grant from the Office of Education (OEC-9-71-0033), a small grant from the Spencer Foundation, and funds from the Department of Sociology at Stanford for faculty research. Some of the methodological work was supported by a grant from the National Institute of Education (NIE-G-76-0082). Finally, during the period that this book was organized in its final form, Hannan was a fellow at the Center for Advanced Study in the Behavioral Sciences and was supported by National Science Foundation Grant BNS76-22943.

In addition to the work included in this book, we intended to include two additional chapters, but publication costs made this impossible. Interested readers may wish to consult them. A general review of our data as they bear on the description of international equality and inequality can be found in John W. Meyer, John Boli-Bennett, and Christopher Chase-Dunn, "Convergence and Divergence in Development," *Annual Review of Sociology,* 1 (1975): 223–46. And a study of the effects of the international system on income inequality within countries appears in Richard Rubinson, "The World-Economy and the Distribution of Income within States," *American Sociological Review*, 41 (1976): 638–59. Other studies from our project are referred to throughout the book.

Some of the material in this book is taken or adapted from papers previously published. We thank the following journals for their permission to republish copyrighted material:

Chapter 3 is slightly adapted from "The World Educational Revolution, 1950–1970," *Sociology of Education,* 50 (1977): 242–58.

Chapter 4 appeared originally in the *American Sociological Review,* 42 (1977): 479–90.

Chapter 8 is adapted from "The Effects of International Economic Dependence on Development and Inequality: A Cross-National Study," *American Sociological Review,* 40 (1975): 720–38.

Chapter 9 appeared originally in the *American Sociological Review,* 42 (1977): 795–808.

Chapter 10 is a revision of "The Permeability of Information Boundaries and Economic Growth": A Cross-National Study, *Studies in Comparative International Development* 12 (Spring 1977):3–28.

Chapter 12 is a revised version of a paper by Richard Rubinson, "Dependence, Government Revenue, and Economic Growth, 1955–1970," *Studies in Comparative International Development* 12 (Summer 1977): pp. 3–28.

Finally, we wish to acknowledge our indebtedness to the many agencies that publish comparative data on nations, particularly the Inter-University Consortium for Political and Social Research.

John W. Meyer and Michael T. Hannan

I INTRODUCTION

ONE · National Development in a Changing World System: An Overview

John W. Meyer and Michael T. Hannan

The modern world is dominated by the social changes which generate the rationalized and technical division of labor, the powerful bureaucratic nation-state, and the world culture of educated individual choice and responsibility. These worldwide institutions define enormous inequalities, both internal to societies and between them.

Explaining all this has been a major enterprise of the social sciences which themselves arise as part of the larger process. The great theoretical ideas of these disciplines arose as casual interpretations of modernization. Squadrons of conservative and radical economists created theories of the evolutionary explosive power of technological innovation and liberated market forces, and saw such forces as the engines of the other changes. Partly in reaction, other social scientists emphasized the causal power of particular patterns of culture—once religious ideas, but now more commonly education and mass communications. Still other social scientists see the rise of rationalized political systems and political competition as central forces.

Almost all these ideas have a common frame: there are entities called societies in which the hypothesized forces operate. Societies are internally interdependent systems, such that the transformation of one subsystem leads to the transformation of all the others. True, external factors operate at the boundaries of each society, generating market pressures, political threats and opportunities, and social and technical innovations. But once these factors impinge on a society, the main consequences occur through the internal structural processes that maintain the coherence of the society as a bounded system.

Leave for later the defects of this perspective, which clearly takes too seriously as distinct units the national political states that are created and become dominant as a *product* of the history of modern development. Consider, rather, the evidentiary history of the core issues of the theory of social and economic development.

What do we know about the effect of the culture and norms of rational individualism—the Protestant ethic or the modern educational system—on economic development? Weber's account was based mainly on argument, with a good many examples of entrepreneurial sentiment and ac-

3

tivity in which Protestantism may have played a role, and with comparative observations on a few historical societies which varied in the availability of an appropriate ideology, but which may or may not have been comparable on other relevant variables. The literature since Weber has nibbled on his thesis, arguing about particular instances, mostly at the individual or subgroup level, and only infrequently examining the development of societies. The literature on the effects of education has similarly dealt primarily with evidence on the behavior of educated individuals, particularly the observation that they commonly receive higher incomes than others. Studies of these kinds do not address the question of overall institutional effects.

Similarly, what do we know about the independent impact of expanded markets and complex technologies on the economic or social development of societies? Following the original economists, we mostly assume the causal relationships involved and examine case histories with an eye to illustrating theory rather than testing it. We observe associations between developed economies, expanded states and rationalized cultural systems and assume that economic factors must play a role.

This brings us to the main thing we do know in comparative macrosociology. We know that in comparing many societies the dimensions of social and economic "development" are highly interrelated. Richer societies have more elaborate institutional structures, more extended states and political participation, more "modern" cultures and individuals, and greatly expanded educational systems. Societies fall, by and large, on an evolutionary scale. What the engines of "progress" on this scale are, we do not know. We have the treasured theories which, when assembled, argue that everything causes everything else. Particular causal variables have devotees, but little evidentiary status.

How does this situation arise? Essentially out of a series of methodological difficulties. Very little research employs a research design that is appropriate to the questions formulated in the grand macrosociological theories. These theories consist of assertions of the effects of societal or system-level variables on changes in certain features of social, political, or economic organization. Thus appropriate research designs must provide variations over time in societal characteristics for one or more societies. We discuss the design and analysis issues in more detail in chapter 2. However, it is worth noting here the main tendencies of the designs that have been employed.

Most of the studies that purport to speak to the issues or that are interpreted as speaking to the issues are at the individual or subgroup level.[1] They examine relationships among individuals *within* one or more societies (prominent examples include Almond and Verba 1963; Inkeles and Smith 1974). But the difficulties in making inferences from such designs to macrosociological relationships are well known (see Hannan 1971). Are Protestants more likely to act like capitalists? We have a long debate on the question (see, for instance, Samuelsson 1961). Whatever the outcome of this debate, it bears only indirectly on the larger question. Weber's argument concerned the impact of one institutional system on another. His argument could be correct even if Protestants are unlikely to behave like capitalists. It could be wrong even if every Puritan behaves entrepreneurially.

Similarly, even if educated persons earn more income, we cannot conclude that societies with higher levels of education have higher aggregate products (see the papers in Blaug 1968, 1969 for an argument to this effect, and Hannan 1976 for a counterargument). Nor can we conclude, as did Jencks et al. (1972), that because quality of schooling has slight effect on earnings, the structure of educational opportunity has no effect on the *distribution* of income in society.

Most of the relevant quantitative research that incorporates institutional variation is cross-sectional. Prominent examples are Lipset (1960) and Harbison and Myers (1964). The problems here are also well known. As long as the causal structure is not well understood, cross-sectional analysis cannot tell us if education causes economic growth, say, or economic growth causes high levels of educational expansion, or both (unless we are willing to make very strong and usually implausible assumptions).

The available longitudinal studies of institutional phenomena typically study one society over time or compare a few societies. Prominent examples are Bendix (1956), Moore (1966), and Smelser (1959). Most often, we observe independent and dependent variables changing together over time. In the absence of careful multivariate analysis, it is difficult to convincingly isolate causes and effects. There are, however, several important examples of multivariate time series analysis of such institutional variations: Kuznets (1971) and Tilly and his collaborators (Snyder and Tilly 1972).

We are aware of no large-scale attempts to apply panel analysis to the issues in question. The panel design incorporates both variation between nations and variation over time for each nation. This feature of the design enables one to utilize a broad range of institutional variation (obtained by using many nations) to model institutional change. Moreover, this design (as we discuss in chap. 2) provides estimates of the existence of causal effects that are under most usual conditions more dependable than those produced by either cross-sectional or time series analysis. It is not that there is any "free lunch" associated with the use of panel analysis in the sense that strong causal inferences are produced without strong assumptions. Rather, the assumptions required for valid inference concerning the existence of causal effects in a panel model are more realistic and plausible in this research context than are those required for the same inference in either a cross-sectional or time series design.

THE MOTIVATION OF THE PRESENT STUDIES

We set out as a research group in 1970 to address directly and empirically some of the major issues raised by theories of national social development. We believed at the time that the main justification for the gap between comparative research and macrosociological theory, the lack of adequate data on many societies over time, no longer held. While it is still true that research of this sort is plagued by data problems—what research is not?—the main international data-gathering agencies and other research organizations have built up longer and longer time series on most nations and have invested heavily in refining earlier series, thus avoiding recognized errors in the collecting of later data. The studies in this book are built on the premise that it is time to investigate what these data, defective though they may be, can tell us with respect to the main ideas of our field. Throughout, with few exceptions, we formulate and estimate panel models for these data. It is in fact the application of this design to institutional analysis that most distinguishes this research from other social science research on the issues.

Such a direct assault on the major issues in the theory of social development brings great costs, a contemplation of which has led others to employ data which are more limited, but much more indirectly related to the main theoretical issues.

Most of these difficulties have to do with measurement. The panel design places severe constraints on the data that can be used. For the most part, we must use available measures which are often less than ideally linked to underlying theoretical concepts. This problem is discussed in chapters in which it is salient. However, we have not relied on existing data sources alone. Rather, we have devised and measured variables that have not been used previously, e.g., features of national constitutions (chap. 13), information load of exported products (chap. 9), ubiquity of a nation's exchange network (chap. 10), various measures of economic dependence recoded from existing data (chap. 8), number of cabinet posts (many chapters), and national control of educational systems (chap. 5). In fact, within the constraints imposed by the design (that data be available over time for many nations) we have made a large investment in constructing measures of large-scale social and political organization. We have no doubt that these measures can and will be improved on. We hope that this research suggests some ways in which the existing data and widely available primary sources (e.g., constitutions and national yearbooks) can be used to construct other measures of social and political structure.

It is widely believed that the available data contain considerable error. Our investigations suggested that this is a problem, but no more so than in sociological research on within-nation processes. Both our discussions with statisticians at UNESCO and ILO and our own methodological research (chap. 7; Hannan, Rubinson, and Warren 1974; Rubinson 1974) indicate that measurement error is not so strong in these data as to completely obscure causal effects.

Inevitably, our research is mainly restricted to the post–World War II period in which systematic data on many societies became available. This period is unique in many ways, and findings which apply to it may be of limited generalizability. As time goes on and data files accumulate, more and better data covering more time periods will make possible much more complete analyses.

Given the limited number of national societies in the world, we cannot attend to every possibility that the causal processes involved in national development are completely different in different types of societies—an idea which is the stock-in-trade of case-study researchers. We can look for overall effects, or for differential effects in only a few, grossly defined, subgroups of national societies. For instance, we try to discover if the factors affecting economic development differ in rich and poor nations (chaps. 6 and 7).

Our attempt to make direct tests of prevailing macrosociological ideas, then, required a tolerance for ambiguity and error which other researchers might consider foolhardy. We approached the task with the view that rational angels will acquire more reasonable fears about where to tread only if fools experiment. It also seemed clear that the retreat to more trustworthy data and safer analyses which characterizes much comparative research is often also a retreat from some of the most obvious and important intellectual issues of the field.

THEORETICAL PERSPECTIVES

We began our research with agreement on one theoretical issue and disagreement on another. We shared the view that social structural variables have origins and consequences at the aggregate level that are distinct from their individual-level causes and effects. We differed in our view of the central aspects of social structures: some of us (we came to call it the institutional view) saw these as operating as rules or social realities, while others (we called it the ecological view) saw them as organized networks of actual social relations and exchange. In order to illustrate these two general views of social structure, and to contrast both with styles of social structural reasoning which emphasize more the properties of individuals, we consider below the variety of explanations available for the causal effects of increases in the scale of formal educational systems on national productivity. We classify these into three general categories.

Aggregate Individual Approaches

The most common intellectual strategy is to propose that the national-level effects of education occur via a two-step process. First, education is thought to change the individuals who experience it. Two types of intraindividual change are often identified: learning of specific skills (e.g., literacy) and socialization to modern standards and rules (e.g., bureaucratic norms). Such changes presumably affect individual productivity upon entry into the labor force. So literate individuals, as well as those having modern Western time orientations, become more productive.

The second step in the explanation involves aggregation. As education increases the stock of more productive individuals (i.e., those with the appropriate learning and socialization) and as these individuals enter the labor force, there is an increment in productivity as they replace less productive workers.

The general form of such explanations, that Stinchcombe (1968) termed "demographic," is to argue that aggregate outcomes reflect the changing composition of populations on relevant characteristics. In a very gross sense, demographic explanation may prove profitable for the analyses we conduct. If the assertions at the individual level are accurate, it is reasonably likely that a qualitatively similar relationship will hold at the national level. But it is not at all certain. It is not difficult to imagine circumstances in which increasing the stock of more productive individuals does not foster productivity gains (e.g., if an attempted shift away from traditional agriculture toward more industrial activity results in the production of goods that are not competitive in the world market). Productivity might also increase through mechanisms having nothing to do with the knowledge or socialization of individuals (e.g., a technical change or a change in world prices).

If it is established that the process stipulated at the individual level is true, then demographic explanations for any observed aggregate relationship involving the same variables cannot be dismissed out of hand. On the other hand, it is entirely plausible (as we shall argue below and in chap. 6) that increases in education will generate aggregate productivity gains even if there is no relationship between education and productivity at the individual level. If we are interested in explaining changes that occur in national societies, demographic or aggregative individual approaches can serve as only very tentative substitutes for theories that take characteristics of national societies explicitly into account. We shared, in our research, a commitment to do this, but there are a number of different possible lines of approach.

Institutional Approaches

The creation and expansion of educational systems may activate modern norms and values within a society both among those who experience education and those who do not. For example, Meyer (1977) has argued that the existence of national educational systems serves to legitimate both the status and the actions of modernizing elites. It also makes possible the dissemination through the population of distinctly modern purposes such as industrial development. In other words, in the competition of values and rules, the creation and expansion of formal educational systems alters the competition in favor of certain more modern symbolic elements.

The difference between the institutional perspective and an aggregative individual approach stressing socialization of modern norms crystallizes around the population presumably affected. From a socialization perspective, only those exposed to the socializing institutions ought to be affected, while from an institutional view the creation of status of "educated person" or "college graduate" may alter the views of many persons with little or no schooling. The referent is to *the normative structure of a nation* rather than to the norms of individuals. The institutional view adds the premise that a change in normative structure imposes constraints on action for broad classes of actors in systems.

By focusing on normative structure, an institutional perspective abstracts out one particular feature of social organization. This view is organizational. The organization studied is *symbolic* and *normative*. Production is socially organized activity. As such it is doubtless subject to the same kind of normative constraints as in other collective action.

Ecological Approaches

Ecological explanation emphasizes the organizational, environmental, and technological constraints on collective action. The central theme concerns the adaptation of human populations to social and nonsocial environments through collective organization. The environment together with technology poses a set of constraints on collective action that greatly limit feasible alternatives. Among the great diversity of cultural and organizational responses available to human populations, those types of social organization optimally adapted to these constraints survive disproportionately.

Like institutional analysis, ecology concentrates on collective action, i.e., on social organization. However, the constraints identified are *material*, *interactional*, and *relational* rather than normative and symbolic. In other words, an ecological account of adaptation features the role of the material environment and the material aspects of technology along with competition, conflict, and exchange among human populations.

From an ecological perspective, modern educational systems are primarily organizations. As organizations, they accumulate certain valuable resources and alter the distribution of resources in the system. The expansion of an educational system introduces new or expanded elements into the organizational network underlying social systems. Such alterations in the distribution of resources and in organizational networks may affect system productivity. For example, a shift toward industrial production appears to require the subordination of local markets in labor (and other inputs to production) to highly rationalized national systems. If so, any social organizational change promoting the rise of national labor markets (at reasonable cost) will increase productivity. Machlup (1970) has suggested that the expansion of modern forms of schooling has precisely this consequence. By granting credentials to students, educational systems identify those individuals capable of functioning at or above some minimal level in a bureaucratic setting (and perhaps rank individuals in terms of some other abilities). Insofar as these credentials are employed by purchasers of labor, search time for labor is reduced. Further, the extensiveness of the system of education allows efficient allocation of labor throughout an economy. As a consequence, overall productivity ought to rise.

Notice that the argument does not require that anyone learn anything in school. The process is organizational. If, however, individuals do learn productive skills in school, the organizational process will augment or amplify the productivity gains deriving from the aggregate individual process.

This sort of argument is ecological in that it refers to the organizational adjustment of a system to technological and environment (market) demands and constraints. Optimal adjustment promotes system functioning.

Theory in Relation to Data

We had great hopes that our research would enable us to find data differentially supporting ecological or institutional views of macrosocial structure. In this we were disappointed, for the most part; findings which could be interpreted in one way could also be interpreted in the other. We were mostly unable to find evidence with which to convince each other. The different lines of thought are exemplified, however, at several points in the chapters that follow. For instance, chapters 3 and 4 take intellectually contrasting views of the expansion of modern educational systems. In chapter 3 education is seen as a massive institutional classification system in society, while in chapter 4 it is seen as an implemented organizational structure. The views do not conflict very clearly: more important, the data do not really enable us to distinguish between them. Similarly, chapters 9 and 10 take a more ecological view of economic development than does chapter 6. But it is difficult to see that the evidence presented can distinguish between the perspectives.

Similarly, our theoretical commitment to the aggregate level of analysis in contrast to individual or subgroup levels, while exemplified in the studies reported here, is neither strongly supported nor rejected by our empirical findings. Most of these can be interpreted as reflecting processes occurring at the aggregate level, but most of them could also be accounted for by more microsociological ideas.

Because of the absence of previous comparative empirical work in these areas, and because of the limitations imposed by available measures, the theoretical issues which *are* confronted in the studies in this book are more specific in character than the general ones noted above. The studies below examine 1950–70 data relating to some of the specific hypotheses commonly found in comparative theories (whatever their abstract theoretical grounding) about the processes of national development:

1 Do economic development, state power, national independence, and political participation affect the expansion of national educational systems? Chapters 3, 4, and 5 examine the hypothesis that they do.
2 What other institutions affect national economic development? Chapters 6, 7, and 12 explore the hypothesis that such development is affected by educational expansion, the power of the state, and political and social modernization.
3 Do economic and educational growth affect the expansion of the power of the state in society? And do they affect the form of the state? Chapters 11 and 12 present data on these questions.
4 Chapter 14 examines the effects of economic development and state power on the status of women in society.

We have pursued these issues as far as we can, limited by (*a*) the poverty of available measures, (*b*) the limited numbers of countries in the world, and even more limited numbers of countries for which data are available, and (*c*) the short time since World War II for which such data are available.

But as our research progressed, we became increasingly aware of limits on our intellectual perspective, an awareness which shifted the forms of our research as time passed.

Second Thoughts
The intellectual tradition emphasizes the treatment of societies as real units of analysis. So did our basic research design, which involved analyses of changes over time in measures on these societies as units. This is clearly naive. The economies, states, and cultural systems of almost all national societies are historical creatures of the European political economy (e.g., all of the Americas, almost all of Africa). Further, the cur-

rent evolution of most national societies is greatly affected by the economic, political, and cultural events which occur entirely outside their
boundaries. Economic developments in Africa, the Near East, or Latin
America are clearly resultants, for better or for worse, of dominant
world markets and technologies. Similarly, political events in such areas
(e.g., the Nigerian civil war, the creation of an independent Angola)
are also creations of the world system. Modern states, economies, and
cultural systems are obviously ongoing constructions of worldwide processes—affected by internal processes, true, but also by external ones.
We cannot treat as independent units the nation-state entities imposed
on the societies of the world over the last century or two. Our awareness
of these issues was greatly sharpened by the recent work of Wallerstein
(1974a) and Tilly (1975) and their collaborators. Both scholars have
made us more aware of the impact of events in the wider world system
on the structures of particular national societies and states.

How are we to study the impact of the wider world system? The most
immediate step is to look for the impact *internal* to societies of the variable which most clearly captures their differentiated relation to the wider
system: dependence. Some national societies are clearly more dependent
on the wider context than others and are caught in roles which continue
dependence relationships. Available theories argue that this dependence
creates great limitations (and in some theories, opportunities) for their
development. The studies in this book investigate such questions in
detail:

5 Does national dependence lower and restrict economic development,
   independent of other factors (chaps. 8, 9, and 10)?
6 Does national dependence weaken the power of the state in society
   (chaps. 11 and 12)?
7 Does national dependence restrict educational expansion (chap. 3)?

The issue of the effects of dependence merely introduces the study of
the structure of the larger world system. Countries are not only affected
by their dependence or dominance in this system. Clearly, the economy,
political system, and culture of the world system penetrate all societies,
structuring their internal institutions in response. As we consider such
issues, our basic research design loses its force. Simple panel analyses
of the relationships among features of national societies provide no information on larger system processes affecting *all* subunits. Inasmuch as
all national societies are reactive or reflective entities responding to the
evolving wider system, all may be expected to change over time in many
similar ways. Properties of national units are acquired by the diffusion
of the structures of the wider system. This takes us in the direction, not
of causal comparative analysis (for we really have but one case evolving
over time), but toward historical description and time series analysis
(see Meyer, Boli-Bennett, and Chase-Dunn 1975). Chapter 13, and to

some extent chapter 3, follows this path and shifts away from the design underlying the other studies. Here the attempt is to describe features of the whole system: the evolution of its dominant political forms (chap. 13 on state structure) and the spread of its (relatively standardized) educational system (chap. 3). These topics take us beyond the structure of our research and ultimately suggest quite different research designs.

Theoretical Papers
The burden of developing and presenting empirical analysis of a great many of the most obvious issues of substantive comparative sociology limits our ability, in the empirical studies below, to develop some of the lines of theoretical speculation which seem to us relevant for the future. Several theoretical papers in the last section of the book take on this task unrestricted by much empirical information.

Chapter 15 formulates an ecological theory of the effects of the increasing connectedness of the world economy on the construction and defense of social boundaries, i.e., emerging and continuing ethnic and national solidarities as they are created by the wider system.

Chapter 16 reviews the emerging literature on the evolution of the modern world system over the last few centuries, attempting a description of some relevant properties, not of individual national subunits, but of the system as a whole, and defining some of the ways in which these properties are thought to be interrelated.

And chapter 17, in reviewing and summarizing our work, considers the nature of the modern world system and the processes that maintain its structure or are changing it. This chapter attempts to address two larger questions. What forces (economic and—the more difficult question—noneconomic) have produced the recent wave of rather homogeneous social structural modernization around the world? And what changes in and reactions to these forces can we foresee?

AN OVERVIEW OF OUR FINDINGS AND CONCLUSIONS
The research reported in the studies that follow leads us to the following tentative conclusions about national and world development during the 1950–70 period:
1 The explosive expansion of national systems of education proceeds very rapidly in all sorts of societies during the 1950–70 period (chaps. 3 and 4; Meyer, Boli-Bennett, and Chase-Dunn 1975). Educational expansion may at one time have been highly contingent on political structure. However, we find little evidence for such effects. Even the effects of economic growth are smaller than might have been expected (chaps. 3 and 4). To some extent, the growth of educational systems appears to proceed of its own momentum. However, while the push toward expansion may be universal, success in expanding education

in any society is constrained by history and by features of educational organizational structure (chap. 4). Educational growth occurs very much under the aegis of states, and strong states exercise tight control over the operation of education (chap. 5). But the engines that create this growth appear to lie outside the properties of particular countries and to reflect exigencies of global social organization whose logic and purposes are built into almost all states.

2 Nation-states tend to be organized around modern economic purposes, and economic growth occurs almost everywhere (chap. 6; Meyer, Boli-Bennett, and Chase-Dunn 1975). The expansion of formal systems of primary and secondary education tends to increase economic growth rates, though the expansion of university systems does not (chap. 6). However, many measures of political and social modernization appear not to affect economic growth during this period (chap. 6). Perhaps this is because rationalized orientations and economic growth are built into market structures and into the structure and purposes of the state organizations which have become the dominant organizations in virtually all societies. In any event, the power of the state to organize and control action in the society aids in economic growth (chaps. 6, 7, and 12), especially in less developed nations (chap. 7).

It may be that economic growth rates are high for most nations because of the rapid growth and articulation of a world economic system. But national growth is affected by status and position *within* this system. Nations that are dependent grow less rapidly than others (chaps. 8 and 10). However, we find no evidence for the view that position in the world division of labor, in terms of the nature of the products produced (raw materials versus processed goods), affects economic growth (chap. 9).

3 States tend to expand their power and authority within society in all types of countries through the modern period (chaps. 12 and 13; see also Meyer, Boli-Bennett, and Chase-Dunn 1975). Their capacity to do this is affected by economic development and educational expansion, but is limited by dependence on other nations (chap. 12).

The rapid expansion in the power of states, and the externally imposed extension of the state system to almost all societies in the world, generates a situation in which state dominance often takes the form of unitary (or one-party) states in some measure freed from internal societal controls (chap. 11). Perhaps as a result, political participation may rise, but it is organized more by states and less by the diverse interests built into society. Thus formal democracy does not expand, and both political participation and democracy are, during our period, affected less by economic development and educational expansion than they are by the state organization and dominance.

4 The modern economic system generates great inequalities within societies, but also generates strong nation-states which tend to lower
inequality (chaps. 14 and 15; see also Rubinson 1976). Strong states
tend to eliminate primordial inequalities in the interest of rules of
citizenship (chaps. 13 and 14; but see chap. 15).

5 The world as a whole shows increasing structural *similarities of form*
among societies without, however, showing increasing *equalities of
outcomes* among societies. A pattern of expanded states, urbanization, industrialization, and educational systems is widespread (chaps.
3–7, 11–14; Meyer, Boli-Bennett and Chase-Dunn 1975). But the
stratification processes of the world system generate forces which keep
international inequalities at very high levels (chaps. 8, 10, and 12).
The world as a whole seems to look like a society of raw unregulated
capitalism. Great growth, great cultural homogeneity, and great inequality are dominant features.

Overall, we are impressed with the extent to which strong state organization has succeeded in this period. The strengthening of the world
market economy has altered the balance of power within states between
political centers and other organizations, institutions, and regions. For
many reasons, the shift of economic activity and decision-making to a
world-wide level has increased the likelihood that strong state structures
will emerge victorious in political competition. These strong state centers attempt to manage relations between nations, and as this system
of relations expands in scope and importance, these political centers
gain greater power and autonomy within societies. The actions that such
states typically undertake, including the expansion of education, the
expansion of citizenship, elimination of some primordial identities, and
the management and planning of production, seem to aid economic
growth during this period.

On the other hand, the system of strong states seems to contain few
mechanisms for controlling the unequalizing forces of the capitalist
world system. And, the very success of central state organizations may
create the conditions for successful resistance to state power. Increasingly, such resistance appears to activate agencies in other nations or
in the world system itself to limit the ability of states to control certain
segments of the population or certain types of activity. For example,
ethnic or nationalist movements rely increasingly on the support of other
states and the UN in their conflict with the state that controls them.

The picture that emerges from this research may be quite specific to
a period of great economic expansion and extension of markets. The
forms of state structure and state action that we see appear to be quite
specialized to such expansion. A period of sustained world-wide economic contraction, or a long-term stabilization, might alter the picture
considerably. Moreover, continued expansion of a capitalist world sys-

tem whose actors are states controlled by mostly "socialist" one-party regimes may recapitulate the fate of capitalism within nations. That is, a larger set of political organizations might emerge, controlling exchanges between states, and regulating and eliminating competition and some inequalities.

NOTES

[1]Giving microsociological relationships research priority is sometimes even made a methodological canon of comparative research (Przeworski and Teune 1970).

TWO · Issues in Panel Analysis of National Development: A Methodological Overview

Michael T. Hannan

PERSPECTIVES ON PANEL ANALYSIS

Though sociologists have employed panel designs for some time, there is little agreement about the formulation and estimation of panel models. In part this lack of agreement reflects the varied purposes that sociologists bring to panel analysis. Our motivations for choosing this design were sketched in the previous chapter. The purpose of this chapter is to outline the class of models and estimators we use and our reasons for using them. To place our research in a broader methodological context, I contrast our procedures with certain widely used alternatives.

As we discussed in the previous chapter, our goal is to study the effects of various institutional sectors on each other. The literature on national development suggests that effects may run in all directions—that is, that feedback effects occur more often than not. For simplicity I treat the case where there are only two variables of concern, X and Y. We might think of school enrollments and national production, or national production and economic dependence, etc. Suppose further that the variables are measured at only two points in time, t_0 and t. Then the operative question is how to model the causal relations among the four variables, X_0, X_t, Y_0, and Y_t.

Suppose we had the ability to experiment. We would hold X_0 constant (through either randomization or nonvariation), introduce variation in Y_0, and observe the consequences for X_t. In another experiment we would similarly vary X_0 and observe consequences for Y_t. In each case we would examine the impacts of variation in one lagged variable on changes in the other variable. The nonexperimental model that we and most other social scientists use is a simple analogue to this pair of experiments. We write a two-equation system in which variation in each outcome variable at time t is a linear function of its initial level and of the initial level of the other variable:

$$Y_t = \alpha_0 + \alpha_1 Y_0 + \alpha_2 X_0 + u, \tag{1}$$
$$X_t = \beta_0 + \beta_1 X_0 + \beta_2 Y_0 + v. \tag{2}$$

For shorthand, I refer to the model in equations (1) and (2) as the *basic model*.

17

Each equation states that the outcome depends on the pair of causally predetermined variables and on a disturbance that we assume is uncorrelated with the right-hand-side variables (but see below). Our interest focuses on α_2 and β_2. These parameters indicate the degree to which variations in one variable affect another, holding constant initial levels. If $\alpha_2 = 0$, we conclude that X does not affect Y over time; and if $\beta_2 = 0$, we conclude that Y does not affect X over time.

But this is just the usual structural equation or causal modeling perspective. The pair of equations, (1) and (2), embody assumptions both about the nature of the process and about the behavior of disturbing factors (summarized in u and v). Quality of inferences about the causal relations obviously depends on the accuracy of both types of assumptions. There is no magic in panel analysis. Nor is there a special theory of statistical inference for panel analyses. Once the model is formalized in a set of structural equations, the methods used are identical to those used for structural equation models generally.

This perspective differs from that which informs much social-scientific work on panel analysis. It is more common to propose specialized methods for panel inference. Most of this work follows the tradition begun by Lazarsfeld (see Lazarsfeld, Pasonella, and Rosenberg 1972), which poses the methodological problem as follows. Given that X and Y are correlated, construct measures of effect that permit one to conclude that X causes Y *or* Y causes X (but not both). Lazarsfeld and his students constructed indices (for sixteenfold tables) that seek to answer this question.[1] This approach has been generalized to quantitative analysis in the form of cross-lagged correlation (see Campbell and Stanley 1963; Pelz and Andrews 1964; Kenny 1973).

Undoubtedly there are some situations in which X causes Y but not vice versa. But, in general, "Does X cause Y *or* Y cause X?" is not the right question. As we argued in the previous chapter, for many macrosociological questions it is reasonable to begin with the assumption that X causes Y *and* Y causes X. This issue is not merely rhetorical. Attempting to choose either X *or* Y as the causal variable leads to testing procedures that are far from optimal when both variables have effects.[2] Thus we eschew this approach to panel analysis.

So we work squarely in the structural equation tradition. We presume familiarity with the logic and procedures of this approach at the level of Duncan (1975). In several cases, we use more advanced methods. They are noted below and discussed in the chapters in which they arise. The remainder of this chapter is devoted to a consideration of alternative specifications of the relations among X_0, Y_0, X_t, *and* Y_t, and to various methodological issues that arise in our work. The purpose of this discussion is to place our work in a broader methodological context, to note limitations on our findings, and to suggest ways in which future researchers can improve on our work.

WHY NOT USE CHANGE SCORES?

In discussing our work with other sociologists we are often asked why we do not relate *changes* in X to *changes* in Y, and vice versa. Addressing this question leads to consideration of issues that clarify the interpretation of estimates of the parameters of the model in equations (1) and (2). It will facilitate exposition to consider separately using change scores as dependent variables and using them as causal variables. To keep the algebra simple we will consider only the Y-equation.

The first model we consider relates changes in Y over the period of observation to the initial levels of X and a disturbance w:

$$\triangle Y_t = Y_t - Y_0 = \alpha_0' + \alpha_2' X_0 + w. \tag{3}$$

But the model in equation (3) is just the special case of equation (1) where $\alpha_1 = 1$. So two things can happen. The restriction that $\alpha_1 = 1$ may be correct, in which case estimation of equation (1) will give approximately that result. Then it does not matter whether one estimates equation (1) or (3). On the other hand, the restriction may be incorrect. In that case estimation of the change score model usually gives biased estimates of the effect of X_0 on Y_t. To see this, note that by subtracting Y_0 from each side of equation (3) we obtain

$$Y_t - Y_0 = \alpha_0 + \alpha_1 Y_0 + \alpha_2 X_0 + u - Y_0,$$
or

$$\triangle Y_t = \alpha_0 + \alpha_2 X_0 + q, \tag{4}$$
where

$$q = (\alpha_1 - 1)Y_0 + u.$$

Equation (4) has exactly the same form as the change score model except that the disturbance q contains Y_0. If X and Y are causally related over time, it will almost always be the case that they will be correlated cross-sectionally. If so, the disturbance q is correlated with X_0, and least-squares estimates of equation (4) will be biased. The bias is zero only when the constraint is true, i.e., $\alpha_1 = 1$. The model in equation (1) avoids such bias.

What about changes in X over the period of observation? As long as the two-equation model in equations (1) and (2) is appropriate, both X and Y will change over the study period. In an experiment we can study one process at a time. Lacking such controls, we cannot presume that X, say, is fixed at X_0 over the period we observe. To do so leads to an obvious inconsistency when we shift attention to the X_t equation.

That is, if equation (2) models change in X over the period (t_0, t), we cannot maintain that X is constant in the equation for Y_t.

From the perspective of causal analysis the real issue is whether changes in X over the study period affect Y_t (holding Y_0 and X_0 constant). This important question has far-reaching implications, as we shall see below. We can place the methodological problem in clear focus by writing a model that incorporates the effects of changes in each variable:

$$Y_t = \gamma_0 + \gamma_1 Y_0 + \gamma_2 X_0 + \gamma_3 (X_t - X_0) + u', \tag{5}$$
$$X_t = \delta_1 + \delta_1 X_0 + \delta_2 Y_0 + \delta_3 (Y_t - Y_0) + v'. \tag{6}$$

For the moment we presume that the model in equations (5) and (6) is the true model. Note that the original model in equations (1) and (2) is a special case of this model with $\gamma_3 = 0$ and $\delta_3 = 0$.

It turns out to be more convenient to rewrite the model as follows:

$$Y_t = \gamma_0 + \gamma_1 Y_0 + \gamma_2' X_0 + \gamma_3 X_t + u', \tag{7}$$
$$X_t = \delta_0 + \delta_1 X_0 + \delta_2' Y_0 + \delta_3 Y_t + v', \tag{8}$$
where

$$\gamma_2' = \gamma_2 - \gamma_3, \delta'_2 = \delta_2 - \delta_3.$$

This new model has an obvious advantage over the basic model; it permits causal effects over lag periods shorter than (t_0, t). But it introduces a new methodological problem. While the original model was recursive, the model in equations (7) and (8) contains simultaneous causation. Both X_t and Y_t appear as both independent and dependent variables in a pair of equations. So we have lost an important type of simplicity. More important, the model in equations (7) and (8) is not identifiable (to use the language of econometrics). Its parameters cannot be uniquely estimated from any data set.

The literature on simultaneous equations estimation commonly advises two procedures for repairing underidentified models (see Johnston 1971, esp. chap. 12). One can use theory or prior research to place constraints on the parameters of the model. Unfortunately we cannot avail ourselves of this strategy as we lack such theory and evidence. The second alternative involves the use of instrumental variables. The model in equations (7) and (8) can be identified by finding a pair of variables that are uncorrelated with u' and v' such that one of them affects Y_t but not X_t directly and the other affects X_t but not Y_t. Inserting these variables into estimators will resolve the indeterminacy of the model. But again we find ourselves blocked by the lack of prior theory. As the literature argues that almost everything affects everything else, it is hard to argue authoritatively a priori that some variables behave as instruments (that is, they affect only some of the variables in the model).

In the long run, the resolution of the problem under discussion will likely involve these sorts of strategies. Our assessment was that the field was not sufficiently well developed for us to rely on theory and prior research for the strong assumptions that must be used to motivate the simultaneous equations methods. Thus we decided to settle for simpler methods.

Our situation is as follows. We propose to use the model in equations (1) and (2) to draw inferences about institutional and structural change in nations. However, we realize that this model is not completely general and that strong arguments can be made for the superiority of the model in equations (7) and (8). So we must defend the choice of the basic model over the more complex alternative. I just argued that the more complex model cannot be uniquely estimated as it stands. But that is not a justification for the simpler model. Are there any general arguments that favor the model in equations (1) and (2)? I will advance three.

One line of argument claims that changes during the study period do not have effects; that is, the basic model is correct. This amounts to arguing that all the causal effects have a lag at least as long as twenty years. But, it is easy to show that if the lags are longer than twenty years we will not observe systematic effects with this model. Therefore, this position requires that one know exactly the structure of the lags in the effects. This sort of reasoning motivated Heise's (1970) treatment of panel analysis.

This position has some appeal. Some social scientists argue that twenty years is too short a period over which to observe interinstitutional effects. Readers who take this view will not be troubled by our neglect of effects with lags shorter than twenty years. However, we observe that some institutions, notably political structures, change literally overnight. Such changes can have strong and almost immediate effects on other institutions. So we cannot always rest assured that twenty years is a conservatively short period that rules out effects of shorter lag.

We find another aspect of this position disturbing. It presumes that the process operates over discrete time intervals. In formal terms the model implied is a difference equation with a twenty-year lag. I prefer the view that adjustments to institutional changes are continuous in time and not specialized to any particular causal lag. What happens if we model the process in this fashion, that is, as a continuous time process? Our general argument presumes that changes in X and Y depend on the levels of both variables. The simplest continuous time model that is consistent with this argument is the linear system

$$\frac{dY(t)}{dt} = a_0 + a_1 Y(t) + a_2 X(t), \tag{9}$$

$$\frac{dX(t)}{dt} = b_0 + b_1 X(t) + b_2 Y(t). \tag{10}$$

But the differential equations (9) and (10) cannot be estimated directly. Instead we solve the system subject to appropriate initial conditions (see Coleman 1968). The solution to this system has exactly the same form as our basic model, equations (1) and (2). That is, it is a two-equation model in which X_t depends linearly on X_0 and Y_0, and Y_t depends linearly on Y_0 and X_0. The parameters of the panel model can thus be considered as nonlinear functions of the parameters of the differential equation model (see Coleman 1968; Doreian and Hummon 1976; Hannan and Freeman 1978).

This relationship may surprise readers trained in classical panel-analysis traditions. It shows that the basic model is less restrictive than conventional treatments imply. Despite the fact that it ignores effects of $\triangle X_t$ and $\triangle Y_t$, it turns out to be an implication of a model in which X and Y adjust *continuously* to levels of X and Y during the entire period. For details, see Kaufman (1976).

The linear system in equations (9) and (10) can be shown to be a reasonably good approximation to a variety of more complex change models. This seems a good argument in favor of the model in equations (1) and (2). However, we cannot assert that the basic model is *the* correct model for panel analysis. Other, more complex differential equation models will give rise to different panel specifications. Nonetheless, it is comforting to learn that the basic model has more general value than is commonly acknowledged in discussions of panel analysis.

Both these arguments have a "best case" flavor. That is, they depend on nature's working in the interests of valid inference. But, what happens if the more complex model is correct? More concretely, what are the consequences of estimating the basic model when $\triangle X_t$ and $\triangle Y_t$ have causal effects?[3] If the qualitative implications of the basic model hold over plausible ranges of the parameters of the model with change effects (eqs. [7] and [8]), this argues strongly in favor of the basic model. If, on the other hand, results from the basic model change radically with alterations in parameters of equations (7) and (8), we must proceed cautiously. In particular, we must identify those ranges of parameter values over which inferences from the basic model have some validity, and restrict our attention to empirical contexts that meet the conditions.

The first two arguments treat the basic model as a structural model in its own right. But in the present discussion, it must be considered as the *reduced form* of the model in equations (7) and (8). That is, we reconceptualize the basic model as an algebraic rearrangement of equations (7) and (8). It is obtained by solving equations (7) and (8) for Y_t and X_t:

$$Y_t = C^{-1}[(\gamma_0 + \gamma_1 \delta_0) + (\gamma_1 + \gamma_3 \delta'_2) Y_0 + (\gamma'_2 + \gamma_3 \delta_1)X_0 + (\gamma_3 v' + u')], \tag{11}$$

$$X_t = C^{-1}[(\delta_0 + \delta_1\gamma_0) + (\delta_1 + \delta_3\gamma'_2)X_0 + \delta'_2 + \delta_3\gamma_1)Y_0$$
$$+ (\delta_3u' + v')], \tag{12}$$

where

$$C = 1 - \gamma_3\delta_3.$$

Equations (11) and (12) provide a new interpretation of the coefficients of the basic model in terms of the parameters of the change model.

Recall that the change effects model is not identified. Thus one cannot use reduced-form coefficients to obtain unique estimates of the α's and β's. But as long as u' and v' are well behaved (i.e., uncorrelated with X_0 and Y_0), we can always obtain good estimates of reduced-form coefficients. That is why we investigate the usefulness of the reduced form for informing us about causal relations holding under the more complex model.

In using the basic model, we report estimates of α_2 as the effect of X_0 on Y_t and β_2 as the effect of Y_0 on X_t. We confine attention to the former as treatment of the two cases is completely parallel. According to equation (11),

$$\alpha_2 = C^{-1}(\gamma'_2 + \gamma_3\delta_1). \tag{13}$$

Thus we investigate whether the quantity in equation (13) is a reasonable measure of the effect of X on Y over time.

The quantity in parentheses in equation (13) is familiar to structural equation analysts. It is the sum of a direct effect and an indirect effect. The direct effect, γ'_2, is the so-called cross-lag effect. The indirect effect, $\gamma_3\delta_1$, is the effect of X_0 on Y_t via X_t. Thus the reduced-form effects summarize both direct and indirect effects. The total effect of X_0 (the sum of the direct and indirect effects) is multiplied by C^{-1}. This multiplier adjusts the total effect for the cycle of causation implied by the model. According to the model, any increment in X_t produces a change in Y_t, which in turn affects X_t, etc. So effects of X_0 are propagated over an infinite cycle of causal loops joining X_t and Y_t. The multiplier is the appropriate rescaling of the effects of X_0. Thus to understand the reduced-form coefficients we must consider both the total effects and the multiplier.

Since the model is underidentified, we cannot conduct an exhaustive analysis. The reader can always choose some combination of γ's and δ's that will cause trouble. However, it is informative to consider a series of special cases.

CASE 1 *X has no effect on Y_t: $\gamma_2 = 0$, $\gamma_3 = 0$.*
Clearly $\alpha_2 = 0$ for this case. This result, though obvious, is important.

It tells us that when X has no effect, we will not mistakenly identify effects of Y or $\triangle Y_t$ on X_t as effects of X on Y.

CASE 2 X_0 *affects* Y_t *but* $\triangle X_t$ *does not:* $\gamma_2 > 0$, $\gamma_3 = 0$.
Again the result is simple: $\alpha_2 = \gamma_2$, the cross-lag effect of X_0 in the structural form. This holds even when $\triangle Y_t$ has an effect on X_t.

Now we consider more troublesome cases. Throughout we assume that the autoregression δ_1 is positive, since this is the case in our empirical work. Without loss of generality, we assume that the effect of X_0, γ_2, is positive as well. In the general case, the multiplier, C^{-1}, can take on any value. Until further notice we assume that C^{-1} is also positive.

CASE 3 X_0 *and* $\triangle X_t$ *have the same sign effects:* $\gamma_2 > 0$, $\gamma_3 > 0$.
In this case the reduced form contains both a direct and an indirect effect. Since for the moment we assume a positive multiplier, the sign of the reduced-form effect is the same as that of

$$\gamma'_2 + \gamma_3\delta_1 = \gamma_2 + \gamma_3(\delta_1 - 1). \tag{14}$$

If both $\gamma_2 > 0$ and $\gamma_3 > 0$, the quantity in equation (14) is positive when

$$\delta_1 > 1 - \frac{\gamma_2}{\gamma_3}. \tag{15}$$

We will consider three cases. When the lagged effects and change effects are equal, i.e., $\gamma_2 = \gamma_3$, the requirement for the quantity in equation (15) to be positive is $\delta_1 > 0$. This amounts to requiring negative feedback in the process generating the X_t. I mentioned earlier that we do not find this problematic in our research.

Similarly, when $\gamma_2 > \gamma_3$, the criterion is that δ_1 exceed some negative quantity, $(1 - K)$, where K is the ratio of γ_2 to γ_3. So neither is this case problematic.

Finally, there is the case in which the change term effect exceeds the lagged effect: $\gamma_3 > \gamma_2$. The criterion for the reduced-form effect to be positive, that δ_1 exceed $1 - K$, is now potentially problematic. Since $\gamma_3 > \gamma_2$, $0 \leq K \leq 1$. Thus δ_1 must exceed some positive quantity. For example, if γ_3 is twice γ_2, then we require that $\delta_1 > 1/2$. So we will run into trouble when γ_3 is much larger than γ_2 and the autoregression of X is small. Such cases do not seem likely in our research as the autoregressions are rarely small. Nonetheless, we must recognize that the effect of X_0 in the reduced form will have opposite sign from the effects of S_0 and $\triangle X_t$ in the structural form (but see below).

So in all but exceptional circumstances, we expect that the sign of α_2 will agree with those of the relevant structural parameters. However, quantitative estimates of the effect of X_0 will be wrong for two reasons. Using the reduced form gives X_0 credit for the causal effects of $\triangle X_t$.

This is a mistake as far as inferences about X_0 are concerned. But it is not wrong as regards the effect of X considered globally. We attach no special significance to the 1950 levels of variables. We have chosen the time points out of design convenience. So it does not upset me in this stage of inquiry to confuse effects of $\triangle X_t$ with those of X_0. The second reason why the quantitative estimates of α_2 differ from the structural parameters involves the multiplier. We delay discussion of this issue.

CASE 4 *The system is close to equilibrium: X_0 and $\triangle X_t$ have the same effect as do Y_0 and $\triangle Y_t$; $\gamma_2 = \gamma_3$; $\delta_2 = \delta_3$.*
When systems are close to equilibrium, the effects of (small) changes are close to the effects of initial levels. In this special case,

$$\alpha_1 = \gamma_1 C^{*-1},$$
$$\alpha_2 = \gamma_2 \delta_1 C^{*-1},$$
$$\beta_1 = \delta_1 C^{*-1},$$
$$\beta_2 = \delta_2 \gamma_1 C^{*-1},$$

where

$$C^* = 1 - \gamma_3 \delta_3 = 1 - \gamma_2 \delta_2.$$

Notice that $\gamma_2 = \alpha_2/\beta_1$ and $\delta_2 = \beta_2/\alpha_1$.

If, as is often the case in our research, the reduced-form autoregressions β_1 and α_1 are close to unity, the reduced-form cross-effects are close to the structural-form cross-effects.

CASE 5 *X_0 and X_t have opposite sign effects: $\gamma_2 > 0$, $\gamma_3 < 0$.*
Here we find real problems, as well we should. If lagged effects are positive and change effects are negative, any attempt to come up with an overall effect of X will mislead. The relevant expression is again expression (15). The autoregression coefficient in the X_t equation, δ_1, again plays a central role in determining the sign of the reduced-form effect. If $\delta_1 < 1$, then (15) is positive and the reduced-form effect has the same sign as the structural effect of X_0. When $\delta_1 = 1$, the situation is even better; it is the same as case 2. However, when δ_1 exceeds unity, expression (15) is the sum of a positive and a negative quantity and expression (15) can be either positive or negative depending on the relative size of γ_2 and γ_3 (holding δ_1 constant). The qualitative result is similar to that in case 3. When γ_3 is much larger than γ_2, we can obtain the wrong sign effect (here we also need $\delta_1 > 1$).

Up to this point we have seen that inferences from the basic model have at least the proper sign as long as the effect of $\triangle X_t$ is not much larger than the effect of X_0. This conclusion is reinforced when we focus on the multiplier. Recall that $C^{-1} = 1/(1 - \gamma_3 \delta_3)$. Thus it is positive when $\gamma_3 \delta_3$ is less than unity. If $\gamma_3 \delta_3 > 1$, the system will grow explosively. Any exogenous impact on X_t, say, will be amplified through each cycle of $X_t \rightarrow Y_t \rightarrow X_t$. The system is unstable and cannot long maintain this causal structure.

This is not to say that it can never happen in nature. Many of the structural properties we study grow exponentially during the period. However, in many analyses we adopt log transforms to linearize such growth. (See substantive chapters for more details, especially chap. 6.) In light of such transformations, it does not seem likely that $\gamma_3 \delta_3$ exceeds unity for the cases we consider. Nonetheless, we recognize that violations of this condition wreak havoc with inferences from the reduced form. It is difficult to establish precisely the implications of explosive growth for reduced-form estimates since it is not obvious that other parameters, e.g., δ_1, would remain unchanged under large increases in γ_3 and δ_3. All I can do is caution the reader that the value of even the qualitative inferences from our basic model may be incorrect if this condition is not met.

This third perspective on the basic model, then, leads to more cautious conclusions. In general, it tells that we will not go far wrong when the effects of $\triangle X_t$ and $\triangle Y_t$ are small relative to those of X_0 and Y_0 and the growth is stable (in the transformed variables).

So the class of models we use can be justified from any of three perspectives: (1) that the basic model in equations (1) and (2) approximates the true causal structure, operating with a certain lag; (2) that equations (1) and (2) are the solution of a differential equation system relating levels of X and Y to changes in X and Y; or (3) that the basic model is the reduced form of the proper model which allows for causal effects over the study period. At the time we began our research, the sociological literature emphasized the first of these perspectives. However, none of us believed that the lag periods we used correspond with any fundamental feature of the processes under study. Thus we are forced to either of the other positions. I favor the second; other members of our research group incline more toward the third. We agree, however, that empirical analyses of the sort we report are necessary preliminaries to adequate specification of the dynamics of national development.

Issues in Estimation

Our research context poses some special methodological issues. These issues hold with equal force whether the basic model is viewed as a structural model or whether it is considered a reduced form for a more complex model. In this section I will identify the issues, outline our strategies for addressing them, and cite relevant technical literatures that contain more detailed treatments.

So far I have assumed that the disturbances (the total effect of all omitted variables) were well behaved. In particular I assumed that they were independent of the variables appearing on the right-hand side of the basic model. If this is so, ordinary least-squares (OLS) estimators are consistent (see Johnston 1972, chap. 9). If, in addition, the disturbances have constant variance, OLS is also asymptotically efficient. The first two complications we consider involve likely failures of the independence and constant-variance assumptions.

Autocorrelation

Most readers are undoubtedly sensitive to the possibility that the disturbances are not independent from period to period. The problem is endemic to panel studies, and the studies we report are no exception. Consider the composition of the disturbances. In our research, the set of omitted variables includes material infrastructure (e.g., national systems of transport, communication, and so on), technology, cultural organization, national history, and so on. Each of these features of social organization has two properties: (1) It is stable; that is, it does not shift radically from period to period. (2) It affects many of the processes we study. As long as these causal effects are not included in the model, they are forced into the disturbance terms. And, given the pair of properties identified above, the disturbances will be correlated from period to period. Nations with unobserved characteristics that generate exceptionally high levels of some outcome in one period will tend to have exceptionally high levels in the next period. The more enduring are the unobserved causal forces, the stronger will be the autocorrelation of the disturbances and the dependence from period to period.

The impact of autocorrelation of disturbances on OLS estimators is well known (see, for example, Johnston 1972, chaps. 8 and 10; Hannan and Young 1977). We must consider two effects. First, autocorrelation implies some nonindependence of observations; the analyst using such data has less information about the process than would be given by the same number of independent observations. But, OLS assumes that the observations are independent; and calculations of confidence intervals and tests of significance reflect this assumption. Thus use of OLS with autocorrelated disturbances biases standard errors toward zero and thus gives inflated levels of statistical significance.

The second effect applies particularly to models, like the basic model, that include lagged dependent variables. It is easy to show (by writing the basic model for the period from $-t$ to t_0 and making appropriate substitutions into the basic model) that autocorrelation of disturbances implies that the disturbances at time 0 will be correlated with both X_0 and Y_0. In this case OLS estimators are biased and inconsistent.

We are concerned with the properties of OLS estimators in small samples. We have some relevant evidence from Monte Carlo simulations. In regressions of a variable on only the lagged dependent variable, autocorrelation (of the type termed "first-order autoregressive") produces an upward bias in the slope associated with the lagged dependent variable (Malinvaud 1970). Addition of another regressor reduces this upward bias. Nerlove (1971) and Hannan and Young (1977) obtained similar results using a different error structure (a variance-component model with random but constant individual-specific effects; see below). The slope of the lagged dependent variable is biased upward while the slope of an exogenous variable is biased downward. The latter effect reflects the negative correlation of estimators for positively correlated regressors. The autocorrelation biases the slope of the lagged dependent variable upward and thereby pushes the slope of a correlated regressor downward.

The results of the simulation studies do not apply directly to our model. Here both X_0 and Y_0 are correlated with the disturbance in each equation while in the simulation studies the additional regressor was not correlated with the disturbance. Nonetheless, the results seem to hold approximately. Take equation (1), for example. The enduring portion of the disturbance affects both Y_0 and Y_1 directly but X_0 only indirectly through effects on Y_{-t} and effects of Y_{-t} on X_0. These indirect effects will usually be much smaller than the direct effects. Consequently the correlation of Y_0 with the disturbance should be considerably higher than that of X_0 with the same disturbance. Then the coefficient of Y_0 will be more affected by autocorrelation bias. It is not clear what will be the effect of autocorrelation on the slope of X_0. This depends on the magnitudes of the various effects and the strength of autocorrelation. I cannot assert that the slope of X_0 will be biased toward zero as in the simulation studies. Nonetheless it seems highly unlikely that the bias in this slope would be positive. In the cases we analyze, I expect this bias to be relatively small and unsystematic.

All but two of our empirical studies use OLS estimators. The results just cited imply that their estimates of slopes of the lagged dependent variables will be biased upward. The estimates of the cross-effects on which we base our inferences may be biased in complex ways. But it seems unlikely that any such biases will systematically distort our inferences across the multiple analyses that we report.

In two cases, chapters 4 and 7, we correct for the most pervasive form of autocorrelation bias. In chapter 4 we pool several waves of panel observations and estimate models that include disturbance terms that are specific to each nation. The nation-specific factors summarize the most enduring features of social organization and are assumed to be constant over the study period. The model should also control for unobserved causal factors that change slowly relative to the processes under study. Use of a pooled model enables us to identify the causal structure and to form generalized least-squares estimators of causal effects. These estimators have been shown to have good small-sample properties (Hannan and Young 1977).

Chapter 7 also treats the factors producing autocorrelation as unobserved latent variables. Use of multiple indicators permits identification of a model with latent variables producing autocorrelation for each indicator of the dependent variable. The model is estimated by maximum likelihood using Jöreskog's (1969, 1973) procedures for analyzing linear structural equation models.

Heteroscedasticity

The assumption of constant error variance is also problematic for some of the outcomes we study. Some of our outcomes measure the scale of a system, for example GNP, or school enrollments. It is unlikely that Guyana, say, has the same error variance in either outcome as the Soviet Union or the United States. A small percentage deviation for the latter is larger than the initial level for the former. In general, period-to-period fluctuations for giant nations will be much larger than those for small nations. In other words, we expect the error variance for such scale variables to be increasing functions of the scale.

Suppose the error variance of u_t in equation (1) is proportional to, say, the square of X_0; i.e.,

$$\text{Variance } (u_t) = \theta X_t \sigma^2_u$$

Then, it is straightforward to correct for heteroscedasticity by forming weighted least-squares estimators (WLS). The procedure is as follows. Divide the entire structural equation by X_0 (this transforms the disturbance to u_t/X_0, which has the variance $\theta^2\sigma^2_u$—constant across values of X_0). Apply OLS to the transformed equation but treat the coefficient of X_0^{-1} as the constant, the constant as the coefficient of X_0, and the coefficient of Y_0/X_0. In other words, we continue to focus on the original structural equation and introduce the transformation only to repair a problem in the distribution of the disturbances.

This procedure has a superficial similarity to use of structural equation models for ratios of components to scale factors, for example, enrollment ratios or GNP per capita. Much published research and some of our research deals with relations among such ratios. Alternatively we treat the relevant scale factors, for example population size, as causal variables in their own right. Using the first strategy, we might regress per capita GNP on lagged per capita GNP and some political variable. In the second we would regress GNP on lagged GNP, the political variable, and population size (perhaps at both time 0 and time t). Since the latter strategy is used much less widely than the former, the matter deserves some comment.

Ideally our theories would arbitrate between these formulations. Since our theories lack such precision, we must use other criteria for choosing between them. Use of ratio variables is commonly defended as a method for adjusting or controlling for scale. But the second formulation does this as well, though the nature of the adjustment differs. Are there any other grounds for choosing between the two? Some sociologists have recently argued that the use of ratio variables may complicate inference (Freeman and Kronenfeld 1973; Schuessler 1973; Fuguitt and Lieberson 1974). They have noted particularly the difficulty that arises when one regresses, say, the ratio of expatriated profits to GNP on GNP (or GNP per capita). Since the same variable, GNP, appears in the numerator on one side of the equation and as a denominator on the other, the relationship between the two ratios is constrained. So, for example, a hypothesis that two variables are negatively related, does not face much likelihood of being rejected.

A more general problem has not been addressed in the sociological literature. Consider a model in which 1970 GNP/Pop depends on 1950 GNP/Pop and 1950 primary enrollment ratio (number of primary students divided by size of the relevant age group). The coefficient for the cross-effect of the enrollment ratio on per capita GNP summarizes a number of possible effects: the effect of size of 1950 enrolled population on 1970 GNP, a (nonlinear) effect of 1950 enrollments on 1970 population, a (nonlinear) effect of 1950 school-age population on 1970 total population and on 1950 GNP. I would not attribute the same substantive significance to each of these effects. Therefore, I am unwilling to summarize all these effects in a single term. I prefer to model the process in terms of primitive variables for this reason.

My argument hinges on my substantive orientation. Other members of our research group are more comfortable formulating arguments in terms of ratio variables. So we do not speak with one voice on this issue.

Measurement Error

Much of the work of our research project concerned measurement. We were constrained by the availability of data gathered by international organizations and, in several instances, by research groups. However, we devoted considerable effort to comparing estimates of the same quantity from numerous sources, checking the internal consistency of various indices (both over time on the same index and across indices of the same construct at a point in time), and so on. As a result of this work we believe that most of the data we use are of high quality.

However, the sources of error in reports of population size, GNP, and school enrollments are well documented. Although we have eliminated many gross errors (and during the period of our research the UN published revised and corrected figures for the entire span we cover), we have certainly not eliminated measurement error. And even random measurement error biases OLS estimates of structural parameters. Elsewhere (Hannan, Rubinson, and Warren 1974) we discussed at length the likely patterns of random and nonrandom errors in these data. We proposed and crudely estimated some models with multiple indicators of unobservable variables. Use of these models enables one to adjust estimates of structural parameters for both random and specified nonrandom errors in variables. Chapter 7 contains a more refined analysis of similar models using maximum-likelihood procedures.

We have not, however, widely used models with latent variables in our research. They demand the use of multiple indicators. For several of the variables we study, particularly political structure and economic dependence, measures are available for only small numbers of nations on any one indicator. Using several indicators at once reduces the effective sample size below the levels at which a multivariate analysis can be trusted at all. This constraint is currently losing force as gaps in the data are being filled. As chapter 7, the most recently completed of the empirical papers, documents, sufficient data on political organization are now available for the sensible use of unobservable variable models with multiple indicators. We expect the use of such models to become increasingly important in future research on these issues. In the meanwhile, we take consolation in the findings in chapter 7 and in Hannan, Rubinson, and Warren (1974) that many of the variables we analyze are measured quite reliably by sociological standards.

Functional Form of Relationships
Structural equation models are sometimes criticized for limiting attention to linear-additive relationships. Such a charge has no basis in logic or fact. A structural equation model can have any functional form. Some of the models we estimate are linear in both variables and parameters, as in equations (1) and (2). Others are linear only in the parameters, as in regressions of logarithms of variables on lagged variables and other variables. The reader can establish that such relations are nonlinear by taking antilogs of the equation. Finally, we estimate some models that are nonlinear in the parameters. For instance, in chapters 4, 6, and 7 we estimate relationships separately for rich and poor nations. The functional forms used are defended in the empirical chapters. This is not the place for any extended discussion. Rather, my point here is to emphasize that the structural equation perspective we adopt does not restrict us to any particular substantive hypothesis such as linear-additive relations.

SUMMARY
Most of our empirical work involves variations on a simple model. We treat each outcome as a function (sometimes linear) of a set of lagged variables, including the lagged dependent variable. This type of model

entered the social science literature as an analog to an experiment. But the model is not completely general and in no sense does it render causal inference unproblematic. We take the position that the model must be treated as a substantive model of the process and that the quality of inferences from the model depends on the quality of the substantive representation. I advanced three justifications for the use of the simple model in our research. In the course of stating these arguments, I indicated possible difficulties with using this model to study national social change.

In large measure, these difficulties involve the strength of the effects of changes in variables during the study period. If the effects of changes are different in sign from the effects of initial levels, the basic model will tend to misstate causal effects. For reasons that I outlined, I do not know and cannot determine empirically whether this is a problem in our research. In effect, we have proceeded under the assumption that the effects of initial levels of variables represent reasonably well the effects of all levels that occur during the period. This, then, is the major substantive assumption underlying our work.

We reject the view that special estimation procedures must be designed for panel studies. Instead, we treat the model as a structural equation model and use structural equation procedures. Our work was conducted during a period in which sociological methodology underwent profound changes. In the early years of our research, the sociological literature did not offer useful guidelines on most estimation issues. However, rapid progress has been made and sociologists have begun to utilize a wider variety of estimators. The empirical chapters completed in different epochs of the project reflect some of these differences. In our earlier research we relied heavily on ordinary least-squares estimators. As our research progressed, we altered procedures to handle certain complications, particularly autocorrelation, heteroscedasticity, and measurement error. In most cases the more complex procedures had never been applied to studies of national social change. Our experience is that more refined analyses generally give the same qualitative picture as did our earlier analyses (with certain exceptions; see chap. 7), but with a sharper focus. I believe that it is important that future research on national social change extend the use of these and related procedures.

NOTES

1 Lazarsfeld's work actually led to two traditions. His treatment of sixteenfold tables (the full cross-classification of two dichotomous variables measured at two points in time) involved the line of thought discussed in the text. At the same time, his treatment of the so-called eightfold table (the cross-classification of later measures on one variable on the earlier

values of both variables) was much closer to the position we take.

2 For example, it is easy to develop simple situations in which such measures fail. For example, suppose X_0 affects Y_t but Y_0 does not affect X_t. Suppose further that X is highly autocorrelated but Y is not and that X_0 and Y_0 are reasonably highly correlated. Then the cross-lag correlation procedure will lead to the inference that Y causes X (the correlation of Y_0 with X_t will be larger than the correlation of X_0 with Y_t). It is equally easy to come up with additional complications that have the same consequence for the cross-correlation test. Kenny (1973) has stated a set of conditions under which a generalization of cross-lag correlation procedure yields valid inferences. These restrictions are exceedingly restrictive and appear to hold only for systems in equilibrium (among other things the contemporaneous correlations among variables must be constant over time). The structural equation approach is suited to a wide range of situations beyond the scope of cross-lag correlation analysis.

3 For reviews of this perspective on panel analysis, see Duncan (1969, 1972, 1975), Goldberger (1971), Hannan and Young (1977), and Heise (1970).

II EXPANSION AND REORGANIZATION OF EDUCATION

THREE · The World Educational Revolution, 1950–70

John W. Meyer, Francisco O. Ramirez,
Richard Rubinson, and John Boli-Bennett

This chapter analyses the extremely rapid expansion of national educational systems that occurred throughout the world between 1950 and 1970 (for analyses from a different perspective see chap. 4). The first section of the chapter reviews those theories which explain educational expansion as a function of variations in national structural characteristics. The second section presents descriptive data which suggest that education has expanded so rapidly and universally that this process is affected by factors exogenous to national societies. The third section addresses this problem by formulating diffusion models which describe the apparently self-generating nature of educational expansion. But diffusion models do not explain why an institution expands; they only describe the process. So the fourth section returns to the issues of explanation to test what national characteristics affect educational expansion. These analyses show that measures of national economic, political, and social modernization account for very little expansion in education The final section confronts the problem of explanation at a different level by identifying some emergent features of the world system which may have caused this world educational revolution.

THEORIES OF NATIONAL EDUCATIONAL EXPANSION
Most theories of educational expansion explain the process in terms of endogenous economic, political, and social characteristics of nations. This section briefly summarizes these arguments. The fourth section analyses cross-national data from 1955 to 1970 to test these propositions.

PROPOSITION 1 *Economic development increases educational expansion.* Many theories assert that economic development increases educational growth through both individual and aggregate mechanisms. At the individual level, many theories argue that in more industrialized countries

This paper originally appeared in *Sociology of Education* 50 (1977): 242–58. Stephen Heyneman, along with our research colleagues, made many helpful suggestions.

labor markets are more thoroughly organized around educational credentials, education becomes more of a human capital investment, and the traditional criteria of status and prestige become less important than in nonindustrialized countries. Consequently, individuals desire and demand more schooling to increase their own economic reward (Blau and Duncan 1967; Boudon 1974; Bowles and Gintis 1976; Collins 1971). Evidence from nonindustrialized countries, however, suggests that labor markets there are also highly organized by educational credentials, that individual rates of return on education are not necessarily lower, and that traditional criteria of status and prestige may not be more valued than in industrialized countries (Currie 1977; Hansen and Haller 1973; Heyneman 1976; Holsinger 1975). The validity of proposition 1 for explaining educational growth through individual mechanisms needs to be empirically verified.

At the aggregate level, economic theories of education assert that advanced industrial economies require higher skill levels in the labor force; and they also have more resources to allocate to education both as an investment and as a consumption good (Blaug 1968, 1969; Dreeben 1968; Machlup 1972). Some long-term historical evidence suggests, however, that there is no close connection between industrialization and educational growth (Lundgren 1976). The validity of proposition 1 with respect to aggregate mechanisms also needs to be empirically tested.

The empirical studies relating educational and economic development are largely cross-sectional in design. These studies find a strong positive relationship between these variables, but longitudinal studies are needed to distinguish the effects of economic development on education from causal effects in the opposite direction (see chap. 6; Steadman 1970).

PROPOSITION 2 *Political and social modernization increase educational expansion.* Theories of modernization argue that education expands for several reasons. First, modern representative polities require high levels of citizen participation and political efficacy. Such political systems, then, expand mass educational systems to create participatory citizens (Almond and Verba 1963; Inkeles and Smith 1974). Second, modern representative regimes are more tolerant of competing status groups, and therefore more such groups are able to gain access to education (Ben-David and Zloczower 1962; Collins 1971). Third, the spread of bureaucratic organization increases the number of positions in society which are governed by universalistic criteria of personnel selection. Modernization theorists argue that the curricula and structural arrangements of schools meet these demands for identifying and selecting individuals on such universalistic criteria (Dreeben 1968; Parsons 1958). Despite the well-known discussions of such theories (Inkeles and Smith 1974), there are virtually no comparative analyses of these hypotheses.

PROPOSITION 3 *Powerful and authoritative states expand education.*

The process of the expansion and consolidation of political authority is often thought to increase education, since such a process requires the creation of a national political culture and ideology, and the creation of national citizenship. Education is a mechanism for producing both of these changes (chap. 5; Bendix 1964). Many historical studies have noted the close relationship between education and state-formation (Merriam 1931; Reisner 1927), and this process should be accentuated in the contemporary world since the power of national states has continued to increase.

PROPOSITION 4 *Ethnically plural societies expand education more slowly.* Analysts generally assume that state-formation, and its effects on increasing education, are more costly and conflictual in an ethnically heterogeneous society. One empirical study finds that education reduces such pluralism, but that pluralism reduces the expansion of education (Warren 1973).

PROPOSITION 5 *Dependent societies expand education more slowly.* Some dependency theories argue that national integration, and consequently its effects on educational expansion, are hampered by colonial or peripheral status in the world system (chap. 16; Frank 1969). This relationship arises from the fact that elites in such societies derive their power from their links to metropolitan centers and not from their success in integrating their populations into a national culture.

WORLD EDUCATIONAL EXPANSION 1950–70

These theories did not prepare us for the educational revolution which occurred after 1950 (Coombs 1968). This educational expansion is described in table 3.1. The figures in the table are the number of students in primary, secondary, and higher education in all countries for which UNESCO (1971) presents statistics. The data are standardized by census estimates of the number of persons in the age group appropriate for each level of education and for the length of schooling at each level.

The data do contain some error. Some enrollment figures may be exaggerated due to internal accounting procedures of some countries. Census reports sometimes underestimate the population bases used as denominators in the enrollment ratios. In some countries, large numbers of overage persons are in primary school, so that enrollment rates in such countries are over 100 percent. Nevertheless, detailed investigation at the UNESCO Statistical Office convinces us that they have assembled the data with considerable skill and care (Rubinson 1974; pp. 149–58). The errors in the data are also decreasing over time, which makes the findings of table 3.1 especially surprising.

The table shows the mean primary, secondary, and higher education enrollment ratios for all countries for which data are available from 1950 to 1970. Since countries vary in size, these means do not describe the experience of the average child. We also divide the countries into a richer and poorer half (at $172 per capita GNP in 1950), and report the mean ratios for each group.

TABLE 3.1   Mean Educational Enrollments as Percentages of the Appropriate
             Age Group Populations

Educational Level	1950 Mean %	1960 Mean %	1970 Mean %	Number of Cases
A. Primary students/age group population				
All countries	58	71	83	117
Richer countries[a]	90	98	102[b]	51
Poorer countries	37	53	72	56
B. Secondary students/age group population				
All countries	12.7	21.5	30.5	102
Richer countries[a]	21.3	35.8	46.4	49
Poorer countries	5.3	9.4	17.0	46
C. Higher education students/age group population				
All countries	1.4	2.8	5.3	109
Richer countries[a]	2.6	5.2	9.2	46
Poorer countries	0.6	1.2	2.6	55

a. Richer countries are defined as those above the median in 1950 GNP per Capita ($172 in 1964 US dollars). Cases do not add to total because of missing data on GNP per capita.

b. Percentage can exceed 100 for several statistical reasons noted in the text.

Table 3.1 shows extraordinary change in a twenty-year period. The mean primary enrollment rate went from 58% to 83%. This mean change could have been even higher, except that many countries reached the ceiling level of 100 percent. The growth in secondary and higher education, which is little restricted by ceiling effects, is even more dramatic. The secondary ratio more than doubled in the richer countries, and more than tripled in the poorer ones. Higher education increased almost four times in both richer and poorer countries. Even more striking is the fact that these large increases in ratios occurred during a time when the absolute size of the age groups involved was increasing by 50 to 100%. Detailed examination of these data also shows that in *no* country did the secondary or higher educational enrollment ratio decline. In some countries the primary ratio declined, but only because the initial pool of overage students without primary education declined. Thus, between 1950 and 1970, the expansion of national educational systems was universal, with greater proportions of rapidly expanding age groups in school.

MODELS OF SELF-GENERATING EDUCATIONAL EXPANSION
It is unlikely that the propositions discussed above can account for such a tremendous, universal increase in education. The growth of education

described above suggests that national educational systems had a self-generating character during this period. Before we can test the effects of national structural characteristics on educational expansion, we must model this process. Then we can determine whether national economic, political, and social characteristics affect educational expansion over and above the expansion which is built into the educational system itself.

With some longitudinal models this task is straightforward. In modeling economic growth, for example, one can propose that a country's GNP in 1970 is a simple linear function of its GNP in 1950. And in fact, this is a reasonable first approximation of economic growth from 1950 to 1970 (chap. 6).

But educational systems are subject to complications that make such simple models inappropriate. First, varying rates of population growth affect the size of the available pool of children. In richer countries, the number of children of primary school age has expanded rather slowly since 1950. In most poorer countries, this age group has expanded much more rapidly. Second, because enrollment ratios have a ceiling limit of 100%, the expansion in a country already at this level will be limited by the growth of the age-group population.[1] Third, educational expansion is much less limited by structural properties of a society than are other characteristics like economic growth. The latter requires tangible resources and effort, while the redefinition of many people as pupils and some people as teachers is much less difficult to achieve. Fourth, for secondary and higher education, the pool of available persons is defined not only by the whole age-group population, but also by the number of persons graduating from the preceding level of schooling.

These considerations suggest that, in establishing baseline models of educational expansion, we can employ ideas from diffusion research. Two diffusion models are relevant: a model of contagion and a model of diffusion from a constant source (Rogers 1963). Contagion models imply that education expands into the previously uneducated sectors of the population at a rate determined by the original proportion of educated people. Contagious diffusion theory predicts that education expands according to an S-shaped curve. Models assuming diffusion from a constant source imply that education expands at a rate determined by the size of the previously uneducated population. Such models predict an increasing but decelerating curve of educational enrollments over time, with a ceiling level of 100%. Our descriptive model of self-generating educational expansion employs a combination of both types of processes. The empirical question we wish to answer with these models is, How much does educational expansion depend on both the available uneducated population and the initial size of the educated population? Such models can tell us to what extent the population characteristics already built into the educational system create further increases in enrollments. It is for this reason that we see such models as reflecting a self-generating process.

Primary Education

The model of primary educational expansion is built around the following four assumptions:

1 The maintenance of a constant proportion of the age group in primary school is not problematic. What is to be explained is the increase in enrollment beyond this level. Therefore, the dependent variable in this analysis is the primary enrollment ratio in 1970 minus the same ratio in 1955.

2 Diffusion from the extant educational system is modeled by assuming that the rate of growth of the primary education ratio is proportional both to the initial size of the ratio and to the proportion of the age group not in school. This model produces the classic S-shaped curve of diffusion theory. The rate of diffusion, then, depends both on the number of elements *from* which it takes place and the number of elements remaining *to* which it can take place. This part of the model thus specifies that the primary enrollment ratio (p) expands at some constant function of $p_1(1-p_1)$.

3 To model educational expansion at a constant rate from a constant source to the uneducated population assumes that education diffuses not from schools and teachers but from the structure of the world system and the nation-state. If a switch were thrown in 1950, after which education expanded everywhere independent of the initial presence of schools and teachers and customs within particular countries, then the primary ratio (p) would expand at some constant function of $(1 - p_1)$. This part of the model represents the classic diffusion-theory idea of expansion into the unconverted population at a constant rate.

4 Our models also require two methodological additions. First, two other terms are included. One is a constant term to capture aggregate tendencies of the models to over- or underpredict enrollments. The other is the rate of growth of the primary age-group population, under the hypothesis that rapid population growth inhibits the growth of the primary enrollment ratio. This implies that the primary enrollment ratio expansion is a negative function of the rate of expansion of the primary age-group population, ($PPop_{70}/PPop_{55}$). Second, we include in the model the term $(1/PPop_{70})$ to make these models parallel to weighted least-squares estimates of total enrollments in order to correct for possible biases from the use of ratio variables in the analysis (Freeman and Kronenfeld 1973; Fuguitt and Lieberson 1974; Schuessler 1973). However, we find it more theoretically meaningful

to interpret the results in terms of ratio variables; so we will use such interpretations throughout.

In summary, primary educational expansion is estimated by the following equation:[2]

$$p_{70} - p_{50} = a + b_1 p_{55}(1 - p_{55}) + b_2(1 - p_{55} + b_3 PPop_{70}/PPop_{55} + b_4/PPop_{70},$$

where p_{55} = primary enrollment as a proportion of the primary age-group population, 1955, and $PPop_{55}$ = primary age-group population, 1955.

Secondary and Higher Education

The models for secondary and higher, or tertiary, education are the same as for primary, with three differences:

1 Since most countries are not approaching the ceiling limit of 100% enrollment in secondary and tertiary education, the terms which capture this effect, $(1 - s_{55})$ and $(1 - t_{55})$, are dropped from the model.[3]

2 Secondary and tertiary educational expansion depend on earlier expansion of the preceding educational level. We incorporate into the model of secondary education the term $p_{55}(1 - s_{55})$, which represents expansion into the previously uneducated secondary sector as some linear function of the earlier primary rate. The model for tertiary enrollments similarly incorporates an analogous term, $s_{55}(1 - t_{55})$.

3 Since we do not have accurate data on secondary and tertiary education age-group populations, we use total population growth. We also use total population as the weighting term in the equations. These alterations should make little difference in the findings.

In summary, secondary educational expansion is estimated by the following equation:

$$s_{70} - s_{50} = a + b_1 s_{55}(1 - s_{55}) + b_2 p_{55}(1 - s_{55}) + b_3 Pop_{70}/Pop_{55} + b_4/Pop_{70},$$

where s_{55} = secondary enrollment as a proportion of the secondary age-group population, 1955 and Pop_{55} = total population, 1955.

The equation for tertiary educational expansion follows the same specifications as for secondary education.

Data Exclusions

In analyzing primary education, we exclude all countries which have 90% or more of their eligible age-group population in primary school in 1955. These countries are so near the ceiling limit that further increases or decreases may indicate measurement error more than substantive change. This eliminates thirty-seven of 118 cases from the analysis of primary enrollment. In analyzing tertiary education, we exclude the United States, since its extremely high rate of enrollment in higher education could distort the analysis. In fact, parallel analyses without this exclusion show no substantive differences.

Findings

Table 3.2 presents the results from estimating these models with data from 1955 to 1970. Each row of the table reports the findings for one level of education, with the slope, standardized slope, and the standard error of the slope given for each independent variable. To aid in interpretation, we group the independent variable terms according to whether they (*a*) reflect the process of contagious diffusion, (*b*) reflect the process of a constant rate of penetration, or (*c*) reflect both of these processes simultaneously.

The results of this analysis can be summarized as follows. First, these diffusion processes account for a substantial proportion of the variance in educational expansion at all levels. The explained variances (R^2) for primary, secondary, and tertiary levels are 0.27, 0.36, and 0.60. The R^2 for primary education is the lowest, probably because of measurement error in those countries which near the 100 percent ceiling level by 1970. These results show that the size and rates of growth of the populations in school and in the uneducated age groups of school age explain significant amounts of the expansion of education between 1955 and 1970. That is, much of the expansion of education follows a self-generating process based on the demographic characteristics of the school populations, independent of national economic, political, and social characteristics.

Second, the classic S-curve describes a large component of educational expansion: countries having very low ratios in 1955 expand more slowly; those in the middle of the scale expand very rapidly; and those near the ceiling expand more slowly again.

Third, the size of the available uneducated population sector is important for primary educational expansion; and the available population produced by the preceding education level is even more important for secondary and tertiary education. To this extent, then, the process of a diffusion force converting the available population at a constant rate also applies.

These models do not really explain, in a theoretical sense, the expansion of education. They simply show how this increase occurred during this particular time period. The classic S-curve describes much of this process, as does the idea that education expands by a constant rate of absorption of the available uneducated population. For primary education, the rate of growth of the primary age-grade population is important

TABLE 3.2 Models of Educational Expansion, 1950–70: Ordinary Least-Squares Estimates[a,b]

Dependent Variable	Independent Variables					Constant	R^2	Number of Cases
	Contagion Term	Constant Rate of Penetration Term	Mixed Term	Population Growth	Control[a] Term			
A. Primary Enrollment Ratio Growth[b]	$P_{55}(1-P_{55})$	$(1-P_{55})$		$\dfrac{Prim.Pop.70}{Prim.Pop.55}$[c]	$\dfrac{1}{Prim.Pop.70}$			
	1.96**(0.38).58	0.25**(0.09).31		−0.21**(.09)−.25	39(54).07	0.13	.27	81
B. Secondary Enrollment Ratio Growth	$s_{55}(1-s_{55})$		$P_{55}(1-s_{55})$	$\dfrac{Pop.70}{Pop.55}$[d]	$\dfrac{1}{Pop.70}$			
	0.26(0.16).17		0.22**(0.05).48	0.08**(0.04).19	0.85(23.6).00	−0.108	.36	96
C. Higher Ed. Enrollment Ratio Growth	$t_{55}(1-t_{55})$		$s_{55}(1-t_{55})$	$\dfrac{Pop.70}{Pop.55}$[d]	$\dfrac{1}{Pop.70}$			
	0.64**(.18).38		0.12**(0.03).47	0.01(0.01).05	−1.30(5.8)−.02	−0.001	.60	89

** $p < .05$

a. Table entries are slopes, standard errors in parentheses, and standardized slopes. As noted in the text, the raw slopes may be interpreted as weighted least squares estimates of raw enrollments in 1970, as an alternative to the ratio interpretation given here.

b. Cases above 90% on primary enrollment ratio in 1955 are excluded from the analysis of primary enrollment growth.

c. Primary age group population calculated from UNESCO data on raw enrollments and enrollment ratios.

d. Population growth rates, rather than the growth rates in age group population, are used in the equations for secondary and higher education because data on many more countries are available.

in determining the rate of primary educational expansion. And the size of the preceding educational level is important in determining the rate of expansion for secondary and tertiary enrollments. These analyses show that, no matter what the substantive causes of educational expansion were up to 1950, after this time education expanded significantly merely as a consequence of the population characteristics of schools and the uneducated populations. In this sense, then, we have demonstrated that educational expansion between 1950 and 1970 was due to a self-generating process. Our problem in the next section is to see if the economic, political, and social characteristics of countries can contribute to the explanation of educational expansion over and above that which is self-generating.

Economic, Political, and Social Effects

This section returns to the theories discussed at the beginning of the paper to test the effects of structural characteristics of countries on educational expansion. The aim is to estimate the effects of such characteristics on educational expansion, independent of the effects of diffusion as described in Table 3.2.

Variables

We employ a large number of indicators designed to test the five propositions of educational expansion. Here we merely list these indicators. Details are presented in the appendix to this chapter. We use three indicators of economic development: the logarithm of gross national product per capita in 1955, the logarithm of kilowatt-hours of electricity consumed per capita in 1955, and the percentage of the male labor force not in agriculture in 1950. We use four indicators of political and social modernization: an index of formal political representation averaged from 1950–55, an index of political participation 1957–62, the percentage of the population living in cities of 100,000 or more in 1950, and a political modernization index. We use three indicators of the power and authority of the state: an index of state centralization, the size of the national cabinet averaged from 1949 to 1951, and government revenue as a percentage of gross domestic product in 1955. We use one indicator of social heterogeneity: an ethnolinguistic fractionalization index. And we use two indicators of dependence: export partner concentration in 1955, and a country's date of political independence. These indicators are all standard and well-known measures of national structural characteristics. (For a discussion of the interrelations of the indicators within the groups defined above, see chap. 6 and tables 6.1, 6.2, and 6.3.) Much research has shown that they explain many facets of political and economic change. Our aim here is to test whether or not they also explain educational expansion as the theories predict.

Analysis Model

We now include these indicators in our models of self-generating educational expansion in order to test the initial propositions we described. We employ the basic panel model which examines the effects of time-1 independent variables on time-2 dependent variables, controlling for the values of the time-1 dependent variable (chap. 2). Based on the findings in the previous section, we examine educational growth scores, since education expands so rapidly and universally during this time period. We also include in the equations the complex of diffusion variables to test whether national structural characteristics explain educational expansion independent of the diffusion processes.

One further methodological issue requires discussion. We do not simply add the indicators of national characteristics to the models, leaving each coefficient free to vary with the inclusion of each new indicator. In such analyses, multicollinearity becomes intolerably severe. Consequently we treat those equations and their coefficients as fixed, entering them in their entirety as single terms in the regression equations examined below. Thus, the first entry in the first column of table 3.3 shows that log GNP per capita 1955 has an effect (i.e., the standardized slope) of 0.10 on growth in the primary enrollment ratio, in an equation in which the entire set of variables and coefficients defined in the diffusion model in table 3.2 is entered as a single term. In this particular equation, this set of variables has a standardized slope of 0.63, which is not included in table 3.3.

Findings

The findings of table 3.3 are unexpected. Only six of the forty-two coefficients are significant at the 0.10 level. This result is little more than would be expected by chance. The major finding from these analyses is that the specific properties of nation-states do not substantially affect educational expansion over and above that which is affected by the diffusion processes.

All three economic indicators show positive effects on all three educational levels. But these effects are considerably smaller than the literature suggests. The small and insignificant effects on primary education may be explained by the fact that many countries are nearing the 100% ceiling limit, so that much of the remaining variance consists of error. The economic effects on secondary education are the strongest effects in the entire table.

There are no significant positive effects of modernization. A third of these effects are, in fact, negative. Given this overall pattern, we dismiss the single significant negative coefficient in the table as an anomaly, and we conclude that there is no evidence of any effect of political and social modernization on educational expansion.

TABLE 3.3   Effects of Economic, Political, and Social Variables
             on Educational Expansion, 1955–70[a]

	Dependent Educational Variable		
	Prim. Ratio[b] Growth (1970–55)	Sec. Ratio Growth (1970–55)	Higher Ed. Ratio Growth (1970–55)
Effects of Economic Variables[a]			
Economic Indicator:			
Log GNP/Capita 1955	.10 (62)	.21*(88)	.13 (84)
Log KWH/Capita 1955	.10 (51)	.24*(78)	.24**(69)
% Male Labor Force Not in Ag. 1950	.09 (78)	.18*(95)	.02 (89)
Effects of Political and Social Variables[a,c]			
Indicators of Political and Social Modernization:			
Urbanization, 1950	.13 (61)	−.02 (88)	−.02 (84)
Formal Political Rep. 1951–55[d,e,f]	.17 (27)	.04 (44)	.25 (41)
Polit. Particip. 1957–62[d,f,g]	−.03 (42)	.23 (51)	.20 (43)
Political Modernization	−.35**(59)	.03 (85)	.09 (81)
Indicators of State Power and Authority in Society:			
Government Rev./GDP 1955[d,f]	−.09 (32)	.17 (48)	.02 (44)
Cabinet Size 1950[f]	.01 (34)	.12 (54)	.03 (48)
State Centralization	.00 (62)	.08 (88)	−.03 (84)
Ethnolinguistic Fractionalization	−.09 (62)	−.04 (88)	−.05 (84)
Economic and Political Dependence:			
Independent 1945–57 vs Pre-1945[h,i]	−.10 (43)	−.02 (61)	−.12 (56)
Not Ind. by 1957 vs. Ind. Pre-1957[h]	.16 (62)	−.10 (88)	−.11 (84)
Export Partner Concentration, 1955	.16 (43)	−.26**(69)	−.07 (64)

*p < .10
**p < .05

a. Partial effects (standardized slopes) of economic variables, holding constant the models of endogenous educational expansion defined in Table 2. Throughout these analyses the factors defined (and coefficients derived) in Table 2 continue to show significant positive effects on educational expansion. For simplicity these effects are not reported here. Number of cases given in parentheses.

b. Countries over 90% on primary enrollment ratio in 1955 excluded.

c. Log GNP per Capita also held constant. In these analyses Log GNP per Capita usually continues to have positive but insignificant effects on educational expansion. When Formal Political Representation is introduced these effects reverse in sign, but this appears to be an artifact of the particular set of cases involved and not an indication of a spurious relationship.

d. Communist countries excluded because of measurement ambiguities.

e. Data mostly on richer countries.

f. Independent countries only.

g. Data mostly on poorer countries.

h. Countries independent more recently coded high.

i. Countries not independent by 1957 excluded.

Similarly, the three indicators of state power and authority show no effects. Ethnolinguistic diversity has negative effects on the three levels of educational expansion, but none of these effects approach statistical significance. National dependence has slight negative effects on secondary and higher educational expansion, but certainly not on primary education. These last findings suggest that peripheral countries utilize their metropolitan countries for elite education, and that metropolitan powers are cautious in expanding elite education in colonies. But these effects are small.

Our major substantive conclusion is that the propositions which specified variations in national structural characteristics as producing educational expansion receive little empirical support. Even economic development, which most theories emphasize as the major factor, has only small effects. We should also underline the fact that the indicators of social and political modernization had no effects on educational expansion. This is a very important finding given the large amount of theoretical literature which emphasizes such effects. Any effect of modernization on educational expansion must inhere in the self-generating aspect of the process. This set of diffusion effects is common to all countries in the world, independent of their variations on other structural characteristics.

In considering these findings, it is important to remember that we are explaining the process of educational expansion during a specific period in history, 1955–1970. The fact that we found that variations in structural characteristics of countries had no effect on educational expansion during this time period does not mean that they had no effect during other periods. Since the *cross-sectional* correlations between many of these indicators and educational enrollments are relatively high, it is likely that such characteristics of countries played a strong role in producing educational expansion at earlier times. It is the absence of such effects during the post–World War II period which needs to be explained. For our major finding is that national educational systems have expanded from 1955 to 1970 primarily as a function of the population and organizational characteristics of the educational system itself, and not as a function of the political, social, and economic characteristics of countries.

THE MODERN WORLD AND THE EDUCATIONAL REVOLUTION

The absence of effects of national structural characteristics and the importance of educational diffusion processes leads to a consideration of general properties of the modern world as a locus of explanation for the educational expansion since 1950. One relevant and striking feature of the modern world is that it is made up almost entirely of independent nation-states, whose number has grown rapidly from 65 in 1940 to 142 in 1970 (Meyer, Boli-Bennett, and Chase-Dunn 1975). This network of states is the dominant organizational structure of the world. Almost all states play a central role in funding, constructing, controlling, and expanding educational systems (see chap. 5). Perhaps it is the parceling of the world among these organizational units that accounts for the universal expansion of education. In table 3.3 we found no evidence of a positive effect of state power on education, but we did find small negative effects of state dependence and colonial status. We explore this issue here.

If the formation or existence of an independent state in a country affects education, then we should expect two findings. First, throughout this period colonies should have low educational enrollment ratios, and they should be slow to expand education. Second, the period following independence should show an unusual spurt in enrollment ratios as the state organization takes control and expands education. The literature on newly independent countries suggests that such countries give disproportionately great attention to educational expansion (Coleman 1965).

To test these hypotheses, we classify countries by their date of political independence, distinguishing those which became independent during each five-year period from 1945 to 1970. We also have a group of colonies which did not become independent by 1970. We divide the "old" countries (that is, pre–1945) into two groups on the basis of gross national product per capita. Since most new countries are relatively poor, it makes sense to compare their enrollment ratios with those of the poorer group of older countries. For each group of countries we calculate primary, secondary, and tertiary enrollment ratios at five-year intervals from 1950 to 1970. This calculation enables us to see, first, if the poorer older countries are generally higher in enrollment rates with colonies much lower; and second, if each group of countries shows unusually sharp increases in enrollments after becoming independent. Figure 3.1 presents these analyses.

The findings in figure 3.1 do not support these expectations. The colonies which are not independent by 1970 have educational enrollment ratios and rates of growth similar to the other groups of countries. Also, there are no discernible spurts in the rates of educational growth following the time of political independence for countries. All groups of countries show remarkably similar patterns of growth, especially considering the small case numbers in the groups. The different groups of countries in the table begin at different enrollment ratios but follow similar upward paths.

In summary, during the period from 1950 to 1970, the presence of an independent state in a territory did not significantly affect educational expansion. The hypothesis that the universal expansion of education resulted from the organization of the world into a set of nation-states is

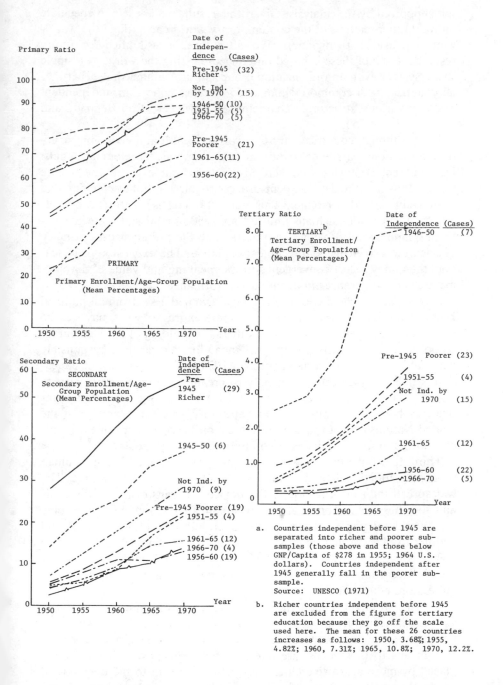

Fig. 3.1   Growth in Educational Enrollment Ratio, 1950–70, by Date of
Independence of Country[a] (mean percentages)

not supported by the analysis. Given this result, we are left to speculate on what other features of the contemporary world can explain the world-wide expansion of education. We offer three possibilities for future research. Each of these is based on conceptualizing the world as a single social system, with an organizational and cultural milieu that penetrates all countries with common demands to increase education, independent of their various structural characteristics (Meyer, Boli-Bennett, and Chase-Dunn 1975).

First, although countries vary in terms of wealth and economic structure, all nations pursue common national economic development goals. Development strategies vary across countries, but every national elite understands that the development process requires rational planning and technically trained personnel. This understanding is reinforced by networks of international loans and aid and widespread state-directed national planning, all of which help perpetuate the present world primacy of scientific knowledge and technical expertise. The expansion of education, then, may reflect convergence in the meaning and value of development despite differences in economic performance.

Second, an educated citizenry is a highly valued asset from all political perspectives. The Tanzanian leader Nyerere expressed what may well be a universal sentiment: "If I leave to others the building of our elementary school system they [the people] will abandon me as their responsible national leader" (quoted in Thompson 1971). The expansion of education is politically desirable, not only to create good citizens but also to legitimate responsible government. In a world that organizationally emphasizes both citizenship and state authority (as, for example, in the United Nations), the expansion of education becomes convenient political shorthand for articulating a commitment to both goals.

Third, the contemporary world not only praises, but insists on "human progress." Individuals and countries are not static but improvable. The widespread faith in education as the device for transforming individuals and societies has led one critic to complain that schooling has become the "world religion of the modernized proletariat" (Illich 1970), and another to observe that people act as if there were "no salvation outside higher education" (Shils 1971). The "new person" and the "new society"—according to Mao, Nyerere, Nkrumah, Castro—inevitably require more education.

Fourth, all of this occurs in a capitalist world economy in which development occurs from success in economic competition. Elites that do not pursue economic and political development as ends, and education as a means to those ends, are likely to fall from power. They are replaced by more aggressive elites who better conform to the demands of the world market and actively champion its goals and methods. These elites vigorously promote education as a means of national mobilization.

CONCLUSION

We have shown that cross-national differences in levels of economic, political, and social development do not adequately explain the massive postwar expansion of national educational systems. Rather, between 1950 and 1970 education has expanded everywhere as a function of the available population to be educated and of the level of education existing in 1950. Education everywhere expanded independent of the constraints and stimuli that economic, political, and social structures provided in previous times. This universal increase in education has led us to speculate that the causes of this expansion lie in characteristics of the contemporary world system, since such characteristics would affect all nations simultaneously. We offer these speculations as directions for further research.

APPENDIX

VARIABLES, INDICATORS, AND SOURCES FOR ANALYSES PRESENTED IN TABLE 3.3

1. Indicators of economic development
   A. *Logarithm of gross national product per capita 1955.* Data are from the World Tables (International Bank for Reconstruction and Development [hereafter IBRD] 1971), measured in 1964 U.S. dollars. The measure is logged because its distribution is skewed.
   B. *Logarithm of kilowatt-hours of electricity consumed per capita 1955.* Data on energy consumption are from Taylor and Hudson (1971).
   C. *Percentage of the male labor force not in agriculture 1950.* Data are from International Labor Office ([hereafter ILO] 1971) which provides the best comparative data on labor forces.
2. Indicators of political and social modernization
   A. *Formal political representation index.* This index, developed by Cutright (1963), reflects the extent to which legislators and chief executives are popularly elected and the degree to which the legislature reflects diverse party interests. Only independent countries are included in this measure; Communist countries are not coded because of ambiguity in the meaning of these criteria for those countries. The index is coded for the years 1950–55.
   B. *Political participation.* This measure is from Adelman and Morris (1973). It covers the period 1957–62 for 74 non-Communist developing countries. Countries are coded on both their formal political structure and the actual level of participation within and among parties and interest groups.
   C. *Political modernization.* We use C. E. Black's (1967) coding of the degree to which (and recency with which) elites committed to modernization control a country.

  D. *Urbanization.* We use the proportion of the national population
     in cities of over 100,000 as of 1950. The data are taken from
     Davis (1969).
3. Indicators of state power and authority
  A. *State centralization.* This index combines three indicators from
     Banks and Textor (1963): power concentration within the state,
     the presence of a single political party, and the presence of a
     "system style" mobilized around national purposes. The measure
     reflects the extent to which political authority is centralized in the
     national state. Data are coded for the late 1950s.
  B. *Size of the national cabinet.* Data are from Banks (1971), aver-
     aged for the years 1949–51. This measure, in some degree, indi-
     cates the extent to which the state has penetrated institutional
     structures of society by linking interest groups to the state bu-
     reaucracy. Communist and other mobilized states usually receive
     high scores.
  C. *Government revenue as a percentage of gross domestic product
     1955.* Data are from International Monetary Fund ([hereafter
     IMF] 1972) with some supplemented from Banks (1971). This
     indicator measures the extent to which the state controls eco-
     nomic resources.
        We employ these three weakly interrelated indicators because
     they capture important, but distinct, aspects of what expanded
     state power entails: the centralization of control, state penetration
     of society, and the rational bureaucratization of state authority.
4. Indicator of social heterogeneity
  A. *Ethnolinguistic fractionalization index.* This measure is from Tay-
     lor and Hudson (1971). Higher scores indicate greater ethno-
     linguistic diversity.
5. Indicators of dependence
  A. *Export partner concentration 1955.* This indicator is the percent-
     age of a country's exports which go to that country's largest ex-
     port partner. Data are from the *Yearbook of International Trade
     Statistics* (United Nations, 1950–55). Data are averaged from
     1950 to 1955. Countries which became independent in this period
     show no distinctive changes in their scores on this indicator.
  B. *Date of independence.* This indicates, to some extent, political de-
     pendence. We distinguish between those countries independent
     by 1945 and those which became independent between 1945 and
     1957.

NOTES

  1 Alternatively, education can become more intense, for example, in
terms of time spent in classrooms. But this is an aspect of education on
which comparative data are unavailable.
  2 We use the time lag 1955–70 because it provides enough time for sub-

stantial changes in enrollments while avoiding data from 1950, which are available for fewer countries and likely to be distorted by the aftermath of World War II. In other analyses we have used the time lag from 1950–65, without substantially different results.

3 Omitting these terms also allows us to avoid severe problems of multi-collinearity between these terms and the terms $s_{55}(1 - s_{55})$ and $t_{55}(1 - t_{55})$.

FOUR · The Expansion of National Educational Systems: Tests of a Population Ecology Model

François Nielsen and Michael T. Hannan

Most research on organization-environment relations concerns itself with the effects of environmental variations on well-established organizations. However, Stinchcombe (1965) has argued persuasively that environmental impacts are strongest at the period of founding. If so, the impacts of environments on organizations will be seen most clearly on new or emergent organizations. Following Stinchcombe, we propose to study environmental impacts by examining the societal conditions for organizing. The creation and expansion of formal organization demands both the existence of certain social organizational features (for example market economy, bureaucratic state administration and so on) and the mobilization of personnel and other resources. Resources can be mobilized only at the expense of other existing or potential forms of organization. That is, if certain material and human resources are to be devoted to a certain form of organized activity, they are not available to other forms of activity. Consequently, forms of organization compete for resources. Insofar as forms of organizations both compete for resources and differ in their demands on the environment, the theoretical strategy of population ecology can be employed to model the differential expansion of the various forms of organization (Hannan and Freeman 1974, 1977).

We focus on the expansion of one particular class of organization: educational organizations. Formal schooling has expanded enormously in every nation in the world over the past twenty-five years (chap. 3). However, the rate of expansion varies greatly from nation to nation. We propose to use this variation to test an elementary population ecology model.

The expansion of education is most commonly explained by reference to the demands of modern industrial and bureaucratic production systems. Education viewed from the perspective of the individual consumer is an asset in competition for scarce rewards. Viewed from the perspective of the labor market or the firm, education is either a productive

This chapter appeared originally in the *American Sociological Review* 42 (June 1977): 479–90.

asset or a signal of some learning or productive ability (Machlup 1970). Expansion of those forms of activity that demand skills in processing information will tend to increase the demand for education. Even if schooling does not affect productivity, its use as a signal for productive skills will tend to activate a competition for education that will lead to increasing levels of investment by individuals in education (Collins 1971; Boudon 1974). In either case, education is treated as a property of individuals that affects their relationship to the production system.

The expansion of education also has strategic value to political elites committed to changing the relationship of the individual to the state or polity. There is a good deal of evidence that education is used to define or redefine status categories in the population and thereby regulate or alter the position of those obtaining education in the polity (chap. 5; Meyer 1971). Insofar as there are advantages to state controllers to mobilize the populations politically, and as long as the expanding of educational systems is a convenient or effective way to this end, education will be expanded. Although this argument is quite different from productivity and signaling arguments, it too treats education as a property of individuals that affects their relationship to the larger system.

We do not dispute either explanation. The trend toward greatly increased schooling undoubtedly reflects increased demands for knowledge, increased reliance on formal certification, status and class competition for jobs and other scarce rewards, and changes in the relationship of the state to its members. Yet we are unwilling to presume that any social system obtains any outcome it needs, in this case increased schooling, simply by virtue of needing it. Nor do individuals automatically find schools or places in schools by virtue of desiring schooling. Schooling is an organized activity, and the expansion of schooling represents an organizational achievement. Schooling expands in a system only when there is demand (from either the controllers of the system or the members) for additional schooling *and* an organizational capacity to incorporate more students. Previous research has emphasized the former at the expense of the latter. We propose that the expansion of formal educational organizations in any society be analyzed in specifically organizational terms.

Educational organizations differ on at least two variables of organizational significance. The first, *complexity,* particularly complexity of the division of labor, increases regularly from primary schools to universities. The second dimension is *unit cost,* the amount of resources needed to process one student. Differences in costs for staff and equipment and the increasing burden of the indirect cost entailed by the nonproductivity of a more valuable fraction of the potential labor force means that unit cost also increases from primary schools to universities.

We can thus define three *forms* of educational organizations: primary, secondary, and tertiary, distinguished by their relative positions on the scales of complexity and unit cost. If the environments of educational organizations are delimited by national boundaries, the collection of schools at a given level within a particular country constitutes a *population* of organizations. Finally, the three populations of organizations (primary, secondary, and tertiary schools), interacting within the same national environment, constitute a *community* of organizations.

Organizational forms, populations, and communities of organizations constitute three basic ingredients of a population-ecological analysis of organizations, as explicated by Hannan and Freeman (1974, 1977). In this paper, we focus on the *aggregate size* of populations of organizations, measured as the national enrollment in a given educational level.

AN ELEMENTARY PROCESS MODEL OF EDUCATIONAL EXPANSION

We discuss first the simple demographic and resource processes introduced above. This simple model is then embedded in a dynamic model that characterizes the manner in which enrollments grow. Finally, we employ organizational dimensions of the three forms of educational organizations to derive a series of inequalities among the parameters of the models applied to each level.

Demographic and Resources Effects

To a large extent, the educational career of an individual takes the form of a rigid processing, with a fixed sequence of steps to be taken in turn. From an aggregate perspective, therefore, the total student enrollment at one level will set an upper limit to the number of suitable candidates for the next level, and thus on the enrollment at that level at some later point. For primary schooling the upper limit is given by the size of the primary school-age population of the country.

The supply of qualified candidates is only one of the factors that are likely to determine enrollment in a given educational level. As we noted above, all the ingredients of education represent a cost of some kind. The price has to be paid by the community in one way or another, so that we expect that the total amount of wealth in the environment will also constrain enrollment at all three levels: the wealthier the country, the larger enrollments it can afford.

The two arguments can be summarized as follows. The joint action of the availability of candidates, or demand, and resource availability determines a ceiling on the expansion of each level of education. From an ecological point of view, the ceiling may be thought of as the *carrying capacity* of a population of organizations in the national environment. The candidates available and the amount of resources in the system correspond then to the *parameters of the niche* of an organizational form. We do not assume that the size of a population of organizations at a given time always coincides with its carrying capacity. The actual degree of expansion of a population depends on dynamic considerations that are further discussed below.

If we let E_t^* denote the carrying capacity of some organizational form and C_t and R_t the cohort and resources conditions, respectively, the model proposes that

$$E_t^* = f(C_t, R_t). \tag{1}$$

We do not have any a priori knowledge of the functional form of equation (1). So for the present, we adopt the simplest possible, a linear relationship,[1]

$$E_{it}^* = \alpha_i' + \gamma' C_{it} + \delta' R_{it}. \tag{2}$$

The parameter α_i' summarizes the cultural, political, and infrastructural conditions that affect the carrying capacity and vary from nation to nation, but are approximately constant over time for each nation.

Dynamic Considerations

The creation and expansion of formal organizations requires the mobilization of resources. Such an effort requires time. Consequently, organizations cannot react instantly to variations in the optimal levels of service. Moreover, the speed of adjustment to a new level of demand/affordability is likely to depend on the structure of the organization, on characteristics of the environment, and on the magnitude of the required change. We can capture the most obvious features of these processes in a simple dynamic model.

Let E_t^* denote, as before, the carrying capacity of the environment for some form of organization, and let E_t denote the existing degree of expansion. Then the growth of a system that responds to demand will depend on a comparison of E_t^* and E_t. In particular, we argue that

$$E = \beta'(E_t^* - E_{t-\Delta t}), \tag{3}$$

where $E = E_t - E_{t-\Delta t}$, and Δt represents some time interval to be determined.[2]

According to equation (3) not only does the system expand when $E_{t-\Delta t}$ falls below E_t^* and decline when $E_{t-\Delta t}$ rises above E_t^*, but the speed of response is proportional to the distance from the *carrying capacity*. The speed-of-response parameter β' describes the characteristics of the organizations and the texture of the environment. When the individual members of a population of organizations are relatively adaptable and the environment offers much resources and little resistance (competition by other forms of organizations), β' will be close to unity: the actual size E_t of the population fully adjusts to its carrying capacity

$E_t{}^*$ during the time interval Δ_t.[3] Organizational inertia or environmental resistance will decrease β'.[4] Therefore, the *responsiveness* parameter β' may be quite informative about the ecology of a population of organizations.

Finally, we make the obvious substitution of equation (2) into equation (3) to yield the full model:

$$E_t = (1 - \beta')\, E_{t\,-\,\Delta t} + \beta'\alpha' + \beta'\gamma'C_t + \beta'\delta'R_t. \tag{4}$$

Equation (4), a finite difference equation, can be rewritten as

$$E_t = \alpha + \beta E_{t\,-\,\Delta t} + \gamma C_t + \delta R_t, \tag{5}$$

where $\beta = 1 - \beta'$, $\alpha = \beta'\alpha'$, $\gamma = \beta'\gamma'$, and $\delta = \beta'\delta'$.

In equation (5), α, γ, and δ are compounded coefficients that incorporate the effects of demand or resources on equilibrium enrollment multiplied by β', the measure of organizational responsiveness to the exogenously determined carrying capacity. Keeping γ' and δ' constant, the higher β', the higher the net effects of C_t and R_t on enrollment. Since we are mostly concerned in what follows with deriving and testing hypotheses on the value of γ and δ, which represent the net effects of demand and resources on *enrollment at time t*, rather than with γ' and δ', the effects of these two variables on the carrying capacity E^*, we choose to reserve the expressions *cohort* and *resource effects* to refer to γ and δ, respectively. The coefficient β will be called the *inertia* parameter since it is a decreasing function of the responsiveness coefficient β' and therefore indicates the degree of organizational resistance to change. The larger β, the slower the adjustment of an educational level to its carrying capacity.

Empirical Specification of the Model

Equation (5) has the familiar form of a linear equation with a lagged dependent variable. We require data at two or more time periods to estimate the model. In fact, we have observations on national enrollments at five-year intervals from 1950 to 1970 (UNESCO 1971). We measure resources as gross national product in 1964 US dollars (IBRD). Following the earlier discussion, the size of the cohort, C_t, for each level of education is measured as the enrollment in the next lower level of education five years earlier. For primary schooling the relevant cohort is the age population at that time. For a number of reasons the measurement of cohorts for secondary and tertiary education is not ideal. The typical time spent in a level of education is usually different from five years; students may reenter the educational system after some interruption; and so on. To attempt to correct for any resulting distortions we add total national population to the models for secondary and tertiary education and primary enrollments to the model for tertiary.

The three empirical specifications of the general model of educational growth may be represented as follows:

$$\text{PRI}_t = \alpha_P + \beta_P \text{PRI}_{t-5} + \gamma_P \text{ PRIPOP}_{t-5} + \delta_P \text{ GNP}_{t-5} + \epsilon_{Pt},$$

$$\tag{6a}$$

$$\text{SEC}_t = \alpha_S + \beta_S \text{ SEC}_{t-5} + \gamma_S \text{ PRI}_{t-5} +$$
$$\delta_S \text{ GNP}_{t-5} + \xi_S \text{ POP}_t + \epsilon_{St},$$

$$\tag{6b}$$

$$\text{TER}_t = \alpha_T + \beta_T \text{ TER}_{t-5} + \gamma_T \text{ SEC}_{t-5} +$$
$$\delta_T \text{ GNP}_{t-5} + \xi_T \text{ POP}_t + \zeta_T \text{ PRI}_t + \epsilon_{Tt},$$

$$\tag{6c}$$

where PRI_t, SEC_t, *and* TER_t denote the enrollments at time t in primary, secondary, and tertiary education, respectively, POP_t denotes national population at time t, and PRIPOP_t denotes the size of the primary-school-age population at time t.

In equation (6), ϵ_P, ϵ_S, and ϵ_T represent the combined effect on enrollment of variables omitted from the model. Alternative specifications of ϵ, and their implications for estimation, are discussed in section 4. An interesting theoretical feature of equations (6) is that the three equations contain *comparable* parameters of organizational significance: the inertia, cohort, and resource coefficients (β, γ, and δ, respectively). Since the model is defined on three populations of organizations that are assumed to differ systematically on the scales of complexity and unit cost, we can compare these coefficients across populations and generate hypotheses relating their respective values to the assumed positions of the populations with respect to these structural criteria. In other words, from the organizational point of view, *the coefficients of the general dynamic model are the variables of substantive interest.* The next section is devoted to an elaboration of this theme and to the derivation of specific hypotheses.

HYPOTHESES

The general model described in section 1 reduces the growth of national enrollments to three main mechanisms. We first attempt to elucidate how the parameters that characterize these mechanisms would be expected to vary across populations of organizations that differ with respect to their degree of complexity and the amount of resources they require.

The Inertia Parameter

In each equation in (6), β is an *inverse* measure of the speed of adjustment to the carrying capacity. Therefore β characterizes the degree of structural inertia of a population. A larger β means that population size is more dependent on the past, that is, exhibits a higher degree of rigidity with respect to exogenously induced pressures for a change in scale.

We argue that both a high degree of complexity and a high cost per unit lower the speed of adjustment of organizations, and therefore increase the value of β. A highly complex and differentiated structure entails the need for a wide variety of specialized skills, roles, and elements of material infrastructure. Not only does the organization compete more with others to mobilize choice ingredients in shorter supply, and is thus less likely to fulfill its needs quickly, but the efficient coordination of the interdependent whole following growth is also more problematical. Conversely, once the organizational structure is created, the specialized components (people or things) are difficult to reallocate for some alternative use, and one would expect a high degree of resistance of the organization to decline as well as to growth.[5] To take specific examples, such prerequisites of the educational process as libraries, schedules, laboratories, classrooms, and adequate teaching and administrative bodies cannot be created and put together without a series of complex decisions and adjustments. The more differentiated the organization, the more complex the series of decisions involved in growth and the longer the adjustment time.

On the other hand, a high cost per unit limits the rate of organizational expansion in an obvious way. For the same level of success of an organization competing with others for environmental resources, a low-cost organization will expand more (in terms of units) than a high-cost one. To summarize both arguments, the speed of adjustment of the size of an organization is expected to be higher when the cost of an additional unit is low and when the organization can expand by the mere addition of relatively unspecialized segments of human and material infrastructure. Thus we hypothesize that $\beta_P < \beta_S < \beta_T$.

The Cohort Effect

According to the general model embodied in equation (5), the coefficient γ associated with C_t is the product of γ', the effect of the cohort of qualified candidates on E^*, and β', the coefficient of organizational responsiveness. If one assumes for a moment that γ' is the same for all three levels, it follows from the preceding discussion that the composite coefficient γ decreases in magnitude from PRI to TER. This is because the responsiveness coefficient of β' is a decreasing function of the inertia parameter β, so that the discussion of section 2a implies $\beta'_P > \beta'_S > \beta'_T$.

It seems likely, however, that γ' itself is dependent on structural characteristics of the organization. Thompson (1967) argues that, in their efforts to approach bounded rationality, organizations attempt to seal off their core technology from environmental fluctuations. This protective function can be carried out by specialized boundary-spanning components through the buffering, leveling, forecasting, and rationing of environmental demands. Thompson's argument can be extended, at the *population* level,[6] by assuming that the protection requirements of organizations are some increasing function of the complexity and intensity (cost) of the core technology: *the more complex the core technology of an organization, and the more efforts and resources there are invested in each unit of input, the more selective the boundary-spanning components in charge of input.* In the educational context, such boundary-spanning activities manifest themselves in various guises: admission committees, entrance examinations, massive elimination after a short trial period within the organization, and so on. In view of equation (5), it means that the carrying capacity of more complex and resource-intensive organizations will be less dependent on cohort size, so that $\gamma'_P > \gamma'_S > \gamma'_T$. Putting together the expected behaviors of the two component parts of the coefficient γ, $\beta'_P > \beta'_S > \beta'_T$ and $\gamma'_P > \gamma'_S > \gamma'_T$, with $\gamma = \beta' \gamma'$, we hypothesize that the estimated γ will decrease from PRI to TER: $\gamma_P > \gamma_S > \gamma_T$.

The Effect of Resources

The effect of environmental wealth is less easy to cast in terms of straightforward inequalities. The coefficient δ, which is to be estimated, is the product of β', the responsiveness, and δ', the effect of resources on optimal enrollment. If one reduces equation (2) to its simplest form, $E^*_t = \delta' R_t$, the meaning of δ' can be expressed as the average increase in the carrying capacity for enrollments due to an increase of one unit of resources in the system. However, we expect both the strength of the resource effect and the unit cost to increase from PRI to TER. With the present model we cannot distinguish the two effects.

Community of Organizations and Environmental Resources

Our analysis to this point involves comparison of three *populations* of organizations that differ on structural criteria. However, the three populations of organizations within a bounded system are clearly in a relationship of *sequential dependence* (Thompson 1967): each level of education produces the input for the next. To that extent, the three populations interacting within the national boundaries constitute a *community* of organizations. We proceed to investigate the impact on the community of organizations of a major environmental constraint—the relative abundance of resources. To this end, we introduce resources in a nonadditive way by estimating the equations (6) separately for poor and rich countries.[7] This procedure leads to a series of additional hypotheses that take the form of comparisons of coefficients two at a time.

First, resource levels in the environment are likely to improve the capability of the three populations comprising the community to adjust quickly to their respective carrying capacities: more resources in the system mean less competition between organizations for essential ingredients. Thus, for each level of education, the inertia coefficient β will be lower in rich countries (R):

$$\beta^R_P < \beta^P_P; \quad \beta^R_S < \beta^P_S; \quad \beta^R_T < \beta^P_T.$$

Second, in an abundant environment, input fluctuations are likely to constitute a lesser threat for the core technology of an organization, since a temporary disequilibrium is more easily corrected by a reallocation of resources. Within a level of education, γ' is expected to be longer in rich countries. Since in addition the organizational responsiveness β' is also increased by wealth, the composite coefficient γ is expected to be larger in rich countries than in poor ones:

$$\gamma^P_P < \gamma^R_P; \; \gamma^P_S < \gamma^R_S; \; \gamma^P_T < \gamma^R_T.$$

This hypothesis can be readily translated into a property of the educational community as a whole. Since γ represents the effect of enrollment at one level on the size of the next, it provides a measure of the degree of sequential interdependence between the component parts of the national system of education. We argue that environmental wealth increases the interdependence of the three levels within the educational community.

Finally, analysis of the resource effect is somewhat more tractable within the community context. There are two reasons for expecting that δ' will be larger in poor nations. The first is a marginal return argument. When few resources are available, the major constraints on organizational growth are resource constraints. Thus an increase in resources should have maximum impact in this situation. And in richer environments, the bulk of causality presumably shifts to other potentially limiting factors. Second, unlike the case in the population level analysis, the unit-cost effect is in the same direction: a dollar of expenditures can purchase more educational services in a poor nation.

Notice that the coefficients δ that are products of resource and responsiveness effects are still indeterminate in sign. We argue that the resource effect is larger in poor nations, but that responsiveness is higher in rich nations. Thus we must compute δ' explicitly.

METHODOLOGY
Pooled Cross-Section and Time Series Analysis
Rather than estimate equation (6) separately for each of the four five-year lags, we pool all of the data into a single model. This design, discussed extensively by Nerlove (1971) and Hannan and Young (1977), permits us to deal satisfactorily with an estimation problem that plagues

almost all sociological panel analyses: autocorrelation of disturbances. In motivating equation (2) we pointed to the relatively constant features of national cultural, social, and political organization that affect educational expansion. Since these features are not measured here, they are forced into the disturbances in equation (6). Since they presumably operate in every period, the disturbances are correlated over time and with the lagged dependent variables. Consequently, ordinary least-squares estimators applied to equation (6) are biased and inconsistent. If the autocorrelation of disturbances is due only to the constant nation-specific effects (i.e., $\epsilon_{it} = \mu_i + \nu_{it}$, where the ν_{it} are well-behaved random disturbances), two strategies of estimation applied to the pooled model yield consistent and asymptotically efficient estimators. The first treats the μ_i as fixed effects and calculates pooled within-nation regressions. We refer to this as the LSDV estimator. The second, MGLS (modified generalized least-squares), treats the μ_i as random effects whose variance components are to be estimated under the assumption that the μ_i have constant variance. When the constant-variance assumption holds, MGLS has better small-sample properties (Nerlove 1971; Hannan and Young 1977). However, since we are uncertain that the constant-variance assumption is appropriate to these data, we report results from both approaches.

Heteroscedasticity

When the units of observation differ greatly in size, the random portion of the disturbances is unlikely to have constant variances (see the discussion in Freeman and Hannan 1975). In fact, preliminary analysis of these data indicated that the absolute values of disturbances increased sharply with size. Therefore, we introduce a generalized least-squares correction, namely, weighted least-squares. However, implementing weighting in the pooled model is complicated. We have shifted from the Nerlove-type estimators most usually used to those proposed by Henderson (1952, 1963; see also C. R. Henderson, Jr., 1971) which permit us to construct two estimators that simultaneously control for both nation-specific factors and heteroscedasticity.[8] They parallel the two approaches introduced above. We label the fixed-effects estimator WLSDV and the random-effects estimator WGLS. Both are consistent and asymptotically efficient under the stated assumptions. A justification for this procedure and an algorithm are presented in Nielsen (1974).

RESULTS

We begin by presenting estimates of equation (6), which we call the reduced-form model for the population and community-level hypotheses. Then we calculate estimates of the underlying dynamic model.

Cross-Population Analysis

We start by investigating the hypothesized ordering of inertia and cohort effects in equation (6) across the three populations of organizations. Table 4.1 gives the relevant results for the two estimators and two samples (rich and poor nations). Consider first the inertia effect. For both estimators and both samples we find the hypothesized effect: the estimated inertia parameter increases from primary to secondary to tertiary. For example, the WLSDV estimates are 0.169, 0.694, and 0.872 for primary, secondary, and tertiary in rich nations and 0.552, 0.747, and 0.935 in poor ones. This result lends support to our theoretical expectation: at the population level, more complex organizations, with a higher unit cost, adjust more slowly to their carrying capacities.

The hypothesis concerning the cohort parameter is that it should decrease from primary to tertiary. This hypothesis also fits the data perfectly. Therefore, more complex and costly educational organizations tend to incorporate a smaller fraction of the supply of qualified candidates.

We argued that the dimensionality of the linear resource parameter made its meaning ambiguous. It is nevertheless interesting to examine the empirical results to see if the coefficients exhibit some systematic pattern across educational levels. The resource coefficient for secondary enrollments is the highest for all four sample-estimator combinations. This seems to suggest that the two effects (in opposite directions) of complexity and cost on the resource parameter indeed take place in reality. The low coefficient of primary would then be explained by a low "dependence" on resources, the low tertiary coefficient by a high "cost" effect in the opposite direction, while the higher resource parameter of secondary would result from a combination of more dependence on resources not yet offset by a parallel increase in cost. This interpretation is of course ad hoc, but the empirical results strongly suggest the existence of a curvilinear relationship.

Cross-Community Hypotheses

To test the effect of the abundance of the environment on the inertia, cohort, and resource parameters, we compare estimates for rich and poor countries. For example, by the WLSDV method the inertia parameter of primary is estimated as 0.169 for rich countries and 0.552 for poor ones; the inertia coefficients are 0.694 and 0.747 for secondary and 0.872 and 0.935 for tertiary. The same pattern holds for the WGLS estimates. Thus our first community hypothesis is confirmed: the inertia parameter tends to be lower in wealthier environments.

The cohort coefficients are analyzed by similar techniques. For both estimators the postulated inequality holds: for each educational level the cohort effect is higher in rich environments than in poor ones. That

TABLE 4.1 Estimates of the Reduced Form Model (Eq. [6]) of Educational Growth[a]

Dependent Variable	Sample	Method	Independent Variables							R²	Number of Cases
			PRI_{t-5}	SEC_{t-5}	TER_{t-5}	GNP_{t-5}	POP_t	$PRIPOP_{t-5}$	Constant		
PRIMARY Enrollment$_t$	Richer Nations	WLSDV	0.169 (0.052)[a]	...	...	-0.106 (0.025)[a]	...	1.073 (0.063)[a]	0 ...	.893	28 28
		WGLS	0.473 (0.054)	...	...	0.015 (0.022)	...	0.598 (0.051)	-186.96 (183.01)	.987	28 28
	Poorer Nations	WLSDV	0.552 0.087	...	...	0.145 (0.177)	...	0.584 (0.082)	0 ...	.982	28 28
		WGLS	1.015 (0.046)	...	...	-0.275 (0.141)	...	0.165 (0.028)	92.17 (181.40)	.982	28 28
SECONDARY Enrollment$_t$	Richer Nations	WLSDV	0.275 (0.062)	0.694 (0.084)	...	0.190 (0.049)	-0.385 (0.017)	...	0 ...	.877	29 29
		WGLS	0.077 (0.031)	0.962 (0.052)	...	0.054 (0.019)	-0.015 (0.041)	...	15.82 (33.26)	.977	29 29
	Poorer Nations	WLSDV	0.106 (0.047)	0.747 (0.110)	...	0.235 (0.093)	0.042 (0.085)	...	0 ...	.855	29 29
		WGLS	0.036 (0.020)	1.119 (0.082)	...	0.029 (0.062)	0.023 (0.015)	...	-23.57 (48.76)	.948	29 29
TERTIARY Enrollment$_t$	Richer Nations	WLSDV	0.018 (0.015)	0.035 (0.019)	0.872 (0.112)	0.035 (0.014)	-0.016 (0.045)	...	0 ...	.899	29 29
		WGLS	0.017 (0.008)	0.013 (0.011)	1.160 (0.068)	0.013 (0.005)	-0.023 (0.010)	...	-0.96 (4.72)	.972	29 29
	Poorer Nations	WLSDV	-0.023 (0.009)	0.002 (0.024)	0.935 (0.094)	0.040 (0.019)	0.068 (.017)	...	0 ...	.832	29 29
		WGLS	0.005 (0.004)	0.012 (0.008)	1.165 0.061	0.005 (0.011)	-0.000 (0.003)	...	-4.42 (6.57)	.958	29 29

a. Standard errors in parentheses.

is, in wealthier countries the educational system is more responsive to the demographic pressure of the pool of qualified candidates.

The last set of hypotheses concerns the effect of the abundance of the environment on the resource parameter of the educational system. Recall that the resource effect is defined on δ', the effect of R_t on E^*; and that δ is a composite coefficient, the product of parameters δ' and β' that are expected to be found in reverse orderings when compared across environments. The situation, however, can be approached through the following a fortiori argument: if δ is larger for poor countries, then δ' must be larger also, since the smaller responsiveness coefficient β' would tend to diminish the value of δ and obliterate the difference between poor and rich countries. Keeping this possibility in mind, we compare the estimates of δ across the two samples. For the first time we encounter substantial disagreement between estimators. For WLSDV the resource effect is larger for poor nations for each level of education. However, exactly the reverse pattern holds with the WGLS estimates. We have not been able to determine why this difference arises. It may have something to do with small-sample properties of the WGLS method in that unweighted generalized least squares estimates (not reported here) agree with those of WLSDV. Clearly, this matter deserves deeper study.

The Determination of Carrying Capacities

We have managed, so far, to verify most of the propositions of section 2 without explicitly computing the parameters of equation (2) for the equilibrium enrollment, γ' and δ'. These coefficients, however, can be easily recovered from equation (5): β' is first computed as $1 - \beta$, and then γ' and δ' as γ/β' and δ/β', respectively. Given our results, these calculations are meaningful only for the WLSDV estimates, for reasons we discuss below. The calculations are reported in table 4.2. Across the levels of education both β' and γ' exhibit the expected decrease from primary to tertiary, and the behavior of δ' remains curvilinear, with the highest resource effect in the secondary equations. The rich-poor comparisons are also all in the expected direction (the one exception is γ' for primary, where the effect for poor nations is slightly larger). More important, we finally get a clean test of the community-level resource hypothesis. As we had predicted, the resource effect for each level of education is larger for poor nations.

We could not make similar calculations from the WGLS estimates because the estimated β exceed unity in four of the six equations. This implies that the responsiveness parameter is negative. A negative responsiveness parameter implies substantively meaningless dynamics. This problem likely stems from any combination of three complications: (1) the functional form of the dynamics may not be appropriate, especially for more complex organizations (the problem seems worst for tertiary education); (2) the hypothesis that the transitory portions of the disturbances of equation (6) are not autocorrelated may be wrong; and (3) the constant portion of the disturbances in equation (6) may not have constant variance. Each of these issues demands further study. It is particularly important that the dynamic structure be clarified further. In the meantime, our results must be considered a first approximation.

TABLE 4.2 Estimates of Parameters of the Dynamic Model of Educational Growth (WLSDV)[a]

Parameter	Level of Education	Richer Nations	Poorer Nations
Responsiveness:	Primary	0.831	0.448
$\hat{\beta}'$ $(=1 - \hat{\beta})$	Secondary	0.306	0.253
	Tertiary	0.128	0.065
Effect of Cohort on Equilibrium:	Primary	1.291	1.304
$\hat{\gamma}'$ $(= \hat{\gamma}/\hat{\beta})$	Secondary	0.899	0.419
	Tertiary	0.273	0.031
Effect of Resources on Equilibrium:	Primary	−0.128	0.324
$\hat{\delta}'$ $(= \hat{\delta}/\hat{\beta})$	Secondary	0.621	0.929
	Tertiary	0.273	0.615

a. Calculated from estimates in table 4.1. See text for explanation.

DISCUSSION AND CONCLUSION

This paper focuses on the aggregate size of populations of organizations. This point of view enabled us to propose a simple dynamic model of educational growth, independent of individual variations in organizational strategies due to mechanisms of intrapopulation competition (see note 6, above). Since the model could be specified for three populations of organizations (the primary, secondary, and tertiary levels) within two types of environments (rich and poor), we could meaningfully compare general mechanisms of change (inertia, cohort effect, and dependence on resources) across populations and environments.

The results confirm, on the whole, our population ecology model of organizational growth. The maximum size of a population of organizations within a bounded environment is determined by the *carrying capacity* of the environment for a particular organizational form. In our simplified model of educational expansion, we specified the carrying capacity as a function of two *niche parameters*: the supply of qualified candidates and the amount of resources in the environment. An immediate goal for further research consists in identifying other parameters of the niche of an organizational form (for example, political and cultural factors). A population of organizations, however, cannot react instantly to an expansion or contraction of the carrying capacity of the environment because of both the inherent structural inertia of individual organizations and competition between populations for resources and membership. In our model, structural inertia and the effect of competition are lumped together in the inertia parameter β. We showed that this coefficient, and the dynamic mechanisms it represents, could be meaningfully compared across populations and environments. Further work should attempt to analyze the process of growth by explicitly modeling the mechanisms of competition.

NOTES

1 The linear approximation has the defect that it implies nonzero enrollments when either C or R is zero. However, as we are considering the behavior of these systems far away from zero, we do not think this is a serious problem. Alternatively, we can specify that the relation in equation (2) is a power function and estimate the model under a logarithmic transformation. Our experience is that a log-log specification gives qualitatively similar results. We retain the linear specification since it leads to the simplest dynamic structure.

2 Models similar to equation (3) are often written as

$$\Delta E = \beta'' \Delta t (E^*_{t - \Delta t}),$$

where β'' represents the response of the system during a unit time interval $\Delta t = 1$ (see, for example Hummon, Doreian, and Teuter 1975). In the present context, we are not attempting to estimate the underlying continuous process. We chose to define $\beta' = \beta'' \Delta t$, and to focus on the coefficient β', which permits us to formulate the dynamic properties of the model (for example, the conditions of stability) in a simpler way. As Samuelson (1970, Appendix B) points out, the time variable in a difference equation can always be redefined so as to make the time interval Δt equal to unity.

3 The assumption that enrollment adjusts itself to E^*_t places constraints on the acceptable range of values of the coefficient β', which has to be between 0 and 2. If β' is negative, the size of the population of organizations and its equilibrium value diverge over time. A β' greater than 2 implies that E_t exhibits oscillations of increasing amplitude over time. In the stable case, $1 < \beta' < 2$ entails oscillations of decreasing amplitude until $E_t = E^*$, while $0 < \beta' < 1$ corresponds to a monotonic convergence of E_t to E^* (Blalock 1969, chap. 5; May 1973a, Appendix III).

4 One major mechanism of environmental resistance is competition with other forms of organizations. Competition between forms of organizations occurs when their respective carrying capacities depend on the *same* environmental variables, so that the expansion of one form decreases the carrying capacity, or maximum size, of others. Competition depends therefore on the

relevant niche parameters. For example, the three levels of education do not compete for candidates, since their prospective students are likely to belong to very different groups, so that an increase in enrollment at one level does not threaten the expansion of other levels. By contrast, they are likely to compete for *resources* (particularly money), since allocated environmental resources for the expansion of one level of education are unavailable for other levels. In our simplified model of educational expansion, the net effect of competition is forced into the dynamic coefficient β, which is treated here as a purely phenomenological, descriptive parameter. We argue that competition decreases the speed of response of the populations involved.

5 For all the nations we are studying enrollments increased over the period. Therefore, we do not address the likelihood that decline processes differ from growth processes for these forms of organizations (Freeman and Hannan 1975).

6 This extension of Thompson's argument is one instance of a hypothesis that is more readily justified at the population level than for individual organizations. Considered separately, individual members of a population of organizations have available a variety of strategies, ranging from extreme exclusiveness to minimal boundary-spanning intensity. Whatever strategy is chosen will presumably depend in part on mechanisms of intrapopulation competition between organizations for membership and resources, so that one would expect the individual coefficients γ' to vary widely within the population. At the aggregate level of a population, by contrast, general constraints on the functioning of a given organizational form are likely to appear in a sharper light. From a deeper point of view, the issue is intimately connected with the problem of collective rationality (Hannan and Freeman 1977): there is no guarantee that a course of action that is adaptive for a single organization will be optimal when many competing organizations adopt a similar strategy.

7 Nations are assigned to the poor or rich sample according to their position below or above the median GNP per capita measured in 1950, the earliest time point in the data. We exclude from the sample countries that were not independent in 1950.

8 The weighting factors are $PRIPOP_t$ in the PRI_t equation and POP_t in equations for SEC_t and TER_t.

FIVE · Creating Members: The Political Incorporation and Expansion of Public Education

Francisco O. Ramirez and Richard Rubinson

The preceding two chapters on the expansion of educational enrollments have analyzed the factors which affected the *size* of national educational systems. In this chapter we turn to an analysis of one of the *structural* features of educational systems, their relationship to the national state. We refer to this relationship as the political incorporation of education. We contend that expanded state authority and power leads to a greater degree of educational incorporation. The first part of this chapter discusses the conceptualization and measurement of this characteristic of educational systems. We then present our analyses of the effects of expanded state authority and power, and other factors, on our primary, secondary, and tertiary political incorporation scales. The second part of this chapter advances an interpretation of the role of education in modern states which is based on the empirical findings of the analyses of the expansion and political incorporation of education.

THE POLITICAL INCORPORATION OF EDUCATION
Conceptualization

The political incorporation of education refers to the degree to which the national state regulates education. Such political regulation takes the form of a series of rules by which the state controls education. Educational institutions vary considerably in the degree to which they are organized by such rules. In some countries, there is a national ministry of education which regulates all aspects of the educational system. Schools must acquire a political charter; teachers must have certification from a national organization; the curriculum is organized and distributed by a national agency to all schools; and the rules and regulations regarding the admission and graduation of students are regulated at the national level. In such countries, the educational system can be characterized as having a high level of national political incorporation. In other countries, there is no national ministry of education regulating activities. Schools may be set up by private groups with little regulation from the state. Decisions regarding curriculum, admissions, and graduation requirements are made by local authorities. Teachers need not be certified by the state, but need meet only local requirements. There are no national standards or curriculum uniformity in the country. In such countries, the educational system can be characterized as having a low degree of national political incorporation. The degree of political incorporation may vary by levels of schooling and by the different features of education just described, so any measure of political incorporation must take these different factors into account.

This structural dimension of political incorporation should be distinguished from institutional differentiation, which refers to the degree to which educational activities have been separated from other activities and organized by a functionally specific institution. In the present world system, education is institutionally differentiated in all nation-states.

Measurement

The data from which we constructed measures of national political incorporation were created by a content analysis of detailed descriptions of educational systems as reported in the UNESCO World Survey of Education handbooks. The procedure was as follows: First we created a list of seven features of education which we wished to code. These features were (1) the political level with general responsibility for education, (2) the political level with general control over education, (3) the political level which controls student admissions, (4) the political level which controls curriculum, (5) the political level which controls examinations, (6) the source of funding for students, and (7) the source of funding for the schools. This information was coded for each country for which data were available; and the information was coded separately for primary, secondary, and tertiary schooling. These data describe the educational systems of countries around 1965.

Each of the seven items was scored on a scale of zero to seven. Each item was given a score of 0 if there was no political control over the item; a score of 1 if there was only local political control; a score of 2 if there was a combination of local and provincial control; a score of 3 if there was only provincial control; a score of 4 if there was a combination of local, provincial, and national control; a score of 5 if there was a combination of local and national control; a score of 6 if there was a combination of provincial and national control; and a score of 7 if there was only national political control of the item. This scoring system was designed to produce a scoring in terms of increasing degree of national political control over each feature of education coded.[1]

A country's scores for the degree of national political incorporation of primary, secondary, and tertiary education were computed by summing the score for each item on which there was information and then dividing by the number of items used. Only those countries with at least five items of information were used. This procedure produces a score of national political incorporation for each of the three levels of schooling,

with a score of 7 representing the highest degree of political incorporation and a score of 0 representing the lowest degree of incorporation.[2]
There is a high correlation between the degree of political incorporation
of primary and secondary education ($r = .72$), but only a moderate
correlation between either primary or secondary and tertiary educational incorporation ($r = .38$ for primary and $r = .34$ for secondary).
Thus, while countries with high degrees of national political incorporation of education tend to be high on all three levels of education, they
tend to control primary and secondary education in a similar fashion and
tertiary less.

Findings

Table 5.1 presents the means and standard deviations for the measures
of national political incorporation for primary, secondary, and tertiary
education. The striking finding in this table is that the mean levels of
national political incorporation of education are quite high throughout
the world. The mean level of national political incorporation is 5.46 for
primary education and 5.41 for secondary education. The mean level
for tertiary education is considerably lower at 3.81, but this still represents a rather high degree of national political control. These measures
tell us, then, that during the period we have been analyzing, national
states have controlled much of the educational activity associated with
formal schooling, and that this national control is more heavily concentrated at the primary and secondary than at the tertiary level. Although
we know of no other analogous study of the degree of national control

TABLE 5.1   Means and Standard Deviations for the Political Incorporation
of Education Scales

Level of Education	Mean	Standard Deviation	Number of Cases
Primary	5.46	1.52	119
Secondary	5.41	1.50	116
Tertiary	3.81	1.74	72

of other institutions, we suspect that education tends to be especially
highly politically controlled by the national state. Examples of countries
with highly incorporated tertiary educational systems as of 1965 include
the USSR and Eastern European countries with the exception of Yugoslavia; France and Sweden in Western Europe; Algeria and the UAR in
the Middle East; Indonesia in Asia; Cuba and Brazil in Latin America.
Countries with low levels of tertiary educational incorporation include
Switzerland, Ireland, Nigeria, India, Japan, Canada, and the USA. The
incorporation score of the USA for primary and secondary education is
also lower than the national mean scores for these levels.

We next turn to an examination of the societal factors which might be associated with the degree of national political incorporation of education. Our main interest is to test the proposition that expanded state authority and power leads to higher levels of educational incorporation. Because the modernization literature emphasizes the importance of economic and educational growth in promoting state involvement in the educational system, we estimate the effects of these variables. Because competition or conflict among ethnic groups is often viewed as an important influence on the political character of education, we also estimate its effect. Thus, table 5.2 presents a series of cross-sectional multivariate analyses of the effects of political, economic, and social variables on the primary, secondary, and tertiary educational incorporation scales. The indicators used in these analyses are described in chapter 3.

TABLE 5.2   Zero-Order Correlations among Primary, Secondary, and
Tertiary Educational Incorporation Scales[a]

	Primary	Secondary	Tertiary
Primary	1.0	.72	.38
Secondary		1.0	.34
Tertiary			1.0

a. 61 cases.

The pattern of results is quite clear: (1) Higher levels of state authority and power lead to higher levels of national educational incorporation. The positive association is significant for seven out of nine coefficients and strongest at the tertiary level. (2) The greater the degree of economic rationalization (as measured by the proportion of the male labor force outside the agricultural sector), the lower the degree of national educational incorporation. The negative association is significant for five out of nine coefficients. (3) The degree of ethnic diversity also negatively affects the national incorporation of the educational system. The negative association is significant for seven out of nine coefficients. (4) The level of enrollment relative to the appropriate age group is not systematically related to the degree of educational incorporation. Expanded primary enrollment tends to show a positive association, while expanded tertiary enrollment tends to show a negative sign. The enrollment coefficient, however, tends not to be significant.

Before we discuss these findings, some clarifying points need to be made: (a) More extended analysis, including factors not reported in this paper, does not alter the results in table 5.3 nor offer additional findings. (b) The initial construction of the educational incorporation scales included 1955 measures for all three educational levels. However,

TABLE 5.3   Effects of Political, Economic, and Social Variables
on the Political Incorporation of Education, 1965[a]

Dependent Variables	Political Variable	% Males not in Agriculture 1960	Ethnolinguistic Fractionalization	Educ. Enroll. Ratio 1965[b]	No.of Cases
		Independent Variables			
Equation (A)	Gov. Rev./ GDP 1961-67				
Primary Incorp. Scale	.44***	-1.02***	-.28***	.17	64
Secondary Incorp. Scale	.22**	- .03	-.19**	-.57	67
Tertiary Incrop. Scale	.38***	- .46***	-.05	-.26	55
Equation (B)	Cabinet Size 1965				
Primary Incorp. Scale	-.14	- .60***	-.20**	.19	72
Secondary Incorp Scale	.10	- .07	-.18**	-.34**	77
Tertiary Incorp. Scale	.41***	- .44***	-.12	-.01	64
Equation (C)	State Centralization Index				
Primary Incorp. Scale	.21**	- .62***	-.19	.18	66
Secondary Incrop. Scale	.30***	- .16	-.27***	-.32**	65
Tertiary Incrop. Scale	.59***	- .18	-.13	-.07	61

** $p < .05$
*** $p < .01$

a. Standardized slopes.
b. Primary, secondary, and tertiary educational enrollment ratios are used as
   independent variables depending on whether the dependent variable is primary,
   secondary, or tertiary incorporation. More complex analyses in which, for
   example, secondary and tertiary enrollment ratios are both included in the
   analysis of tertiary educational incorporation do not differ substantially
   from those given here.

the autoregressions are too high to allow us to engage in panel analysis
except in a few instances; in these cases, the results are very similar to
the ones reported in this paper (Ramirez 1974). (c) In many panel
analyses, the educational incorporation scales used as independent variables fail to show systematic effects on educational, economic, or political development measures. Thus, although in this paper we employ a
cross-sectional design, direction of causality is not a serious issue in
these analyses. (d) In some analyses in table 5.3, problems of multicollinearity probably result in overestimating the size of the coefficients.
This is least problematic in the analyses of tertiary educational incorpo-

ration and most problematic in the other analyses where the intercorrelations among independent variables—educational and economic development, for example—sometimes tend to be moderately high (around .7).

EXPLANATIONS OF NATIONAL EDUCATIONAL EXPANSION AND INCORPORATION

The empirical studies of education in these three chapters produce two major findings: First, educational enrollments have expanded everywhere during the post–World War II era as a function of national participation in a world cultural and organizational milieu which mandates educational expansion (chap. 3), and as a consequence of the demographic features of the educational institutions themselves (chap. 4). This phenomenal growth takes place relatively independent of the constraints and stimuli that economic, political, and social structures provided in previous periods. Second, educational systems tend to be heavily politically organized and controlled by the national government. The degree of national educational incorporation is higher in countries with high levels of state authority and lower in countries with high levels of economic development and in those with much ethnolinguistic diversity.

How do these findings square with the major explanations of national educational expansion and incorporation in the social science literature? Consider first the functional or modernization perspective. Within this broad theoretical framework, the expansion of education is conceptualized as a societal response to the increasing institutional differentiation entailed in development. The primary mechanism through which differentiation leads to educational expansion is through an increase in the demand for actors to fill increasingly complex roles, in terms of both cognitive or technical and affective skills. But the findings in chapter 3 have shown that a number of hypotheses derived from such a theoretical framework are not supported in the period being analyzed. The expansion of educational enrollments was found not to be related to most measures of societal modernization or differentiation. In a functional or modernization model, the national political process intervenes in education only if schooling is not expanding at a rate commensurate with other features of development. But the findings in chapter 3 suggest that education is expanding everywhere at a rate much greater than the expansion of other societal institutions.[3] Thus, one cannot derive from modernization theory the high level of national educational incorporation reported in table 5.1. Moreover, the negative association between economic development and educational incorporation is an anomaly from the modernization perspective. If, as this perspective emphasizes, education is a rational individual and societal investment, why should the greater development of the industrial and service sectors (economic rationalization) be associated with a lower level of state involvement with the educational system (political rationalization)?

Next we turn to status-competition or class-conflict models. Within these frameworks, educational expansion is conceptualized as a consequence of competition or power struggles among various groups in society. In status-conflict versions, education is viewed not primarily as an institution preparing actors for effective role performance, but as a mechanism of allocation to maintain the pattern of unequal distribution of prestige and material reward among groups in society (Collins 1971). In class-conflict models, education is seen as a mechanism to discipline and socialize the working classes toward the structure of authority and control in industrial organizations (Bowles and Gintis 1976). Such theories do not seem capable of explaining the two sets of findings with which we are concerned. First, it is highly unlikely that the uniformities of educational expansion shown in chapter 3 could have been produced by such status- or class-conflict processes. For these national uniformities in the expansion of enrollments would have had to be generated by uniformities in both the degree and timing of either status conflict or class conflict across countries. Second, neither status- nor class-conflict theories adequately explain the processes that affect the national incorporation of education. Status-conflict theories assume a negative relationship between educational centralization and educational expansion (Collins 1971; Ben-David and Zloczower 1962). In table 5.2, the relationship between these two variables is weak and unstable in direction. Furthermore, to the extent that much ethnic diversity implies much status competition, this perspective would lead to the prediction that countries with much ethnicity would experience much educational growth. The finding in chapter 3 clearly does not support this contention. Status- and class-conflict theories alike view the rise in educational centralism in the United States as an elite response to waves of ethnic immigrants. Table 5.3, however, shows that high levels of ethnicity do not promote but rather hinder the national incorporation of education.

In summary, we do not argue that the processes detailed in either functional or conflict theories of education never occur. Rather, we contend that such processes do not seem capable of explaining the findings we have shown during this period. In the section that follows, we sketch a theoretical alternative to modernization and conflict models of education. This alternative emphasizes the expansion of state authority and the role of education in the institutionalization of citizenship. This alternative views education as a contemporary initiation ceremony and conceptualizes its incorporation and expansion as the national construction of citizenship and its extension throughout the population. We call this alternative the creating-members model.

CREATING MEMBERS

Our starting point is an observation by Reinhard Bendix, who noted that historically the expansion and political control of education have tended to be closely related to the extension of national citizenship (Bendix 1964). Bendix also noted that education was the only "right" of citizenship that was actually a duty. That is, while rights of assembly, organization, and voting were voluntary, the right of primary education was everywhere made compulsory. This observation of the compulsory nature of education in contrast to the voluntary nature of the other components of citizenship is still strikingly true today. And since the expansion of citizenship rights and their extension to more and more of a nation's population is a process that tends to characterize countries in our period of study, it seems profitable to look for part of the key to understanding education by focusing on national citizenship (see chap. 14).

Citizenship is that social status which places each individual in a direct and equal political relationship to the state. In this sense, citizenship is that social status which confers membership in the state; and citizenship is the defining characteristic of a particular type of status group whose organizational basis is the state. Citizenship is the social status which both confers and defines a particular social identity—what we commonly call the national identity—and as such can be analyzed as part of the process of the formation of the nation-state. That education is the one aspect of citizenship made compulsory everywhere for everyone suggests that it plays a key role in the formation of a national identity.

The understanding of education as a mechanism of national identity formation is an aspect of education that is in some ways obvious but is also an aspect almost totally overlooked in functional and conflict theories of education. But in all countries, educational curriculum and organization tend to emphasize the transmission of a national culture, the construction and glorification of the national history, and the teaching of the national symbols and the national language. Education, then, is an institutional agency for creating national uniformities among the heterogeneous status and class groupings in society. We are not here arguing that education is always successful in creating a national identity and national identification at the expense of ethnic, religious, or class identifications, though doubtless it sometimes is successful. Rather, we are arguing that the expansion of education and of its national political control reflects the pressures toward national identity and national culture.

Education serves the ends of national identity formation not only through its emphasis on national culture and symbols, but also through its role as the primary mechanism legitimating the economic and political allocation of individuals in society. Numerous studies have shown that education is the major mechanism linking individuals from their status and class backgrounds to their adult economic and political positions. And this linking mechanism of education operates in developed as well as in underdeveloped countries (see, for example, Currie 1972; Hansen and Haller 1973; Heyneman 1976; Holsinger 1975). Education not only alters patterns of economic and political allocation in society, but it has become the primary legitimate way for such allocation to proceed. The possession of educational credentials, then, becomes the primary mechanism by which individuals are defined as full and legitimate societal members. Education, then, is an agency for the creation of national identification and culture at the societal level, and also an agency for the legitimation of national membership at the individual level.

Systems of mass schooling may thus operate like contemporary initiation rites, symbolically separating individuals from their families of origin and orienting them toward the acceptance of a broader and impersonal collective authority (Hart 1963; Dreeben 1968). Many studies of education in developing countries (as well as historical accounts of the rise of education in what are now developed countries) show that school systems have the power to transform individuals into citizens with higher levels of political participation and a stronger sense of attachment to the nation-state (Inkeles and Smith 1974; Almond and Verba 1963). We conceptualize this transformation as a process of institutional certification that works independent of any changes in the internal states of the initiates. In both initiation ceremonies and mass schooling, the content of the socialization (and whether it is learned) is less instrumental to the endowment of membership status than the institutional mandate to create the new person. What takes place within the classroom and the schoolyard may not be intrinsically relevant to becoming a citizen. But if the school or school system is nationally chartered to confer citizenship status, then many routine activities are politically reconstituted to become meaningful citizenship training functions. The products of the school system are then certified to act, and be treated, as citizens.

The likelihood and dramatization of initiation rites varies across societies (see, for example, Young 1965; Cohen 1964). National societies also vary in the extent to which they can politically utilize their educational institutions to create new persons and legitimate the national culture. At issue is the nature of the relationship between state and society —that is, the degree of state authority and power. State authority is the sphere of legitimated state jurisdiction, and state power is the probability that the state as an organization can effectively act upon society. We recognize that the historical trend is in the direction of increasing state authority and power (see chaps. 11 and 13). But cross-national variations continue to exist, and this factor seems to constitute an important influence on the extensiveness and structure of education. Briefly, we contend that the expansion of the symbolic authority and bureaucratic power of the state intensifies the degree to which the interests and rights of the national collectivity permeate the population, transforming one and all into good members. Within such a political framework no individual or group can legitimately fall outside the moral boundaries of the corporate nation-state and no aspect of schooling can be entrusted to anyone other than the national authority.[4]

This perspective leads to two general hypotheses. At higher levels of state authority and power, a country is more likely to (1) extend standardized mass schooling to all within its population; and (2) nationally incorporate the structure of education by locating educational institutions within a network of national rules and resources. The analysis of the expansion of primary educational enrollment in chapter 3 does not support the first hypothesis. However, in analyses that distinguish between the development of public primary versus private primary enrollment, Ramirez (1974) finds that the former is positively influenced by the level of state authority and power while the latter is negatively affected. These analyses are exploratory, and much more work needs to be done to assess the first hypothesis.

Unlike the functionalist and conflict perspectives, the creating-members argument predicts the high level of national educational incorporation by conceptualizing it as the consequence of expanded state authority and power. Although some states enjoy more authority and power than others, most state organizations wield historically unprecedented authority and power. It is therefore not surprising that most educational systems are closely linked to the nation-state. Furthermore, table 5.2 clearly shows an association between state authority and power and educational incorporation at the primary, secondary, and tertiary levels.

What further research implications are suggested by this perspective? First, one should expect to find a positive association between the strength of the state and the extent to which peripheral status groups are transformed into regular members of society (chap. 14). Second, there should be less within-nation variation in educational organization, curriculum for instance, under conditions of expanded state organization. Third, in a society with strong institutional linkages between state and educational organization, educational aspirations and plans should be less private and idiosyncratic; that is, entry into many branches of higher education will be predicated upon passing a national exam, and withdrawal from higher education (dropping out) should be relatively low. Fourth, student organizations and student political movements should be more directly linked to national political parties and to agencies of the national state. Lastly, although our research shows that nationally incorporated educational systems are neither more nor less likely to grow, we suspect that they may be less variable over time—that is, less likely to engage in experimentation and innovation.

NOTES

1 For a detailed discussion of the content analysis, coding procedures, and scoring system, see Ramirez (1974) and Rubinson (1974).

2 Other analyses using scores from scalogram and factor analyses produce results similar to those using this arithmetic scale.

3 In fact, this argument was often used to support the implementation of universal compulsory education. Studies of compulsory education in western Europe have concluded, however, that education was not lagging at the time of the implementation of state-enforced elementary education. For example, Blaug concludes for England, "External benefits, parental incompetence and equality of opportunity do not stand up as arguments for state-provided education" (Quoted in West 1970, p. 12).

4 These ideas are discussed in greater depth in Ramirez (1974) and Rubinson (1974).

III STUDIES OF ECONOMIC GROWTH: EDUCATION, MODERNIZATION, AND STATE POWER

SIX · National Economic Development, 1950–70: Social and Political Factors

John W. Meyer, Michael T. Hannan,
Richard Rubinson, and George M. Thomas

In this chapter we examine social and political factors affecting national economic growth from 1950 to 1970. The literature on this subject, with a few notable exceptions, consists mostly of case studies. The exceptions typically consist of time-series analyses of one or a few Western nations (Kuznets 1971) or cross-sectional analyses of many nations (Harbison and Myers 1964). There are almost no studies that are both longitudinal and broadly comparative. We study all nations for which data are available over this period.

We consider three broad categories of social and political factors: the scale of national educational systems, levels of social and political modernization, and the degree to which power and authority are organized in a state structure. We include little information on properties of the economies in question. Therefore we cannot analyze the processes by which social and political factors affect economic growth. Instead, our interest lies in the classic problem of whether social and political organization affects economic growth and development.

In the first section we discuss the expansion of a world system as it affects the ways in which social and political organization within the nation in turn affect economic growth. This discussion leads to the formulation of three broad hypotheses concerning the relationship of social and political structures of nations to levels of economic growth, and a description of the indicators of the social and political variables and of our research design. The third section contains the results of four different but parallel analyses. Each analysis arises from a different hypothesis concerning the functional form of the relationship of social and political variables to national economic growth. Only three of the models that we estimated give substantively meaningful results. These are presented in detail in the tables. In the text we focus on the patterns of findings that hold across indicators and across models.

86 STUDIES OF ECONOMIC GROWTH

BACKGROUND AND THEORY

The World Context

As pointed out in chapter 1, the 1950–70 period was one in which national societies became increasingly organized around state structures. During the period the number of independent states rose from 93 to 142. These states exist in a world economy that has great power and very high rates of exchange. Dominant elites in almost all states orient to the world economy and to the goal of economic growth. They adopt economic growth as an explicit national goal, attempt to manage it, and engage in national planning to this end (chap. 13; Waterston 1965). The system as a whole *does* grow. Both richer and poorer countries more than doubled their per capita gross national products (in constant prices) from 1950 to 1970 (Meyer, Boli-Bennett, and Chase-Dunn 1975).

The fact that the world is organized in part as a system of states struggling to grow in a world economy changes the terms of theories of economic development. To put the matter in the simplest way: Weber and Marx are not made irrelevant, but one must use Weber and Marx differently from most social science literature on economic growth. Weber's ideas on the cultural factors that induce individuals and communities to engage in rational economic action become less relevant than his theory of organization as economic growth processes become organized by the state. Similarly, ideas about the nature of the struggle between capital and labor within a national context become less relevant than ideas about international capital and imperialism. Furthermore, earlier discussions of the role of traditional political systems—organized around agrarian empires and the maintenance of given distributions of power and status—as inhibiting economic growth have little relevance in a world of states organized in a larger capitalist system (Wallerstein 1974a).

Two other features of the world context are relevant: (1) The 1950–70 period is one of sustained growth in the world (and national) economies. Theories and findings about the factors which would operate in a period of contraction might be quite different from those discussed here. (2) The state system has relatively high legitimacy in the world, and few attempts are made to build political empires or to break up extant states (although many external attempts are made to influence or alter their regimes). State survival is in good part ensured by the network of agreements in the system, and the advantages of sheer size are attenuated.

Hypotheses

The Power and Authority of the State States are organized around economic growth. As they achieve dominance in society, they are able to organize society around this goal, breaking down the power of resistant subunits. Strong states are able to maximize societal positions in the overall world economy even if entrenched internal groups are alienated. Therefore, hypothesis 1 is that in the modern world context, the dominance of the state in society will lead to increased economic development.

The Educational Reconstruction of Populations and Societies An elaborate literature argues that educational expansion increases economic growth (see the review by Machlup 1970). First, education is thought to *socialize* people to the skills and values of modern economic action. It is thought to socialize workers and technicians to their work roles, and to socialize the population at large to demand and accept the social changes involved in economic development.

Apart from socialization, the modern educational system is thought to serve as an *allocation* system. In principle, this could simply be a replacement for traditional personnel allocation, providing no net benefits to the economy as a whole, but arguments have been advanced that education benefits the economy by serving as an efficient method of sorting and selecting people with the appropriate skills and values (Spence 1973; Thurow 1975).

Beyond this, education functions as a *legitimating* system, reconstructing the population so that everyone (whether educated or uneducated) tends to see modern economic organization and action—the labor market, rational organization, investment, technology, and so on—as appropriate. Further, modern educational systems provide similar categories of people and types of knowledge around the world, and they reorganize societies so that penetration by the world culture and market is easier and more legitimate (see Meyer 1977 for an extensive discussion of these ideas).

An empirical literature in the economics of education has arisen attempting to infer the aggregate contribution of education to economic development by adding up the differentials education creates in the income of individuals (see the papers in Blaug 1968, 1969; Bowman and Anderson 1966; Machlup 1970). Since university graduates make a great deal more money than primary school dropouts, even with background held constant, this "returns to education" method usually produces optimistic conclusions.[1] But these inferences make sense only if education is simply a socialization system. If it is an arbitrary allocation system (see Berg 1971), huge income differences may result in no aggregate benefits. If it is a legitimating system, aggregate benefits may greatly exceed the individual gains of the educated. Aggregate data, of the type examined here, are necessary to test these ideas.[2] Therefore, hypothesis 2 is that the expansion of (*a*) primary, (*b*) secondary, and (*c*) tertiary educational enrollments increases economic growth.

Only a few relevant studies have been done. Following the early lead of Anderson and Bowman (1966), McClelland (1966) shows that countries higher on tertiary education showed higher growth rates. Steadman (1970) shows such effects for primary and secondary education. These studies lend some support to hypothesis 2, but alternative causal variables are not considered.

Theories of educational effects on economic development ordinarily suppose these effects to differ with level of development (for example, Harbison and Myers 1964; Steadman 1970). A common argument is that more developed economies benefit especially from higher levels of education which produce technical and managerial personnel for advanced industries, while less developed countries benefit more from mass education which helps modernize the lower levels of the labor force. Steadman (1970) shows some data suggesting such interaction effects.

Finally, it should be noted that theories expressing skepticism about educational effects on economic development (or even suggesting negative effects) have appeared in the last decade. The argument is that education expands the expectations of the population and (a) produces demands which act as a drag on growth, and/or (b) generates political instability and thus economic slowdown. No real evidence has been produced supporting these ideas,[3] but they may play an ideological role in legitimating the restriction of educational expansion.

Social and Political Modernization Modernization was a main theme in discussions of economic development a decade or two ago. The idea is that social arrangements such as urbanization, mass communication, and political participation bring individuals into active and expanded societal participation and provide them with modern orientations which make them more effective creatures of and contributors to economic growth. The major study by Inkeles and Smith (1974) with comparative data on individuals makes this argument. A large number of intervening processes connecting social modernization with economic growth have been discussed, but most of them operate through changes in the attitudes and values of the individual members of society. Thus, social modernization "modernizes" individuals, who then change their reproduction, child-rearing and family patterns, economic behavior, political behavior, and so on, in such ways to generate orientations and capabilities toward economic productivity. Hypothesis 3, then, is that modernized social and political participation increases economic growth.

In recent years, some skepticism about this line of reasoning has developed. With the widespread emergence in the world system of national aspirations to economic development, this variable no longer seems so significant in distinguishing societies. Social scientists recently have attended more to the organizational power and effectiveness of the state as a critical variable affecting economic development than to the degree to which modern goals and values are shared in populations. Among other consequences, this skepticism has led to many doubts about the economic effectiveness of political democracy in the modern world.

All of these doubts have been intensified by a few empirical studies suggesting little relation between such variables as birth rates, and urbanization (clearly conceptually related to social modernization) on the one hand and economic development on the other. We consider evidence on the hypothesis, however, because the line of thought involved has been an important one in the field.

MEASURES

We take our measures from available cross-national data files and yearbooks:

Economic Development

Three indicators of economic development over time are employed: *Gross National Product* GNP data are compiled from national accounts, and are estimates of the value of the goods and services produced per year. The data are taken from the IBRD World Tables (1971) and are transformed into constant (1964) US dollars. There are great difficulties in making these accounts comparable across countries, but biases are relatively stable for each country over time, so the resultant errors in our analyses are moderated. For a number of our analyses gross national product per capita is computed to adjust for variations in population sizes. We sometimes take the logarithm of the statistic to produce an indicator of economic development with a distribution more appropriate for regression analysis. The relative rankings of countries on GNP are highly stable: for 104 cases, the correlation between log GNP per capita in 1950 and 1970 is .92. We employ data for 1950, 1955, 1965, and 1970.

Energy Consumption Data on energy consumption in kilowatt-hours of electricity are also widely available (Taylor and Hudson 1971; IBRD 1971). This indicator closely parallels GNP. The correlation between log GNP per capita and log KWH per capita is .88 for 1950 (81 cases) and .92 for 1970 (111 cases). The correlation between log KWH per capita 1950 and log KWH per capita 1970 is .80 (79 cases).

Percent of the Male Labor Force Not in Agriculture This variable, available from the ILO (1971) for 1950 and 1960, describes the economic structure, rather than production levels. As Kuznets (1971) notes, changes in structure may be decreasingly associated with economic growth. Nevertheless, economic development in most of the world means shifting the population out of the agricultural sector into industrial production and services. The variable is closely related to log GNP per capita (.85, 105 cases, in 1950; .90, 129 cases, in 1960) and to log KWH per capita (.78, 98 cases, in 1950; .86, 110 cases, in 1960). The variable is very highly autocorrelated between 1950 and 1960 (.99, 144 cases).

The Power and Authority of the State in Society

Unlike economic development, there is little conceptual agreement or empirical relation among indicators of the power of the state. States vary in their resources with respect to society, but also in the degree to which they are integrated with (and represent the interests of) groups in society, and these two dimensions are by no means closely related. In the measures discussed below, of course, we consider only states which are formally independent through most of the period from 1950 to 1970. We use government revenue as a percentage of gross domestic product, the index of state centralization, and the size of the cabinet. For the description and sources for these measures, see chapter 3.

Communist countries tend to receive high scores on the index of state centralization and on the size of the cabinet variable. They also grew more rapidly during the 1950–70 period than did most other countries. Part of this growth, however, may be related to measurement biases. Their national account statistics differ from the conventional Western format. As a near equivalent to GNP, we use net material product. But this measure (compared to GNP) is biased toward growth resulting from industrial rather than service production. This bias may help create some of the positive effects of our index of state centralization and size of the cabinet variables that we report later. It does not affect our estimates of the effect of government revenue, since communist countries are not given scores on this variable.

Table 6.1 presents a correlation matrix of these various indicators and shows the relation of each to log GNP per capita in 1950. The table shows the difficulties in defining state power. The indicators range from the one most indicative of state *resources,* government revenue as a percent of GDP, which is closely related to level of economic development, to our index of state centralization, which is negatively correlated with economic development and with government revenue. This tells us something about the modern political world: less developed states attempt forced mobilization and/or control in competing in the world system, while more developed ones tend to absorb (or be absorbed in) their societies through nation-building.

The point here is that we cannot consider state power and authority as a unitary phenomenon in the modern world; we must look for empirical evidence on the economic effects of its several indicators to decide how to further evaluate its dimensions.

TABLE 6.1   Intercorrelations of Indicators of State Power and Authority, and Correlations with Log GNP per Capita, 1950[a]

	Gov. Rev./ GNP 1955	Cabinet Size	Index of State Centralization	Log GNP per Cap. 1950
Government Revenue/GNP 1955	1.0	.02(58)	-.13(59)	.47(60)
Cabinet Size 1950		1.0	.52(66)	.08(68)
Index of State Centralization			1.0	-.39(82)

a. Number of cases in parentheses; correlations based on all cases for which data are available. As noted later, some countries are excluded in further analyses.

Educational Expansion We use the data on educational enrollments at primary, secondary, and tertiary levels that we used in chapter 3. Table 6.2 shows that these educational ratios are highly intercorrelated with each other and with economic development.

Social and Political Modernization There is relatively little agreement on the meaning of modernization, except for the understanding that it involves social differentiation and the consequent elaboration of individual roles and extension of individual participation in social institutions. But its indicators are rather highly intercorrelated. As indicators of modernization we use urbanization, formal political representation, political participation, and political modernization. All these variables have been described in chapter 3. The correlation among these variables and log GNP per capita 1950 are shown in Table 6.3.

Control Variables

In various analyses below, we hold constant other variables which may be of substantive interest, or which may contaminate effects in which we are interested:

Population and Population Change Our measures of economic development sometimes are standardized on population. They may in any case be affected by population, since national accounts are often based on estimates affected by population size, and since population growth may offset economic development. We try several tactics for controlling such effects, using population data taken from Taylor and Hudson (1971).

Capital Formation as a Proportion of Gross Domestic Product This is a standard economic variable thought to affect subsequent growth. It may be an intervening variable for the effects of interest, or may be an independent variable creating other effects as artifacts. In either event, we perform some analyses holding it constant: data are taken from Taylor and Hudson (1971).

Ethnolinguistic Fractionalization This measure, as described in chapter 3, is also used.

Exclusions

In analyses considering the effects of political variables, we examine data on only those countries which are independent through the period under investigation. Political variables may have quite distinct meanings in colonies. Even when political variables are not explicitly involved, we report some analyses for independent countries only, for the same reason.

Throughout our analyses, we eliminate those countries with a large proportion of their GDP derived from oil and mining. Specifically, this excludes those countries in which over 20% of the GDP was derived

TABLE 6.2   Intercorrelations of Educational Enrollment Ratios, and Correlations with Log GNP per Capita, 1950[a]

	Pri. Enroll. Ratio 1950	Sec. Enroll. Ratio 1950	Univ. Enroll. Ratio 1950	Log GNP per Cap. 1950
Primary Enrollment/Age Group 1950	1.0	.64(112)	.58(115)	.74(91)
Secondary Enrollment/Age Group 1950		1.0	.74(109)	.72(87)
UniversityEnrollment/Age Group 1950			1.0	.64(87)

a. Number of cases in parentheses; correlations based on all cases for which data are available. As noted later, some
    countries are excluded in further analyses.

TABLE 6.3   Intercorrelations of Indicators of Social and Political Modernization, and Correlations with Log GNP per Capita, 1950[a]

	Urban. 1950	Polit. Modern.	Polit. Particip. 1960	Formal Polit. Rep. 1946-50	Log GNP per Cap. 1950
Urbanization 1950	1.0	.54(127)	.48(72)	.62(51)	.54(104)
Political Modernization		1.0	.33(73)	.71(53)	.68(100)
Political Participation 1960			1.0	.53(29)	.47(54)
Formal Political Representation 1946-50				1.0	.82(50)

a. Number of cases in parentheses; correlations based on all cases for which data are available. As noted later, some countries are excluded in further analyses.

from extractive sources (IBRD 1971), or in which this changed during the 1950–70 period by over 10%.[4]

The logic of this exclusion is simple. While we are interested in the economic effects of the larger world system in the 1950–70 period, those effects merely due to the accidental availability of mineral resources are so exogenous to a given country's social structure as to constitute simply a source of extraneous error.

Throughout our analyses, we eliminate data from the United States for statistical reasons. The US has disproportionate scores on several economic, and especially educational, variables, and we wanted to avoid analyses which might be affected by extreme values.[5]

ANALYSES AND RESULTS

We pursue our analyses with four different models, each designed to take into account different methodological issues and possible specifications. We discuss each in turn, and show the relevant results.

Conventional Ratio Analysis

We have five different economic indicators at time 2 which permit time lags long enough to show the potential effects of independent variables. To make possible ordinary least-squares estimates, the five indicators of economic growth are transformed and standardized so that they are (a) reasonably distributed, and (b) corrected for population size. They are (1) The percentage of the male labor force not in agriculture 1960; (2) log GNP per capita 1965; (3) log GNP per capita 1970; (4) log KWH per capita 1965; and (5) log KWH per capita 1970. With the GNP and KWH variables, we select time 1 variables about 15 years earlier (so that peculiar distortions in given time 1 measures cannot affect all the analyses).[6] We test the hypotheses using panel analysis as discussed in chapter 2.

Table 6.4 shows a set of multiple regression equations for each dependent variable. Each row of the table reports a separate equation, with the raw slope associated with each independent variable and the standard error of each slope.

Primary, secondary, and tertiary educational enrollment ratios are included in each equation. We also include the ratio of time 2 to time 1 population to control for population growth, since population is included as a standardizing factor in the formulation of each of our dependent variables. The various analyses then add our indicators of political and social factors hypothesized to affect economic development.

Results The findings relevant to each of our hypothesized (and control) factors are presented in one of the columns of table 6.4. Examining the entries in the relevant column shows the direction, degree of consistency, and significance of the hypothesized effect.

TABLE 6.4   Panel Analyses of Factors Affecting Economic Development[a]

Eq. No.	Political, Social and Control Variable Names	H 1: State Power & Control Authority	H 3: Social & Political Modernization[b]	H 2a: Prim. Enrollment Ratio	H 2b: Sec. Enrollment Ratio	H 2c: Univ. Enrollment Ratio	$\frac{\text{Pop.T2}}{\text{Pop.T1}}$	Control Vars.	Auto-Regression Term[c]	Constant	No.of Cases	Comments
	Dependent Variable: Log GNP per Capita; Time Lag 1950-65											
1				0.21(0.06)**	0.38(0.14)**	-0.00(0.87)	-0.18(0.06)**		0.78(0.06)**	0.71	63	
2	State Centralization	0.07(0.02)**		0.22(0.07)**	0.39(0.11)**	-2.0(0.85)**	-0.03(0.06)		0.85(0.06)**	0.36	42	d
3	Government Rev. 1955	0.009(0.003)**		0.23(0.07)**	0.30(0.12)**	-1.9(0.83)**	-0.08(0.06)		0.74(0.07)**	0.60	36	d,e
4	Cabinet Size 1950	0.01(0.004)**		0.15(0.08)*	0.31(0.13)**	-2.3(0.99)**	-0.01(0.07)		0.84(0.06)**	0.30	42	d
5	Capital Formation 1950			0.13(0.09)	0.41(0.14)**	0.12(0.94)	-0.18(0.07)**	0.010(0.004)**	0.66(0.08)**	0.94	27	e
6	Ethno-Ling. Fract.			0.17(0.06)**	0.33(0.13)**	0.46(0.85)	-0.18(0.06)**	-0.0014(0.0006)**	0.77(0.06)**	0.82	63	
7	Formal Polit. Rep. 1950		-0.002(0.003)	0.16(0.08)**	0.01(0.20)	0.79(1.1)	-0.25(0.07)**		0.86(0.10)**	0.74	30	d,e
8	Urbanization 1950		0.002(0.002)	0.21(0.06)**	0.36(0.14)**	-0.27(0.93)	-0.18(0.06)**		0.76(0.06)**	0.75	62	
9	Polit. Modernization		0.04(0.01)**	0.19(0.06)**	0.42(0.13)**	-0.80(0.85)	-0.13(0.06)**		0.70(0.06)**	1.05	60	
10	Colonies 1950 Only			0.23(0.09)**	0.03(0.57)	3.5(3.2)	-0.38(0.16)**		0.71(0.14)**	1.10	20	f
	Dependent Variable: Log GNP per Capita; Time Lag 1955-70											
11				0.13(0.07)*	0.36(0.13)**	-0.50(0.85)	-0.19(0.08)**		0.99(0.07)**	0.37	73	
12	State Centralization	0.05(0.02)**		0.26(0.09)**	0.38(0.13)**	-1.8(0.91)*	-0.07(0.10)		1.0(0.09)**	0.06	46	d
13	Government Rev. 1955	0.001(0.004)		0.28(0.09)**	0.57(0.14)**	-1.9(0.86)**	0.00(0.10)		0.89(0.09)**	0.19	38	d,e
14	Cabinet Size 1950	0.010(0.004)**		0.25(0.11)**	0.33(0.13)**	-1.9(0.94)**	-0.01(0.12)		0.98(0.09)**	-0.04	44	d
15	Capital Formation 1950			0.17(0.14)	0.40(0.16)**	-0.86(1.1)	-0.18(0.17)	0.009(0.005)	0.82(0.12)**	0.60	25	d
16	Ethno-Ling. Fract.			0.07(0.08)	0.32(0.13)**	-0.20(0.84)	-0.18(0.08)**	-0.0013(0.0006)**	1.0(0.07)**	0.43	73	
17	Polit. Particip. 1960		-0.002(0.005)	0.14(0.12)	0.76(0.21)**	-1.7(1.1)	-0.03(0.15)		1.0(0.12)**	0.04	28	d,g
18	Formal Polit. Rep. 1955		0.002(0.003)	0.28(0.10)**	0.45(0.14)**	-1.3(0.91)	-0.11(0.09)		0.83(0.10)**	0.54	35	d,e
19	Urbanization 1950		0.003(0.001)**	0.14(0.07)**	0.33(0.13)**	-0.69(0.81)	-0.24(0.08)**		0.93(0.07)**	0.54	73	
20	Polit. Modernization		0.03(0.01)**	0.11(0.08)	0.39(0.13)**	-0.98(0.89)	-0.14(0.09)		0.95(0.08)**	0.55	70	
21	Colonies 1955 Only			-0.05(0.13)	0.50(0.47)	-0.66(3.0)	-0.12(0.18)		1.1(0.17)**	0.06	24	f

Eq. No.	Political, Social and Control Variable Names	H 1: State Power & Authority[b]	H 3: Social & Political Modernization[b]	H 2a: Prim. Enrollment Ratio	H 2b: Sec. Enrollment Ratio	H 2c: Univ. Enrollment Ratio	Pop.T2/Pop.T1	Control Vars.[b]	Auto-Regression Term[c]	Constant	No. of Cases	Comments
	Dependent Variable: Log KWH per Capita; Time Lag 1950-65											
22				0.29(0.13)**	0.50(0.26)*	0.04(1.7)	-0.26(0.12)**		0.68(0.06)**	1.25	57	
23	State Centralization	0.08(0.02)**		0.17(0.11)	0.35(0.16)**	-0.84(1.2)	-0.05(0.09)		0.78(0.04)**	0.85	40	d
24	Government Rev.	0.01(0.005)**		0.21(0.10)**	0.22(0.17)	-0.91(1.2)	-0.16(0.09)		0.68(0.05)**	1.07	34	e
25	Cabinet Size 1950	0.01(0.005)**		0.08(0.11)	0.31(0.17)*	-0.93(1.3)	-0.06(0.10)		0.76(0.04)**	0.90	40	d
26	Capital Formation 1950			0.30(0.18)*	0.37(0.25)	0.11(1.6)	-0.17(0.13)	0.15*(0.009) 0.0015(0.0011)	0.59(0.10)**	1.12	25	e
27	Ethno-Ling. Fract.			0.31(0.13)**	0.54(0.26)**	-0.48(1.7)	-0.26(0.12)		0.70(0.06)**	1.15	57	
28	Formal Polit. Rep.1950		-0.001(0.006)	0.10(0.13)	-0.09(0.27)	0.91(1.8)	-0.25(0.10)**		0.85(0.07)**	1.09	29	d,e
29	Urbanization 1950		-0.006(0.004)	0.29(0.13)**	0.55(0.26)**	0.71(1.8)	-0.23(0.13)*		0.72(0.06)**	1.21	56	
30	Polit. Modernization		0.00(0.03)	0.32(0.13)**	0.47(0.25)*	-0.46(1.7)	-0.23(0.12)*		0.67(0.07)**	1.24	55	
	Dependent Variable: Log KWH per Capita ; Time Lag 1955-70											
31				0.36(0.23)	0.36(0.33)	-0.32(2.5)	-0.55(0.23)**		0.66(0.10)**	1.66	51	
32	State Centralization	0.04(0.026)*		0.05(0.15)	0.40(0.18)**	0.02(1.4)	-0.26(0.18)		0.83(0.07)**	1.06	32	d
33	Cabinet Size 1950	0.009(0.005)*		-0.17(0.15)	0.37(0.15)**	0.24(1.2)	-0.22(0.15)		0.81(0.07)**	1.18	30	d
34	Ethno-Ling. Fract.			0.42(0.23)*	0.43(0.34)	-0.86(2.5)	-0.55(0.23)**	0.002(0.002)	0.68(0.10)**	1.53	51	
35	Formal Polit. Rep. 1955		0.001(0.005)	0.01(0.16)	0.29(0.21)	0.35(1.5)	-0.32(0.17)*		0.80(0.08)**	1.28	25	e
36	Urbanization		0.003(0.003)	0.38(0.23)*	0.31(0.34)	-0.34(2.4)	-0.63(0.25)**		0.62(0.11)**	1.81	51	
37	Polit. Modernization		-0.04(0.05)	0.38(0.23)*	0.29(0.35)	0.75(2.8)	-0.60(0.25)**		0.69(0.11)**	1.46	50	
	Dependent Variable: Log KWH per Capita; Time Lag 1955-70											
38				3.3(2.0)*	7.3(4.5)	-20(28)	-6.0(2.7)**		0.99(0.04)**	10.57	70	
39	State Centralization	1.8(0.54)**		4.9(2.8)*	8.4(4.9)*	-50(33)	-0.79(3.3)		1.0(0.04)**	1.28	43	d
40	Government Rev. 1955	-0.07(0.15)		5.5(2.9)*	6.9(5.4)	-82(36)	1.7(3.6)		1.0(0.06)**	-1.23	36	d,e
41	Cabinet Size 1950	0.60(0.10)**		2.9(2.4)	4.7(4.0)	-98(30)**	4.4(3.0)		1.0(0.04)**	-9.01	42	d
42	Capital Formation 1950			7.4(5.5)	15(8.4)	-50(48)	-2.6(5.1)	0.31(0.25)	0.84(0.11)**	5.07	27	e
43	Ethno-Ling. Fract.			2.4(2.1)	6.5(4.5)	-12(28)	-5.9(2.7)**	-0.03(0.02)	0.99(0.04)**	12.05	70	e
44	Formal Polit. Rep.1950		0.22(0.13)*	3.2(3.4)	-7.6(8.4)	51(48)	-3.8(3.5)		0.94(0.07)**	7.27	30	d,e
45	Urbanization		0.00(0.07)	3.2(2.0)	7.2(4.6)	-20(30)	-5.9(2.8)**		0.99(0.04)**	10.50	69	
46	Polit. Modernization		0.22(0.41)	3.2(2.3)	7.5(4.7)	-26(30)	-5.7(2.9)**		0.98(0.04)**	11.90	66	
47	Colonies 1950 Only			4.0(1.9)**	-12(13)	182(75)**	-8.7(4.2)**		1.0(0.04)**	13.05	26	f

*p < .10, **p < .05; a.Ordinary least-squares estimates of slopes; standard errors in parentheses. A typical equation (e.g., Eq. 2) regresses log GNP per capita 1965 on earlier state centralization, educational enrollment ratios, population growth, and log GNP per capita;
b.Variable names in left column; c.Autoregression term is dependent variable at time 1;
d.Countries independent by time 1 only; e.Communist countries excluded because of measurement ambiguities;
f.Analysis of colonies if more than 20 cases; g.Mostly developing countries.

Overall, the results are surprisingly consistent, given the defects of our measures and the limited case numbers involved in the analyses. It is particularly convincing that the effects in the five different sets of analysis—each with a different indicator of economic development (or an indicator at a different time point)—show such similarity. This gives us confidence that the particular economic indicators chosen, or the particular lags involved, are not accounting for our results. Some of the sets of variables (particularly log KWH per capita 1970 and the non-agricultural labor force, which is highly autocorrelated over time) tend to show fewer significant effects than others, but the direction of the effects is consistent in all of them. We review the findings in terms of our particular independent variables.

HYPOTHESIS 1 *The power and authority of the state* The results are shown in the first column of the table. Despite the conceptual and empirical unrelatedness of these indicators, they all show consistent—and often significant—positive effects on each indicator of development. Government revenue, the index of state centralization,[7] cabinet size—all show consistent effects. This consistency is a major finding; it does not, however, enable us to distinguish among these disparate indicators.

HYPOTHESES 2A, B, AND C *Educational enrollments* Again, the consistency of the effects is impressive. Secondary education shows positive effects on economic development—very often significant ones.[8] Primary education also shows effects, though often not significant.[9] University education expansion, on the other hand, almost always shows *negative* effects, contrary to our hypotheses. Apparently it is the reorganization of the masses through mass education, rather than the reorganization of elite populations, which is the main economic significance of the modern educational system. We discuss this finding at the end of this chapter.

HYPOTHESIS 3 *Social and political modernization* The data provide little support for ideas along these lines. The effects are not consistently positive, and not usually significant. Neither urbanization nor our three political measures show consistent effects throughout these analyses.

Autoregression The autoregression terms are very large. This is to be expected, given the continuity in economic structure and production built into national societies. It is of little immediate substantive interest here. The surprising result of these analyses is the consistency of other effects, given the enormous continuity in economic data through the period of investigation.

Population growth rates show negative effects in these analyses. This should not be given a substantive interpretation because of ambiguity in the meaning of the analyses. (*a*) Population growth is entered because it might show a negative effect of substantive interest. (*b*) But this effect might be artifactual, in a sense, since population denominators are built into our economic dependent variables. (*c*) And further, positive biases are built in because estimates of GNP in national accounts sometimes include inferences based on productivity per worker. (*d*) Finally, negative biases are built in when estimates of the agricultural work force are based on subtractions of other workers from the adult male population.

Capital formation shows a few positive effects in these analyses, as we would expect. But these effects are not large enough to alter inferences from the other findings.

Ethnolinguistic fractionalization shows weak and inconsistent effects. Clearly, the inclusion or exclusion of this variable does not alter our other findings.

Some equations include only independent countries; others include all countries for which we have data. A few analyses are based on the limited data available for countries which were colonies during at least part of the period. Comparisons of these analyses suggest that our educational effects are not strikingly different for these groups of countries.

Overall, (*a*) the five economic indicators behave similarly; (*b*) the effects of independent variables show a consistent pattern. Measures of state power and authority, and of mass education, show positive effects. A measure of elite education shows insignificant negative effects. And measures of modernization show no consistent effects.

Differences between Richer and Poorer Countries Many theories argue that factors affecting economic development are different in rich and poor countries. Most arguments suggest that primary and secondary education, and perhaps state power (see chaps. 7 and 12), are most important for poor countries, while university education matters more for rich countries.

To study such effects we separate our countries on 1955 GNP per capita into the *richer* 40% (those above $278 in 1964 US dollars GNP per capita) and the poorer 60%. We then repeat our analyses of log GNP per capita 1970 separately for the two groups of countries.[10]

Data are presented in table 6.5. We include only those equations for which at least twenty cases are available. Of course, the limited case numbers are a problem in all the analyses.

Most findings parallel those of table 6.4. For both rich and poor countries, secondary education affects growth positively, and tertiary education has (often insignificant) negative effects. Unlike the combined analysis, these data show no effects at all of primary enrollments.[11] The effects of modernization variables tend to be slightly positive in both groups of countries. The effects of state power indicators are generally insignificant, and in poorer countries there seems to be no effect. In later analyses we will be interested to see if this interaction effect holds up. While the data are clearly fragile, and few significant findings appear, they do not support the idea that there are significant differences between the factors affecting growth in rich and poor countries (but see chap. 7).[12] The main difference from the overall analyses is that the effects of state power indicators seem to disappear.

TABLE 6.5   Panel Analyses of Factors Affecting Economic Development for Richer and Poorer Countries[a]

Eq. No.	Political, Social, and Control Variable Names	H 1: State Power and Authority (roman type)[a] / H 3: Social and Political Modernization (italic type)[a]	H 2a: Prim. Enrollment Ratio	H 2b: Sec. Enrollment Ratio	H 2c: Univ. Enrollment Ratio	Pop. T2 / Pop. T1	log GNP/Cap 1955	Constant	No. of Cases	Comments
					Richer Countries[b]					
1			-0.06(0.14)	0.24(0.11)**	-0.95(0.92)	-0.14(0.13)	0.86(0.11)**	0.93	27	
2	State Centralization	0.03(0.025)	0.10(0.20)	0.28(0.13)**	-2.8(1.2)**	0.04(0.15)	0.95(0.14)**	0.38	23	c
3	Cabinet Size 1950	0.009(0.004)**	-0.09(0.16)	0.21(0.11)*	-3.2(1.1)**	0.08(0.14)	1.0(0.14)**	0.25	23	c
4	Ethno-Ling.Fract.	-0.001(0.001)†	-0.08(0.15)	0.24(0.12)**	-9.3(0.94)**	-0.13(0.14)	0.88(0.12)**	0.90	27	
5	Urbanization 1950	*0.00(0.001)*	-0.06(0.15)	0.24(0.12)**	-0.97(0.95)	-0.12(0.15)	0.87(0.12)**	0.90	27	
6	Polit. Modernization	*0.03(0.02)*	-0.04(0.14)	0.30(0.12)**	-1.6(1.0)	0.00(0.17)	0.81(0.11)**	1.0	27	
					Poorer Countries[b]					
7			-0.01(0.09)	1.3(0.38)**	-1.6(1.6)	-0.13(0.11)	1.0(0.10)**	0.19	46	
8	State Centralization	0.01(0.04)	0.04(0.16)	1.7(0.82)**	-3.9(2.3)*	-0.06(0.17)	1.0(0.15)**	0.06	23	c
9	Government Rev. 1955	-0.007(0.006)	0.40(0.15)	2.0(0.70)**	-4.8(2.2)**	-0.00(0.18)	1.1(0.14)**	-0.08	22	c,d
10	Cabinet Size 1950	-0.004(0.007)	0.03(0.14)	2.1(0.57)**	-4.2(1.8)**	-0.06(0.17)	1.2(0.14)**	-0.33	21	c
11	Ethno-Ling. Fract.	-0.001(0.001)†	-0.05(0.09)	1.2(0.39)**	-1.0(1.7)	-0.14(0.11)	1.0(0.10)**	0.26	46	
12	Polit. Partic. 1960	*-0.001(0.006)*	0.80(0.16)	1.3(0.90)	-3.1(2.6)	-0.02(0.22)	0.99(0.19)**	0.09	23	d,e
13	Urbanization	*0.004(0.002)***	0.05(0.09)	0.64(0.15)	-0.64(1.7)	-0.16(0.11)	0.97(0.11)**	0.35	46	
14	Polit. Modernization	*0.029(0.017)**	-0.06(0.10)	1.3(0.39)**	-2.0(1.7)	-0.11(0.11)	1.0(0.11)**	0.39	43	
15	Colonies 1955 Only		-0.03(0.14)	0.48(0.73)	23.(14.)	-0.20(0.20)	1.0(0.18)**	0.35	20	

* $p < .10$

** $p < .05$

† Control variable.

[a] Variable names in left column.

[b] Dependent variable is log GNP per capita 1970; Time 1 is 1955 except as indicated. Ordinary least-squares estimates of slopes; standard errors in parentheses. Equations with less than 20 cases omitted. Richer countries are those above median 1955 GNP per capita ($278 US).

[c] Countries independent by 1955 only.

[d] Communist countries excluded due to measurement ambiguities.

[e] Mostly developing countries.

Analysis of Raw Economic Variables

Two methodological criticisms of the analyses reported above are considered here. First, we have taken the logarithm of two economic variables: GNP per capita and KWH per capita. This amounts to a major *and arbitrary* transformation of each of these variables from the natural —and clearly intelligible—units in which they are originally formulated. Although this transformation is common, it is practically never justified with substantive arguments. The usual justification is that the original distribution of GNP per capita and KWH per capita are too skewed for most common statistical procedures to make sense. But extraordinary and arbitrary transformations of clearly defined variables may be questioned: the log transform compresses values at the upper end of their distributions very greatly.

Second, the analyses above are, strictly speaking, analyses of joint economic-demographic variables, since GNP per capita and KWH per capita combine both attributes. Any positive findings of a variable could in principle result from either positive effects on economic growth or negative effects on population. This problem is compounded by the fact that population terms are built into the denominator of most of our independent variables—the time 1 economic indicators, education enrollments, urbanization, and so on. This means that a whole series of biased relations among independent variables and between them and dependent variables are *built into* our analyses, since all these variables are divided by population terms—terms which are clearly likely to involve correlated errors of differing and unknown magnitudes. Analyses employing such ratios have been criticized in the literature (Freeman and Kronenfeld 1973; Fuiguitt and Lieberson 1974; Schuessler 1973). We attempt to deal with these problems here. They have been discussed more formally in chapter 2.

One solution is to estimate equations predicting, say, raw GNP—not logged, and not corrected for population. Consider a reasonable equation along these lines:

$$\text{GNP}_{1970} = a + b \, \text{GNP}_{1955} + c \, \text{Primary enrollment}_{1955}$$
$$+ \, d \, \text{Secondary enrollment}_{1955} + e \, \text{Univ. enrollment}_{1955}$$
$$+ \, f \, \text{Population}_{1970} + g \, \text{Political variable} \times \text{Population}_{1955}.$$

This equation seems to be a straightforward application of our hypotheses without (*a*) logging GNP or (*b*) incorporating many ratio variables. The only term requiring explanation is the interaction term involving the political variable. This is made plausible by the simple idea that the effects of state power on raw dollars of GNP ought to be related to the number of people involved. The other independent variables are already scaled to population and do not require this correction.

Analyses of the sort represented by the equation above do not often appear in the literature because (*a*) the variables are highly *skewed*—violating the assumptions of regression analysis; and (*b*) the variance in the residuals in such analyses is highly correlated with independent variables. For instance, examination of ordinary least-squares estimates of equations like the one above shows that the absolute values of the residuals in GNP_{1970} are correlated .70 or more with GNP_{1955}. This violates another assumption of ordinary least-squares.

However, weighted least-squares estimates, with every term including the constant weighted by $1/\text{Population}_{1955}$ (or $1/\text{GNP}_{1955}$) are possible, and *do* reduce both distributional anomalies and the correlation between residual variances and independent variables.

We have examined *many* such analyses. In almost none of them do any independent variables (except, of course, GNP_{1955}) show significant effects. Even the direction of effects seems random in these analyses.

Some reflection suggests an explanation: these models formulate a series of arguments that, for instance, the addition of one secondary graduate should increase national GNP by so many dollars. This makes little sense. One would imagine that such effects should be relative to the wealth of the country. Secondary graduates might be expected to add X dollars to the GNP of a country which starts at a GNP per capita of $100; but they should add perhaps $50X$ to a country which starts at $5000 in per capita GNP. In principle, that is, the effects on raw GNP (and KWH) of independent variables of the sort we consider ought to be interactive.[13] In ordinary analyses such interaction creeps in inadvertently through the logging of GNP and KWH, which, aside from its methodological virtues, transforms variables and effects in just this interactive way. We turn to more explicit ways of doing the same thing without moving to ratios or logarithms.

Interactive Analyses of Raw Economic Variables

As a result of the previous section, our arguments now take the following interactive form:

$GNP_{1970} = a + b\,GNP_{1955} +$
$\qquad c$ Primary enrollment$_{1955} \times$ GNP per capita$_{1955} +$
$\qquad d$ Secondary enrollment $_{1955} \times$ GNP per capita$_{1955} +$
$\qquad e$ University enrollment $_{1955} \times$ GNP per capita$_{1955} +$
$\qquad f$ Population$_{1970} +$
$\qquad g$ Political variable $\times$ Population$_{1955} \times$ GNP per capita$_{1955}$.

That is, the effect of each independent variable is thought to be proportional to the 1955 per capita GNP of a country.

All the variables in this model are of course highly skewed. And the variance in the residuals is highly correlated with GNP in 1955 (and other independent variables). For this reason, estimates are in the form of weighted least squares, with every term in each equation weighted by $1/GNP$ at time 1.[14]

Analyses for GNP_{1970}, GNP_{1965}, KWH_{1965}, and KWH_{1970} are shown in Table 6.6. The results closely parallel those for the conventional analyses shown earlier. Secondary education shows positive, and usually significant, results. (Equations [8] and [30] show insignificant negative effects because of the particular sample of countries included with formal representation, not because this variable renders secondary education spurious.) Primary education shows more consistently positive and significant results than in the earlier analyses.[15] Most indicators of state power show significant positive effects. The modernization variables show few consistent (and few significant) effects, though urbanization may have positive effects. The control variable effects conform to the earlier analyses.[16]

Tables 6.7a and 6.7b show what happens when the countries are subdivided on GNP per capita into the richer 40% and the poorer 60%.[17] The effects of secondary education remain in both subsamples. The effects of primary education disappear in the richer countries, perhaps for the methodological reasons noted earlier. The effects of university education are insignificantly negative in both subsamples. Of considerable interest is the fact that the effects of indicators of state power are generally positive (and often significant) in both subsamples. This suggests that the absence of such effects in the poorer countries in the conventional analyses should not be taken too seriously. Again, the effects of modernization indicators are generally insignificant (and often negative) in both subsamples. The overall pattern of these findings suggests that our earlier conclusion that there are not substantial differences in effects between richer and poorer countries is sustained.

With the arbitrariness of logged economic measures removed and with the biases of ratioed measures practically eliminated, the results of these analyses show a pattern of results strikingly similar to the conventional analyses above, and add considerably to our confidence in the conclusions we are reaching. We examine, however, data from one more kind of analysis.

Dynamic Analyses

So far we have reported standard panel analyses which employ time as a methodological device to permit causal inferences. *Change* is not incorporated in measures but is used methodologically. But the causal imagery we employ is clearly dynamic in character. It implies that changes in independent variables (and different states of independent variables) will generate changes in dependent variables.[18]

We therefore turn to models involving change in the formulation of variables. We take as a dependent variable the ratio of a country's GNP in 1970 to its GNP in 1965 (in constant dollars), and thus measure an economic growth rate. We hold constant the growth rate in GNP from 1950 to 1955 and examine the effects of our independent variables of interest: aspects of state power, educational enrollments, and social modernization.[19]

Table 6.8 shows the relevant data. We have examined some similar analyses for KWH, but few significant results of any kind appear. This may have substantive significance, but KWH, especially for poor countries, tends to be a somewhat arbitrary measure of economic growth, since it is rather easily affected by a few policy changes. Growth rates

TABLE 6.6   Interaction Models: Panel Analyses of Factors Affecting Economic Development[a]

Eq. No.	Political, Social and Control Variable Names	H 1: State Power & Authority Var. xGNP[b] $_1$	H 3: Social & Polit. Modern. Var. xGNP $_1$	H 2a: Prim. Enrollment xGNP/Cap. $_1$	H2b: Sec. Enrollment xGNP/Cap. $_1$	H 2c: Univ. Enrollment xGNP/Cap. $_1$	Pop. T2[c]	Control Vars.[b] xGNP $_1$	GNP$_1$[d,e]	KWH$_1$[f]	Constant	No. of Cases	Comments
				Dependent Variable: GNP[d]; Time Lag 1950-65									
1				0.66(0.28)**	1.2(0.60)**	-1.0(6.3)	0.03(0.01)**		1.3		-30	79	
2	State Centraliz.	0.29(0.08)**		0.70(0.38)*	1.7(0.68)*	-10.(7.4)	0.02(0.02)		0.96		122	55	g
3	Gov. Rev. 1955	0.01(0.01)		0.69(0.32)**	1.1(0.59)*	-10.(6.6)	0.03(0.01)**		0.92		87	49	g,h
4	Cabinet Size 1950	0.08(0.02)**		0.89(0.33)**	1.1(0.56)**	-13.(6.5)**	0.02(0.01)**		-0.11		187	57	g
5	Capital Form. 1950			0.24(0.47)	0.71(0.79)	-2.1(9.3)	0.03(0.02)	0.01(0.02)	1.4		-16	37	h
6	Ethno-ling. Fract.			0.54(0.28)*	0.91(0.61)	-6.1(6.3)	0.03(0.01)**	-0.006*(0.003)	1.6		-30	79	
7	Polit. Part. 1960		0.01(0.02)	0.68(0.39)*	2.2(0.80)**	-9.6(9.3)	-0.02(0.03)		0.92		-153	30	g,h,i
8	Form. Polit. Rep. 1950		-0.03(0.01)**	0.70(0.31)**	-0.11(0.73)	-1.0(6.0)	-0.03(0.03)		2.1		-52	39	g,h
9	Urbanization 1950		0.007(0.005)	0.63(0.28)**	1.1(0.61)*	-9.1(6.3)	0.03(0.01)**		1.2		-24	78	
10	Polit. Modern.		-0.01(0.08)	0.68(0.29)**	1.1(0.68)	-8.9(6.7)	0.03(0.02)		1.3		-32	75	
11	Colonies 1950 Only			0.70(0.47)	3.8(1.7)**	-20.(20)	0.06(0.03)**		0.84		-59	20	j
				Dependent Variable: GNP[d]; Time Lag 1955-70									
12				0.53(0.25)	1.3(0.56)**	-2.9(5.9)	0.008(0.014)		1.7		-57	91	
13	State Centraliz.	0.22(0.08)**		0.91(0.34)**	2.0(0.63)**	-7.6(6.8)	0.01(0.02)		1.1		-5	60	g
14	Gov. Rev. 1955	-0.02(0.02)		1.1(0.36)**	2.2(0.65)**	-10.(7.5)	0.02(0.02)		1.1		-24	52	g,h
15	Cabinet Size 1950	0.05(0.02)**		1.0(0.35)**	1.6(0.60)**	-10.(6.9)	0.02(0.02)		0.35		64	59	g
16	Capital Form. 1950			0.30(0.46)	1.4(0.82)*	0.33(9.6)	0.03(0.03)	0.02(0.02)	1.4		-138	37	h
17	Ethno-ling. Fract.			0.42(0.25)*	1.1(0.57)*	-1.4(5.8)	0.01(0.01)	-0.006**(0.003)	2.1		-57	91	
18	Polit. Part. 1960		0.01(0.02)	0.85(0.34)**	4.2(0.78)*	-1.7(7.6)	0.00(0.02)		1.4		-30	37	g,h,i
19	Form. Pol. Rep. 1955		-0.02(0.02)	1.1(0.44)**	2.3(0.74)**	-9.5(8.2)	0.03(0.03)		1.1		-77	47	g,h
20	Urbanization 1950		0.009(0.005)*	0.54(0.25)**	1.2(0.57)**	-4.0(5.9)	0.01(0.01)		1.6		-49	90	
21	Polit. Modern.		-0.11(0.066)*	0.61(0.26)**	1.4(0.60)**	-4.8(6.3)	0.00(0.02)		1.4		-154	87	
22	Colonies 1955 Only			-0.09(0.51)	1.6(1.7)	8.6(19)	-0.01(0.03)		2.4		-38	25	j

Independent Variables

Eq. Nr.	Political, Social and Control Variable Names[b]	H 1: State Power & Authority Var. xGNP[1]	H 3: Social & Polit. Modern. Var. xGNP	H 2a: Prim. Enrollment xGNP/Cap.[1]	H 2b: Sec. Enrollment xGNP/Cap.[1]	H 2c: Univ. Enrollment xGNP/Cap.[1]	Pop. T2[c]	Control Vars. x GNP[1]	GNP[d,e][1]	KWH[f][1]	Constant	No. of Cases	Comments
				Dependent Variable: KWH[f]; Time Lag 1950-65									
23				1.19(0.65)*	1.5(1.4)	-13(14.)	0.06(0.04)		-0.40[k]	2.7(0.26)**	-33	66	
24	State Centraliz.	0.79(1.6)**		0.52(0.72)	2.9(1.3)**	-7(14.)	0.05(0.04)		-0.71	2.9(0.23)**	89	51	g
25	Gov. Rev. 1950	0.06(0.02)**		0.53(0.50)	1.6(1.0)*	-9(10.)	0.08(0.03)**		-1.2	2.6(0.17)**	-14	44	g,h
26	Cabinet Size 1950	0.18(0.04)**		0.84(0.69)	1.9(1.2)	-9(14.)	0.08(0.04)**		-3.2	2.6(0.23)**	330	51	g
27	Capital Form. 1950			0.96(1.26)	3.1(2.2)	-13(25.)	0.20(0.11)*	0.10(0.07)	-2.5	2.4(0.37)**	137	32	h
28	Ethno-Ling. Fract.			1.08(0.66)	1.2(1.5)	-9(15.)	0.07(0.04)*	-0.008(0.007)	-0.11	2.7(0.26)**	-51	66	
29	Polit. Part. 1960		0.01(0.04)	0.45(0.73)	3.4(1.6)**	-4(17.)	0.01(0.05)*		-0.04	2.5(0.52)**	-29	26	g,h,i
30	Form. Pol. Rep. 1950		-0.02(0.02)	1.12(0.53)**	-1.0(1.2)	-12(10.)	0.005(0.06)		0.64	2.6(0.13)**	-182	38	g,h
31	Urbanization 1950		0.01(0.01)	1.13(0.67)*	1.4(1.5)	-11(15.)	0.07(0.04)*		-0.63	2.7(0.27)**	-3	65	
32	Polit. Modern.		0.11(0.17)	1.14(0.66)*	1.6(1.4)	-11(15.)	0.05(0.04)		-0.76	2.7(0.26)**	-52	65	
				Dependent Variable: KWH[f]; Time Lag 1955-70									
33				1.4(1.1)	2.5(2.1)	6(28.)	0.11(0.07)		-1.0[k]	2.1(0.36)**	-139	62	
34	State Centraliz.	0.85(0.28)**		0.5(1.4)	5.2(2.2)**	12(31.)	0.09(0.09)		-1.4	1.9(0.32)**	-135	42	g
35	Gov. Rev. 1955	0.06(0.05)		1.6(1.5)	7.1(2.1)**	-24(38.)	0.26(0.10)**		-3.7	2.0(0.31)**	-157	34	g,h
36	Cabinet Size 1950	0.21(0.07)**		0.4(1.6)	5.1(2.1)**	8(36.)	0.21(0.09)**		-4.8	2.0(0.34)**	596	39	g
37	Capital Form. 1950			0.02(1.9)	4.7(3.1)	37(48.)	0.33(0.20)*	-0.01(0.09)	-2.0	2.1(0.50)**	57	31	h
38	Ethno-Ling. Fract.			1.2(1.1)	1.7(2.2)	12(28.)	0.12(0.07)*	-0.01(0.01)	-0.44	2.1(0.36)**	-115	62	
39	Form. Pol. Rep. 1955		-0.10(0.053)*	1.0(1.8)	5.6(2.3)**	16(39.)	0.11(0.09)		-0.51	2.2(0.36)**	-196	34	g,h
40	Urbanization 1950		0.01(0.02)	1.4(1.1)	2.3(2.2)	7(29.)	0.11(0.08)		-1.1	2.1(0.37)**	-123	62	
41	Polit. Modern.		-0.42(0.26)	1.1(1.1)	2.4(2.1)	18(30.)	0.04(0.08)		-2.3	2.1(0.36)**	-219	61	g,h

* p <.10 ; ** p < .05; a. Weighted least-squares estimates of slopes; standard errors in parentheses. Equations with less than 25 cases omitted. A typical equation (e.g., Eq. 2) regresses GNP 1965 on earlier state centralization, educational enrollment ratios, population, and GNP; all terms are then weighted by dividing by earlier GNP.

b. Variable names in left column; c. In thousands; d. GNP in millions of 1964 $US; e. Standard error and significance not estimated by computer program.

f. In millions; g. Countries independent by time 1 only; h. Communist countries excluded due to measurement ambiguities;

i. Mostly developing countries; j. Analysis of colonies if more than 20 cases; k. Weighting by 1/GNP yields a coefficient for GNP even in equations estimating KWH .

TABLE 6.7a Interaction Models: Panel Analyses of Factors Affecting Economic Development for Richer Countries Only[a]

Eq. No.	Political, Social and Control Variable Names	H 1: State Power & Authority[b] Var. xGNP_1	H 3: Social & Polit. Modern.[b] Var. xGNP_1	H 2a: Prim. Enrollment xGNP/Cap._1	H 2b: Sec. Enrollment xGNP/Cap._1	H 2c: Univ. Enrollment xGNP/Cap._1	Pop T2[c]	Control Vars.[b] xGNP_1	GNP[d,e]	KWH[f]	Constant	No. of Cases	Comments
				Dependent Variable: GNP[d]; Time Lag 1950-65									
1				0.14(0.37)	1.8(0.58)**	-2.1(6.8)	0.26(0.05)**		0.88		- 95	42	
2	State Centraliz.	0.05(0.11)		0.29(0.52)	1.6(0.69)**	-4.9(8.7)	0.21(0.07)**		0.92		- 52	33	g
3	Gov. Rev. 1955	0.04(0.02)**		-0.20(0.51)	1.6(0.65)**	1.1(8.8)	0.26(0.07)**		0.51		- 12	28	h
4	Cabinet Size 1950	0.03(0.02)		0.31(0.48)	1.6(0.61)**	-4.9(8.1)	0.19(0.06)**		0.37		41	33	g
5	Capital Form. 1950			-0.17(0.46)	1.5(0.68)**	2.5(9.1)	0.30(0.07)**	0.07**(0.02)	-0.25		- 78	25	h
6	Ethno-Ling. Fract.			0.08(0.37)	1.6(0.59)**	-1.1(6.6)	0.25(0.05)**	-0.0065*(0.0038)	1.2		- 93	42	
7	Form. Pol. Rep. 1950		-0.02(0.02)	0.34(0.37)	0.94(0.81)**	-7.1(6.6)	0.11(0.09)		1.6		- 51	26	g,h
8	Urbanization 1950		0.004(0.005)	0.16(0.38)	1.8(0.59)**	-2.5(6.8)	0.25(0.05)**		0.77		- 80	42	
9	Polit. Moderniz.		-0.07(0.09)	0.20(0.40)	1.6(0.60)**	-2.9(7.2)	0.25(0.06)**		0.71		-146	41	
				Dependent Variable: GNP[d]; Time Lag 1955-70									
10				0.14(0.43)	1.8(0.67 **	1.4(7.3)	0.31(0.08)**		1.3		-118	40	
11	State Centraliz.	0.21(0.13)		0.81(0.66)	2.7(0.84)**	-7.6(9.9)	0.28(0.10)**		0.44		-160	34	g
12	Gov. Rev. 1955	0.03(0.02)*		-0.15(0.67)	2.5(0.76)**	4.4(9.6)	0.47(0.11)**		0.27		-129	27	g,h
13	Cabinet Size 1950	0.06(0.03)**		0.75(0.57)	2.4(0.71)**	-8.0(8.8)	0.27(0.09)**	0.07**(0.02)	0.30		+ 4	34	g
14	Capital Form. 1950			-0.37(0.47)	2.4(0.78)**	8.4(10)	0.49(0.09)**	-0.002(0.005)	-0.21		-194	24	g
15	Ethno-Ling. Fract.			0.15(0.43)	1.7(0.70)**	1.5(7.4)	0.30(0.09)**		1.3		-123	40	
16	Form. Pol. Rep. 1955		0.009(0.04)	0.81(0.68)	3.0(0.85)**	-8.7(9.8)	0.35(0.12)**		0.43		-174	28	g,h
17	Urbanization 1950		-0.005(0.006)	0.16(0.43)	1.8(0.67)**	1.3(7.3)	0.31(0.08)**		1.4		-138	40	
18	Polit. Moderniz.		-0.11(0.11)	-0.03(0.50)	1.7(0.68)**	2.9(8.0)	0.26(0.10)**		1.2		-129	39	

Independent Variables

Eq. No.	Political, Social and Control Variable Names	H1: State Power & Authority Var. xGNP$_1$	H3: Social & Polit. Modern.[b] Var. xGNP$_1$	H 2a: Prim. Enrollment xGNP/Cap.$_1$	H 2b: Sec. Enrollment xGNP/Cap.$_1$	H 2c: Univ. Enrollment xGNP/Cap.$_1$	Pop T2[c]	Control Vars.[b] xGNP$_1$	GNP[d,e]	KWH[f]	Con-stant	No. of Cases	Comments
			Dependent Variable: KWH[f]; Time Lag 1950-65										
19				0.34(0.96)	2.5(1.4)*	7.7(17)	0.40(0.10)**		-1.5[i]	2.8(0.26)**	-13	46	
20	State Centraliz.	0.35(0.20)*		0.42(0.97)	2.5(1.2)**	-2.4(16)	0.22(0.13)*		-1.1	2.8(0.21)**	35	32	g
21	Gov. Rev. 1955	0.13(0.03)**		0.10(0.79)	2.50(0.97)**	-7.5(14)	0.41(0.12)**		-3.4	2.8(0.16)**	-172	26	g,h
22	Cabinet Size 1950	0.08(0.04)**		0.61(0.96)	2.0(1.2)*	-2.6(16)	0.22(0.13)*		-2.4	2.7(0.21)**	160	31	g
23	Capital Form. 1950			-1.2(1.4)	2.9(1.9)	32(26)	0.50(0.14)**	0.06(0.06)	-2.4	2.7(0.34)**	924	26	g
24	Ethno-Ling. Fract.			0.35(0.97)	2.3(1.5)	8.4(17)	0.39(0.10)**	-0.005(0.009)	-1.3	2.8(0.27)**	-22	46	
25	Form. Pol. Rep. 1955		-0.01(0.04)	0.86(0.68)	-0.21(1.5)	-11(12)	0.03(0.17)		0.33	2.6(0.14)**	-74	25	g,h
26	Urbanization 1950		0.003(0.01)	0.37(0.98)	2.4(1.5)	7.6(17)	0.40(0.10)**		-1.6	2.8(0.27)**	-4	46	
27	Polit. Moderniz.		-0.19(0.21)	0.04(1.0)	2.3(1.4)	13(18)	0.37(0.10)**		-1.8	2.8(0.26)**	-55	46	
			Dependent Variable: KWH[f]; Time Lag 1955-70										
28				-1.4(1.6)	4.0(2.1)*	50(31)	0.68(0.28)**		-1.2[i]	2.1(0.38)**	293	34	
29	State Centraliz.	0.98(0.40)**		-0.46(2.3)	7.0(2.7)**	30(44)	0.48(0.29)*		-3.3	3.2(0.41)**	393	29	g
30	Gov. Rev. 1955	0.11(0.07)		1.8(2.6)	8.9(2.9)**	-18(53)	0.54(0.36)		-6.9	2.2(0.42)**	-82	23	g,h
31	Cabinet Size 1950	0.19(0.09)**		-1.2(2.3)	5.2(2.5)**	37(46)	0.48(0.30)		-4.8	2.2(0.43)**	895	28	g
32	Capital Form. 1950			-1.1(2.7)	5.3(3.6)	51(59)	0.35(0.43)	-0.10(0.13)	-0.87	2.4(0.65)**	1027	23	g
33	Ethno-Ling. Fract.			-1.6(1.5)	2.4(2.1)	58(29)***	0.61(0.26)**	-0.04(0.01)**	0.21	2.1(0.35)**	254	34	
34	Form. Pol. Rep. 1955		-0.18(0.12)	2.1(2.8)	8.3(3.0)**	-5(54)	0.10(0.39)		-0.46	2.1(0.44)**	250	23	g,h
35	Urbanization 1950		-0.01(0.02)	-1.4(1.6)	4.3(2.2)*	47(31)	0.66(0.29)**		-0.73	2.0(0.39)**	253	34	
36	Polit. Moderniz.		0.18(0.36)	-1.2(1.7)	4.3(2.2)*	46(32)	0.77(0.34)**		-1.1	2.1(0.38)**	324	34	

*p < .10; **p < .05; a. Weighted least-squares estimates; standard errors in parentheses. Equations with less than 25 cases omitted. All equations weighted by dividing by earlier GNP. Cases are only those countries above median GNP per capita; b. Variable names in left column; c. In thousands; d. GNP in millions of 1964 $US; e. Standard error and significance not estimated by computer program; f. In millions; g. Countries independent by time 1 only; h. Communist countries excluded due to measurement ambiguities; i. Weighting by 1/GNP yields a coefficient for GNP even in equations estimating KWH.

TABLE 6.7b   Interaction Models: Panel Analyses of Factors Affecting Economic Development for Poorer Countries Only[a]

Eq. No.	Political,Social and Control Variable Names	Independent Variables									Con-stant	No.of Cases	Comment
		H 1: State Power & Authority Var. xGNP$_1$	H 3: Social & Polit. Modern. Var.xGNP$_1$	H 2a: Prim. Enrollment xGNP/Cap.$_1$	H 2b: Sec. Enrollment xGNP/Cap.$_1$	H 2c: Univ. Enrollment xGNP/Cap.$_1$	Pop. T$_2^c$	Control Vars.^{b} xGNP$_1$	Control Vars. GNP$_1^{d,e}$	KWH$_1^f$			
		Dependent Variable: GNP^d; Time Lag 1950-65											
1				0.83(0.39)**	2.01(1.5)	-6.3(10)	0.00(0.02)		1.4		-29	37	
2	State Centraliz.	0.31(0.11)**		0.81(0.48)*	8.6(3.8)**	-23(12.)*	0.00(0.02)		0.72		125	22	g
3a	Gov. Rev. 1955	0.01(0.03)		0.91(0.44)**	1.3(3.1)	-12(9.2)	0.02(0.02)		0.81		123	21	h
3b	Cabinet Size 1950	0.10(0.02)**		0.96(0.36)**	5.2(2.0)**	-22(8.6)**	0.005(0.013)		-0.52		247	24	g
4	Ethno-Ling.Fract.			0.66(0.41)	1.9(1.4)	- 1.3(11)	0.01(0.02)	-0.005 (0.004)	1.6		-28	37	
5	Urbanization 1950		-0.00(0.02)	0.87(0.46)*	2.1(1.5)	- 6.8(11)	0.00(0.02)		1.5		-32	36	
6	Polit.Modern.		0.10(0.10)	0.55(0.41)	6.5(2.5)**	-11(9.9)	0.02(0.02)		1.5		101	34	
		Dependent Variable: GNP^d; Time Lag 1955-70											
7				0.52(0.31)*	3.1(1.1)**	- 7.3(9.5)	-0.00(0.02)		1.8		-66	51	
8	State Centraliz	0.07(0.12)		0.67(0.44)	4.2(2.8)	-14(10)	-0.01(0.02)		1.4		-26	26	g
9	Govn. Rev. 1955	-0.03(0.03)		0.88(0.45)*	4.1(1.8)**	-18(11)	-0.00(0.02)		1.6		- 2	25	g,h
10	Cabinet Size 1950	0.01(0.03)		0.77(0.40)	4.9(1.8)**	-17(9.6)*	-0.02(0.02)		1.4		-16	25	g
11	Ethno-Ling. Fract.			0.39(0.32)**	2.7(1.1)**	- 4.6(9.5)	-0.00(0.02)	-0.005* (0.003)	2.1		-64	51	
12	Polit. Part. 1955		-0.00(0.02)	0.75(0.38)**	3.6(1.8)**	-15(10)	0.01(0.02)		1.4		5	27	g,h,i
13	Urbanization 1950		0.04(0.01)**	0.60(0.25)**	2.1(.93)**	13(7.8)*	0.02(0.01)**		1.3		-44	50	
14	Polit. Modern.		0.01(0.09)	0.33(0.35)	5.5(1.7)**	-20(10)**	-0.01(0.02)		2.2		-143	48	
15	Colonies 1955 Only			-0.28(0.43)	0.50(1.5)	141(34)**	-0.01(0.02)		2.2		- 4	20	j

				Independent Variables									
Eq. No.	Political, Social and Control Variable Names	H 1: State Power & Authority Var. xGNP$_1$	H 3: Social & Polit. Modern. Var. xGNP$_1$	H 2a: Prim. Enrollment xGNP/Cap.$_1$	H 2b: Sec. Enrollment xGNP/Cap.$_1$	H 2c: Univ. Enrollment xGNP/Cap.$_1$	Pop. T$_2$[c]	Control Vars.[b] xGNP$_1$	GNP$_1$[d,e]	KWH$_1$[f]	Con-stant	No. of Cases	Comment
				Dependent Variable: KWH[f]; Time Lag 1950-65									
16				0.56(0.70)	2.2(4.5)	−12(15)	0.08(0.04)**		−1.5[k]	4.9(0.55)**	61	20	
17	Cabinet Size 1950	0.21(0.04)**		0.45(0.65)	14(3.7)**	−31(15)**	0.01(0.05)		−3.4	3.4(0.83)**	337	20	g
18	Ethno-Ling.Fract.			0.79(0.64)	5.0(4.3)	−25(15)*	0.07(0.04)	0.012**(0.006)	−2.3	5.0(0.50)**	187	20	
				Dependent Variable: KWH[f]; Time Lag 1955-70									
19				0.40(1.4)	5.2(6.0)	−1.8(54)	0.04(0.07)		−0.93[k]	5.1(0.69)**	−42	28	
20	Ethno-Ling.Fract.			0.03(1.3)	12(6.8)*	−33(54)	0.02(0.07)	0.02**(0.01)	−1.5	5.2(0.66)**	138	28	
21	Urbanization 1950		0.03(0.03)	1.2(1.6)	0(7.4)	9.7(55)	0.07(0.07)		−1.9	4.8(0.72)**	−11	28	
22	Polit. Modern.		−0.96(0.30)**	0.93(1.2)	−2.6(5.6)	97(55)*	−0.04(0.06)		−5.9	4.9(0.59)**	−80	27	

* $p < .10$
** $p < .05$

a. Weighted least-squares estimates of slopes; standard errors in parentheses. Equations with less than 20 cases omitted. All equations weighted by dividing by earlier GNP. Cases are only those countries below median GNP per capita (for 1950, $195; for 1955, $278; 1964 $US).

b. Variable names in left column.

c. In thousands,

d. GNP in millions of 1964 $US.

e. Standard error and significance not estimated by computer program.

f. In millions.

g. Countries independent by time 1 only.

h. Communist countries excluded due to measurement ambiguities.

i. Mostly developing countries.

j. Analysis of colonies if more than 20 cases.

k. Weighting by 1/GNP yields a coefficient for GNP even in equations estimating KWH.

TABLE 6.8　Change Models: Factors Affecting Rates of Economic Growth[a]

Eq. No.	Political, Social and Control Variable Names	H 1: State Power & Authority	H 3: Social & Political[b] Modernization	Independent Variables								
				H 2a: Prim. Enrollment Ratio 1955	H 2b: Sec. Enrollment Ratio 1955	H 2c: Univ. Enrollment Ratio 1955	Pop.1970 / Pop.1955	Control Vars[b]	GNP 1955/ GNP 1950[c]	Con-stant	No.of Cases	Com-ments
				ALL COUNTRIES								
1				0.15(0.12)	0.34(0.26)	-0.39(1.7)	-0.08(0.17)		0.21(0.17)	1.2	73	
2	State Centraliz.	0.06(0.04)		0.36(0.19)*	0.47(0.32)	-1.9 (2.0)	0.08(0.25)		0.04(0.22)	1.0	46	d
3	Gov. Rev. 1955	-0.007(0.007)		0.30(0.17)*	0.85(0.31)**	-2.8(1.9)	0.14(0.25)		0.32(0.29)	0.67	38	d,e
4	Cabinet Size 1950	0.009(0.01)		0.38(0.21)*	0.35(0.32)	-1.8(2.2)	0.06(0.32)		0.07(0.25)	0.93	44	d
5	Capital Form. 1950			0.29(0.27)	0.70(0.32)**	-3.7(2.1)*	0.35(0.34)	0.01 (0.009)	0.07(0.23)	0.47	25	e
6	Ethno-Ling. Fract.			0.06(0.13)	0.29(0.26)	0.12(1.7)	-0.07(0.17)	-0.002 (0.001)	0.21(0.16)	1.3	73	
7	Polit. Patt. 1960		0.007(0.012)	0.05(0.26)	1.2(0.49)**	-3.1(2.6)	0.36(0.34)		0.24(0.38)	0.43	28	a,d,f
8	Form.Polit.Rep.1955		-0.002(0.006)	0.25(0.15)*	0.67(0.23)**	-3.5(1.5)**	0.00(0.18)		0.37(0.19)*	0.87	35	a,d
9	Urbanization 1950		0.005(0.002)**	0.10(0.12)	0.24(0.26)	-1.0(1.7)	-0.15(0.17)		0.21(0.16)	1.3	73	
10	Polit. Modern.		0.03(0.03)	0.11(0.13)	0.34(0.27)	-1.2(1.8)	-0.02(0.19)		0.21(0.17)	1.3	70	
11	Colonies 1955 Only			-0.02(0.19)	0.28(0.81)	0.59(5.5)	-0.02(0.35)		0.28(0.35)	1.1	24	
				RICHER COUNTRIES[g]								
12				-0.29(0.34)	0.27(0.30)	-1.5(2.2)	-0.04(0.34)		-0.02(0.24)	2.0	27	
13	State Centraliz.	0.12(0.06)		0.31(0.50)	0.51(0.37)	-4.3(2.7)	0.34(0.45)		-0.25(0.28)	1.2	23	d
14	Cabinet Size 1950	0.02(0.01)**		-0.20(0.36)	0.34(0.36)	-4.6(2.6)*	0.44(0.43)		-0.37(0.29)	1.5	23	d
15	Ethno-Ling. Frac.			-0.29(0.35)	0.27(0.30)	-1.5(2.3)	-0.04(0.35)	-0.00 (0.003)	-0.02(0.24)	2.0	27	
16	Urbanization 1950		0.002(0.004)	-0.26(0.35)	0.25(0.30)	-1.6(2.2)	-0.17(0.40)		-0.04(0.26)	2.0	27	
17	Polit. Modern.		-0.03(0.06)	-0.31(0.35)	0.31(0.31)	-2.3(2.7)	0.11(0.44)		-0.01(0.24)	2.0	27	

| | | | | Independent Variables | | | | | | | | |
Eq. No.	Political,Social and Control Variable Names	H 1: State Power & Authority	H 3: Social & Political Modernization[b]	H 2a: Prim. Enrollment Ratio 1955	H 2b: Sec. Enrollment Ratio 1955	H 2c: Univ. Enrollment Ratio 1955[h]	Pop. 1970/Pop.1955	Control Vars.[b]	GNP 1955/GNP 1950[c]	Constant	No.of Cases	Comments
					POORER COUNTRIES[h]							
18				0.07(0.18)	0.47(0.84)	-0.61(3.5)	0.05(0.25)		0.26(0.29)	0.97	46	
19	State Centraliz.	0.03(0.09)		0.23(0.35)	-0.26(2.1)	0.18(5.8)	0.23(0.41)		0.24(0.57)	0.64	23	d
20	Gov. Rev. 1955	-0.009(0.02)		0.36(0.37)	0.76(1.9)	-2.0(6.0)	0.11(0.51)		0.01(0.56)	1.1	22	d,e
21	Cabinet Size 1950	-0.02(0.02)		0.37(0.39)	0.57(1.8)	0.86(5.8)	-0.23(0.57)		0.17(0.59)	1.5	21	d
22	Ethno-Ling. Fract.			-0.02(0.18)	0.13(0.86)	0.83(3.6)	0.01(0.25)	-0.002 (.002)	0.32(0.29)	1.1	46	
23	Polit. Part. 1960		0.004(0.014)	0.04(0.36)	-0.30(2.0)	1.1(6.1)	0.56(0.46)		0.36(0.55)	0.06	23	d,e,f
24	Urbanization 1950		0.01(0.004)**	0.16(0.17)	-1.2(1.1)	2.2(3.6)	0.00(0.24)		0.13(0.28)	1.2	46	
25	Polit Modern.		0.03(0.04)	0.05(0.20)	0.40(0.88)	-1.1(3.7)	0.04(0.26)		0.28(0.30)	1.1	43	
26	Colonies 1955 Only			-0.04(0.29)	0.69(1.5)	1.1(30)	-0.21(0.45)		0.28(0.45)	1.3	20	

* p < .10
** p < .05

a. Dependent variable in all equations is GNP 1970/GNP 1965. Ordinary least squares—estimates of slopes; standard errors in parentheses. Equations with less than 20 cases omitted.

b. Variable names in left column.

c. GNP in millions of 1964 $US.

d. Countries independent by 1955 only.

e. Communist countries excluded due to measurement ambiguities.

f. Mostly developing countries.

g. Countries above median 1955 GNP per capita ($278; 1964 $US).

h. Countries below median 1955 GNP per capita.

in it used as measures of economic development tend to contain, we believe, high levels of error.

The variables in table 6.8 are relatively unskewed in distribution, and the equations are estimated with ordinary least squares.

The findings of table 6.8 generally parallel our earlier results. For the combined set of countries, primary and secondary enrollments tend to positively affect growth. University enrollments have generally insignificant negative effects. The indicators of state power show weak effects, however. As in all the previous analyses, the modernization indicators show weak effects. Interestingly, the table also shows that our measure of economic growth has little stability over time. This could simply reflect high measurement error, but seems substantively plausible: while GNP has a very high autocorrelation over time, there is no reason to suppose that in the modern world context the rate of change in GNP has such stability.[20]

A few separate analyses for richer and poorer countries are also reported in table 6.8, and even in these, only limited numbers of cases are available. The results are almost entirely insignificant, but conform in pattern to our earlier findings. Again, primary education shows some negative effects in the richer countries, and the effects of measures of state power disappear in poorer ones. We do not know whether to give these differences substantive interpretations.

In short, these results, obtained by a procedure considerably different from the earlier analyses, lend support to our overall conclusions.

CONCLUSIONS

Our data can be summarized simply. Proceeding through a number of different analysis models, and with several different indicators of economic growth, we consistently find the following:

1 Our conceptually and empirically disparate indicators of state power and authority in society all seem to show positive effects on economic growth in the 1950–70 period.[21]

2 As regards mass education, primary and especially secondary enrollments also affect economic growth. University level educational expansion consistently shows insignificant negative effects.

3 Measures of modernization, urbanization, and political modernization and participation show no effects on economic development.

We further find that these results tend generally to describe the expansion of both richer and poorer countries during this time period. Or at least, putting it more conservatively, we do not find convincing differences in patterns of effects between the two types of countries.

In interpreting these patterns, it is clear that they are very much conditioned by the world context of the 1950–70 period. Social modernization may have been an important source of economic development in a world in which development (and modernization) were not built-in, official goals of the dominant powers. Similarly, state power may be quite destructive of unrestrained economic growth in an imperial system (or any system in which political forces can command the whole larger system of exchange). The effects of state power in our data (especially given unclearly conceptualized variables and measures of uncertain measuring) give testimony to the fact that modern states are organized around economic development as a goal. Economic Calvinism is the official religion of modern states; perhaps modernizing individuals and societies with "modern" values is no longer needed.

It is important to note that this finding does *not* mean that in the modern world larger units grow more rapidly. In fact, other analyses consistently show little relation between the population or economic size of a country and its economic growth rate.[22] The evidence shows, rather, that the dominance of a state *within* its society is the relevant factor. Economic success apparently involves the ability of a state to effectively organize its population rather than its ability to compete with other states. This may tell a good deal about the underlying organization of the contemporary world.

Finally, the effects of education that we found make sense in a context in which schooling is a development-oriented institution. Modern schooling systems are controlled by *states,* not by religious or private groups, and they are designed to channel people and values into rationalized economic activity (see chap. 5). In a world in which education was organized differently, different effects might ensue. Perhaps that is why primary and secondary education (which, in most societies, send most school-leavers into the economic labor force) show positive economic effects. Tertiary education, in most societies, channels people almost entirely into the high professions and the civil service, not into the economy.[23] Perhaps this absence of a direct organizational connection between higher education and the economy accounts for the utter absence of any indication of a positive effect in our findings.

In any event, the simplest summary of our findings seems to be that in a world in which the goal of economic development is built into the dominant political structures, the nation-states, the power and authority of these states and their ability to reorganize their citizens for economic action through the mass education system seem to be causal factors of some significance in determining the degree of economic development. We have not learned *what* about state power and mass education creates these effects, but the effects themselves seem to be present.

NOTES

1 These conclusions play an important ideological role in justifying the expansion of education in developing countries, and the intellectuals producing

them get more attention in such countries than in their own. The method usually involves some additional corrections (for example, for income foregone, and for earnings obtainable from alternative investments to education) beyond those reported here. But the fundamental flaw of aggregation remains.

2 It is also possible to approach such studies with data over time on a single case. This is made less plausible by the existence of very strong trends upward in both educational enrollments and economic variables. Thus a "residual" approach arises in the economics of education attributing economic growth not easily explained by ordinary economic factors to education (see, for example, Denison 1962). Few alternatives are considered.

3 The only evidence produced for this hypothesis is the observation that destablizing social and political movements are led by educated people. But this is true for most other structures in modern society too.

4 This excludes Algeria, Liberia, Libya, Mauritania, Surinam, Iran, Kuwait, Saudi Arabia, Congo (Zaire), Gabon, Guyana, Nigeria, Swaziland, Trinidad-Tobago, and Venezuela. A number of these countries would have been excluded anyway because of missing data on other variables.

5 This exclusion made very little difference in our findings.

6 We choose, thus, some lags from 1955 to 1970 and others from 1950 to 1960 or 1965. This has the advantages of (a) avoiding the use of the same particular measurement points in all of our analyses; and (b) having some lags starting ten years after World War II to try to remove temporary effects of the war from our analyses.

7 Communist countries receive high scores on the index of state centralization, and also tend to grow more, economically, during this period. Even when they are removed, however, this variable continues to show positive (though nonsignificant) effects. They are removed from analyses including government revenue, and cannot account for its effects.

8 In equations with formal representation, the effect of secondary education sometimes disappears entirely. This can be seen to result from the particular selection of cases when this variable is included, because the variable itself has little effect and thus cannot render other effects spurious.

9 Primary enrollment data contain several biases which may produce these results—particularly when we divide the countries. While gross differences between more and less developed countries in primary enrollments probably have meaning, within both groups error variance may dominate— because more developed countries cluster around the ceiling of 100%, while less developed ones have enrollment ratios which may be inflated by the overenrollment of overaged persons.

10 Such analyses for the other economic indicators do not produce very different results.

11 As noted above, ambiguities in this measure may make interpretation difficult. Richer countries vary around a very high mean, and perhaps their variance is not substantively meaningful. Poorer countries often have technically inflated values during periods of rapid expansion.

12 The slopes associated with secondary education differ sharply between the two groups of countries, but since we use the log of GNP in these analyses, it is hard to make a substantive interpretation—a larger slope in poorer countries may mean a much smaller dollar effect than a small slope in rich ones.

13 Economic production functions are ordinarily interactive, not additive: they treat the value of a given unit of one factor of production as highly dependent on the presence of other production factors. This kind of reasoning has not been a major theme in the economics of education, which has tended to deal in case studies and has not often confronted the problem.

14 We use this weight even in equations estimating KWH. GNP data seem to be somewhat more stable, especially for poor countries, in which KWH can be greatly affected by a given policy decision (for example, to build a large dam). For the same reason, we interact our independent variables by GNP_1 even in the equations estimating KWH_2 as a dependent variable.

15 This variable may show more effects in overall, than in subdivided, analyses because dividing the sample on GNP eliminates much of the meaningful variation, as noted earlier.

16 The negative coefficients associated with GNP in the KWH equations are of no substantive interest. This term is simply used as a weighting term in these equations. Similarly, the effects of population should not be taken seriously, for some of the methodological reasons noted earlier.

17 The cutting point for 1950 is $195. In 1955 it is $278.

18 Strictly speaking, each of the models we estimate is dynamic since they are all difference equations. The models described in this section introduce more complex dynamic elements. For a statement of the correspondence between panel models and dynamic differential equation models, see Coleman (1968).

19 Sophisticated dynamic models would measure *changes* in these independent variables, but measures of their change are often unavailable or imprecise, and do not always correspond closely to our conceptualizations. Changes in educational enrollments, for instance, may only slowly alter the stock of educated personnel. When included in panel analyses such as those of table 6.8, changes in educational enrollment ratios are unrelated to subsequent changes in economic growth.

20 It would undoubtedly have more stability in a world context in which some countries were not organized around development at all. In the present world context, which seems to penetrate practically all societies, rates of growth are rather similar.

21 In addition to the data reported above, a measure of the relative size of a country's internal security forces shows rather consistent positive effects on economic development (see Meyer, Hannan, and Rubinson 1973). Too few cases are available to lend much confidence to this result, however.

22 Through the 1950–70 period, there is some tendency for growth rates to be highest in communist societies (perhaps partly for artificial measure-

ment reasons noted above), and in other societies in the "upper middle" part of the GNP per capita scale. Growth rates are lower in countries at the top of the scale (especially in the US) and in those at the very bottom of the scale. See Meyer, Boli-Bennett, and Chase-Dunn 1975.

23 This is in contrast with the United States, in which the enormously expanded higher educational system is a main training ground for many positions in the economy.

SEVEN · Political Mobilization and Economic Development: A Confirmatory Factor Analysis

Yilmaz Esmer

National economic development is one of the major themes characterizing the post–World War II era. Although interest in "inquiries into the nature and causes of the wealth of nations" is by no means recent, it is difficult to overemphasize the popularity and the importance the subject has gained among both academicians and politicians over the last few decades.

Parallel to this growing concern over economic growth and development, the role of the state in inducing and leading national development has also expanded considerably. Today's national state—particularly, although by no means only, in newly independent countries—is assigned the major responsibility in seeing that a fast rate of economic growth is achieved. The masses are mobilized by the central political authority around the goal of economic development and are asked to make political as well as economic sacrifices in the name of this goal. Almost every country has a central plan for economic and social development, stating the principles according to which national resources are to be allocated and setting forth concrete goals such as an exact growth rate to be achieved. In Waterston's (1965, p. 2) words, "Today, the national plan appears to have joined the national anthem and the national flag as a symbol of sovereignty and modernity."

The basic question we wish to answer in this paper is the same as the one asked in chapter 6: Are more powerful, centralized, and authoritative states that can mobilize their citizens more efficiently and expediently likely to accelerate economic growth? Furthermore, should we expect the direction and magnitude of this effect (that is, the effect of political mobilization on economic development) to be similar in underdeveloped and developed societies?

The independent variable in this study, political mobilization, is generally used in reference to two different processes. In the more common usage of the term, the state is the passive actor. Social groups mobilize themselves around certain goals and demand recognition from or action by the central political authority. The aim here is to influence and put pressure on the state. The working classes, for example, may demand participation in the political system or legislation to further their economic interests and mobilize their members to achieve these goals. The object of this type of mobilization is action (or sometimes inaction) by the political authority. Campaigns for universal suffrage and education are perhaps better illustrations of demands by the masses directly upon the state. Ethnicity, religion, color, language, social class, occupation, and geographic location have frequently served as the bases of such mobilization efforts.

It should be noted, however, that the state is not only the passive object but can also be the active instigator of political mobilization. In varying degrees, all states attempt to mobilize their citizens or certain groups of citizens around "national goals." Tilly (1975, p. 34) notes, for example, that socialist regimes actively promote working-class mobilization. In this instance, the direction of mobilizational efforts is reversed. The present study is an attempt to assess the effects of political mobilization, in this latter sense, on economic development.

The research design of this study is based on two metatheoretical assumptions which should be made explicit. We assume that (a) more powerful and centralized states will be more successful in mobilizing their citizens around any desired goal, and (b) national economic development is one of the major goals of all contemporary states. As expressed in chapter 6, states are organized around economic growth.

The relationship between powerful, mobilizational states and economic development has been the subject of much discussion and research (see, for example, Adelman and Morris 1967, 1973; Aitken 1959; Emerson 1963; Hirschman 1958; Meier 1976; Rostow 1962). Chapter 6 enumerates the reasons for expecting accelerated economic growth in countries where the political authority is powerful and centralized. The authors of that chapter conclude that power and authority of the state indeed have positive effects on economic development, and that these effects are similar in wealthy and poor countries.

In this paper we attempt to test further the conclusions reached in chapter 6 using different techniques of analysis. A powerful, centralized, mobilizing state is expected to positively affect economic growth mainly for the following reasons. Where voluntary savings fail to reach adequate levels the state can force savings more successfully through taxation, restrictions on consumption, price policies, and compulsory lending; it can control the labor force more effectively, preventing interruptions in production; it is under less pressure in allocating available resources; it is in a better position to build the infrastructure required for economic growth. However, with respect to all these factors, the situation is clearly different in developed and underdeveloped countries. In the former, not only has the initial critical capital accumulation been realized, but incomes are sufficiently high to allow voluntary savings; the marginal effects of a few "political investments" are much lower; basic infrastructure consisting of transportation, communication facilities, and so on is already completed; and, to use Baran's (1957) words, "investing in road-building, financing construction of canals and power stations, organizing large housing projects, etc." do not "transcend . . . the financial and mental horizons of capitalists" in developed countries. Students of economic development frequently note such differences in the structure and working of the economies of developed and underdeveloped countries.

HYPOTHESIS 1 *In underdeveloped countries, political mobilization will have positive effects on economic development.*

HYPOTHESIS 2 *In developed countries, political mobilization will have no significant effects on economic development.*

RESEARCH DESIGN AND METHODOLOGY

To test these hypotheses, I use a basic panel design (see chaps. 1 and 2). However, to avoid the biases in the estimation procedure that correlated error terms could cause in a standard panel model (see chap. 2), a multiple-indicator design is employed. Thus, both political mobilization and economic development are treated as unmeasured variables. Such a model has certain advantages:

1. The biasing effects of measurement errors can be reduced by proper use of multiple indicators (see, for example, Duncan 1975, chap. 10).

2. The researcher no longer has to assume that the error term in the equation is uncorrelated with the independent variables, for the use of multiple indicators usually allows the identification of models which incorporate correlated error terms.

3. An overidentified model provides additional information with which the fit of the model to the data can be assessed.

4. Aside from these methodological considerations, use of the multiple-indicator model is appropriate for our analysis on theoretical grounds as well. Both political mobilization and economic development are multidimensional processes. Thus, a model that includes indicators of various dimensions of these processes will reveal more information about the relationship in which we are interested.

Jöreskog (1969, 1970, 1973) has developed a technique for the analysis of covariance structure involving unmeasured variables. The technique is called confirmatory factor analysis and, unlike ordinary factor analysis, requires that the underlying structural model be completely specified before estimation. Parameters in the model can be fixed to a predetermined value, can be free, or can be constrained to be equal to other parameters (Jöreskog 1970; Werts, Jöreskog, and Linn 1973).

Jöreskog (1972, p. 243) has shown that the variance-covariance matrix Σ of observed variables in a multiple-indicator model can be written as

$$\Sigma = \beta(\Lambda^\Phi\Lambda' + \Psi^2)\beta' + \theta^2,$$

where β is a matrix of structural parameters between unobserved factors, Λ is a matrix of factor loadings, Φ is the variance-covariance matrix of factors, and Ψ and θ are diagonal matrices.

Jöreskog has authored a series of computer programs for estimating the parameters of the general model. Of these programs, ACOVS (analysis of covariance structures) will be used in this study. ACOVS yields statistically efficient least-squares and maximum likelihood estimates of unknown parameters and a goodness-of-fit test statistic (Jöreskog, Gruvaeus, and van Thillo 1971).

MEASUREMENT AND THE BASIC MODEL

Throughout the analysis, two indicators are used to measure the level of national economic development: gross national product per capita and kilowatt-hours of electricity consumption per capita. The seven measures of political mobilization, on the other hand, are the Banks and Textor (1963) power concentration index; number of political parties; internal security forces as a proportion of working-age population; political control of primary and tertiary education; and primary and tertiary students in public schools as a percentage of total number of primary and tertiary students.[1]

Thus, in the analyses that follow, I estimate the following equation:

$$\text{EconDev}_{t_2} = p_0 + p_1\text{EconDev}_{t_1} + p_2\text{PolMob}_{t_1} + u_{t_2}.$$

This basic model (fig. 7.1) is estimated with different sets of indicators of political mobilization and for five, ten, fifteen, and twenty-year lags. The two additional factors, F_1 and F_2, on figure 7.1 represent the collection of variables which affect both GNP_{t_2}, and KWH_{t_1} and KWH_{t_2}, respectively. Thus the model takes into account the correlation between the residuals of GNP and KWH over time while estimating the random error terms (e_1, e_5, e_6, e_7) as well. It will be noted that in the model h_1, h_1', h_2, and h_2' are not separately identified but that only the products h_1h_1' and h_2h_2' are.

For purposes of comparing the goodness of fit of our model to one which assumes that error terms are uncorrelated, each run was repeated leaving out F_1 and F_2. As we shall see, taking into account the fact that the residuals of GNP and KWH actually consist of two parts, one random and one correlated, improves the fit of the model considerably.

As I have already noted, ACOVS gives both maximum likelihood (ML) and least-squares (LS) estimates for each parameter. In this

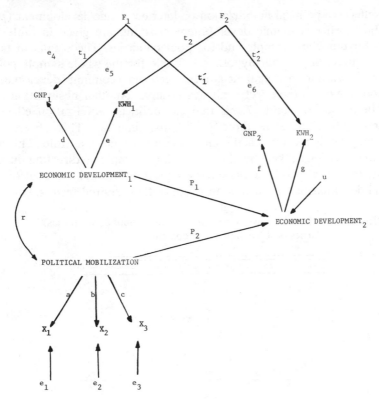

Fig. 7.1   Basic Panel Model of the Effects of Political Mobilization on
Economic Development

paper, I shall be reporting only maximum likelihood estimates. However, it should be mentioned that although in some instances there are considerable differences in the magnitude of the two, all the inferences that we make using the ML estimates are also confirmed by the LS estimates. One advantage of using the ML estimates is the fact that they yield a χ^2 test with which one can judge the degree of fit between the hypothesized model and the data.

To test the hypothesis that political mobilization is related to economic development only in poor countries, I shall estimate each model twice: once for the whole sample of countries and once for the lower 75% of the sample (with respect to GNP per capita in 1950). Unfortunately, due to missing data, the number of cases for the upper quartile of the sample is too few for any meaningful statistical analysis.

RESULTS OF THE ANALYSIS

The first model that we estimate includes two indicators of political mobilization: power concentration and the number of political parties.

The effects of political mobilization on later economic development (p_2), holding earlier economic development constant, are given in table 7.1 both for the whole sample and for poor countries. The results in table 7.1 strongly support our hypotheses. While for the whole sample political mobilization has small negative effects on economic development, in poor countries the effect is always positive. Another observation that can be made from table 7.1 is that the political mobilization effect in poor countries increases directly with the time lag. This observation generally holds throughout the analysis and is quite plausible. The mobilizing decisions taken by the state (for example, redirecting investments to capital goods or organizing education around the goal of national development) need time to produce their desired results.

TABLE 7.1   Effects of Power Concentration and Number of Political
Parties on Economic Development[a]

Time Lag	Entire Sample	Poorer Nations
1950–55	$-.026^b$ (56)	.107 (36)
1950–60	$-.001$ (57)	.152 (37)
1950–65	$-.014$ (56)	.197 (36)
1950–70	$-.009$ (48)	.711 (28)

a. Standardized path coefficients; number of cases in
    parentheses.

b. For this run the ML function did not converge after
    500 iterations. The coefficient reported is thus
    the standardized LS estimate.

The estimates obtained from the model which assumes that the error terms of GNP_{t_1} and GNP_{t_2}, and KWH_{t_1} and KWH_{t_2} are uncorrelated yields results similar to our basic model (table 7.2). To decide which model fits the data better we need to compare the χ^2 obtained from the ML estimates. We would expect that the more complicated model, which takes into account the correlation between residuals, gives a better fit, but that the fit of the simpler model will improve as the time lag increases since correlations between the residuals should be inversely related to the lag. The χ^2 values reported in table 7.3 confirm both expectations. Clearly, even taking into account the difference in the degrees of freedom, there is no question about which model gives us a better approximation. In addition, χ^2 values for the simpler (residuals uncorrelated) model do decrease steadily as time lag increases, pointing to a decreasing correlation between error terms over time. This finding is consistent in all the runs that were completed.

TABLE 7.2   Effects of Power Concentration and Number of Political Parties on Economic Development, Residuals Not Correlated[a]

Time Lag	Entire Sample	Poorer Nations
1950–55	$-.029^{b}$ (56)	.062 (36)
1950–60	-.003 (57)	.116 (37)
1950–65	.006 (56)	.190 (36)
1950–70	-.007 (48)	.260 (28)

a. Standardized path coefficients; number of cases in parentheses.

b. For this run the ML function did not converge after 500 iterations. The coefficient reported is thus the standardized LS estimate.

Our next set of estimates includes the number of internal security forces as an indicator of political mobilization in addition to power concentration and the number of parties. We think this variable is a good indicator of the sheer coercive power of the state. Unfortunately, data on internal security forces exist for a very limited number of countries for earlier times. As a result, the sample size becomes too small to be meaningful. Therefore, while attaching no significance to the results obtained from runs including the internal security forces variable, we note that they confirm all the observations made from the previous set of estimates.

The next four indicators of political mobilization that we use are measures of the control the state has over education. We rotate these four variables as the third indicator of political mobilization in a model which already includes power concentration and the number of parties.

TABLE 7.3   Comparison of χ^2 Values for Tables 7.1, 7.2[a]

Time Lag	Residuals Correlated: χ^2 with 3 d.f.		Residuals Not Correlated: χ^2 with 5 d.f.	
	Entire Sample	Poorer Nations	Entire Sample	Poorer Nations
1950–60	9.36	10.29	137.05	53.69
1950–65	3.70	11.10	99.30	51.15
1950–70	7.83	7.88	63.46	20.21

a. Indicators of political mobilization: power concentration and number of political parties.

Table 7.4 compares the effects of political mobilization on economic development for the whole sample and for poor countries in a model which includes the political control of primary education measure, while table 7.5 gives a comparison of the χ^2 values between the simpler model and our basic model. Both tables conform to our expectations. From table 7.4, once again we observe that, while for the whole sample effects are around zero regardless of time lag, for the lower 75% of the sample they are positive and are related directly to the time lag. As expected, for both the whole sample and the poor countries there is a significant difference between the fit of the model that correlates the residuals of economic development indicators over time and the one that does not, to the advantage of the former, with the latter improving as lag increases.

Table 7.6 summarizes the effects of political mobilization when the remaining three measures of the control of education are added to power concentration and number of parties, one at a time. Thus, in column

TABLE 7.4   Effects of Power Concentration, Number of Political Parties and Political Control of Primary Education on Economic Development[a]

Time Lag	Entire Sample	Poorer Nations
1950–55	.005 (44)	.091 (27)
1950–60	.049 (45)	.179 (28)
1950–65	.029 (44)	.349 (27)
1950–70	.025 (40)	.415 (23)

a. Standardized path coefficients; number of cases in parentheses.

TABLE 7.5   Comparison of χ^2 Values for Models Adding Political Control of Primary Education as an Indicator of Political Mobilization[a]

Time Lag	Residuals Correlated: χ^2 with 8 d.f.		Residuals Not Correlated: χ^2 with 10 d.f.	
	Entire Sample	Poorer Nations	Entire Sample	Poorer Nations
1950–55	24.65	12.65	207.87	73.23
1950–60	23.30	20.31	181.49	47.85
1950–65	17.45	25.80	129.41	52.23
1950–70	14.48	14.81	62.71	19.01

a. Power concentration and number of political parties remain in all analyses as indicators of political mobilization.

TABLE 7.6   Effects of Political Mobilization on Economic Development[a]

	Additional Mobilization Indicator Included		
Time Lag	Control of Tertiary Ed.	Public Primary Ed. as % of Total	Public Tertiary Ed. as % of Total
	Entire Sample		
1950–55	.053 (36)	−.035 (52)	−.023 (45)
1950–60	.078 (37)	−.002 (53)	.011 (46)
1950–65	.103 (37)	.025 (52)	.008 (46)
1950–70	.132 (31)	.053 (44)	−.003 (38)
	Poorer Nations		
1950–55	.142 (22)	.096 (34)	.095 (29)
1950–60	.216 (23)	.180 (35)	.210 (30)
1950–65	.286 (23)	.535 (34)	.250 (30)
1950–70	.449 (17)	.212 (27)	.289 (22)

a. Standardized path coefficients; number of cases in parentheses. Power concentration and number of political parties remain in all analyses as indicators of political mobilization.

(1), both for the whole sample and for the poor countries, political control of tertiary education is used as an indicator of political mobilization in addition to power concentration and number of parties. In columns (2) and (3), this variable is replaced by the percentage of primary students in public schools and the percentage of tertiary students in public schools, respectively. It will be noted that the results in table 7.6 are consistent with our previous findings.

DISCUSSION

The results reported in this paper support the hypothesis that the positive effects of state power on economic development are in play only in poor nations. What could cause the discrepancy between these findings and those reported in chapter 6? Here is one possible explanation. An examination of the correlation coefficients among the indicators of state power and economic development shows that the nature of the relationship between the two is significantly different in poor and rich countries. Measures of state power are positively related to economic development in poor countries, but they are negatively correlated with both indicators

of economic development in rich countries. We have noted before that
when the error terms are correlated, the least-squares estimates are
biased. Hannan (1973) shows that when the independent variables are
positively correlated this bias will inflate the magnitude of the effects of
the lagged variable while deflating the effects of the other independent
variable. In poor countries, the positive correlation between indicators
of state power and economic development will suppress the political
mobilization effects. On the other hand, since the measures of state
power are negatively correlated with economic development in rich
countries, the insignificant effects in these countries could not be the
result of this bias in the estimation procedure.

In this type of multivariate analysis, it is always possible that an uncontrolled variable is responsible for the findings. This possibility, need-
less to say, can never be eliminated—at least in practice. However, it is
reassuring to note that the inclusion of one such variable that is likely
to produce a spurious relationship between political mobilization and
economic development, namely the level of education in the society,
does not alter our findings.

Throughout this paper, conclusions were drawn from comparisons of
standardized coefficients or β's. It is, however, known that comparing
standardized coefficients across samples can frequently be misleading.
Given that

$$\beta_{yx} = b_{yx}\frac{\sigma_x}{\sigma_y},$$

a change in the variance of either the dependent or the independent
variable can cause a comparison of β's across samples to be meaningless. However, it can also be seen from this equation that a change in
the variances of dependent or independent variables cannot change the
sign of the coefficient. Also, a slope of zero cannot be affected by the
differences in variances across samples. The results we obtained for
the whole sample showed the effects to be almost always around zero.
Furthermore, when the whole analysis was repeated for the upper third
of the sample, the effects of political mobilization were in most instances
found to be slightly negative.

CONCLUSIONS

In this study we used a confirmatory factor-analytic model to estimate
the effects of powerful, mobilizing states on economic development. Although a number of indicators of political mobilization were used, the
results were consistent throughout the analysis. Our major findings can
be summarized as follows:
1. Powerful, centralized mobilizing states accelerate economic development only in countries whose per capita incomes are relatively low.

2. This effect is felt not immediately but after a certain time lag—generally, after at least ten years.
3. On the methodological side, the panel design we used was significantly improved when the assumption that $E(uX_i) = 0$ was relaxed.

NOTES

1 For an explanation of these variables and the sources from which they were coded see chapters 3 and 6.

2 The probability level of the χ^2 value is the probability of getting a χ^2 value larger than that actually obtained, given that the hypothesized structure is true (see Jöreskog, Gruvaeus, and van Thillo 1971).

IV STUDIES OF ECONOMIC GROWTH: NATIONAL ROLES IN THE WORLD SYSTEM

EIGHT · The Effects of International Economic Dependence on Development and Inequality

Christopher Chase-Dunn

INTRODUCTION

Dependency theorists claim that international economic dependence produces the "development of underdevelopment" in peripheral areas of the world economy. At the same time, the core-periphery distinction has led to revisions in the theory of capitalist development which focus on the world system, rather than national societies, as the relevant unit of analysis. In combination these two ideas imply that Marx's law of uneven development and pauperization, while it may have been wrong for the core nations, is correct for the world economy as a whole, and for the peripheral nations in particular.

The gap between core and periphery and the gross inequalities within peripheral countries suggest that this is indeed the case. The hypothesis that dependence retards development has not been adequately tested by formal comparative research, however. Case studies have found evidence both contradictory and supportive of this hypothesis, as have the few previous comparative studies that have been done.[1] The related hypothesis that dependence increases inequality within peripheral countries has not at all been subjected to comparative test. This paper reports the results of a panel analysis of the effects of two kinds of international economic dependence on economic development, and a cross-sectional test of the effects of dependence on income inequality.

WHAT IS INTERNATIONAL ECONOMIC DEPENDENCE?

International power-dependence relations range from direct military force, through formal political subjugation (colonialism), to more subtle economic forms of power and influence such as foreign investment, foreign aid, and trade relations based on a vertical division of labor. Although it is clear that these different forms are functionally interrelated, the focus of this research is on the more subtle neocolonial types

This chapter is adapted from a paper published in the *American Sociological Review* 40 (1975): 720–38.

of economic dependence which predominated in the period studied—the "Pax Americana" from 1950 to 1970.

International economic dependence itself varies from direct penetration to indirect dependence resulting from location in a larger structure. The most direct economic penetration of peripheral areas by core nations is through private investment by transnational corporations which own and control the process of production. Less direct influence is exercised by foreign aid programs and credit agencies. Indirect economic dependence results from a nation's location in a restricted position in the world trade network or specialization in a marginal role in the international division of labor.

This research examines the economic effects of two specific types of dependence: investment dependence and debt dependence. These two types of economic dependence are positively correlated (0.63), and we are interested to see if they have similar effects on economic development and income inequality.

THEORETICAL APPROACHES TO DEPENDENCE AND DEVELOPMENT

Uneven Development and International Power-Dependence Relations

Myrdal (1957) points out that capitalist development unleashes market forces that create both "spread" effects, by which growth in one area or sector creates development in other areas, and "backwash" effects which drain resources out of the hinterland and concentrate them. In the developed nations (comprising what Wallerstein [1974a] calls the "core" of the world system) class struggle and political processes have strengthened spread effects, resulting in a more even distribution of employment. In the periphery, however, backwash effects have been dominant, resulting in the concentration of development in the core and in enclaves attached to the core. At the level of the world system as a whole, uneven development remains the dominant trend.

The operation of control structures between core states and peripheral areas may reinforce this uneven development. Direct colonial control of peripheral areas has been replaced by the neocolonial mechanisms of direct foreign investment and credit. It is my hypothesis that penetration by external control structures, other things being equal, has a negative effect on economic development through the mechanisms reviewed below. The period studied in this research, 1950 to 1970, was a period of world economic expansion in which almost all national economies were growing (Meyer, Boli-Bennett, and Chase-Dunn 1975). The hypothesis is, then, that dependent nations grow less than others.

Before discussion of theories which predict the effects of dependence on development, it is necessary to clear up three possible misunderstandings. First, what many theorists understand to be simply resource flows between largely unconnected societies are considered by other theorists to be control structures which link superordinate to subordinate units in the same interactive system. This is especially true of the types of dependence studied here—dependence on foreign investment and foreign credit. These radically different ways of perceiving the same reality lead, of course, to completely different predictions about the consequences of such relations.

The second problem in discussing different theoretical approaches is that some theorists propose very long-run structural mechanisms by which dependence may affect development, while others propose short-term effects. Both long-run and short-term hypotheses are reviewed because the research design used in this study is germane to both.

Third is the problem that, while some theories deal with the effects of international power-dependence relations in general, others deal specifically with investment and debt dependence. Again, both types are discussed because research is relevant to both, although more directly to the latter.

The Theory of Imperialism Marx (1967) saw the historical relationship between the centers of capitalist development and the hinterlands of the world in terms of the notion of primitive accumulation. Part of the impetus for the emergence and domination of the capitalist mode of production was the appropriation by European powers of the wealth of Africa, Asia, and the Americas. Marx thought that the domination of the capitalist mode of production would spread throughout the world economy, battering down all Chinese walls with the cheap prices of its commodities. Colonialism would destroy the precapitalist modes of production and each nation would develop the way England had.

Lenin (1965) introduced the concept of imperialism into the Marxist analysis of capitalist development. He pointed out that the exploitation of peripheral areas was an important dimension of capitalist development, rather than a passing phase. Lenin saw monopoly capitalism as needing to export capital and to appropriate raw materials and markets in the periphery. He predicted interimperialist wars resulting from the division and redivision of the periphery by the advanced capitalist powers. Lenin expected that the original centers of capitalist development in Europe would become decadent and that the source of industrial strength would move to the periphery.

Dependency Theory The persistence of underdevelopment in the periphery led to the reexamination of the theory of imperialism and monopoly capitalism by Baran (1957). Baran put forth the theory that penetration of the periphery by core capitalism actually creates obstacles to development. Later Frank (1969) was to term this idea the "development of underdevelopment," implying that the poverty of the periphery is an ongoing modern process, not a primordial state. The literature on the mechanisms by which interaction between core and periphery has retarded the latter has grown greatly in recent years. There are three main topics: exploitation, structural distortion, and suppression of autonomous policies.

Exploitation of the Periphery by the Core

Capitalist development on a world scale involves competition among different actors (capitals and states) for shares of the economic surplus. New resources are created, but at any point in time the amount of extant surplus is finite. Frank (1969) argues that penetration of the periphery by foreign investment drains surplus from the periphery to the core through the repatriation of profits and interest. This "backwash" effect accumulates capital in the core and underdevelops the periphery.[2] Amin (1974) contends that this "decapitalization" results from a continuing process of primitive accumulation in which political and military force backs up economic advantage in core-periphery relations.

Emanuel (1972) contends that exploitation is hidden in the prices at which commodities from the periphery are exchanged for commodities from the core. This "unequal exchange" stems from the different wage structures in the core and the periphery. In the periphery a worker must work, say, two hours to produce what is exchanged for a product which a core worker produces in one hour—and this at the same level of productivity. Thus, the market prices of core-periphery exchange contain a transfer of value to the core.

Some theorists argue that unequal exchange and uneven development will occur in any system of interaction in which the distribution of power is unequal (Baumgartner, Buckley, and Burns 1975). This happens because more powerful actors will use their power to determine outcomes to their advantage. This approach seems to apply to any situation in which the welfare of the less powerful is not heavily protected by social or political institutions. Certainly the world economy is such a system. If foreign investment and credit are control structures between superordinate and subordinate actors in a competitive system, they should cause uneven development.

Thus, exploitation of the periphery by the core is hypothesized to occur by means of decapitalization, unequal exchange, and subordination to external controls in a competitive system. These mechanisms are thought to retard the development of the periphery.

Structural Distortion of the Peripheral Economy

A number of dependency theorists argue that the economic structure which emerges in the periphery as a result of the world division of labor is distorted in such a way as to create obstacles to development (Amin 1974; Dos Santos 1970). An outward-oriented economy specializing in the production of raw materials for export does not develop a differentiated internal structure. Frank (1969) observes that the infrastructure created by colonialism and foreign investment is oriented toward the ports of exit. Railroads, roads, telegraph lines, and so on all function to carry raw materials out of the country and return processed goods. This retards the integration of the national economy by linking the different areas and sectors of the peripheral countries with the external world rather than with one another (Ehrensaft 1971). The multiplier effect, by which demand in one sector or area of a country creates demand in another, is weak because externally oriented linkages soon transfer demand out to the international economy (Singer 1950).

The peripheral areas have been integrated into the world economy as producers of raw materials for export to the industrial countries. Peripheral areas often specialize in a single raw material export, either agricultural or mineral. Galtung (1971) argues that an economy which is specialized in the production of raw materials will grow less than one in which production is more differentiated. Production which involves high levels of processing creates greater demand for inputs and greater opportunities for related economic activities on the output side of production (Hirschman 1958).

Prebisch (1950) maintains that any national economy which remains undifferentiated will suffer from the vicissitudes of the international market, and that this is especially true of those specialized in the production of raw materials because the terms of trade for these commodities decline relative to manufactured goods and capital equipment produced in the core. Also, as there is more fluctuation in price for raw materials in the world market, instability makes economic planning (private or public) more difficult.[3]

In addition Griffin and Enos (1970) argue that dependence on foreign credit reduces the domestic marginal propensity to save and thus negatively affects economic growth by lowering domestic capital formation.

Beckford's (1972) analysis of the role of transnational corporations in plantation economies suggests that the short-term impact of these corporations increases national income and opens new areas of production, but the long-run institutional and structural effect is to distort the use of resources in the peripheral economy. Transnational corporations greatly affect land use, labor markets, and the allocation of investments. Beckford maintains that the logic by which these corporations operate is derived from the scope of the enterprise as a whole, including processing and marketing operations in the core. Thus, they influence the allocation of resources in the periphery from this point of view, using market imperfections (monopoly power in sales and consumption) to guard against the risks of natural or political disaster. Their interest in maintaining relatively cheap labor, low taxes, and the freedom to maneuver is often inconsistent with the balanced development of the peripheral country in which they produce. The distortion of resource use patterns creates what Beckford calls a state of dynamic underdevelopment.

Thus dependence is hypothesized to distort the economic structure of the periphery in the following ways: specialization in raw material production (low differentiation), outward-oriented infrastructure (low integration), and the creation of resource use patterns which retard economic development.

Suppression of Autonomous Policies in the Periphery

Some dependency theorists have argued that dependence retards development through its suppression of autonomous policies in government and business which would mobilize balanced development (Johnson 1972). Baran (1957) contends that dependence distorts the development of a national industrial bourgeoisie. Merchants, with their stake in the export of raw materials and the import of manufactured goods, combine with landed classes (which have similar interests) to prevent the emergence of a domestic manufacturing or industrial bourgeoisie. They do this by politically preventing the introduction of tariffs that would protect infant industries against the competition of already developed producers in the core states. Frank (1969) sees this process in the history of Latin American development. Civil wars occuring in the middle of the nineteenth century in most of the newly independent Latin American republics involved the issue of autonomous versus external orientation. In each case the forces of "free trade" and external orientation triumphed. Wallerstein (1972) makes a similar case for the peripheralization of Poland in the sixteenth century European "world economy."

Other theorists maintain that strong links between elites in the periphery and core elites form what Galtung (1971) calls a "bridgehead" of interests and connections. The external orientation of these "liaison elites" (Hopkins 1969) and the fact that their power and interests are based on connections with the core states means that they suppress policies and leaders seeking to mobilize balanced autonomous development.[4] According to Hayter (1971), international and transnational agencies which lend to peripheral countries (development banks) stand behind the operations of transnational companies in maintaining "a good climate for foreign investment."

Sunkel (1973) claims that the connections of ruling groups in the dependent periphery with core states and transnational corporations create a political structure which keeps wages low and concentrates development in the "international" sector. The links between the core and elites in the periphery increase income inequality by raising the incomes of elites, and keeping the wages of workers low. The power of the elites in dependent peripheral countries is backed by their alliances with the core, so they are able to suppress demands for higher wages and income redistribution (Rubinson 1976).

Thus, dependence creates a political situation which retards development by linking elites in the periphery to the interests of the core. This prevents the emergence of autonomous forces seeking to mobilize balanced development and maintains extreme inequalities in the periphery.

Theoretical Approaches Which Hypothesize Positive Effects of Dependence on Development

Most neoclassical economists and modernization theorists in sociology see what I have been calling dependence as resource flows or the diffusion of modernity from advanced to backward societies. The notion that foreign investment and credit constitute a form of domination is seen as paranoid and reactive and as a remnant of the unfortunate colonial past (Viner 1952). Occasionally the reality of foreign control is acknowledged, however, as more than a political misconception. The following quote from Lester Pearson (1969) compares what I have called debt dependence to dependence on foreign investment.

> Another common misconception is that loan financing leads to less foreign control over the host countries' economies than equity investment. Actually, fixed interest creditors are in a far stronger position with respect to national authorities than are foreign equity investors, who can often be influenced by fiscal, monetary, and other policies.

This comparison of the control aspects of debt and investment dependence is not seen by Pearson as inconsistent with the theories reviewed below, which predict positive effects of dependence on the economic development of peripheral countries.

Neoclassical International Economics In neoclassical international economics the flow of capital from advanced to less-developed nations is understood to be a main engine of economic growth. Capital is capital and its investment should lead to increased production in the enterprise into which it is channeled, as well as economic growth in other sectors due to increased demand. Unrestricted international flow of capital to areas where it will bring the highest return will result in the maximization of growth for the system as a whole, and presumably also for the peripheral areas to which the capital flows. The benefits of foreign investment will spread because of incomes created by new employment and the "trickle-down" effect caused by increased demand for land, labor, and materials (Schelling 1958). The input of foreign aid should result in growth for the same reasons, and because it supplements local savings and makes greater investment possible (Chenery and Strout 1966). The use of aid funds to build public works and infrastructure should have positive effects on later growth.

The theory of comparative advantage holds that specialization in the production of raw materials (one of the correlates of dependence) will not have negative effects on growth if it is more economical to exchange raw materials for manufactured goods than to produce the imported goods domestically. Ricardo put forward the theory of comparative advantage to show why it was mutually advantageous for nations to trade. The example he used was the exchange of English linen for Portuguese wine.[5] The theory holds that "whether or not one of two regions is absolutely more efficient in the production of every good than is the other, if each specializes in the products in which it has a comparative advantage (greatest relative efficiency), trade will be mutually profitable to both regions" (Samuelson 1970). This is in direct contradiction to the idea of "structural distortion" discussed above.

Modernization Theory Most sociologists who study development and modernization focus almost exclusively on processes internal to national societies (Eisenstadt 1966; Stanley 1972; Smelser 1963). The exceptions to this are those theorists who discuss borrowing or diffusion of modern traits from advanced to premodern societies. Bendix (1964) discusses how imperial Meiji Japan modeled its constitution after that of imperial Germany. Parsons (1971), also focusing on diffusion, claims that

> the "imperialist" phase of Western society's relationship with the rest of the world was transitional. The trend toward modernization has now become worldwide. In particular, the elites of most nonmodern societies accept crucial aspects of the values of modernity, especially economic development, education, political independence, and some form of "democracy."

Modernization theorists also emphasize the transfer of advanced technology, modern rational organizational forms, labor habits complementary to industrial production, and "modern" attitudes toward the self, the family, and the society which facilitate economic development (Moore and Feldman 1960). This approach implies that a country which is penetrated by direct foreign investment (has located within it subsidiaries of modern transnational corporations) should develop more than a country that is not so penetrated. Similarly, foreign aid that brings technical assistance and advice regarding fiscal and development policies should also facilitate economic growth.

Summary of Propositions

The dependency literature reviewed above discusses mechanisms by which international power-dependence relations in general have effects on development. The following is an inventory of the propositions which relate specifically to the types of dependence studied in this research—investment and debt dependence.

Mechanisms by Which Investment and Debt Dependence Negatively Affect Economic Growth

a) Exploitation by the core drains resources from the periphery which are needed for its development. Profits on foreign investment and interest on credit transfer value from the periphery to the core and retard the development of the periphery.

b) Externally oriented production and penetration by transnational corporations distort the economic structure of the periphery. Differentiation and integration of national economies are obstructed and a pattern of resource use is created which maintains a state of dynamic underdevelopment.

c) Links between elites in the core and the dependent periphery act to suppress autonomous mobilization of national development.

Mechanisms by Which Foreign Investment and Credit Positively Affect Economic Growth

a) Foreign capital creates production directly in the enterprise in which it is invested and generates demand for other inputs which contribute to economic growth.

b) Foreign credit finances public infrastructure needed for development.

c) Diffusion of technology, work habits, modern organizational forms, modern attitudes, and consumption preferences will stimulate economic development.

Mechanisms by Which Investment and Debt Dependence Affect Income Inequalities within Dependent Countries

a) Positive effect: In peripheral countries penetrated by external control structures, the ruling groups are able to obtain a large share of the national income and to prevent income redistribution because their power is backed up by their alliances with the core.

b) Negative effect: Foreign investment and credit expand the wage-earning working class and the salaried middle class, which enlarges the middle of the income distribution and lowers overall inequality.

Let us turn now to a comparative test of dependence effects on economic development. This research enables us to estimate whether aggregate effects are positive or negative, but does not differentiate between all the mechanisms hypothesized above. Any estimated aggregate effect may be the resultant of the simultaneous operation of different mechanisms, but findings which are consistently negative will direct further attention to dependency theory.

RESEARCH DESIGN

Panel analysis is employed to estimate the effects of dependence on development. This method is particularly important because there is reason to believe that there is reciprocal causation between the two variables. Earlier studies have concluded that dependence has a positive effect on development on the basis of the observed positive cross-sectional correlation. This correlation may be due to the positive effect which level of development has on the influx of foreign capital and aid, however. In the periphery foreign capital tends to flow where there is already greater economic activity and potential for development. Chase-Dunn (1975) has shown that a panel analysis of the effects of level of development on increase in investment dependence supports this contention, and thus the use of panel analysis to estimate the effect of dependence on development is crucial.

Measures of dependence used in the tables reported below have been weighted by population size (per capita) rather than on economic size (per GNP) of the nation in order to make a conservative test of the hypothesis of a negative effect of dependence on development. Weighting with population size rather than economic size should bias the estimate toward the positive if there is an artifact due to ratio measures having common terms.[6]

The theoretical literature on dependence effects focuses on less-developed countries, and so our sample of nations consists of those with less than $406 per capita GNP in 1955. This excludes the richest nations from the analysis while leaving enough cases to allow meaningful regression estimates. Thus we are comparing poor dependent nations with poor independent or isolated nations. A parallel analysis including the rich nations is reported in Chase-Dunn (1975). The results are very similar to those presented below.

MEASUREMENT

International Economic Dependence

1 Investment dependence per capita—the penetration of a nation by direct private foreign capital investment—is measured by employing an item from the International Monetary Fund *Balance of Payments Yearbook*: "debits on investment income" in US dollars. It reports all profits made by foreign direct investment in the "host" country (regardless of whether or not they are repatriated). I computed the average debits on investment income for the period from 1950 to 1955 (to smooth out short-term variation) and divided by the population. This variable, due to its badly skewed distribution, is converted to a logarithmic scale to make it suitable for use in linear regression analysis. Summary statistics on the measures of investment and debt dependence are contained in the appendix.

2 Debt dependence per capita—the dependence of a nation on foreign credit—is measured by the total "external public debt," which is composed of loans to the government and government-guaranteed loans (IBRD 1971). The per capita distribution of this variable is not badly skewed, so it is unnecessary to convert it to a logarithmic scale. Since these data are not available before 1965, we are forced to use a shorter time lag for our panel regression estimates.

Other Causal Variables

There are two additional variables introduced into the equations estimating the effects of dependence on aggregate economic development. They are hypothesized to be related to both dependence and development.

a) Domestic capital formation: This is a measure of local savings, domestic capital formation as a percentage of gross domestic product.[7] It is found for 1960 in Taylor and Hudson (1971).

b) Specialization in mining: The percentage of gross domestic product produced in the mining sector shows the extent to which a national economy is specialized in the production of mineral raw materials. It is found in data presented by the World Bank for 1955 (IBRD 1971).

Measure of Income Inequality

Data on income inequality are not available for different time points, so panel analysis which uses it as a dependent variable is not possible. Thus I have used a cross-sectional design to estimate the relationship between dependence and inequality.

Individual and household income inequality: This is a Gini index computed from the distribution of national income to quintiles of the population, from the poorest 20% to the richest 5%. It has been gathered by Adelman and Morris (1971) and improved by Paukert (1973), resulting in fifty-eight cases available for around 1965.

RESULTS

First let us consider the cross-sectional correlations among debt dependence, investment dependence, and economic development. The correlation between investment dependence and debt dependence is 0.63, indicating that they are somewhat different aspects of economic dependence. Gray (1969), however, claims that foreign aid and credit, rather than displacing foreign private investment, facilitate it by providing public infrastructure which is useful to the foreign enterprise. Hayter (1971) contends that international lending agencies work hand in hand with transnational corporations to maintain open conditions for the foreign investor. Both authors would agree that debt and investment dependence are complementary rather than functional alternatives.

Both investment dependence and debt dependence are positively correlated with measures of economic development in the sample of poor nations. This is because a number of very poor nations are not dependent on foreign investment and credit—that is, they are relatively isolated from neocolonial control structures. Foreign capital tends to flow to where there is already greater economic activity, and thus the correlation between dependence and development is positive. Similarly, debt dependence is higher among more developed peripheral countries because credit is extended on the basis of economic potential. Previous research has interpreted these positive cross-sectional correlations as evidence that dependence facilitates development. Panel analysis enables us to separate the reciprocal effects of dependence and development—that is, to estimate the effect of dependence on development separately from the effect of development on dependence.

Effects of Investment Dependence on Economic Development

Let us look now at the panel regression estimates of investment dependence effects on three measures of economic development in table 8.1. The lags differ between dependent variables so it is difficult to compare the size of the effects. The direction (positive or negative) is the main thing we want to know.

The regression coefficients estimating the effects of investment dependence are negative for all three measures of economic development ($\beta = -.22$, $-.12$, and $-.02$), indicating that investment dependence retards development. For GNP per capita and kilowatt hours of electricity per capita the estimates are statistically significant at the .05 level. The estimated effect on the percentage of the labor force in nonagricultural production is small and not statistically significant, but this measure of occupational structure changes slowly and there is only a ten-year lag, as data are not yet available for 1970.

Beckford's (1971) contention that foreign investment has immediate positive effects, but long-run negative effects, on development is supported by the finding that longer lags with the same dependent variables produce larger negative estimates (Chase-Dunn 1975).

The estimated effect on log kilowatt-hours in table 8.1 is for a fifteen-year lag (1950–65). Data are available for 1970 on this variable, but for fewer cases. The estimate using the 1970 measure of kilowatt-hours is also negative ($\beta = -.15$).

The model examined in table 8.1 assumes that other variables are not interacting with investment dependence and economic development. We need to introduce two variables into the model that are related to both dependence and development.

TABLE 8.1   Panel Analysis of the Effect of Investment Dependence
on Economic Development[a]

Dependent Variable (y_t)	Independent Variables		Constant	Number of Cases
	y_{t-1}	Investment Dependence 1950–55		
Log GNP per Capita 1970	1.32*** (0.13) .99	−0.097** (0.045) −.22	−0.17	38
Log Kilowatt Hours per Capita 1965	0.78*** (0.05) .97	−0.087** (0.041) −.12	1.13	31
% Non-agric. Labor Force 1960	1.02*** (0.03) .98	−1.62 (2.27) −.02	−6.7	46

** p < .05
*** p < .01

a. Y_{t-1} is the lagged dependent variable in 1950; entries are unstandardized slope, standard error of slope in parentheses, and beta.

First, we know that core states need to acquire raw materials, so foreign investment is attracted to countries with substantial mineral resources. This means that the effect of having mineral resources is confounded with the effect of investment dependence in table 8.1.

In table 8.2 we introduce another independent variable, the specialization of a nation in mining, including the production of oil and other minerals. The correlation between investment dependence and specialization in mining is .40, which supports the idea that foreign investment is drawn to areas with mineral resources. Table 8.2 shows the estimated effects on three measures of economic development of both investment dependence and specialization in mining.

The estimates of investment dependence effects are all more negative and statistically significant in table 8.2 than in table 8.1. Thus, the hypothesis that investment dependence has negative effects on development is strongly supported. The effects of specialization in mining are positive on all three development variables and are statistically significant at the .01 level except for the effect on the percentage of the labor force in nonagricultural production. These results provide support for the contention that mineral resources facilitate economic development.

TABLE 8.2   Panel Analysis of the Effects of Investment Dependence
             and Specialization in Mining on Economic Development[a]

Dependent Variable(y_t)	Independent Variables				
	y_{t-1}	% GDP in Mining in 1950	Investment Dependence 1950–55	Constant	Number of Cases
Log GNP per Capita 1970	1.50*** (0.16) 1.05	0.12*** (0.046) .28	-0.187*** (0.059) -.41	-0.39	25
Log Kilowatt Hours per Capita 1965	0.76*** (0.04) .98	0.099*** (0.039) .17	-0.145*** (0.044) -.22	1.27	24
% Non-agric. Labor Force 1960	1.07*** (0.06) .99	0.89 (1.01) .05	-2.27** (1.15) -.12	-13.7	25

** p < .05
*** p < .10

a. Y_{t-1} is the lagged dependent variable in 1950; entries are unstandardized slope, standard error of slope in parentheses, and beta.

Second, it may be that investment dependence is related to the ability to generate local savings. If domestic savings for new investment are low, foreign capital may flow in to take up the available opportunities. At the same time the low propensity to save and invest may be related to other difficulties within a peripheral economy that retard economic development. If this were so it would produce a spurious negative estimate of the effect of investment dependence on economic development when domestic capital formation is not included in the model.

Table 8.3 shows the results of including a measure of domestic capital formation in an equation estimating the effect of investment dependence on development. Because of lack of data in 1950 on domestic capital formation, a shorter time lag for the dependent variable is used in table 8.3. (The longer lag with fewer cases produces results very similar to those shown in table 8.3.) The shorter time lag reduces the size of the estimated effect of investment dependence, but table 8.3 presents the estimate both with and without domestic capital formation. It can be seen by comparing the estimates that the inclusion of domestic capital formation reduces the negative estimate of the investment dependence effect only slightly. This means that investment dependence has negative effects independent of its relationship to domestic capital formation.

The effect of domestic capital formation is positive on both GNP per capita and kilowatt-hours per capita, although only the first estimate is statistically significant. The betas for investment dependence and domestic capital formation are strikingly similar in both equations, except that they have opposite signs. This implies that two types of economic "resources" can, given different structural and institutional conditions, have opposite effects on economic development.

Effects of Debt Dependence on Economic Development

Data on external public debt are not available for most poor countries before 1965. A short-lag panel analysis can be made between 1965 and 1970, however.

Table 8.4 contains the results of an analysis which includes debt dependence and domestic capital formation as independent variables. Domestic capital formation is included because it may be related to the tendency to contract foreign debt, and because it is known to effect economic development. The estimated effects of debt dependence are

TABLE 8.3   Panel Analysis of the Effects on Investment Dependence and Domestic Capital Formation on Economic Development[a]

Dependent Variable (y_t)	y_{t-1}	Independent Variables		Constant	Number of Cases
		Investment Dependence 1950–60	Domestic Capital Formation 1960		
Without Domestic Capital Formation in the Equation					
Log GNP per Capital 1970	1.18*** (0.07) .97	−0.052** (0.027) −.12		−0.24	28
Kilowatt Hours per Capita 1965	.95*** (0.02) .99	0.034 (0.018) −.04		0.19	28
With Domestic Capital Formation in the Equation					
Log GNP per Capita 1970	1.09*** (0.08) .89	−0.044** (0.024) −.11	0.89*** (0.35) .16	−0.16	28
Log Kilowatt Hours per Capita 1965	0.94*** (0.03) .98	−0.031 (0.019) −.04	0.25 (0.29) .03	0.19	28

** $p < .05$
*** $p < .01$

a. Y_{t-1} is the lagged dependent variable in 1960; cases in both equations are those for which data are available on both domestic capital formation and investment dependence. Entries are unstandardized slope, standard error of slope in parentheses, and beta.

TABLE 8.4   Panel Analysis of the Effects of Debt Dependence and Domestic
              Capital Formation on Economic Development[a]

Dependent Variable (y_t)	y_{t-1}	Independent Variables		Constant	Number of Cases
		Debt Dependence 1965	Domestic Capital Formation 1960		
Log GNP per Capita 1970	1.09*** (0.07) .99	-0.007 (0.007) -.05	0.004 (0.27) .001	-0.03	33
Log Kilowatt Hours per Capita 1970	1.19*** (0.14) 1.03	-0.059** (0.028) -.22	-0.49 (1.09) -.05	-0.06	26

** p < .05
*** p < .01

a. Y_{t-1} is the lagged dependent variable in 1965; entries are understandardized
     slope, standard error of slope in parentheses, and beta.

both negative, but only the effect on kilowatt-hours is statistically significant. This is weak evidence that debt dependence has negative effects,
but fairly strong evidence that it does not have positive effects.

The estimated effect of domestic capital formation, which was significant with the longer lag in table 8.3, is not significant in table 8.4 for
either dependent variable.

Effects of Debt and Investment Dependence on Inequality
Dependence is thought to affect development in part through its effects
on the class structure of the peripheral countries. It is hypothesized that
liaison elites in dependent countries are supported by external power,
and thus the distribution of resources is very unequal. Only cross-sectional data on income inequality are available and they are not gathered
at exactly the same time point for each case (Paukert 1973). Even so,
given the theoretical relevance of the proposition that dependence effects
on development are connected with effects on inequality, a preliminary
test of the effect on inequality is justified.[8] Table 8.5 contains the results
of the cross-sectional analysis of the effects of investment and debt dependence on income inequality in peripheral countries. Included as
dependent variables in both equations are specialization in mining and
economic development—both thought to be related to dependence and
inequality.

The estimates of the dependence effects are both positive but not
statistically significant (although nearly so at the .05 level). This is weak

support for the hypothesis that dependence maintains income inequality in peripheral countries.[9]

Summary of Results

The hypothesis that investment dependence retards economic development is strongly supported by tables 8.1 through 8.3.[10] Further investigation of dependence effects on growth in different economic sectors indicates that there are negative effects on production in agriculture and manufacturing, but that investment dependence has a *positive* effect on production in mining (Chase-Dunn 1975). This suggests that dependence effects are not uniform and that further research should be done to determine the loci of effects on development.

It is shown that debt dependence definitely does not facilitate economic development, and there is weak evidence that it retards it. It may require a longer time lag for the negative effects of debt dependence to become measurable by cross-national research. This question can be settled as more complete data are collected.

Table 8.5 provides some support for the hypothesis that dependence causes the unequal distribution of income. It should be added that the estimated effect of investment dependence on the income share received by the top 5 percent of the population is positive, while the effect on the income received by the bottom three quintiles of the population is negative. This is further evidence that dependence provides support for

TABLE 8.5   Cross-Sectional Analysis of the Effects of Investment and Debt Dependence, Economic Development, and Specialization in Mining on Income Inequality[a]

	Independent Variables					
	Dependence Measure	Log GNP per Capita	Specialization in Mining	Constant	R^2	Number of Cases
Eq.(1): Investment Dependence						
	6.11 (3.84) .44	−3.28 (7.6) −.09	0.014 (0.018) .17	38.6	.27	31
Eq. (2): Debt Dependence						
	0.011 (0.008) .31	−1.19 (7.12) −.04	0.021 (0.018) .22	45.6	.18	30

a. Dependent variable: Gini index of income inequality. Entries are unstandardized slope, standard error in parentheses, and beta.

elites in the periphery and keeps wages low relative to the income of elites.

THEORETICAL IMPLICATIONS

The findings reported above indicate that dependency theory must be taken seriously as an explanation for uneven development in the world economy. Power-dependence relations between core and periphery operate to reproduce the inequalities between national societies. In a competitive world economy, subjection to external controls is a disadvantage which retards relative development. This is shown to be true for direct penetration by investment dependence and is also true of indirect forms of dependence resulting from restricted location in the international trade network.[11] This effect may become larger in the period of world economic contraction which began in 1967. Peripheral nations which are more subject to core control may be prevented from taking advantage of opportunities for development which emerge in such a period.[12]

The finding of a negative effect of investment dependence on economic development means that foreign capital must be seen as a form of control as well as a flow of resources. The structural and institutional context in which this economic flow is imbedded produces effects which are opposite those of domestic capital investment. The proposed mechanisms by which dependence retards development are not directly tested herein, and further research focusing specifically on intervening variables needs to be done. The most plausible explanation for the negative effect of dependence is that proposed by Beckford (1971). Nations which are subjected to external controls cannot appropriate their own surplus for investment in balanced development. Transnational corporations operate to further their own growth, but not the development of the countries in which they are located. These corporations use their political and economic influence to keep labor costs and taxes low and to maintain the conditions for their continued profitable operation.

The preliminary finding that dependence maintains income inequalities suggests that one way in which dependence retards development is by linking national elites in the periphery to the interests of the transnational corporations and the international economy. Thus political and economic forces which attempt to mobilize balanced national development are suppressed.

We know that a great deal of foreign investment in peripheral countries goes into the extraction of mineral raw materials. Therefore the finding that investment dependence increases production in the mining sector (Chase-Dunn 1975) suggests that foreign investment has positive effects on the enterprise in which it is invested. In combination with the finding of negative effects on aggregate economic development, this suggests that foreign investment combines positive direct effects on the enterprise in which it is invested with negative effects on the rest of the national economy, resulting in overall negative effects.[13]

In the light of these findings, oppositional movements and national policies in the periphery which stress self-reliance and careful control over inputs from the core must be seen as other than reactive ignorance. Beckford (1971) points out that independence is a necessary but not a sufficient condition for development in the periphery. Autarchy combined with political mobilization for development has been really successful only in large states which control a big internal market, such as China and the Soviet Union. Small nations that cut themselves off from the world economy risk isolation and stagnation, for example Burma. Peripheral countries that try to break their dependency on the core also risk subversion or invasion, for example Chile.

One solution to the problem of dependence would appear to be the control of inputs from the core to assure compatibility with balanced development (Morley 1975). A number of nations have made laws regulating foreign investment in an attempt to gain the benefits without the costs, for example Japan, Mexico, India, and Yugoslavia. This strategy is difficult in a competitive world in which the transnational corporations have the upper hand. The larger scale on which transnational corporations operate gives them the advantage over small peripheral countries (Moran 1973). The balkanization of the periphery, which is the legacy of the colonial empires, makes solidarity among peripheral nations difficult. Competition for foreign investment rather than concerted regulation of it has been the main tendency.

Regional agreements to regulate core inputs, such as the Andean group, may be a good strategy for the periphery (Girvan 1973). The example of the Organization of Petroleum Exporting Countries indicates that effective coordination of policies between peripheral states is possible; and this alternative may be more realizable with the economic downturn which began in 1967. A world-wide contraction of production with increasing competition between core states has compromised the hegemony that the United States enjoyed during the Pax Americana. Increasing economic competition and political pluralism in the world system, with more of a balance between competing core states, may create opportunities for peripheral solidarity which have not heretofore existed.[14]

We have already seen manifestations of such solidarity in OPEC and other producers' combinations, the growth of regional trade, investment and development agreements, and the call for a "new international economic order."

This growing awareness of the core-periphery contradiction and the effects of dependence may be the beginning of a political process which eventually will modify the grossly uneven development of the world economy. Balanced international growth most probably awaits the formation of a reallocative world state. The contradiction between immense productivity and increasing inequality could be the motive force from which such a state emerges.

APPENDIX
Summary Statistics on Measures of Economic Independence
(for nations with less than $406 per capita GNP 1955)

Mean	SD	Skew-ness	Max	Min	N
Log Investment Dependence per Capita 1950–55					
2.06	.75	−.08	3.26	.68	38
Debt Dependence per Capita 1965					
$318	$261	1.2	$1080	$6	55

NOTES
1 There have been a large number of cross-national studies of dependence effects published since this research was completed. A review and comparison of most of these studies is in Bornschier, Chase-Dunn, and Rubinson (1978).

2 Pinto and Knakal (1973) show that, between 1960 and 1968, profit remittances to the United States from Latin America exceeded new investment by 6.7 billion US dollars.

3 Barrat-Brown (1974) has shown that the terms of trade alternately worsen and improve for Third World raw material producers over the last 100 years. Wallerstein (1974b) has argued that opportunities for upward mobility occur for some "semiperipheral" nations during periods of contraction in the world economy. The recent economic downturn and the price rise for raw materials may indicate the return of such a period. Delacroix's (1974) cross-national study finds that specialization in raw materials has no effect on economic growth.

4 Trimberger (1976), in a study of military bureaucrats and economic nationalism in Japan, Turkey, Egypt, and Peru, argues that autonomous leadership can be effective in modifying the worst aspects of dependence.

5 Sideri (1970) has made a historical investigation of the emergence of this exchange and its consequences for the development of the two countries. This exchange was imposed on the Portuguese by the British in exchange for protection of the Portuguese colonial relationship with Brazil. This division of labor is seen by Sideri as one cause of the Portuguese failure to industrialize.

6 In the case of estimating the effects of dependence on development, it is possible that negative effects such as those found by Evans (1972) are artifactual because dependence measures are standardized on GNP to control for economic size, while the dependent variable is GNP per capita. This

is the case in which the same term is in the denominator of one measure and the numerator of the other. In order to provide a conservative test of the hypothesis that dependence has a negative effect on development, the dependence measures are weighted with population. This is because, according to the argument that an artifact results from a common term (Schuessler 1974), the per capita measures should create a positive artifact.

7 Gross domestic product is GNP plus net factor payments going abroad. It includes income which returns to nonnationals, including profit and interest on foreign investment and loans (O'Loughlin 1971).

8 A much more thorough and convincing study of the relationship between dependence and inequality (Rubinson 1976) supports the results reported here.

9 The possibility that this result is due to reciprocal causation—a positive effect of inequality on investment dependence due to low wage policies of the liaison elites—is partly ruled out by a panel analysis which includes income inequality as an independent variable. An estimate of the effect of inequality on investment dependence was computed by regressing investment dependence in 1966 on income inequality in 1965 while controlling for investment dependence in 1955. This revealed no effect of inequality on investment dependence, although this is not a conclusive result because of the time at which inequality is measured. If it may be assumed that inequality is fairly stable over this period, this result rules out the hypothesis of a reciprocal effect which would account for the cross-sectional relationship shown in table 8.5. This is additional support for the hypothesis that dependence causes inequality.

10 A systematic comparison of the contradictory results of cross-national studies of the effects of investment dependence and aid dependence, along with a new analysis, is reported in Bornschier, Chase-Dunn, and Rubinson (1978).

11 Export partner concentration, or the extent to which a nation's exports go to a single other nation, is also found to retard economic development (Chase-Dunn 1975; Rapkin 1976; Walleri 1976).

12 This supported by the results of a recent study by Gobalet and Diamond (1977).

13 Further support for this interpretation is provided by a cross-sectional analysis which estimates the effect of investment dependence on inequality of production in economic sectors. This is measured by the Gini index of the distribution of product per worker across eight economic sectors. The beta coefficient estimating the investment dependence effect on sectoral product inequality is .78 and is significant at the .001 level for a sample of twenty-six poor nations. This is controlling for economic development and specialization in mining. Since this research was completed, two studies have appeared which support the contention that foreign investment has short run positive and long-run negative effects (Bornschier 1975; Stoneman 1975).

14 In earlier periods of contraction and conflict in the world economy, peripheral nations have individually moved toward political and economic independence (Frank 1969; Ness and Ness 1972).

NINE · The Export of Raw Materials and Economic Growth

Jacques Delacroix

The study of economic development is a natural meeting ground for social scientists of the several disciplines. Yet, few practitioners of one social science venture far into the preserves of sister disciplines. Sociologists sometimes give cursory attention to economic variables but rarely include them in the models they test. One economic variable of sociological interest is a country's propensity to participate in international exchange markets as a supplier of raw materials. First, this propensity denotes the occupancy of a particular position in a "world system" (see Wallerstein 1974a) made up of nation states. Secondly, the ability to export goods that are more or less processed depends much on a country's own internal division of labor and on its degree of organization. The latter characteristics, in turn, constitute an important aspect of the social differentiation of the country or nation state.

The specialization of countries in the export of raw materials or unprocessed goods has been of interest to theorists of economic development for a long time. For the present purpose, it will suffice to trace back to Lenin the importance attributed to this variable in economic processes. He called the "capture of the most important sources of raw materials" one of the "four principal manifestations of monopoly capitalism" (1965, p. 123). Most theorists treat specialization in the supplying of raw materials as a position in a world division of labor. The conceptualization nearly always implies a notion of unequal exchange (Prebisch 1950; Emmanuel 1972; Baran 1956; Magdoff 1969; Frank 1971; Galtung 1971; Benot 1973; Amin 1973; Wallerstein 1974a). That is, an inherent inequality between the exchange partners is thought to operate more or less consistently to the disadvantage of the raw-materials exporters. This perspective suggests the plunder of poor countries by a handful of rich industrialized nations, the exploitation of the many by the few (Lenin 1965, p. 124). In other words, it posits surplus value extraction by a macro class that must set the stage for a new, transnational version of the class struggle. The new version of the class struggle in turn heralds the future demise of capitalism in its latest

This chapter appeared originally in the *American Sociological Review* 42 (1977): 795–808.

worldwide expression (see, in particular, Wallerstein 1973, 1974b). This particular version of the relationship between national export specialization and international power relations was already present, though in embryonic form, in Lenin (1916, p. 126) and possibly also in Marx (1853, p. 663). It has sociological implications far beyond the more immediate matter of economic growth to which we now turn.

In the past few years, a large number of social scientists and other writers have affirmed or used the idea that specialization in the export of raw materials has adverse consequences for the national economy of the exporter, with specific reference to areas of the Third World (notably Frank 1965; O'Connor 1971; Galeano 1971 [with references to Latin America]; N'Krumah 1967; Berman 1974 [with respect to Africa]). Some theorists who are not specifically Marxist have adopted the idea (see, for example, Heilbroner 1972, p. 219).

Scholars differ in the degree to which they attribute the specialization of the poor countries in the export of raw materials to the deliberate active intervention of the rich countries. Marxist writers have had a tendency to infer such intervention from a demonstration that it is in the interest of the rich (capitalist) countries to so intervene (Jalée 1965; Magdoff 1969; Dean 1971). Frank writes of the "development of underdevelopment" (1966). Recently, some theorists have focused on the demonstration of a "gatekeeper effect" which involves a rather less conspiratorial view of the rich countries' intervention in the economic affairs of the poor ones. The gatekeeper effect can be summarized as follows: Developed countries maintain underdeveloped countries in their position of raw material suppliers by controlling the latter's access to the outside world. The developed countries control the underdeveloped countries' access to the capital, the technology, and other resources necessary for industrialization. This forced inability to industrialize, in turn, perpetuates the relationship by preventing the poor countries from becoming either self-sufficient or exporters of processed goods. The gatekeeper role is assigned variously to the indigenous bourgeoisie (Berman 1974), directed by foreign capitalist interests and more or less allied to the national military elites (Bourricaud 1966; Galtung 1971, p. 85); to transnational corporations acting directly (Petras 1968; O'Connor 1970; Seidman and Green 1970); to international organizations, principally banks (O'Connor 1970; Payer 1971); or to a mixture of all of these (Levin 1966). A few writers have formulated this effect in purely structural terms (that is, with no implications regarding the gatekeepers' volition—Berman 1974; Baldwin 1966). A very small number imply that the managerial incompetence of the governments of the countries concerned perpetuates specialization in the export of raw materials or the ensuing adverse economic consequences (Leff 1968; Tugwell 1974).

Several processes can be identified as underlying the assumed negative effect of specialization in the export of raw materials on economic health. Empirical evidence in support of the presumed relationship can therefore be brought to bear on the underlying processes or on the relationship itself. In this paper, I summarize the most important underlying processes and review the previous empirical research. I then present and discuss findings of a direct test of the relationship which uses different measures and more up-to-date methods than did the previous research.

PROCESSES

Theoretical explanations of the presumed relationship between specialization in the export of raw materials and national economic welfare pertain to one or a combination of the following processes:

a) The gradual institution of the world–"European" division of labor in the sixteenth century is elaborately described by Wallerstein. The capitalist world system rests on more (and more complex) processes than that resulting in the specialization of areas into exporters of raw and transformed goods. Nevertheless, Wallerstein devotes the better part of one chapter (1974a, pp. 86–126) to tracing the intricate linkages between types of commodities produced, systems of labor control, strength of the state apparatus, availability of urban laborers (pp. 117–18), the success of indigenous bourgeoisies, and the establishment of core capitalism. Wallerstein also describes the varying ability of both peasants and urban workers in the European core areas to share in the ensuing windfall. Hence, *the assignment of what prefigured the present "Third World" to the task of providing raw materials (bullion, then food, then materials for industrial transformation) in the sixteenth century is a prime (though not perhaps a primary) cause of the contemporary world inequality.* That this relationship is historically drawn out and causally complex should not obscure its existence, earlier described in more structural terms by Galtung (1971).

b) *The international demand for raw materials is fundamentally inelastic and increasingly so.* The industrialized countries who are the principal buyers of raw materials experience very moderate population growth. At the same time, their capacity to perform more and more processing operations on the same quantity of raw material is increasing constantly (Magdoff 1969). Improvements in the productivity of raw material exporters resulting in increased supply confronts a nearly fixed demand. This must result, for the raw material exporters, in lower per unit prices rather than in growth of income (Furtado 1965; Gomez 1966; Maizel 1968; Galeano 1971, p. 218).

c) Logically linked to the last explanation but different in its consequences is the observation that *raw materials prices tend to undergo wide fluctuations.* Such fluctuations tend to make rational economic planning difficult or impossible for the private entrepreneur and the government planner. This state of affairs is aggravated by the fact that the external trade flows of underdeveloped countries implicate a larger portion of their GNPs than is typically the case for developed countries. This explanation of the unfavorable consequences of specialization in export of raw materials is broadly and critically discussed by Gleziakos (1973).

d) Fourthly, to the extent that the production of raw materials is financed by nondigenous interests who repatriate their excessive profits (Gomez 1966), *the exports of raw materials may result in actual net outflows of cash* (Berman 1974, p. 6).

e) Finally, Singer (1950), Young (1970), Galtung (1971), and others speculate that *specialization in the export of raw materials results in allocation of national resources that are less than optimal from the standpoint of the exporter's economic growth.* In particular, they allege that such specialization impedes investments in economic and social sectors most likely to have multiplier effects on the exporter's economy.

The net, overall thrust of the collection of arguments summarized above is to deny the validity of one of the major tenets of classical macroeconomic theory. According to the law of comparative advantage (Samuelson, 1970, pp. 645–67), each actor in the world division of labor must concentrate on what *it does best*, whether or not any other actor does it better. Classical economic theory states categorically that this strategy is in the interest of all the actors.

By contrast, a large and growing body of theory astride several disciplines asserts that a country's specialization in the export of raw materials or unprocessed goods adversely affects its economic well-being. In particular, this body of theory views such specialization as a major obstacle to economic growth and development.

PREVIOUS RESEARCH

In spite of its high degree of acceptance in the literature, the idea that specialization in export of raw materials has adverse effects on economic growth and development is supported by little empirical evidence. What little research on the matter does exist is methodologically unsatisfactory, or else it fails to support the hypothesis.

Some researchers have investigated the link between specialization in raw materials export and economic growth from the viewpoint of price instability. Naya (1973) finds no statistically significant relationship between the percentage of export in raw materials and the instability of the income of a country derived from exports. His study, using regression analysis, is based on a cross section of seventeen Asian countries presumed to have experienced greater than average export income instability. Gleziakos (1973), also using cross-sectional regression analysis, fails to show a significant relationship between the export price instability of forty countries and their growth rates. This result agrees with earlier research by Coppock (1962) and McBean (1966).

Quantitative tests lending support to the hypothesis are scarce. Jalee (1965) and Rollins (1956) construct descriptive tables showing that countries that specialize in the export of raw materials are not rich. Galtung (1971) provides positive support for the hypothesis with cross-sectional bivariate correlations based on sixty countries. His dependent variables are gross national product per capita and percentage of the population employed in nonprimary sectors of the economy. Galtung's measure of export specialization *trade composition index* expresses as a ratio the balance between the relative degree of processing of the imports and exports of a country. The trade composition index has two defects as a measure of export specialization: (*a*) As is the case with many compound ratio variables, there are theoretically contradictory ways to get the same score on this measure. (*b*) Galtung himself signals the second defect: "There is no doubt that this index is a crude measure among other reasons because the variable *degree of processing*, so crucial to the whole analysis, has been dichotomized in 'raw materials' vs. 'processed goods' and because the basis for the dichotomization is the division made use of in UN trade statistics" (p. 102). In other words, the dichotomization of products into raw and processed betrays the actual continuity of the theoretical variable *degree of processing*. Any item that reaches a market is the product of human labor on nature (Galtung 1971, p. 86) and an investment of human culture into a natural object. Hence a measure of degree of processing should admit of an infinity of values except zero. Ideally, each individual item should have its own score denoting this labor and this cultural investment. This is difficult to achieve because of obvious limitations on the availability of data. However, it is possible to minimize the costs of categorizing by using finer categories than Galtung's dichotomy. Finer categories tend to make the observed effect of the measure on other variables less dependent on the exact location of each cutting point between categories.

Galtung expresses reservations about his own use of the UN trade statistics as a source of data for his index. However, the Standard International Trade Classification used by the UN is not fatally inappropriate for this purpose if one makes more use of its features than Galtung does, and especially if one uses it more critically. (I will develop this point in a latter section of this chapter.)

Quite aside from the weakness of the trade composition index, Galtung's test of the hypothesis is inconclusive because of its design. The positive correlation he reports between trade composition index and *percentage of the labor force in nonprimary sectors* ($r = .77$) is partly tautological. If, for example, a large percentage of a country's labor force were employed in extractive industries, one would expect that it would be reflected to some degree in the composition of its export, which must include some quantities of raw materials. Therefore, percentage labor force in nonprimary sectors and trade composition index may be, to some extent, two measures of the same internal development variable.

Galtung also reports a high positive correlation between trade composition index and gross national product per capita ($r = .89$). Both measures are for 1967–68. Hence, the test is synchronic rather than diachronic. Such a test leaves open the matter of causation, at least from a narrow, empirical-quantitative viewpoint. Galtung provides rich theoretical argument in support of an interpretation that makes trade composition (or the degree of processing of export) the cause and GNP per capita the consequence. However, it is desirable to test the hypothesis diachronically as well, as he points out (p. 103). Furthermore, since Galtung's test depends on bivariate correlations, the matter of causality cannot be resolved through interpretation of the interrelations of other variables with trade composition and with the dependent variables. In particular, it would be useful to test the hypothesis with a design that would include variables chosen to contribute to the elimination of three alternative interpretations of Galtung's findings: (a) National specialization in the export of goods at a low level of processing is a by-product of poverty; it has no direct effect on it. (b) Countries with a large population enjoy a comparative advantage in specializing in the production and export of labor-intensive low-processed goods. Such countries are primevally poor. (c) While the link between specialization in the export of low-processed goods and poverty is real, such specialization and poverty result from processes *internal* to the country rather than from the operation of the world system.

In the following pages I report on a diachronic test of the hypothesis based on a measure of degree of processing of exports that minimizes the difficulties involved with Galtung's trade composition index. I include in the model tested variables designed to facilitate choice between the original hypothesis of dependency and world system theories and the third interpretation above.

MEASURES

The literature mentions a variety of ways in which specialization in the export of raw materials impedes economic development. Finsterbusch (1973) has shown that gross national product per capita is highly correlated with a multiple-indicator measure of the somewhat diffuse concept of development. In the first equation presented in Table 9.1, I use *GNP per capita* 1970 as a dependent variable. However, there are well-known difficulties of interpretation associated with ratio variables (Kuh and Meyer 1955; Briggs 1962; Schuessler 1974). I therefore present a second equation where (raw) GNP 1970 is the dependent variable. I use a logarithmic transformation of this variable (base 10) because the error variance of this measure may be correlated with other variables in the equation. This second equation also includes a measure of population size in 1955 in order to make the dependent variable in this equation (raw) GNP, comparable to the dependent variable in the first equation, GNP per capita. It can be shown that introducing in a regression with panel design a measure of population size taken at the *same time* as the dependent variable is nearly equivalent to standardizing the dependent variable by population size. On the other hand, population size measured at the late time of my diachronic model (1970) and the same measured at the early time (1955) are highly correlated ($r = 0.96$). Hence the inclusion in the model of *population size* measured in 1955 allows one to interpret the dependent variable (raw) gross national product as a measure of social welfare, functionally equivalent to GNP per capita. It should be noted that the inclusion of this population measure does *not* in any way make equation (2) an adequate test of the effect of population size on economic growth. I attach no substantive meaning to the estimate associated with this measure because of the extreme complexity of the matter (see Easterlin 1967).

The data for gross national product 1970 and 1955 come from the International Bank for Reconstruction and Development's *1971 World Tables* and from its 1973 *World Economic Atlas* (IBRD 1973) (see note 1). The data for the measure of population size in 1955 were obtained from Taylor and Hudson (1971).

Measuring the variable of theoretical interest, degree of processing of exports, is a theoretical problem in its own right. Galtung formulates the hypothesis in these terms: the higher the level of processing of the total export of a country, the greater its economic growth (1971, p. 86). Boulding, in his discussion of "social species" (1970, pp. 20–22), likens the "direct organization of human ideas and knowledge" which goes into the making of an automobile (an act of processing) to the transmission of genetic information. Likewise, in a previous critique of the labor theory of value, Boulding had expressed the idea that raw materials are transformed into products through the injection of social organization in the form of information (1953, pp. 164–66). Stinchcombe remarks that the processing of information generates structural growth (1968, pp. 281–82). At the same time, he makes it clear that the information content of processed goods (for example, general cargo) is higher than that of raw materials (for example, "bulk goods").

Hence, the degree of processing of a marketable product can be expressed in terms of the amount of (social) information invested in it.

In this sense, any product is a vehicle for a certain amount of socially organized information.

To measure the degree of processing of a country's exports is to assign to the commodities that comprise them weights that express the amount of social information invested in them. Ths operation involves two distinct steps:

a) Aggregation of commodities. Theoretically, each individual item contains an amount of information different from that contained in any other item. The problem here is to make use of the information available to regroup items in a way that comes satisfactorily close to respecting the underlying continuity of the processing dimension (that is, to improve on Galtung's simple dichotomization).

b) Devising of a weighting system expressing the amount of social information invested in the commodities aggregated in step (a) above.

Step (a) of my coding procedure consists in aggregating the breakdowns of countries' exports provided by the *UN Yearbook of International Trade Statistics* at the SITC (revised) two-digit "division" level. I chose the two-digit level because it is the finest one at which enough countries report the composition of their export. Choosing an even finer level would have caused the loss of cases below the absolute minimum number necessary for regression analysis with significance tests. At the same time, little improvement in precision would have been gained by adopting a finer level of aggregation. The SITC two-digit divisional level classification contains in crude form an embryonic scale of degree of processing. For example, in division 26, it places "textile fibers (*not* manufactured into yarn, thread or fabrics) and their waste," while division 65 contains "textile yarn, fabrics, made up articles and related products." Likewise, the SITC two-digit level distinguishes between division 28, "metalliferous ores and metal scrap," and division 67, "iron and steel," and 68, "Non-ferrous metals." However, this classification does not array products according to their degree of processing with enough consistency that we may use it as a de facto weighting scheme. Instead, I assign to each division a weight from a scale ranging from 1 (for cattle) to 9 (for transportation equipment). The scale itself is based on a scheme whose basic conceptual unit is the *minimal transformation to which an object must be subjected in order to become a commodity* (that is, marketable). The scheme takes into consideration comparison between transformations, distance between SITC divisions in terms of number of transformations, additivity of transformations (for example, transport equipment contains refined metals "transformed" from ore), and the homogeneity of the contents of each division. The measure of degree of processing is computed by multiplying the value of the content of each SITC division expressed as a percentage of total

by the weight assigned to that division and summing across. The scores
on this measure, called *level of transformation of export* range, in 1955,
from 574 (West Germany) to 128 (Bolivia). Little information seems
seems to have been lost by ignoring imports since level of transformation
of export for 1955 has a rank order correlation of 0.85 with Galtung's
1967–68 trade composition index. I use *level of transformation of export* 1955 as my independent variable of main theoretical interest.[2]

I use level of transformation of export to try to ascertain the *direct*
effect of specialization in the export of raw materials on economic
growth for the 1955–70 period. The problem here is to estimate the
influence of a country's position in the world economy, as denoted by
this measure, *over and above* the possible effects of processes internal
to the country.

World system and dependency theories posit that processes internal
to each nation-state are consequences of location in the world system or
they treat such processes as causally secondary. Alternative interpretations (*a*) and (*c*) above of Galtung's findings depend on the realism of
the assumption that internal factors are secondary. Hence a more complete test of the hypothesis than the one offered by Galtung would incorporate some control for the possible effects of *internal* factors on economic growth.

Following Galtung's general reasoning, the most relevant internal
factor here seems to be the country's initial information-processing
capacity. Galtung argues strongly that specialization in raw materials
hinders the economic development of poor countries *primarily* by deny-
ing them the beneficient "intra-actor effects" that accrue to their industrialized trade partners. In particular, Galtung speculates that specialization in raw materials places countries at a relative disadvantage with
respect to the expansion of their educational systems (1971, p. 87).
Most of the other intra-actor effects discussed by Galtung can be sub-
sumed under the category of internal differentiation corresponding to a
given capacity for processing information.

Galtung's implicit concept of information-processing capacity rejoins
the conceptualizations of Duncan (1964, pp. 39–41), Boulding (1966),
Stinchcombe (1968), Delacroix (1974), and Lenski (1976, pp. 556,
558). Lenski and Lenski (1974), for example, make the existing store
of generalized information available to a group and the group's changing
ability to increase and utilize it the cornerstone of their theory of social
change.

Galtung mentions education as one of the concrete manifestations of
information-processing capacity whose expansion is adversely affected
by specialization in raw materials (1971, p. 87). His assumption that
educational expansion contributes to the economic development of countries is supported by arguments or findings by Sollow (1957), Schultz
(1963), Denison (1962), Meyer, Hannan, and Rubinson (1973), Har-

bison (1973), Hannan and Meyer (1973), and, indirectly, by Inkeles and Smith (1974).[3] Accordingly, I make *secondary school enrollment in 1955* stand for general information-processing capacity. I choose secondary rather than primary school enrollment because, if this variable has an independent effect on economic growth, it is more likely to be discernible over the time period considered (15 years) than would be the case with primary enrollment. In addition, secondary school enrollment has lower correlations with population size than does primary enrollment and lower correlation with GNP than does university enrollment. In equation (1) where the dependent variable is GNP per capita, the measure of secondary school enrollment is expressed as a ratio of the secondary school age population. This measure is taken from the 1971 edition of the UNESCO *Statistical Yearbook*. In equation (2), which includes a measure of population size and where the dependent variable is (raw) GNP, secondary school enrollment 1955 is entered without a control for the appropriate age population. The reason for this omission is that population size measured in 1955 has a correlation of .99 with the measure of secondary school age group measured at the same time. Hence the measure of population size serves the dual purpose of simulating GNP per capita growth (see above) and of controlling for secondary age population.

Finally, it could be argued that equations (1) and (2) constitute an inadequate test of the hypothesis because of the shortness of the lag on which they are based (1955–70). Wallerstein envisages a process unfolding over several centuries. Galtung seems to hypothesize a slow incrementation of negative intra-actor effects whose aggregate consequence is the purported link between specialization in the export of raw materials and a slow economic growth. Given the existing data limitations, not much can be done to extend the lag between measurement of independent and dependent variables. However, it is possible to gain an idea of the *indirect* effect of specialization in raw materials on economic growth. There seems to be a consensus around the idea that educational expansion contributes to economic growth. If raw-materials specialization has a negative effect on educational expansion, then it must also *indirectly* hinder economic growth, through no direct relationship appears for the lag covered. Ideally, one would estimate the effect of the level of transformation of export measured at an earlier point on secondary school enrollment in 1955, but data limitations make this infeasible. The next best solution is to make use of such data as are available by estimating this relationship for the 1955–70 period. The results of this operation are presented in equation (3), which is of the same general form as equation (2).

The cases over which the equations presented and mentioned in this paper are computed vary according to the availability of data. Slightly more than half of the countries included in each set would have been

TABLE 9.1   Pearson Correlation Coefficients[a]

Variable	1	2	3	4	5	6	7	8	9
1. Log GNP 1970	1.0								
2. Log GNP 1955	.97	1.0							
3. GNP per capita 1970	.54	.49	1.0						
4. GNP per capita 1955	.47	.47	.94	1.0					
5. Level of transformation of export 1955	.70	.65	.61	.49	1.0				
6. Secondary enrollment 1970	.71	.65	.82	.74	.68	1.0			
7. Secondary enrollment 1950	.65	.59	.85	.79	.72	.88	1.0		
8. Secondary enrollment 1970 as proportion of secondary age population	.73	.70	.24	.08	.55	.43	.47	1.0	
9. Secondary enrollment 1955 as proportion of secondary age population	.58	.56	.23	.08	.57	.44	.48	.92	1.0
10. Population size 1955	.41	.45	-.12	-.14	.18	.24	-.04	.87	.50

a. Pairwise deletion, for all cases for which data were available on Level of transformation of export 1955 (59 cases maximum).

TABLE 9.2   Effects of Degree of Processing of Export on Economic Growth and Secondary School Enrollment, 1955–70[a]

Equation 1

Dependent Variable	GNP/cap. 1955	Secondary Enroll. Proportion 1955	Level of Transform. of Export 1955	R^2	Constant	Number of Cases
GNP/cap. 1970	2.05	1070.57*	0.001	.90	−0.25	49
	.75	.17	.10			

Equation 2

Dependent Variable	Log GNP 1955	Popn. 1955	Secondary Enroll. Proportion 1955	Level of Transform. of Export 1955	R^2	Constant	Number of Cases
Log GNP 1970	0.90	-0.6×10^{-9}	0.5×10^{-7}**	0.4×10^{-3}	.95	1.25	48
	.90	−.05	.10	.06			

Equation 3

Dependent Variable	GNP 1955	Popn. 1955	Secondary Enroll. Proportion 1955	Level of Transform. of Export 1955	R^2	Constant	Number of Cases
Secondary Enroll. Proportion 1970	0.12×10^{-4}	0.3***	−0.07***	−161.6	.95	1.2×10^5	47
	.90	.42	.57	−.01			

*p < .10
**p < .05
***p < .01

a. For each entry the first row is the unstandardized (b) coefficient and the second row is the standardized (beta) coefficient.

considered underdeveloped in 1955. All sets exclude the US. Close inspection of the residuals associated with each equation shows that while
equations (1) and (2) give very similar predictions, equation (2) gives
a better prediction for poor countries.

FINDINGS AND DISCUSSION

The findings directly relevant to the test of the hypothesis are easy to
summarize. For the fifteen-year period covered, initial wealth is the
main factor in economic growth as evidenced by the high autoregression
terms in equation (1) and (2) ($\beta = .75$ and $.90$ respectively). The estimates of the effect of level of transformation of export on economic
growth do not come close to statistical significance in either equation
(1) or (2). This lack of significance is not an artifactual consequence of
the high autoregression terms in these equations since in both equations,
secondary school enrollment has a significant positive effect ($\beta = .17$,
very close to the .05 level in eq. [1], $\beta = .10$, and above the .05 level
in eq. [2]).

Equation (3) is a less than perfect test of the plausibility of an indirect linkage between specialization in raw materials export and economic growth via information-processing capacity. If level of transformation of export affected secondary school enrollment negatively, it
would indirectly also affect economic growth negatively since secondary
enrollment has a positive influence on the latter. In equation (3), the
beta estimating the effect of level of transformation of export on secondary school enrollment is negative but very small ($-.01$), and no-
where close to statistical significance.[4]

With all their limitations, these findings do not add up to a confir-
mation of the widespread belief that national specialization as raw materials supplier to the world economy is a primary cause of underdevelopment. Rather, these new findings lend some support to reinter-
pretation (c) above of Galtung's previous findings: while there is a
positive association between raw-materials specialization and initial poverty (evidenced by correlations of .51 and .62, respectively, between
GNP per capita 55 and GNP 55 on the one hand and level of transformation of export in 1955 on the other), the former seems to have
little consequence over the short run.

In fact, these findings express inadequately a vastly more complex
situation than suggested by the original hypothesis. Strict space limitations prevent me from exploring this situation adequately, but four main
points should be kept in mind:

1 In the short run, wealth leads to wealth. It is difficult to show the
   effect of anything on national wealth. However, equations (1) and
   (2) show that *something* does affect national economic growth positively, even in the short run. This something, represented by sec-

ondary enrollment, is an internal process rather than an external one as predicted by world system theory.

2 The exceptions to the rule that wealth leads to wealth further contradict world system theory. Equation (2), which gives the best prediction for Turkey, *underpredicts* the economic growth of Libya while it *overpredicts* that of Britain. Libya became *more specialized* in the export of one raw material between 1955 and 1970. Britain's highly processed export in 1955 did not prevent its subsequent downfall.

3 The implicit picture (made explicit by Galtung) of a world neatly divided between poor raw-materials exporters and rich processed-goods exporters is substantially incorrect. Chile, usually thought of as an underdeveloped country, exports mostly *refined* copper products (70% of the value of its export in 1955) and very little ore (6%). On the other hand, everyone knows that the US and Canada are big exporters of raw agricultural products. Even greater reliance on raw commodities on the part of rich countries is not unexceptional. Iceland tripled its GNP between 1955 and 1970. Yet, in 1955, Iceland's export consisted of very lightly processed or unprocessed fish to the tune of 85% of total value. Argentina, whose agricultural export was only 60% of total (foodstuff), only doubled its GNP during the same period.

4 There is no compelling *empirical* reason for ignoring the influence of internal processes on economic development or for treating these processes as mere consequences of position in the world system. Chase-Dunn (1975) and Rubinson (1976) have recently shown some associations between measures of dependency and national income distribution. Nevertheless, some internal *institutional* factors of economic growth enjoy a degree of freedom from the constraints imposed by initial poverty and by position in the world system. Thus, in 1955, the Pearson correlations between secondary enrollment expressed as a ratio of the appropriate population on the one hand and GNP per capita and level of transformation of export on the other were .79 and .71, respectively ($N = 49$). While these associations are not negligible, they indicate that these variables had only about half of their variance in common. This suggests a freedom to maneuver not often acknowledged by exogenetic theories of economic development. Yet, as the OPEC countries have shown, some producers of raw materials do maneuver. In particular, they sometimes succeed in obtaining higher payments for their exports of unchanged quality. The conditions under which the terms of trade can be modified through the deliberate actions of exporters are not well studied. Nevertheless, Tugwell (1974) has described the process by which the governments of oil-producing countries find themselves in a progressively more favorable bargaining position vis-à-vis the foreign

corporations operating on their soil. His demonstration puts into question the widespread assumption that the objective interest of indigenous elites in raw-material-exporting countries is to act as gate-keepers on behalf of alien capitalist interests (see Galtung 1971). What *kinds* of national elites will emerge may depend in part on a country's place within the world economy. The roles these elites will play in their countries' economic development may be a joint product of exogenous variables that more or less facilitate the *management of dependence* as suggested by Tugwell and of evolving internal factors. Among the latter, the information-processing capacity of a country, expressed in such things as the overall educational status of its population, must limit the range of available policies.

Finally, the transformation of wealth accruing from exports into industrial development must be influenced by national informational capacity which seems largely independent of the degree of processing of a country's exports.

NOTES

1 *Coding of gross national product* (GNP)—millions of US dollars. This variable was coded from the International Bank for Reconstruction and Development 1971 *World Tables* (table 4) for the year 1955. For the year 1973, I used the World Bank's *World Economic Atlas*. There are some minor differences between the two sources' methods for computing countries' GNP. For the years 1950 to 1965, the *World Tables* present the GNP at factor cost, expressed in constant 1964 dollars. The *World Economic Atlas* provides figures for 1970 GNP at market prices, using a multiyear period for a base. GNP at market prices includes indirect taxes and is consequently approximately 20% higher, on the average, than GNP at factor cost for the same year. The differences seem, however, to affect all countries about equally. Using a multiyear period for a base for the US dollar reduces temporary distortions. Differences between the 1970 data and those for previous years are unlikely to affect findings at the aggregate level. However, one should exercise caution when taking the figures literally for any given country.

2 A major conceptual defect of this measure is that it counts only material products. According to the logic of considering processing as an investment of information into objects, the export of pure information, in the form of services, should also be counted. However, it is difficult to combine such exports (for which data are at any rate spotty) with commodities. I think that the distribution of scores would not have been much altered by the adjunction of this dimension. I am grateful to the anonymous reviewer who drew my attention to this point, with which I fully agree.

3 While these authors would undoubtedly not agree on the exact nature of the causal path between education and economic growth, they all present evidence in support of the existence of such a link.

4 The findings attached to level of transformation of export tend to be very robust. They are sensitive neither to small variations in the cases nor to time lags over which the equations are computed. Furthermore, controlling for secondary school age population in equations (2) and (3) does *not* change the overall pattern of findings in spite of the multicollinearity this procedure creates. Logging the GNP measures in equation (3) or substituting GNP per capita and secondary enrollment as a ratio of the appropriate age group does not make the coefficients associated with level of transformation of export significant. Finally, logging all the variables to make equations (2) and (3) fully interactive does not alter the conclusions reached.

TEN · The Permeability of Information Boundaries and Economic Growth

Jacques Delacroix

World-system theory does not attribute exclusive causality to economic relationships. Several world-system theorists also hypothesize the existence of more or less deliberate forms of cultural imperialism. According to this view (most systematically presented in Galtung 1971), the developed capitalist countries' superiority in the field of information-communications functions as an adjunct of their economic and political imperialism and may sometimes initiate it (Galtung 1971, p. 91).

A similar hypothesis is formulated in more specific terms by Portes, a scholar not usually associated with world-system theory. According to Portes (1973a), the cultural influence of rich countries over poor ones constitutes a Trojan horse for the introduction of foreign values into the latter. Portes suggests that the import of foreign values from developed countries jeopardizes capital accumulation—and therefore economic growth—in poor countries by encouraging premature mass consumption (a point also made by Horowitz 1972). Moreover, according to Portes the secularity inherent in the cultural imports from developed countries diverts popular support from nationalist development ideologies required by growth. Both world-system theory and Portes's evaluation of the impact of informational imports on the economic growth of countries appear, on the surface, to contradict the tradition of sociocultural evolution.

According to Lenski and Lenski (1978), the accumulation of information about the environment can only enhance a social system's ability to deal with variations in the environment (White 1959, 1960; Cherry 1961; Duncan 1964). But the relevant environment of each nation-state is composed largely of other nation-states (Lenski and Lenski 1974, p. 60). Therefore, in a dynamic world, imports of information from abroad must contribute to the economic success of nation-states, according to evolutionary theory. The negative view of information imports held by world-system theorists and by Portes also implicitly contradicts some aspects of the modernization perspective on economic development.

This chapter appeared originally in *Studies in Comparative International Development* 12 (1977): 3–28.

Modernization theory is largely, if not dogmatically, ontogenetic (Hechter 1975; Rubinson 1976). It locates the processes responsible for economic development within the boundaries of the countries concerned. When modernization-oriented scholars consider the consequences of cross-boundary cultural influences, they generally assume these to be beneficial to economic development or benign (for example, Inkeles and Smith 1974; Bellah 1965; Eisenstadt 1966, p. 65). This positive evaluation of the consequences of developed countries' cultural influence on poor ones is consistent with the general theoretical orientation of this school. Following Weber (1958), most modernization theorists view the spread of rational economic behavior as the determining force in the economic progress of countries. The spread of rational economic behavior, in turn, requires attitudinal changes in the mass of the population away from most of their traditional heritage. Hence the theoretical and empirical stress of modernization-oriented scholars is on values, value changes, and their personality correlates (see, for example, Stephenson 1968; Kahl 1968; Inkeles 1971; Eisenstadt 1973; Inkeles and Smith 1974; also Smith 1973 pp. 87–95; Portes 1973a, b for a review of this literature), rather than on purely economic obstacles to development. With this orientation, it is natural to expect that cultural influences from more modern regions should contribute to "modernization" and therefore to economic progress. This school's emphasis on the benefits of modern values sometimes resembles an entreaty to poor countries to adopt a particular set of foreign, often Western values. A rather extreme version of this propensity is illustrated by Eisenstadt's (1966, p. 65) early definition of modernization as "the process of change toward those types of social, economic and political systems that have developed in Western Europe and North America." (Eisenstadt further restricts Western Europe to England, Scandinavia, and the Netherlands, all countries where Protestants were firmly in control during the crucial phases of their development.)

Modernization-oriented scholars have been criticized on several grounds for attributing a central place to values and to their personality correlates (Horowitz 1972; Godwin 1974; Von Eschen 1975). Nevertheless, the irrelevance of values and personality features to the study of economic development has not been well demonstrated (Bendix 1967; Portes 1973b). Likewise, there are few cross-national empirical studies on the more specific matter of information imports and of their impact on economic growth, though there are some suggestive case studies (Lent 1975; Arnove 1975; Hurley 1975; Breen 1975).

A useful cross-national empirical exploration of this matter would distinguish between the impact of *information imports in general* and the consequences of imports of *cultural values* in particular. Furthermore, such a study would control for some of the economic determinants of development hypothesized by world-system theory. With such controls it could be ascertained whether cross-boundary information transactions have effects on economic growth over and beyond those attributed to economic relationships.

A reason for distinguishing between information imports in general and import of cultural values is suggested by Deutsch's description of the informational strategy of some developing nation-states. Deutsch (1966, p. 83) observes that during a nation-building prelude to economic takeoff, "only the most careful influences from the outside world are henceforth to be admitted . . . without admitting any broader foreign values, habits or culture patterns." In this formulation, value-laden information imports (which must in the present world come mostly from developed countries and should constitute modernizing influences, according to modernization theory) interfere with the mobilization of the national community. If this mobilization is, in turn, instrumental to economic growth, it follows that value-laden information imports should adversely affect economic growth (this formulation seems to underlie Horowitz's 1972 notion of a "compression" effect). Other (that is, non–value-laden) information imports may still play the positive role assigned to them by evolutionary theory.

If this synthetic model of the effects of information imports on economic growth is correct, a strategy of selective permeability of the national informational boundaries should enhance economic growth. Such a strategy would consist in facilitating most imports of information while excluding the importation of foreign values, especially modern ones. The model proposed here reconciles evolutionary theory with the world-system position on the economic impact of cross-boundary information transactions. It does this by distinguishing between more and less value-laden kinds of information. This distinction brings into focus a major area of incompatibility between world-system theory and modernization theory which views cross-boundary information transactions as beneficial.

In the following pages, I present the results of an exploratory test of the hypothesis that *information imports have a positive impact on the economic growth of countries except when they consist mostly of foreign values*. This test will show by implication that the permeability of national informational boundaries affects the economic fates of countries over and beyond their position in a system of economic cross-boundary relationships. In a second part of the chapter I present some findings in support of the additional proposition that evolutionary and world-system arguments help account exogenetically for the previously mentioned findings. Finally, I briefly explore some of the possible policy implications of the same findings.

ANALYSIS OF THE EFFECTS OF TWO KINDS OF
INFORMATION FLOWS ON ECONOMIC GROWTH

Design and Measures

The first hypothesis is that cross-boundary information imports have positive effects on economic growth except when they bear mostly foreign values. This hypothesis is tested through regression analysis with panel design.

Ideally, the respective effects of different kinds of information imports should be estimated within the same equation. However, the problem presented by nonduplicating missing cases makes this infeasible. I therefore estimate each effect in separate but morphologically analogous equations (eq. [1] and eq. [2] in table 10.1). In each equation, the cases included are entirely determined by the availability of data for the 1950–70 period.

Table 10.1 ("first test") shows the beta coefficients, significance levels, and *b* coefficients associated with each independent variable in equations (2) and (3). Table 10.2 shows the list of countries over which equations (1) and (2) are computed, with comments on the representativity of these countries and a brief analysis of the residuals associated with each equation.

I distinguish between imports of general information and imports of value-laden information. Practically, information imports are channeled through print and visual and electronic media. These are reasons to believe that the value load of information imports varies according to the media that channel them. The translation of foreign books into the national language of a country is an instance of general information import. The value component of books varies greatly, but it is small across categories of books. (Generally, large numbers of translations from one language to another are of technical works and legal documents.) I speculate that the import of films from abroad constitutes an instance of a value-laden information import. This is based on three considerations. First, it could easily be argued that the effective (i.e., lasting) cultural content of most commercial films consists almost entirely of values. Second, films but not books are destined for mass consumption. (For example, Yugoslavia in 1962, with a population of less than 16,000,000, registered more than 55,000,000 movie admissions [International Motion Picture Almanac, 1964].) Rogers (1969, p. 155) names the cinema as a source of initial cosmopolite contact that does not require literacy. Therefore foreign values imported into a country via films are subject to wide diffusion. Third, the particular aesthetic-emotional format of film as a medium is probably propitious to uncritical acceptance of the value message it carries. Thus foreign values imported into a country via movies are almost certainly widely and

TABLE 10.1 Effects of Book Translations and Film Imports on Change in GNP per Capita and Export Partner Diversifications, 1950–70[a]

Independent Variables	First Test		Second Test[b]	
	Equation 1 35 cases u = .26 GNP/cap 1970	Equation 2 31 cases u = .62 GNP/cap 1970	Equation 3 30 cases u = .59 Export Partner Diversity 1970	Equation 4 26 cases u = .52 Export Partner Diversity 1970
Export Partner Diversity 1950			.367* (0.184)	.520* (0.107)
GNP per Capita 1950	2.4*** (0.15)	1.83*** (0.39)	-0.021 (0.068)	-0.047 (0.064)
Total School Enrollment per Capita 1950	3634.78* (1928.31)	-621.28 (4244.66)	-0.103 (0.169)	-0.061 (0.155)
Language Pool Book Production 1950 (dummy)	-241.81 (167.05)		0.019 (0.048)	
National Book Production 1950	0.01 (0.02)		0.011 (0.080)	
Translations 1950	0.77*** (0.24)		.105* (0.048)	
Films Shown 1950		0.86 (0.60)		0.211 (0.124)
Films Imported 1950		-0.98 (1.41)		-0.329** (0.149)

*   p < .10
** p < .05
*** p < .01

a. Unstandardized (b) coefficients; standard errors in parentheses. See Table 2 for a list of cases included.

b. Independent variables are logarithmic transformations (base 10) of original measures.

deeply diffused. The same cannot be said of book-borne values.[1] If the deleterious effects of the injection of foreign values described by Portes (1973a) and others have any reality, the adverse consequences of information imports on economic growth must be low when the vehicle is translations, high when it is films.

The independent variable of theoretical interest in equation (1) is *number of (book) translations performed in 1950,* coded from UNESCO (1958). In equation (2), the independent variable of theoretical interest is *number of films imported in 1948–53,*[2] coded from several editions of the *International Motion Picture Almanac.* This measure incorporates all nonduplicating cases for which data were available for this five-year period. The iterating procedure used to avoid duplication gives preference to 1950 data over all others, then to 1949 data, then to 1951 data, then to 1948 data, and so on.

Comment on the residuals associated with equation (1)
Nine of the thirty-five countries over which equation (1) is computed were non-European underdeveloped countries (designated by #) at the beginning of the period considered. Another seven European countries plus Israel would have been considered underdeveloped in 1950 (designated =). Of the total of these two categories of poor countries ($N = 17$) ten are placed above the median line for quality of prediction.

The best prediction associated with equation (1) is for Mexico, an underdeveloped country. The worst prediction is for Austria, a developed country. Thus, equation (1) accounts slightly better for the situation of poor countries than for that of rich countries.

Comments on the residuals associated with equation (2)
Equation (2) is computed over a set of thirty-one countries of which sixteen were underdeveloped in 1950 (# and =). Of these, ten are above the median in terms of quality of prediction. The best predictions are for Poland and Ireland, two poor European countries. The worst prediction is for New Zealand, a developed country. Again, in the absence of any other obvious, systematic pattern, there is no reason to believe that the hypothesis tested in equation (2) misrepresents the process as it aects underdeveloped countries.

Comments on equations (3) and (4)
The set of thirty countries over which equation (3) is computed includes fourteen countries that were underdeveloped in 1950 (# and =). Of these, seven are above the median line for quality of prediction.

Equation (4) is computed over a set of twenty-six countries of which twelve were underdeveloped in 1950. Five of these are placed above the median line for quality of prediction. Of these five, the four that also belong to the set over which equation (3) is computed were also above the median line for the quality of prediction pertaining to that equation. Altogether, equations (3) and (4) have twenty-three cases in common (denoted by ″). (The same twenty-three cases are also common to eqs. [1] and [2].) Equations (3) and (4) give very similar predictions (Rsq;= .59 and .52, respectively) in spite of the difference in the cases covered.

TABLE 10.2   Cases and Residuals in Equations (1)–(4)

Cases in Equation 1 (Ranked by increasing magnitude of residuals)				Cases in Equation 2 (Ranked by increasing magnitude of residuals)				Cases in Equation 3 (Not ranked by increasing magnitude of residuals)		Cases in Equation 4 (Not ranked by increasing magnitude of residuals)	
Country	Sign of Residual	Country	Sign of Residual	Country	Sign of Residual	Country	Sign of Residual	Country	Sign of Residual	Country	Sign of Residual
Mexico[a,b]	-	Japan[b]	-	Poland[c]	-	Netherlands	+	Sweden	+	Sweden	-
Hungary	-	Brazil[a,b]	+	Ireland[c]	-	Yugoslavia[c]	-	France	+	France	+
Portugal[c]	-	Turkey[a,b]	-	France	+	Mexico[a]	-	Italy	-	Italy	-
Spain[b,c]	-	Belgium	-	Italy	-	Turkey[a]	-	Ireland[c]	-	Ireland	-
Ireland[b,c]	-	Sweden[b]	+	Greece[c]	+	Norway	+	Finland	-	Finland	-
Norway[b]	+	United Kingdom	+	Venezuela[a]	-	Austria	+	Denmark	+	Denmark	+
Italy[b]	-	Poland[c]	-	Australia	-	Denmark	+	Yugoslavia[c]	+	Yugoslavia	+
Netherlands[b]	-	Canada[b]	+	Spain[c]	-	Israel[c]	+	Mexico[a]	+	Mexico	+
India[a,b]	+	France[b]	+	Czechoslovakia	+	Japan	+	Canada	-	Canada	-
South Africa[a]	-	W. Germany[b]	+	Chile[a]	-	Argentina[a]	-	W. Germany	+	W. Germany	+
Czechoslovakia	-	Philippines[a]	-	Puerto Rico[a]	+	Canada	+	Austria	+	Austria	+
Finland[b]	+	Australia[b]	+	Taiwan[a]	-	Sweden	+	Argentina[a]	+	Argentina	-
Denmark[b]	+	Argentina[a,b]	+	Finland[a]	+	India[a]	-	India[a]	+	India	+
Bulgaria[c]	+	Yugoslavia[b,c]	+	Brazil[a]	-	W. Germany	+	Brazil[a]	+	Brazil	+
Switzerland[b]	+	USA	+	Ecuador[a]	-	New Zealand[e]	-	Spain[c]	+	Spain	+
Burma[a]	+	Israel[b,c]	+	Switzerland	+			Philippines[a]	-		
Greece[b,c]	+	Austria[b,d]	+					USA	+		
Indonesia[a]	-							Switzerland	+	Switzerland	-
								Norway	+	Norway	-
								Portugal[c]	+		
								Turkey[a]	+	Turkey	+
								United Kingdom	+		
								Israel[c]	+	Israel	+
								Indonesia[a]	+		
								Greece[c]	+	Greece	+
								Japan	+	Japan	+
								S. Africa[a]	-		
								Australia	+	Australia	+
								Netherlands	-	Netherlands	-
								Belgium	+		
										Venezuela[a]	+
										Chile[a]	-
										New Zealand	+

a. Non-European country underdeveloped in 1950. b. Cases common to all equations. c. European country underdeveloped in 1950.
d. More than two standard deviations from regression line. e. More than one standard deviation from regression line.

Equations (1) and (2) estimate the relationship between imports of information and increases in wealth. Wealth is measured by *gross national product per capita* (GNP per capita). While GNP per capita has been criticized on various grounds as a measure of wealth, it is an adequate indicator of the very general concept of growth entertained here (Finsterbusch 1973).

Equations (1) and (2) introduce a measure of *total school enrollment per capita* (primary plus secondary school enrollment) in an attempt to capture the overall initial level of modernity of the population on the one hand (see Inkeles and Smith 1974) and the initial level of social differentiation on the other.[3] Whether or not educational development is an active force in modernization, it should be linked, in a structural sense, with initial conditions as they are conceptualized by most ontogenetic viewpoints.

Equation (1) includes a measure of *total book production* coded from the same source as the measure of translations. This is to take into account the fact that the publishing capacity of a country limits its ability to perform translations. This consideration is important since, as we will see, the size of a country's publishing industry is fairly independent of its wealth. A second reason for this control is that a high publishing activity within the boundaries may reduce the usefulness of information imports.

Finally, a measure of *language pool book production* is also included in equation (1). This is to take into account the fact that a country's propensity to translate foreign works may depend partly on lack of alternatives. One important alternative is the availability of books in one's own language (national or "official"; that is, elite) published outside the country. Other things being equal, Ghana, whose official language is English, needs translations less than Thailand, whose official and main language is Thai. Language pool book production is computed as a dummy variable with values 0 and 1. A value of 1 is attributed to any country that belongs to a multinational linguistic pool. Conceptually, it is difficult to decide exactly what constitutes such a pool, for a variety of reasons we need not go into here. Fortunately there is a reasonable cutoff point beween useful multinational pools and others. For the year 1950, four language pools each boast a total book production over 14,000 units. These are the English (38,175), German (21,490), French (16,229), and Spanish (14,010) language pools. Each country that belongs to one of these four pools obtains a score of 1 on this variable. The next pool, the Portuguese, is far behind (6,532).

The dummy variable language pool book production is necessarily a crude measure of informational-import alternatives to translations. Yet other measurement solutions would involve a false precision not in accord with our understanding of the processes involved. Based on thirty-five cases, this variable correlates moderately and negatively with the measure of translations as one would expect if the two measured alternative paths to the same end ($r = .24$).

I include a measure of *total number of films shown* in equation (2) as inferential evidence of processing capacity, by analogy with the book production measure in equation (1). This measure is coded from the same source and by the same nonduplicating procedure as the measure of films imported. No measure of participation in a language pool is included in this equation because the subtitling and dubbing of films are normally done at the point of origin.

Findings from Equations (1) and (2)

Though they are computed over slightly different sets of cases ($N = 35$, $N = 31$), equations (1) and (2) are quite comparable. The two sets include similar proportions of poor countries (see comments in table 10.2) and they have twenty-three cases in common. The 1950 and 1970 means and standard deviations of GNP per capita are very similar across the two sets. The same is true for their school enrollment per capita in 1950. Likewise, the correlation coefficients between the independent variables of theoretical interest and the variables denoting initial position are of identical signs and small magnitudes in the two equations The correlation of translations in 1950 with GNP per capita is .05 and between films imported in 1950 and GNP per capita is .16.

In both equations, low correlation coefficients between the variables of theoretical interest and the measures of initial wealth—GNP/cap—suggest that information flows are, as hypothesized, fairly free from the usual constraints imposed by underdevelopment.

Not unexpectedly, in both equations GNP/cap has the largest effect upon itself over time. The estimates associated with school enrollment per capita are small, but the estimate is close to significance in equation (1).

The measures of book production and films shown both have small, statistically nonsignificant effects on GNP/cap growth. In equation (1), the estimated effect of language pool book production is small and negative. This finding suggests that this measure may express some lingering effect of past colonial relationships which, according to a world-system perspective, should have negative consequences for economic growth. Since this estimate has low statistical significance, however ($P > .10$), further speculation on this matter may be idle.

In equation (1), the beta associated with the measure of translations is moderate, in absolute terms ($\beta = 0.21$), but it is the third largest estimate in this equation, after the autoregression and error terms. This estimate is significant at the .01 level. The estimate of the effect of film imports occupies an analogous place in equation (2). But, as predicted, this estimate is negative and fairly large ($\beta = -0.24$). It does not reach statistical significance ($P = .17$).

The main finding from this test of the hypothesis is that the respective effects of the independent variables of theoretical interest—translations and films imported—are, as predicted, sizable and of opposite signs, in spite of their similar association with the measures of initial development—GNP per capita. While roughly half of the cases in this analysis are developed countries, analysis of the residuals demonstrates that these findings are more applicable to poor than to rich countries (see comments to table 10.2).

The findings lend some support to the hypothesis that imports of information exert an influence on economic growth. This influence is relatively independent of the usual constraints imposed by initial conditions of development. The negative effect of film imports may be interpreted as an indication that, contrary to the implicit assumption of modernization theories (Rogers 1969, pp. 83,69), the positive influence of flows of information requires a limitation on value imports as described by Deutsch (1966). However, equation (2) constitutes an inconclusive test of this part of the hypothesis since the estimate of the negative effect of film imports fails to reach statistical significance. It is difficult to positively demonstrate any effect in an equation based on so few cases where the influence of wealth itself is controlled for (in fact, only the autoregression estimate is significant in eq. [2]). The low statistical significance of the estimate of the effect of film imports may indicate either that the effect does not really exist or that the time lag covered is inadequate for a clear effect to show up. The latter interpretation is most likely if the process hypothesized in equation (2) is in fact an attenuated (that is, "compressed") form of a more complex one, unfolding over a longer period. In the following pages I present additional findings that lend support to this interpretation of equation (2) in particular and to the hypothesis in general.

Information Imports and Trade Dependence

One of the world-system approach's main innovations is the designation of trade dependence as a principal causal mechanism of unequal development (see, for example, Frank 1965; Galtung 1971; Wallerstein, 1974a). One form of trade dependence is partner concentration, which places underdeveloped countries at the mercy of their export partners and of their economic vagaries (Galtung 1971 and, by implication, Magdoff 1960, pp. 35–37). There are two logical alternatives to partner concentration; one is economic autarky the other is partner diversity. World-system theory seems to favor diversity.[4]

The neat bipartite (tripartite in Wallerstein 1974a) division of the world into core and periphery (and therefore trade-dependent) countries proposed by world-system theory can only be a rough approximation of a dynamic reality. A great deal of rank fluctuation occurs along all dimensions of trade dependence. Between 1950 and 1960, for example, of sixty countries for which data are available, eleven improved by ten or more ranks their *export partner diversity,* measured as the number of countries to which they sent more than 0.05 percent of their export. The range of rank gains and losses for that period was -15 to $+15$ (Delacroix 1974). The world system as a whole is constantly expanding and therefore changing. In evolutionary language, this means that new environmental opportunities are appearing while old ones become available to newcomers. The positive rank alterations mentioned above reflect some countries' adaptation to new environmental opportunities and their capture of old ones from others. *Environmental opportunities* here means such things as new markets, expanding markets, and new products and trade routes.

But as stated earlier, according to evolutionary theory the ability to deal successfully with environmental variations is enhanced by possession of information about the environment (Deutsch 1966, pp. 82–83). If this speculative description of the process underlying the findings presented before is correct, general information imports must make a positive and autonomous contribution to the reduction of trade dependence. Hence book translations should increase export partner diversity irrespective of initial conditions. Greater export partner diversity, in turn, should contribute to growth in GNP per capita.

The import of foreign values should not contribute to the reduction of trade dependence or it should affect it adversely. One argument in support of this hypothesis is implicit in Portes (1973*a*). Like any alteration of a country's world-system location, the reduction of trade dependence must require a mobilization of collective resources. (Resources must be shifted to different productions oriented to markets with different characteristics. Often, new technical and managerial skills must be learned. All this requires active cooperation within the labor force.) The ability to mobilize rests on the existence of a national community (in the sense in which the term is used by Deutsch [1966, esp. chap. 5]). In this perspective, import of values via films interferes with the functioning of the national community, thereby inhibiting the effective mobilization of collective resources. Therefore, if film imports have any effect on export partner diversity, this effect should be, on the whole, negative.

Ideally, this new hypothesis would be tested with a three-waves panel design with trade dependence measured in the second wave and wealth in the third. Data limitations make this infeasible. A reasonable substitute is to show that imports of information autonomously affect the reduction of trade dependence in the manner just discussed.

I test this hypothesis with two equations of the same form and content as equations (1) and (2) except that a measure of *export partner diversity* is substituted for GNP per capita as a dependent variable. Export partner diversity described above is coded from the UN *Yearbook of International Trade Statistics*. Because this measure is skewed, I use logarithimic transformations (base 10) of the variables in the equations in order to avoid violating the assumptions of multivariate normality on which regression-analysis significance tests are based.

Note that by including in equations (2) and (4) a measure of the lagged dependent variable—export-partner diversity 1950—I control for one aspect of initial location within the world system. In addition, the measure of GNP per capita for 1950 is retained as a control for initial wealth.

Table 10.2 shows the list of cases over which both equation (3) and (4) are computed and a brief analysis of the residuals. Equations (3) and (4) are not strictly comparable with the two equations in the first test because the two tests have only twenty-three cases in common. However, these twenty-three cases are a reasonably representative sample of the eighty-odd countries in existence in 1950 (see table 10.2). The same set of twenty-three countries is common to equations (3) (based on 30 cases) and (4) (based on 26 cases), in the second test.

Findings from Equations (3) and (4)

Equations (3) and (4) are quite similar in spite of the fact that they are computed over different sets of cases. The means and standard deviations of the variables shared by these two equations are quite similar. Their error terms are also of similar size ($u = 0.59$ and $u = 0.52$). The error term associated with equation (3) is higher than that associated with equation (1) because the autoregression term of the dependent variable is lower here than in the first test.

Correlation coefficients between the variables of theoretical interest and those denoting initial wealth are, again, reasonably low: the correlations between GNP per capita and translations in 1950 and between GNP per capita and films imported in 1950 are .23 and .32, respectively. This confirms the idea that any effect of information import on export-partner diversity is relatively autonomous. In other words, information flows appear nearly as free from the constraints imposed by initial wealth when one controls for initial export-partner diversity (i.e., trade dependence) as when one does not.

Aside from the autoregression terms, the only estimates to reach a respectable level of statistical significance ($P < .03$) in these equations are those of the effects of translations and films imported on change in export partner diversity. Note that with fewer cases and more variables in this second test, it is more difficult to obtain statistically significant estimates than it was in the test of the first hypothesis.

I will refrain from interpreting here the other estimates since they are of low significance and of little substantive concern in this discussion. The main findings from this test are that the estimates of the effects of translations and films imported are, as predicted, sizable, significant, and of opposite signs. In fact, they are almost symmetrical.

Finally, the estimates attached to the measures of information flows—translations and films imported—are larger than they were in equations (1) and (2) where GNP per capita was the dependent variable (.47 vs. .21 and −.59 vs. −.24, respectively). The greater magnitude of the betas attached to the information measures in this second test suggests that the findings adduced in the first test are but an indirect, and therefore attenuated, representation of the influence of information imports on location within the world system. As predicted, the estimate of the effect of film imports reaches statistical significance ($P = .04$) in equation 4. This new result supports the previous speculation that information imports affect economic growth via export-partner dependency.

These findings are quite compatible with the hypothesis that imports of general information improve the economic status of countries by contributing to the reduction of their trade dependence while imports of value-laden information do not.

THEORETICAL IMPLICATIONS
The findings presented above fall short of producing definite proof of the reality of the processes I outline. For one thing, the epistemic links in the models tested may appear tenuous. Yet low correlation coefficients between the independent variables in the model would make likely alternative interpretations of these findings hazardous. In particular, these low correlation coefficients make it unlikely that the equations presented here show spurious relationships better explained by strictly economic processes of which information exchanges would be but a reflection. However, one could also easily argue that the time period covered by the two tests (1950–70) is too short or too arbitrarily located in history to allow for conclusions about long-term effects of information imports.

This study does not begin to adjudicate between modernization and world-system perspectives on economic development. However, it lends support to the world-system approach against the modernization approach in two distinct ways. First, cross-boundary transactions must not be considered necessarily beneficial or benign since some information imports appear to have negative consequences for economic growth. Neither must nation-states be assumed to be bounded since the permeability of their borders to information imports affects their economic growth and even, apparently, their place in world trade patterns. These two observations help vindicate the exogenetic perspective of world-system theory whether or not one agrees with the interpretations of the differential effects of translations and films I propose; and whether or not one attributes primary importance to economic factors of development. Second, the observed impact of film imports suggests that exposure to foreign values—presumably including modern ones—retards rather than enhances economic growth. Analysis of the residuals indicates that the contrary assumption, implicit in modernization theory, is not better supported for poor countries than for rich ones.

This study, however, shows little about the merits of indigenous modernizing influences, except in two weak and incidental ways. The estimates of the effects of the measure of films shown on both measures of economic progress are positive but not statistically significant. Domestic films shown domestically may be vehicles for modern indigenous values as imported films are vehicles for foreign values. Hence it is possible to find some substantive support for modernization theory in the positive effect of films shown on the two measures of economic progress. Similarly, in equation (1), the estimate of the effect of school enrollment is positive and close to statistical significance ($P = .07$). This finding is in line with Inkeles's (1971) proposition to the effect that education is a major modernizing institution. Nevertheless, it should be kept in mind that the favorable effect of education on economic growth disappears when the injection of foreign values (denoted by film imports) is allowed to play its part (see eq. [2]).

The evolutionary argument linking success in meeting variations in the environment with an aptitude for drawing information from the environment is lent strong support by equations (1) and (3). This is especially true if one accepts the interpretation of the relationship between these two equations that I propose. In this interpretation, the positive effect of translations on GNP/cap growth is explained by their positive effect on diversity of export partners. I assume export-partner diversification to be a contributor to economic growth (following world-system theory), and I take it to indicate success in meeting environmental variations. However, the corresponding negative effects of film imports suggest that the evolutionary argument needs to be refined to take into account the possible noxious effect of some externally generated information on the internal functioning of a social system.

The last statement seems in harmony with some world-system expectations. Nevertheless, the strong positive effects of translations on GNP per capita growth and on export-partner diversification (a measure derived from world-system theory) do not vindicate the pro-autarky bias that can sometimes be discerned, amidst much ambivalence, in the world-system perspective (see note 4). Finally, the overall finding that such things as the translation of books and the import of films influence economic development is not compatible with the economism always latent in world-system theory.

In view of these findings, it is tempting to speculate that nation-states are comprised within multiple boundaries that are imperfectly juxtaposed. These several boundaries, of which the informational is one, are subject to different constraints and do not vary in a unitary manner. The resolution of this unit-character problem is particularly vital for a perspective that calls for a redirection of attention toward relationships between entities.

Resolution of this "unit-character" problem in turn necessarily implies empirical research on the different categories of national boundaries and on their permeabilities. One possible strategy for this endeavor is implicit in Portes's discussion of the function of tradition in serving the structural development of Japan, Turkey, and other countries (1973*a*, pp. 262–65, 267–69). All the cases considered there and elsewhere support the idea that the selectivity of boundary control policies implemented by indigenous elites and by the national state affect economic development. Since there are many different historically documented instances of such boundary control schemes, it should be possible to systematically study their consequences (this strategy leaves entirely open the possibility that the forms of national states result largely from the operation of the world-system as it is described by Wallerstein).

RESTRICTIONS ON INFORMATION FLOWS AND NATIONAL ECONOMIC POLICY

This chapter reports on a very exploratory study. Its conclusions can only be tentative. Nevertheless they would, if confirmed, have potential policy implications. The main implication flows from the light in which they place the national informational policies described by Deutsch (1966). The often extravagant restrictions on the free flow of information practiced by the regimes of many developing countries are difficult to perceive as anything other than expressions of fanatic obscurantism. Could they be, in fact, lucid expressions of a realistic assessment of the situation of these countries? A survey of the implicit policy guidance provided by the major theoretical perspectives on economic development suggests that this interpretation is not absurd.

The modernization view of economic development contains an implicit admonition to poor countries to pull themselves up by their own bootstraps. The admonition is as vain as it is cruel if, in fact, most of the Third World is frozen in its present impoverished condition by its structural position in a global system endowed with its own dynamic. On the other hand, the implications for action of the world-system perspective are not immediately clear. They seem to embrace at once a justification for discouraged immobilism and a call for worldwide revolution, Lin Piao style. Third World countries have amply demonstrated their inability to band together for more than immediate economic gain. Even this they have done only rarely.

Ontogenetic and exogenetic perspectives share implicitly the most profound pessimism regarding short-term prospects for economic development in contemporary poor countries. Only very occasionally does one find a scholar who evokes both the plausibility of the world-system perspective and the feasibility of poor countries' management of their participation in the system (for notable theoretical exceptions, see Horowitz 1972 and Tugwell 1974). An overview of the whole field would lead one to believe that national economic development is either not amenable to political volition or that it is not affected by cross-boundary exchanges. There is abundant evidence to the contrary. Even superficial familiarity with the case of Japan should suggest that successful economic development is both eminently responsive to autonomous political decision-making and vigorously shaped by participation in international exchanges.

In the post–1960s years, we observe a clear Third World political trend toward more or less effective nationalist governments of various ideological (see chaps. 11, 12, and 13) leanings. In their attempts at ruling nations in various stages of formation, these nationalist regimes exercise an unsteady control over what remains, in most cases, a very embryonic state apparatus. A central question facing these regimes is that of the freedom they actually enjoy in the furtherance of the now universal goal of national economic development. According to current theories, their freedom of action must be found somewhere in the narrow channel between their depressed structural position in an inexorable world system and the existing psychosocioeconomic circumstances of the mass of their constituencies. Hence, we may ask if the governments of Third World countries that are interested in economic progress have any resources at their command. Are there any deliberate strategies of economic development that do not require what poor countries usually lack? The findings of this study are compatible with the idea that there exists an area of freedom where such strategies may be played out. All national states may exercise some degree of conscious control over their boundaries and what flows through them. If they wish to, national governments are in a particularly good position to administer information flows because the human and financial investments necessary for controlling such cross-boundary flows are typically small relative to national wealth. This is particularly true of the search for relevant information outside national boundaries. The other aspect of informational boundary control is the containment of damaging influences. The impact of film imports shown in this study lends indirect support to Portes's (1973a) argument to the effect that "modern" attitudes are what poor countries need least. World shrinkage induced by the mass media renders impractical the mode of rejection of foreign values practiced by Japan in the seventeenth, eighteenth, and nineteenth centuries. But the technological advances in the field of communications and the relative cheapness of information production argue for a policy of informational import substitution, especially as concerns values.

NOTES

1 I examine the consequences of information flows from the standpoint of imports only. This choice is dictated by the scarcity of data about information exports.

2 Film imports come from Western sources in approximately 80% of all cases in 1950 (UNESCO 1950–55).

3 I do not use an age-specific measure because I wish to characterize the initial structural position of the country as a sui generis entity rather than the specific economic contributions of individual members of the work force.

4 There are two alternatives to high export-partner concentration: export-partner diversification and a shift to autarky. World-system scholars tend to be ambiguous on the desirability of each alternative (for example Frank 1965, p. 12). Reactions to blockade—enforced autarky—seem to indicate that export-partner diversification is the most favored solution (Hoogvelt and Child 1973, p. 42; Petras 1974, pp. 22–23, 33, n. 8).

V   NATIONAL POLITICAL ORGANIZATION

ELEVEN · Maintaining National Boundaries in the World System: The Rise of Centralist Regimes

George M. Thomas, Francisco O. Ramirez,
John W. Meyer, and Jeanne G. Gobalet

The relationship between state and society is a central concern in comparative political sociology (see Bendix 1968; Eisenstadt 1971). Recently many sociohistorical investigations have sought to identify and discuss the struggles and mechanisms by which the state organization emerged, dominated rival powers such as dynastic and religious institutions, and destroyed unwritten principles and traditions associated with the latter. The essays collected by Tilly (1975), for example, stress that the formation of powerful states in Western Europe typically involved the maintenance of a sufficiently large and well-armed military, the capacity to tax the population effectively, and the expansion of state bureaucracy; that is, it involved an increase in state activities and personnel. This tradition of research is concerned with the extensiveness of the state's power: the control that the state exercises relative to other groups and institutions both within and outside the society (see chaps. 12 and 13).

Another research tradition focuses on the constitutional organization of the state. Swanson (1967, 1971) suggests that states are not merely bureaucratic organizations but also the decision-making bodies of national collectivities. The constitutional organization of the state symbolizes and maintains the types of interests legitimated within the national polity. Specifically, some regimes allow for the representation of diverse constituent interests, while others attempt to institutionalize and articulate a single corporate interest of the whole collectivity. At issue here is not the extensiveness of state power but the location of authority within the society: To what degree is authority centralized in the national regime and what are the factors affecting this level of centralization?

This chapter addresses itself to the latter question. We analyze cross-national variations in the extent to which authority is centralized. The first section makes clear how we conceptualize and operationalize this dimension, and it describes post–World War II trends in the formation of centralized regimes. The second section briefly summarizes some arguments linking other characteristics of nations to the centralization of authority. The hypotheses implied by these lines of thought are tested in the third section.

CENTRALIZATION OF AUTHORITY: CENTRALIST REGIMES

As the world system has become consolidated and rationalized, increasingly powerful state bureaucracies have been constructed. Though not necessarily efficient, these bureaucracies are powerful in terms of the authority, duties, and activities formally given to them (Meyer, Boli-Bennett, and Chase-Dunn 1975; Boli-Bennett 1976a, chap. 13). However, the state has become more than a bureaucracy. It has emerged as the decision-making body of the collectivity and as such symbolizes the formally legitimated "will of the society." This will is often ill-defined and penetrated by various constituent interests. However, the central regime may claim that there is only one national interest which it alone represents. The regime subsequently becomes defined not only as the sole legitimate manager of particular sectors of society but also as the sole holder of authority. Two modern examples of centralist regimes are those which greatly limit the number of political parties and those which are dominated by the military. The former are referred to as centralized party regimes, while the latter are military regimes.

Party Centralization: One-Party Systems

Bergesen (1977) argues that the number of political parties within a polity reveals the extent to which corporate rather than constituent interests are recognized and affirmed. When a party is the only legitimate party within a polity, it usually professes that (1) the society is an integrated collective with one common will, and (2) the state party represents that will (Apter 1963; LaPalombara and Weiner 1966; see especially the chapter by Wallerstein), and, hence, that the corporate will is manifested in the activity of the party (Mazrui 1971). Regardless of their truth, these claims explicitly identify the collective goals and interests of the nation with the purposes and aims of the party. Thus, the Ghanaian leader, Nkrumah, proclaimed, "The Convention People's Party is Ghana, and Ghana is the Convention People's Party" (von der Mehden 1964; see Smith 1971 for other examples). All other parties are outlawed within such a system because they are viewed as representing selfish interests. Given these claims and the fact that the one-party regime controls the state apparatus, the state-party nexus becomes the sole center of authority.

In this comparative study, party centralization is dichotomized: centralized party systems are given scores of *one*, and less centralized ones are scored zero.[1] This dichotomy is used instead of the actual number of legitimate parties because the concept in question is not simply the number of interests institutionalized within the party system, but the presence or absence of an organization which purports that there is a single collective will manifested through the activity of the state.

Military Regimes

The second indicator of centralization of authority is the presence or absence of a military regime. The state constitutes a claim to the monopoly of force within a society, and the military is the differentiated, institutionalized manifestation of that claim. When the military gains control of the entire political sphere, there is an increase in the mobilization and public visibility of legitimate force. But a military's dominance is predicated on a much larger claim. For various reasons such as political corruption, indecision, or ineffectiveness, or external infringement upon sovereignty, the military often comes to see itself as the only true representative of the national interest. It therefore intervenes in the management of public affairs. This may be done in either of two ways. The military plays "kingmaker" by supporting a civilian-controlled party or party coalition which then is able to run the government (Kim 1976; Geertz 1973), or it forms a new party whose leaders usually are both military officers and civilians (Bienen and Morell 1976). In the latter case, the military may abolish all other political parties and institute a regime with a distinct national ideology and rationale, claiming national interest as its motivation and justification, and in many ways coming to resemble a centralized party system.[2]

DESCRIPTION AND TRENDS

Though one-party systems and military regimes are overlapping indicators, their correlations (see Appendix A to this chapter) are low, ranging from .11 to .31.[3] The autocorrelations of party centralization are relatively high, ranging from .79 for the first fifteen-year lag to .65 for the second. This indicates that it is rather stable over time. Military regimes, on the other hand, are unstable, as shown in the variable's low autocorrelations: .26 and .14 for the two fifteen-year lags.

TABLE 11.1   Party Centralization, 1950–75[a]

Level of Centralization	1950	1955	1960	1965	1970	1975
High Centralization	32%	38%	44%	56%	63%	66%
Low Centralization	24	22	29	29	28	30
Not Independent	44	40	27	15	9	4
Total	100	100	100	100	100	100

a.147 cases by 1975.

TABLE 11.2   Type of Regime, 1950–75[a]

Type of Regime	1950	1955	1960	1965	1970	1975
Military Regime	5%	6%	5%	8%	18%	23%
Nonmilitary Regime	52	54	70	79	74	73
Not Independent	43	40	25	13	8	4
Total	100	100	100	100	100	100

a.144 cases by 1975.

The increase in one-party regimes is documented in table 11.1. As more countries became independent in the period 1950–70, multiparty regimes increased by only 25 percent, while centralized party systems increased by 106 percent. Table 11.2 shows a similar increase in military regimes. During this period, nonmilitary regimes increased by 40 percent, while military ones increased by 360 percent.[4] The number of multiparty systems leveled off somewhat in 1960, as did the number of nonmilitary ones in about 1965, whereas the number of centralized party systems increased consistently throughout the period.

The concomitant decline of colonies and rise in both types of centralist regimes over time is striking. This is analyzed further for the party variable in figure 11.1, which shows the party history of states grouped according to their date of national independence. We plot the proportion of states with centralized regimes for each cohort. The proportion with such regimes are stable over time for older countries, those independent before 1951. These are primarily the developed countries of Western and Eastern Europe and North America, and the older Latin American nations. The proportion for this cohort remains close to .6 throughout the twenty-five-year period, a relatively low level of party centralization. (The reader is reminded that the variable itself takes on only two values: 0 and 1.) Those countries which became independent between 1951 and 1955 were incorporated as centralized regimes and remained that way; the 1956 to 1965 groups were also highly centralized upon gaining independence, the 1956–60 group becoming entirely one-party polities.

From these four curves it could be inferred that as the world economic system becomes consolidated and rationalized, authority within new independent countries becomes more centralized. However, the cohorts gaining independence after 1966 show progressively lower levels of centralized authority, although even with this decrease the number of centralized party systems comprising a cohort does not fall below 40 percent. It could be argued that the most recently independent countries have yet to undergo the rapid move toward centralization that the 1956–60 cohort experienced: it is possible that, of these 13 nations, those which are not already centralized may soon become so. However, given the factors possibly unique to the 1956–60 cohort, this should not be taken for granted.[5] It is noteworthy that the majority of the 1956–60 cohort consists of African countries. Figure 11.2 gives the party centralization level by geographical region. As countries become independent, they are added to the calculation of the proportion for that region. As would be expected, North America and Western Europe were less centralized throughout the twenty-five-year period, and Eastern Europe and the Soviet Union remained at the maximum level of centralization. Of the other regions, the history of sub-Saharan Africa is the most in-

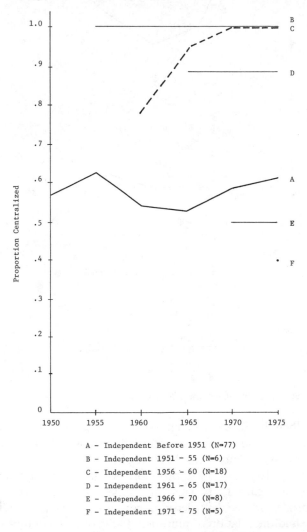

A – Independent Before 1951 (N=77)
B – Independent 1951 – 55 (N=6)
C – Independent 1956 – 60 (N=18)
D – Independent 1961 – 65 (N=17)
E – Independent 1966 – 70 (N=8)
F – Independent 1971 – 75 (N=5)

Fig. 11.1   Centralization of Regimes by Date of Independence, 1950–75

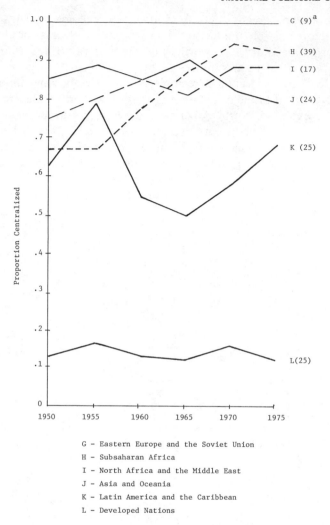

Fig. 11.2   Centralization of Regimes by Region, 1950–75

G – Eastern Europe and the Soviet Union
H – Subsaharan Africa
I – North Africa and the Middle East
J – Asia and Oceania
K – Latin America and the Caribbean
L – Developed Nations

a.   Number of cases in 1975; nations are added to cohorts after becoming
     independent.

teresting. When they became independent from colonial rule, the new African nations were supplied with externally imposed democracies which shortly gave way to more centralized regimes. Their increase in centralization between 1955 and 1970 probably dominates the trends shown in table 11.1 and figure 11.1. This, of course, is not a new finding, for much theorizing in the last decade, concerning the preconditions for democracy and the relation of pluralism to the organization of the polity, was motivated by this shift in African nations to centralized states

(Wallerstein 1969). The following section deals with these theories and a world-system model which attempts to account for this peculiar pattern of centralization of authority.

THEORIES, HYPOTHESES, AND MEASURES

Modernization of Individual Personalities and Activities

Within some theoretical traditions, changes in political organization are seen as the results of changes in individual predispositions to act and participate in certain ways. It is the aggregation of individual changes that results in the modifications at the national level. The purported causes of the change in individual behavior are several. One is economic development. On the one hand, economic growth creates participatory and efficacious individuals (Lipset 1960), and, on the other hand, it gives rise to "modern personalities" characterized by political awareness and sophistication (Inkeles and Smith 1974). Thus, economic development provides a stable atmosphere for democracy and therefore should be negatively related to centralist regimes.

HYPOTHESIS 1 *Economic development has a negative effect on the likelihood of a centralist regime.*

Another cause of individual change is urbanization, which breaks down familial and territorial definitions of the individual, resulting in the modern politicized personality. Thus:

HYPOTHESIS 2 *Urbanization negatively affects the likelihood of centralist regimes.*

As noted by others (see chap. 3), educational expansion is often interpreted as creating participatory definitions of individuals. The more "citizens" the educational system creates, the more stable the democracy. Thus:

HYPOTHESIS 3 *The greater the expansion of the educational system, the less likely the presence of a centralist regime.*

The indicator of economic development used here is per capita gross national product in constant 1964 US dollars (IBRD *World Tables,* 1971). The variable is transformed logarithmically because it is highly skewed. Urbanization is measured by the proportion of the nation's population residing in cities of 100,000 or more (Davis 1969). Three indicators of educational expansion are used: the raw enrollments at the primary, secondary, and tertiary levels divided by the appropriate age-group population. Data are taken from the UNESCO *Statistical Yearbook* (1971).

Institutions and the World System

Another approach emphasizes the organizational and cultural effects which institutions have on a polity. In the history of western development, the rise of a rational market or economic development certainly affected the individuation of everyday life and the establishment of a state which directly incorporated "participating citizens." However, the world has long been consolidated into a unitary economic system—an iron cage (Weber 1958). Variations in economic development no longer systematically affect the political orientation, sophistication, and participation of the people. These qualities have rapidly become the institutional characteristics of any national polity, whatever the level of "development." Economic growth itself is primarily a goal imposed on countries by the world system: growth is necessary for national viability in the larger market, and all countries in the world culture are expected to emphasize economic development as a major priority in their national agendas. Given these institutions and the material and symbolic pressures to conform to them, the poorer the country, the more its regime explicitly mobilizes toward achieving economic growth. The regime mobilizes in part by organizing diverse areas of social life around collective goals so as to direct human and nonhuman resources toward respectable growth targets. In short, in the process of mobilizing, the regime centralizes authority.[6] Therefore, the world-system model also asserts, although for significantly different reasons, the first hypothesis: economic development has a negative effect on the likelihood of a centralist regime.

This framework also emphasizes the organizational impact and meaning of education as an institution. It is the nature of the state to incorporate individuals directly through the category of citizen. The educational institution provides a rite of passage by which citizenship is conferred on people, though the definition of citizenship may vary across polities (see chaps. 5 and 14). Therefore, contrary to hypothesis 3, the extent of education should have little effect on centralization.[7]

Within an institutional approach it is often argued (see, for example, Swanson 1958) that the greater the diversity of a society the greater the development of unifying cultural symbols and integrating structures. The world-system perspective revises and extends this argument. Within the world economy the definition of "nation" is imposed on various territories which otherwise would be comprised of several different polities. Given competitive market processes within the larger system, economic interests within the territory, in conjunction with external economic and political powers, attempt to create strong states in order to protect their economic viability (see Wallerstein 1974a). Once so defined, the nation and state are supported not only by the international economic processes, but also by the other nation-states: in the world culture, nations are seen as real sovereign entities whose continued existence is taken for granted. The result is a hiatus between the strong state and the "fragmented" society which results in a boundary crisis. That is, the state makes increasingly incredible claims concerning the unity of the society. This causes the national boundary to be questioned as witnessed by the fact that strong states often create more intense ethnic conflicts. Various nation-building factions within the collective, often rooted in economic or "state" interests, attempt to maintain the national boundary by bridging the gap between state and society. This increases the likelihood that social authority will become centralized in the state by means of a single-party or military regime. These regimes then may destroy the diverse subgroups and interests symbolically, physically, or both.

HYPOTHESIS 4 *Given the external economic and political pressures within the world system to maintain nation-states, the greater the diversity of society, the greater the likelihood of a centralist regime.*

The concept of population diversity refers to a broad range of characteristics, including ethnic, linguistic, and religious diversity. The indicator used here is ethnolinguistic fractionalization as reported in Taylor and Hudson (1971) and described in chapter 3.

Dependency theory, a specialized theory within the world-system framework, asserts that the greater the economic and political dependence of one nation on other nations, the lower that nation is in the world stratification system (see chaps. 8 and 12). Within such states two economic factions emerge. One opposes dependence and pushes for stronger state controls in order to encourage home industrialization. The second, and often dominant, faction, usually sponsored by outside interests, channels state controls toward protecting the raw production sector. Which movement wins affects the future probability that the country will move into the semiperiphery. In the first case a strong state emerges which mobilizes the population around national goals of economic growth by centralizing authority. In the second, more dependent, case, the state is likely to be weak, though centralized around the maintenance of external interests and the suppression of local ones.

The dependency approach in part parallels the economic development argument. The latter reasons that the higher the level of development, the less likely a centralist regime will exist, regardless of the nation's position in the world stratification system. On the other hand, the economic dependency argument asserts that position in the world structure is the key causal factor.

HYPOTHESIS 5 *Economic dependence increases the likelihood of a centralist regime.*

The indicators of economic dependence are per capita dependence on foreign investment, transformed logarithmically because it is skewed (IMF, Balance of Payments Yearbook, 1957, 1966); and export partner concentration, the percent of a nation's exports which goes to its largest trading partner (UN *Yearbook of International Trade Statistics*, 1951, 1963).

The world system model emphasizes the external factors impinging on a society. Similarly, Stinchcombe (1965) argues that the environment in which an organization is created determines the formal structure of that organization. Even with changes in the environment, the formal structure is in part still affected by the period in which the organization was formed. An extension of this reasoning related to our problem is that causal relationships may be different for countries which became independent before and after World War II, and that the date of independence may have a continuing influence on the nature of the central regime (see Lieberson and Hansen 1974). For these reasons, all of the analyses are made first for the whole sample and then for countries gaining independence after 1944.[8] Also, a dummy variable for date of independence—before or after 1945—is used as an independent variable.

HYPOTHESIS 6 *Causal effects are different for newer nations than for older ones; and the newer the nation, the more likely the presence of a centralist regime.*

MODELS

We test the above hypotheses with regression analyses of panel models. The problem of autocorrelation of error terms probably is not a factor in these analyses because of the low degree of multicollinearity between the independent variables and the time 1 dependent variables, and because of the low level of stability of the centralist regime variables— especially for military regimes. In this paper, we employ simple linear models, since the theories and hypotheses reviewed suggest straightforward additive effects. Other analyses, not reported here, have explored the possibility of more complex interaction effects which differ according to the level of development of a country. The results of these analyses are not appreciably different from those reported here.[9]

We examine the effects of the independent variables on the two different indicators of centralization of authority: party centralization and military regimes. Each effect is assessed over two different time lags: 1950–65 and 1960–75. Therefore, countries gaining independence after 1960 do not figure in the analyses. In all cases, those independent variables which change over time are assessed as of the initial point in the time lag. We then repeat these analyses for countries which became independent after 1944.[10]

RESULTS

Table 11.3 shows some results of our analyses. The table presents the unstandardized regression coefficient and its standard error for each of the independent variables. In all cases the coefficients for the autoregression terms are substantial for the measure of the one-party regime, and are small for the indicator of the military regime. We review the results in terms of the various hypotheses.

HYPOTHESIS 1 *Economic development*. In the entire sample, development shows substantial and significant negative effects on the existence of centralist regimes. Clearly, less developed countries are more likely to move toward or remain under centralized party systems and military regimes. These effects remain no matter which variable or set of variables is included in the equation. For party centralization this effect is reduced for the newer nations. However, it remains substantively significant; the lack of statistical significance most likely is due to the dramatic loss of cases. It therefore is clear that economic development negatively affects the centralization of authority for all nations.

HYPOTHESES 2 AND 3 *Urbanization and education*. Independent of economic development, these variables have little influence on the centralization of authority. In general the analysis for the newer nations shows larger, but still insignificant, effects of these variables. Overall, the results support the view that while education and urbanization might give risc to sophisticatcd, participating citizens, such definitions of individuals are almost universally established and built into all nation-state organizations, making irrelevant any historical effects these variables might have had.[11]

HYPOTHESIS 4 *National boundary crisis and diversity*. The idea that centralist, mobilizing regimes evolve to control populations not yet integrated into unified nationalities receives little support in our data. In no instance does the measure of ethnolinguistic fractionalization show a statistically significant effect, although there are slight indications of a positive influence. We believed that this measure might not indicate the degree to which partitions in the population are actively recognized and observed in a given society. The new-nation sample can help rectify this: the newer the country the less likely that internal subgroupings are blurred or made irrelevant to the organization of the state. There is in fact an increase in the coefficient for those countries independent since 1945, although it is still nonsignificant.[12]

HYPOTHESIS 5 *Economic dependence*. In the 1950–65 period the data show no effects of national economic dependence over and above the influence of economic development. In the 1960–75 period, for both old nations and new nations, there is good indication that dependence increases the centralization of authority. Export-partner concentration primarily affects party centralization. Log investment dependence per capita has large effects on military regimes, and it also positively affects party centralization. The lack of statistical significance in some of the equations is due largely to the small number of countries for which there are data, especially for the newer nation analysis.

TABLE 11.3   Panel Analysis of Factors Affecting Centralist Regimes[a]

All Nations: 1950–65

Structural Variable Names	Dep. Var.: Party Centralization — Structural Variable t_1	Log GNP/Capita t_1	Party Central. t_1	Constant	No. of Cases	Dep. Var.: Military Regime — Structural Variable t_1	Log GNP/Capita t_1	Military Regime t_1	Constant	No. of Cases
		-0.026(0.10)**	0.66(0.09)***	0.78	71		-0.24(0.09)***	0.30(0.11)***	0.68	72
Primary Enroll.Ratio[b]	-0.06(0.17)	-0.26(0.14)*	0.62(0.11)***	0.83	61	-0.17(0.17)	-0.13(0.14)	0.29(0.12)**	0.55	62
Secondary Enroll. Ratio[b]	0.20(0.29)	-0.36(0.14)**	0.63(0.10)***	1.02	58	-0.15(0.31)	-0.22(0.13)*	0.42(0.13)***	0.69	58
Tertiary Enrpll.Ratio[b]	-0.54(2.3)	-0.32(0.15)***	0.56(0.11)***	0.98	55	-0.80(2.5)	-0.26(0.14)*	0.26(0.13)**	0.80	56
Urbanization[b]	-0.09(0.33)	-0.24(0.12)**	0.69(0.09)***	0.74	70	0.03(0.38)	-0.25(0.12)**	0.30(0.12)***	0.70	71
Ethnoling.Fract.	0.05(0.14)	-0.25(0.10)***	0.66(0.09)***	0.75	71	0.15(0.15)	-0.22(0.09)***	0.30(0.11)***	0.60	72
Date of Ind.: 1945[c]	-0.06(0.12)	-0.28(0.12)**	0.64(0.09)***	0.85	71	-0.11(0.13)	-0.27(0.09)***	0.28(0.12)**	0.77	72
Export Partner Concen.	-0.11(0.18)	-0.27(0.13)**	0.59(0.12)***	0.84	50	-0.08(0.18)	-0.26(0.10)**	0.06(0.14)	0.77	49
Log Invest.Depend./Cap.	-0.01(0.06)	-0.32(0.13)**	0.54(0.11)***	0.92	55	0.00(0.06)	-0.28(0.11)**	0.20(0.13)	0.81	56
Subsaharan Africa[c]	-0.11(0.30)	-0.26(0.10)**	0.66(0.09)***	0.79	71	-0.07(0.32)	-0.24(0.11)***	0.30(0.11)***	0.68	72
North Africa/Middle East[c]	0.04(0.12)	-0.25(0.11)**	0.66(0.09)***	0.75	71	0.11(0.13)	-0.21(0.09)**	0.32(0.12)***	0.61	72
Asia and Oceania[c]	-0.01(0.11)	-0.27(0.12)**	0.66(0.09)***	0.80	71	-0.16(0.12)	-0.32(0.10)***	0.28(0.11)**	0.91	72

All Nations: 1960–1975

Structural Variable Names	Dep. Var.: Party Centralization — Structural Variable t_1	Log GNP/Capita t_1	Party Central. t_1	Constant	No. of Cases	Dep. Var.: Military Regime — Structural Variable t_1	Log GNP/Capita t_1	Military Regime t_1	Constant	No. of Cases
		-0.41(0.09)***	0.37(0.08)***	1.45	102		-0.45(0.09)***	0.14(0.15)	1.36	102
Primary Enroll.Ratio[b]	0.26(0.17)	-0.57(0.13)***	0.36(0.09)***	1.66	93	-0.08(0.20)	-0.43(0.16)***	0.17(0.15)	1.41	93
Secondary Enroll.Ratio[b]	-0.19(0.29)	-0.35(0.15)**	0.33(0.09)***	1.39	93	-0.16(0.35)	-0.43(0.17)**	0.16(0.16)	1.38	93
Tertiary Enroll.Ratio[b]	-0.78(1.0)	-0.37(0.12)***	0.32(0.09)***	1.44	94	0.29(1.3)	-0.51(0.14)***	0.10(0.15)	1.53	94
Urbanization[b]	-0.23(0.33)	-0.34(0.11)***	0.39(0.08)***	1.31	101	0.27(0.40)	-0.50(0.13)***	0.14(0.15)	1.44	101
Ethnoling. Fract.	-0.01(0.12)	-0.41(0.09)***	0.37(0.08)***	1.46	102	0.14(0.15)	-0.42(0.09)***	0.14(0.15)	1.24	102
Date of Ind.: 1945[c]	0.02(0.08)	-0.39(0.10)***	0.37(0.08)***	1.41	102	-0.03(0.10)	-0.47(0.11)***	0.13(0.15)	1.42	102
Export Partner Concen.	0.50(0.20)**	-0.36(0.10)***	0.38(0.09)***	1.16	92	0.14(0.24)	-0.51(0.10)***	0.09(0.15)	1.51	92
Log Invest.Depend./Cap.	0.12(0.08)	-0.64(0.15)***	0.29(0.12)***	2.22	65	0.17(0.08)**	-0.55(0.15)***	0.15(0.16)	1.92	65
Subsaharan Africa[c]	0.04(0.10)	-0.39(0.10)***	0.37(0.08)***	1.40	102	0.26(0.11)**	-0.35(0.10)***	0.21(0.15)	1.07	102
North Africa/Middle East[c]	0.00(0.10)	-0.40(0.09)***	0.37(0.08)***	1.45	102	-0.02(0.13)	-0.45(0.09)***	0.15(0.16)	1.37	102
Asia and Oceania[c]	-0.15(0.09)	-0.46(0.09)***	0.37(0.08)***	1.62	102	-0.47(0.11)***	-0.61(0.09)***	0.07(0.14)	1.86	102

Independent Variables

New Nations: 1960-75

Structural Variable Names	Dep. Var.: Party Centralization					Dep. Var.: Military Regime				
	Structural Variable t_1	Log GNP/Capita t_1	Party Central. t_1	Constant	No.of Cases	Structural Variable t_1	Log GNP/Capita t_1	Military Regime t_1	Constant	No.of Cases
Primary Enroll.Ratio[b]	0.13(0.26)	-0.28(0.20)	0.21(0.13)*	1.31	36	-0.28(0.36)	-0.73(0.29)**	0.18(0.28)	1.93	37
Secondary Enroll.Ratio[b]	-0.61(0.60)	-0.38(0.27)	0.24(0.15)	1.42	34	-1.2(0.87)	-0.56(0.42)	0.12(0.29)	1.77	35
Tertiary Enroll.Ratio[b]	-2.7(2.0)	-0.13(0.27)	0.17(0.14)	1.10	33	-2.2(3.4)	-0.45(0.39)	0.17(0.28)	1.51	34
Urbanization[b]	-1.1(0.62)*	-0.05(0.24)	0.13(0.13)	1.05	33	-0.15(1.1)	-0.68(0.36)	0.17(0.30)	1.90	34
Ethnoling. Fract.	0.11(0.18)	-0.24(0.21)	0.24(0.12)*	0.92	36	0.23(0.27)	-0.70(0.37)*	0.19(0.29)	1.88	37
Date of Ind.: 1945[c]	::	::	0.23(0.13)*	1.16	36	::	-0.66(0.30)**	0.19(0.29)	1.68	37
Export Partner Concen.	0.54(0.29)*	-0.27(0.21)	0.19(0.13)	1.10	33	0.03(0.49)	-0.80(0.30)***	0.13(0.31)	2.11	34
Log Invest. Depend./Cap.	0.08(0.17)	-0.34(0.53)	0.29(0.27)	1.50	15	0.22(0.17)	-0.39(0.56)*	0.36(0.30)	2.69	16
Subsaharan Africa[c]	0.14(0.10)	-0.20(0.21)	0.22(0.13)*	1.08	36	0.43(0.16)***	-0.47(0.28)*	0.41(0.27)	1.18	37
North Africa/Middle East[c]	0.07(0.14)	-0.33(0.23)	0.20(0.13)	1.42	36	0.21(0.24)	-0.86(0.33)***	0.06(0.32)	2.17	37
Asia and Oceania[c]	-0.11(0.10)	-0.33(0.21)	0.20(0.13)	1.48	36	-0.52(0.14)***	-0.90(0.25)***	0.15(0.24)	2.48	37

* $p < .10$
** $p < .05$
*** $p < .01$

a. Ordinary least-squares estimates of slopes; standard errors in parentheses. A typical equation regresses party centralization in 1975 on earlier economic development, primary enrollment ratio and party centralization.

b. In hundreds.

c. Dummy variables.

HYPOTHESIS 6 *Period of independence.* The positive effect of ethno-linguistic fractionalization on centralist regimes is slightly higher for the newer nations subsample, but this is primarily because diversity is measured better for this subsample. Education expansion and urbanization tend to have larger negative effects in the newer countries, but they remain small and insignificant. The dummy variable for newness itself shows no effect on centralization of authority. Perhaps the older countries need to be broken down according to date of independence, and the most recent cohort needs to be considered, in order to better examine this hypothesis.

Controls for Geographical Region

In addition to these variables we also controlled for geographical region in order to see if regional and larger cultural differences are operating. While there are some expected significant effects, we feel that these are overshadowed by the effects of economic development and dependence.

CONCLUSIONS

Various factors appear to affect the rise and maintenance of centralist regimes.[13] One factor is the period in which the nation-state was formed. Specifically, most of the countries entering the world system after 1944 had centralized party systems or military regimes at independence, or quickly moved to such regimes. This makes sense if such nation-states are viewed as new organizations adapting to a rationalized and competitive market environment in which centralized authority at least symbolically maintains the sovereign boundary of the nation-state. Yet, our panel analyses show no subsequent causal effect of recency of independence on centralization of authority. This also makes sense. Emergence in the modern rationalized world economy may be a sufficient condition for the centralization of authority, but it is by no means a necessary one: there are many older nations which all along have been or became centralist. These interpretations will be clarified by a better classification of the most recent cohorts and an analysis of their future organization.

As predicted, there is a large effect of economic development on centralist regimes. This, of course, does not allow us to distinguish directly the two general approaches being considered. However, the fact that urbanization and the various educational enrollment variables have no consistent, substantive effects on the centralization of authority provides little support for modernization theories. While economic development, along with the rise of cities and the expansion of education, may under particular historical conditions provide the impetus for the rise of participatory systems, such systems are universally established in the modern world. Economic development is itself a universally imposed goal around which the regimes of poor countries mobilize. That education does not give special support to a democracy in the modern world implies that all types of regimes incorporate individuals via the educational system. To put it most strongly, the educational system is a ritual process universal to modern nation-states which links individuals directly to the sociopolitical organization, though the content of the ritual is determined by the nature of the regime.

The underlying assumptions of the world-system approach are also supported by the analyses of social diversity. This variable has small positive effects on centralization of authority in the newer nations which have more significant internal cleavages and more problematic national boundaries, but which face great external pressures to affirm a cohesive and unitary sovereign entity. The results of the economic dependency analysis give even clearer credence to the world-system model. The positive effects of dependence on centralist regimes over and above economic development and the time of formation support the idea that the lower the country falls in the world stratification system, the greater the likelihood of a centralist regime.

While these analyses leave some unsolved questions, certain inferences can be made. The world system establishes and maintains nation-states which define and directly incorporate "citizens." Nation-states of themselves would not have evolved universally, but in an interconnected and competitive system these externally imposed sovereignties are irresistible. Internal organizational factors therefore are largely uninterpretable unless examined in this context. Problems of maintaining definitions of the national boundary and of reconciling state and society arise within the historical processes of the larger economic and cultural system. The problems result in boundary-maintaining activity by various factions which have material and symbolic interests vested in the state organization. These nation-building groups centralize authority in the state regime. The degree of centralization as measured by one-party and military regimes is a function of (1) the period in which the nation-state was formed, (2) the success of the country in meeting externally imposed goals (most importantly, economic development), and (3) the degree to which the country is autonomously and successfully carrying out economic activity in its own interest within the worldwide division of labor.

APPENDIX A

Correlation Matrices, 1950–65 and 1960–75[a]

1950–65

Variable			1	2	3	4	5	6	7	8	9	10	11	12	13
Party Centralization,	1950	1	1.0												
Party Centralization,	1965	2	.79	1.0											
Military Regime,	1950	3	.13	−.09	1.0										
Military Regime,	1965	4	.09	.21	.26	1.0									
Log GNP per Capita,	1950	5	−.58	−.64	−.07	−.26	1.0								
Primary Enrollment Ratio,	1950	6	−.53	−.57	.04	−.16	.74	1.0							
Secondary Enrollment Ratio,	1950	7	−.46	−.49	−.02	−.16	.72	.70	1.0						
Tertiary Enrollment Ratio,	1950	8	−.50	−.53	.06	−.09	.64	.66	.73	1.0					
Urbanization,	1950	9	−.46	−.40	.06	−.04	.58	.57	.61	.76	1.0				
Export Partner Concentration,	1950	10	.09	.09	−.18	.04	−.23	−.21	−.28	−.04	−.25	1.0			
Log Investment Dependence per Capita,	1950	11	−.22	−.24	−.20	−.13	.37	.15	.03	−.35	.24	.21	1.0		
Ethnolinguistic Fractionalization	1950	12	.12	.17	−.07	−.00	−.30	−.42	−.30	−.22	−.29	−.02	−.20	1.0	
Independent After World War II		13	.20	.30	−.28	−.04	−.39	−.44	−.49	−.48	−.38	.13	−.19	.30	1.0

1960–75

Variable			14	15	16	17	18	19	20	21	22	23	24	25	26
Party Centralization,	1960	14	1.0												
Party Centralization,	1975	15	.65	1.0											
Military Regime,	1960	16	.11	−.04	1.0										
Military Regime,	1975	17	.03	.31	.14	1.0									
Log GNP per Capita,	1960	18	−.52	−.55	−.09	−.45	1.0								
Primary Enrollment Ratio,	1960	19	−.51	−.44	−.11	−.35	.78	1.0							
Secondary Enrollment Ratio,	1960	20	−.48	−.49	−.09	−.36	.83	.71	1.0						
Tertiary Enrollment Ratio,	1960	21	−.42	−.43	−.05	−.36	.68	.56	.80	1.0					
Urbanization,	1960	22	−.35	−.36	−.02	−.26	.67	.64	.66	.63	1.0				
Export Partner Concentration,	1960	23	.04	.23	−.10	−.23	−.22	−.24	−.31	−.23	−.32	1.0			
Log Investment Dependence per Capita,	1960	24	−.48	−.33	−.18	−.09	.64	.42	.36	.32	.37	.12	1.0		
Ethnolinguistic Fractionalization	1960	25	.13	.22	.01	.15	−.36	−.42	−.35	−.22	−.32	.11	.00	1.0	
Independent After World War II		26	.22	.22	−.07	.11	−.47	−.36	−.47	−.47	−.36	.16	−.33	.30	1.0

a. Pearson zero-order coefficients.

APPENDIX B
Nations Independent after World War II
1945–75

1946	Jordan		Senegal
	Lebanon		Somalia
	Philippines		Togo
	Syria		Upper Volta
1947	India		Zaire
	Pakistan	1961	Kuwait
1948	Burma		Sierra Leone
	North Korea		Tanzania
	South Korea	1962	Algeria
	Israel		Burundi
	Sri Lanka		Jamaica
1949	Indonesia		Rwanda
1951	Egypt		Trinidad and Tobago
1952	Libya		Uganda
1953	Cambodia	1963	Kenya
1954	Laos	1964	Malawi
	North Vietnam		Malta
	South Vietnam		Zambia
1956	Sudan	1965	Gambia
	Tunisia		Maldive Islands
1957	Ghana		Rhodesia
	Malaysia (Malaya)		Singapore
1958	Guinea	1966	Barbados
1960	Benin		Botswana
	Cameroon		Guyana
	Central African Empire		Lesotho
	Chad	1967	South Yemen
	Congo (Brazzaville)	1968	Mauritius
	Cyprus		Swaziland
	Gabon	1970	Fiji
	Ivory Coast	1974	Guinea-Bissau
	Malagasy Republic	1975	Angola
	Mali		Mozambique
	Mauritania		Papua
	Niger		Surinam
	Nigeria		

APPENDIX C
At a general level we are concerned with the structural factors, both
internal and external to the nation-state, which affect the type of regime.
We formulate the problem by looking at centralizing regimes. Previous
studies concerned with this general issue take a slightly different approach and concentrate on prerequisites for stable democratic govern-

ments (for example, Lipset, 1960). This approach emphasizes the necessity of politically sophisticated individuals actively participating in the polity in order for democracies to emerge and remain stable, although other historical factors are recognized. Several indices of a "stable participatory democracy" have been made. Cutright (1963; Cutright and Wiley 1969) constructed a scale of formal political representation, and Adelman and Morris (1973) combined various indicators into an overall measure of political participation. Cutright's index is ambiguous for communist countries, and these nations therefore are excluded in the following analyses. Adelman and Morris coded primarily less developed and noncommunist countries (see chap. 3 for a discussion of these variables).

In order to establish some continuity with these studies, we analyze these two variables using equations similar to the ones reported in the text. We examine the influence of many variables on the Adelman and Morris index (1963–68) while controlling for its prior values (1957–62), and on the Cutright index (1961–65) while controlling for its initial values (1946–50). The countries that became independent after World War II show higher levels of political participation as measured by Adelman and Morris. The dummy variable for the date of independence has a positive effect with a slope of 2.08 and a standard error of 1.37 (N = 32). Ethnolinguistic fractionalization also positively affects political participation (slope, .04; standard error, .02, N, 43). No other variable has any effect on this index. Urbanization, economic development, and education have no effects on Cutright's formal political representation measure, although in some equations the coefficient of primary educational enrollments approaches significance (slope, .06; standard error, .04; N, 42). Export-partner concentration also approaches significance with a negative effect (slope, −.06; standard error, .04; N, 35).

These findings do not offer much support for conventional modernization arguments. Cross-national variations in mass political participation and formal political democracy (in noncommunist countries) are not strongly associated with levels of economic, social, or educational development. Earlier we argued that mass political participation was increasingly an institutional characteristic of all national polities. The mean country score on each political index is greater for the later time period (Meyer, Boli-Bennett, and Chase-Dunn 1975). In part, this phenomenon arises as a response to a world system which legitimates state and citizenship authority (see chap. 3). Newness of state organization and ethnic cleavages, variables often discussed as barriers to the development of democratic participation, may actually promote participation among the poorer countries.

Clearly, additional theoretical and empirical treatments of these issues are necessary. Participatory citizenship as a collective definition may be more important than actual behavior. The relation between this and factors such as newness, ethnic cleavages, and type of central regime then need to be analyzed, possibly moving to more complex interactive models.

NOTES

1 The regime is considered centralized when all parties are outlawed, or there is only one legal party, or there are one or more weak parties, or there is one main party and other weak parties. When there are two or more parties with significant power, the regime is considered less centralized. Zero-party systems are usually dictatorships headed by one person or the military, and since the military organization and the charisma of the dictator perform functions similar to the political party, they are classified as centralized or one-party systems. When more than one party is legal but one controls most of the power, it is likely that the weak parties are tolerated precisely because of their weakness, and if they were to gain strength they would probably be suppressed.

2 The military infrequently takes direct active control for long periods of time. Rather, it attempts to right the situation by creating or supporting a political organization capable of maintaining order and the military's own conceptions of the polity.

3 The necessary information on these variables was obtained from Banks (1976). Nations were coded at five-year intervals from 1950 to 1975. In 1950, five of the seven military regimes were categorized as centralized party systems; forty-two of the seventy-five nonmilitary regimes were so categorized. In 1970, thirty-one of the thirty-three military regimes and sixty-six of the one hundred eight nonmilitary regimes had centralized party systems.

4 For a discussion of this expansion in Latin America, see Horowitz and Trimberger (1976).

5 Several of the recently independent countries have begun to make this shift. The uniqueness of the post-1966 countries is also relevant. For many of these nations, "becoming independent" was and is a completely different experience from that of previous nations, establishing seemingly qualitatively different relations with the original colonizing power. See Appendix B for the listing of the countries and their dates of independence.

6 The effectiveness of this mobilization varies across polities, but, in general, it seems that centralist regimes promote economic growth, especially among the poorer countries (see chaps. 6 and 7).

7 It could be argued that, given a highly developed educational system, regimes can mobilize without centralizing authority, causing a negative relation between educational expansion and centralization. This nevertheless would imply a much smaller effect of education on centralization than that predicted by previous lines of thought; it also would suggest more complicated analyses not explored here.

8 East and West Germany and Taiwan are classified as old countries. Figure 11.1 suggests that there may be three distinct environmental periods: before 1945; 1945 to about 1965; and after 1965. However, countries which gained independence after 1960 do not enter into the causal analyses, as noted below.

9 It should be noted that multiple regression analysis is not entirely appropriate to the analysis of dichotomized dependent variables, such as those studied here. More complex analyses, or complex transformations of such dependent variables, are somewhat more appropriate. But in the present situation, in which dependent variables are not dichotomized near 0% or 100%, multiple regression models are more likely to be accurate, and we use them for simplicity.

10 In the new nation subsample there are too few cases for the 1950–65 lag. Therefore only the 1960–75 lag is reported.

11 For the 1960–75 lag, the results for primary and secondary enrollments must be qualified by pointing out their high correlation with economic development. This may be depressing the estimated coefficients of these variables. It should, however, be noted that the multicollinearity for the 1950–65 lag and for the newer-nation subsample is much more reasonable, and essentially the same pattern of results is obtained.

12 In addition to ethnolinguistic fractionalization, we used religious pluralism and a scale combining the two indices. In no case were significant results found.

13. In addition to these results, Appendix C reports parallel analyses for dependent variables which tap the traditionally examined concept of a "stable participatory democracy."

TWELVE · Dependence, Government Revenue, and Economic Growth, 1955–70

Richard Rubinson

Within the context of dependency theory, a number of empirical cross-national studies have investigated the effects of international economic relationships on the economic growth of countries. Chase-Dunn demonstrated in chapter 8 that foreign investment and aid have negative effects on the rate of economic growth. Similar conclusions have been reached by Bornschier (1978) and Stoneman (1975). In chapters 9 and 10, Delacroix analyzed some effects of the composition of trade on economic growth. One conclusion which emerges from such studies is that the effects of trade on economic growth vary by the character of the commodity, while the effects of foreign investment and aid on the rate of economic growth are consistently negative (Bornschier, Chase-Dunn, and Rubinson 1978).

In attempting to understand the reasons for the effects of dependence on growth, it is important to separate the short-term and direct effects of dependence from its long-term and indirect effects. For example, while increased aid and foreign private investment likely have immediate positive effects on GNP, the long-term effects of such dependence operate to retard growth. The short-term effects occur because an influx of aid or foreign investment becomes the immediate capital to increase production and consequently economic growth. However, the long-term negative effects occur because such transactions alter the political and economic structure of a country in such a way as to retard growth. In explaining exactly why dependence has had a negative effect on growth, these studies suggest that the reasons lie in the ways that dependence affects the political and economic structure of a country. Among these structural changes which are presumed to occur as a consequence of dependence are changes in the relative economic and political positions of different classes, changes in the type of production, and changes in the structure and strength of the state.

While the studies reviewed above have demonstrated that there is a negative effect of economic dependence on economic growth, they have not attempted to study the intervening structural changes which are

This is a revised version of a paper which originally appeared in *Studies in Comparative International Development* 12 (1977): 3–28.

thought to produce this effect. This paper specifies this negative relationship between dependence and growth by studying the role of the strength of the state. We test the hypothesis that one of the ways that dependence affects economic growth is through its effects on the strength of the state. If the hypothesis is correct, dependence should have a negative effect on state strength, and state strength should have a positive effect on economic growth when dependence effects are controlled. The first section of the empirical analysis studies the effects of four types of economic dependence on government revenues, our measure of state strength. The second section of the analysis then proceeds to study the effects of government revenues on GNP, our measure of economic growth.

DEPENDENCE AND STATE STRENGTH: CONCEPTS AND MEASUREMENTS

Economic dependence refers to the degree to which a country is subject to economic factors controlled by foreign actors. Consequently, relationships of dependence are not features of underdeveloped economies only, but developed economies are also dependent, though the degree of dependency and its consequences may differ in developed and underdeveloped countries. Used in this way, dependence is a variable feature of *relationships* among units (not a feature of countries), and its effects must be judged empirically. It was one of the contributions of dependency theory, however, to argue that such economic interrelationships were also power relationships, and to hypothesize that their effects had been to relatively retard the rate of economic growth. The studies reviewed above explicitly tested that hypothesis, and the results showed that the effects of those relationships on the rate of economic growth were negative. Such studies need not be interpreted as "proving" or "disproving" dependency theory per se; rather, they should be seen as supporting the assertion that from 1950 to 1970, the greater the degree of foreign economic control, the lower the rate of economic growth. Our concern now is, given the findings of these negative effects, to investigate the hypothesis that state strength is one of the mechanisms by which dependence negatively affects economic growth.

We use measures of four types of dependency that have been employed in previous research. The first type of dependence we use is simply trade, measured as the value of trade per gross national product. Trade of commodities is one of the most basic ways in which countries are dependent on one another. Trade does imply some degree of external control, although trade relationships are often not asymmetrical. A measure which better characterizes asymmetry in trade relations is export-partner concentration, our second indicator of dependence. Export-partner concentration is the percentage of nation's total exports that goes to its largest export partner. To the extent that a country is dependent on one country for sale of its exports, then that exporting country is more subject to constraints imposed by its export partner, since the exporting country has fewer market alternatives (Galtung 1971). Analyses by Chase-Dunn (1975) show that export-partner concentration does have significant negative effects on growth in gross national product per capita, but that the volume of trade does not have such effects. These results emphasize the important point that it is not the volume of transactions per se which are important to consider, but rather the political and economic control of transactions which produce the negative effects of dependence on economic growth. The third and fourth measures of dependence, used by Chase-Dunn in chapter 8, are external public debt and debits on investment income.

State strength refers to the degree to which a state is able to control the activities of the population within its boundaries. Since physical force is an unstable means of control, strong states are those which have transformed their monopoly of physical violence into a stable set of authority relations which give to the state the rights of regulation and control over the activities of its population. Thus, the mark of a strong state is not the size of its army or the centralization of power in the hands of an oligarchy, but the degree to which the state has come to expropriate to itself the rights to control action, among the most important of which are the rights to regulate and control economic activity (see, for example, the papers in Tilly 1975). We measure state strength by government revenue as a percent of gross domestic product, as described in chapters 3 and 6.

There are several reasons why it is particularly important to study the role of the state in the interrelationships between dependence and economic development. First, it has been shown that the formation of strong, centralized states was crucially important to the development of the core countries within the world-system, and that which countries developed strong states and which ones developed weaker states was to some extent a function of the different types of economic dependencies which linked actors of different states (Wallerstein 1974a). Second, it is also clear that several cases of "late development" (for example Germany and Japan) were accomplished through aggressive state action combined with militarism (Moore 1966; Trimberger 1976). And third, in recent years there has been a new wave of state formation combining aggressive state action and militarism in many peripheral states; and this is occuring in precisely those states which are most dependent (Horowitz and Trimberger 1976). In order to begin to understand these recent events and to develop an explanation of state formation within the world system, then, it is necessary to study the interrelationships among economic dependence, state strength, and economic growth.

DEPENDENCE, STATE STRENGTH, AND ECONOMIC DEVELOPMENT
This section reviews the reasons that have been suggested as to why
dependence can be expected to have negative effects on the strength of
states, and why state strength has positive effects on economic growth.

Effects of Dependence on State Strength
The arguments that suggest that dependence negatively affects state
strength are based on three different processes: the process of center
formation, the process by which loans and aid are offered, and the
process of political leverage exerted by foreign-owned businesses.

The basic idea behind the process of center formation is that every
state consists of a coalition of dominant economic interests (Moore
1966). In highly dependent countries the dominant economic elites that
have traditionally developed are those whose primary interests have been
tied to foreign economic actors through mutual interests in the control
of production for export or through production based on foreign capital
(Furtado 1973; Girling 1973). The political interests of such groups
have tended to rest with maintaining little political interference in internal production in order to create a favorable climate for foreign investment and in limiting governmental interference in the economy (Horowitz and Trimberger 1976, p. 228). Demands on the government from
economic groups whose interests lie in the direction of political policies
which would promote indigenous as opposed to foreign-assisted development or in the direction of nationalization of foreign industry are suppressed. Also, states dominated by such types of economic interests tend
to be more able to resist demands for the expansion of social services
and welfare programs. Consequently, the nature and types of center
elites created by relations of dependency produce state structures which
fulfill a smaller range of political demands generated by their populations, and thus they produce weaker state structures.

The second process by which dependence negatively affects state
strength occurs through the particular ways in which foreign aid and
loans have been granted to countries. Hayter (1971) argues, for example, that the primary aid and lending agencies (IBRD, USAID, and
IMF) have policies which both encourage and force recipient countries
to favor private and nongovernmental forms of economic production.
Thus, such agencies use the leverage created by their control over funds
to promote private-sector as opposed to state-sector development. Consequently, such forms of economic dependency can be expected to have
negative effects on the degree of state strength.

The third process by which dependency effects state strength is a result of the fact that dependency often creates the presence of a
powerful group of foreign actors within the country. Such groups will
often be opposed to any increases in state authority over production,

since such increases imply ability to nationalize foreign firms, tax the repatriation of profits, replace foreign personnel with indigenous personnel, and constrain the operation of the foreign firms (Johnson 1972). Consequently, such groups attempt to use their economic leverage to prevent increases in political authority, and thus tend to negatively affect the strength of the state.[1]

Effects of State Strength on Economic Development

If the hypothesis is true that one of the ways that dependence affects economic growth is through its negative effects on state strength, then this implies that a strong state has positive effects on economic growth. There are several reasons for positing such effects, and these reasons are based on a renewed understanding of the important role that states have had in creating economic development in the capitalist world-economy (see, for example, Hobsbawm 1968; Moore 1966; Wallerstein 1974a).

First, strong states are effective mechanisms for protecting economic actors from the risks and uncertainties generated by the world market. They accomplish this task in part through the regulation of the economic production that occurs within their borders. For example, many of the poorest areas in Latin America today were at one time highly active centers of raw material production in the world economy. But when the demand for these materials declined, the capital and organization which exploited these resources were withdrawn (Frank 1972; Stein and Stein 1970). Strong states, however, are effective mechanisms for preventing such occurrences. They can erect barriers to prevent external control of production by forcing ownership into the hands of indigenous groups. They can regulate the flow of capital and profit to ensure that the gains of production are not withdrawn from the country but channeled into other economic activities within the national economy. And through trade and tariff policies they can stimulate a diversification of production. Thus strong states typically have elaborate rules and regulations controlling the production within their boundaries, and much political activity is directed toward controlling economic activity. Second, states are effective mechanisms for securing privileged access to resources and markets, including their own national markets. Economic actors engaged in producing consumption goods, for example, often attempt to influence the state to protect the home market from economic penetration of the manufactures of groups in other states. Similarly, groups attempt to influence the state to secure foreign markets as outlets for their goods and to secure a steady supply of the materials needed for production. Most of the trade and commercial policies of states are directed toward these two ends (Hobsbawm 1968). Third, states are effective mechanisms for organizing economic actors to work in concert in the world economy. States provide a means for pooling the resources of economic actors and achieve the benefits that large scale has in a market system. These benefits can be achieved either through advantage in direct competition or through control over prices.

The ability of states to function in these ways is a consequence of the strength of the state in relation to its own population and in relation to other states. A strong state structure, therefore, is one of the major means by which economic production in a country is organized and expanded. Consequently, if economic dependence does tend to reduce the strength of states, then we should expect that the effect of dependence on economic growth is negative, since states have a positive effect on growth. The next two sections empirically test these hypotheses.

EFFECTS OF DEPENDENCE ON GOVERNMENT REVENUE

The analyses are done by the method of panel analysis with the estimation by weighted least-squares as discussed in chapters 2 and 6. The countries in the analyses include all those which had data on the needed variables in 1955 and 1970.[2]

Table 12.1 shows the effects of the four measures of international economic dependence on government revenue. There are two sets of equations in table 12.1. The first four equations show the effects of the four measures of dependence on government revenue, controlling for the effects of government revenue at the initial point in time and population and gross national product at the initial point in time. The second set of equations adds the percentage of gross national product produced in the mining sector to these equations.

The first four equations show that trade and debits have small positive effects on government revenue, but the effects of neither variable are statistically significant.[3] According to the previous discussion, we expected that trade would have either a zero or positive effect, but we also expected that debits would have a negative effect. External public debt and partner concentration have their expected negative effects, but only the effect of partner concentration is statistically significant. At this point, the hypothesis that dependence has negative effects on government revenue is only weakly supported.

However, these results are altered when we include in the equations the percentage of gross national product in mining. We included the value of mining for two reasons. First, Chase-Dunn showed in chapter 8 that the value of mining interacts strongly with dependence measures, and therefore it should be controlled. Second, inspection of our raw data showed that the highly specialized oil-producing countries had scores on government revenue as a percentage of GNP which were either extremely high or which had extremely large percentage changes from 1955 to 1970. For example, in 1970 Saudi Arabia had government revenues which were 68% of its gross national product, which was

TABLE 12.1 Effects of Economic Dependence on Government Revenue, 1955–70[a]

Measure of Dependence	Independent Variables						
	Dependence Measure 1955	Gov. Rev. 1955	Popn. 1955	GNP 1955	Mining as % GNP 1955	R^2	Number of Cases
Total Trade	18.61 (1.03)	2.20* (3.55)	-0.06 (0.915)	14.35* (2.84)	...	.46	45
Partner Concentration	-37.41* (2.32)	2.13* (3.82)	-0.10 (1.64)	35.31* (3.42)	...	.51	45
External Public Debt	- 0.007 (1.26)	2.62 (4.61)	0.05 (0.347)	18.14* (2.95)	...	.47	35
Debits on Invest. Income	16.10 (1.22)	2.42* (4.21)	0.06 (.868)	16.70* (2.92)	...	.47	44
Total Trade	-3.02 (0.149)	2.34* (3.85)	0.07 (1.09)	17.25* (2.94)	0.09* (2.02)	.51	45
Partner Concentration	-32.92* (2.12)	2.03 (3.78)	0.10 (1.68)	32.59* (3.21)	0.09 (2.09)	.56	45
External Public Debt	-0.007 (1.36)	2.48* (4.54)	0.02 (1.68)	17.19* (2.93)	0.08* (2.10)	.53	39
Debits on Invest. Income	-38.9 (1.53)	2.03* (4.25)	-0.08 (1.26)	17.14* (2.92)	0.20* (2.48)	.54	44

*$p < .10$

a. Weighted least-squares estimates (unstandardized coefficients); t-scores in parentheses. Dependent variable in all equations is government revenue in 1970.

almost twice as high as the next largest figure for any country. And between 1955 and 1970 both Saudi Arabia and Iran doubled their scores on government revenue as a percentage of GNP. This 100% increase was much larger than the increase for any other country in the sample. Therefore, it is necessary to investigate the role of the value of mineral products produced (in which petroleum is included) in order to understand the interrelationship between dependence and government revenue.

The second set of equations in table 12.1 presents these results. In all four equations there are large, positive effects of mining on government revenue. We also note that the effects of both trade and debits become negative when mining is included. The effect of trade is very small and is essentially zero. The effect of debits, however, is both negative and statistically significant. Thus, our initial concern about the interaction of mining with dependence is demonstrated, since the inclusion of mining changes the effect of debits from positive to significantly negative. The effects of external public debt and partner concentration are not affected by the inclusion of mining. They both remain negative, with partner concentration being statistically significant and external public debt having a small negative effect. We also note here the strong positive effects of gross national product and the weak positive effects of population.

From table 12.1 we conclude that all three dependence measures have negative effects on government revenue and that mining has large positive effects. This table also demonstrates an interesting interaction between debits and specialization in mineral production. Debits represent profits made by foreign-owned firms. Without controlling for mining, we see that the effects of debits on government revenue are positive; but with mining controlled these effects become negative. Under the assumption that the effects of mining are really effects of petroleum, these findings demonstrate two well-supported facts: first, that there is a close and mutual interrelationship between the oil-exporting states and the foreign-owned oil companies, such that a significant amount of the profits from petroleum production accrue to those states (Tanzer 1969); and second, these findings suggest the unique position of oil as a commodity within the world economy. Because of this unique position of oil within the world economy, we will continue the analysis by excluding the two oil countries in the sample, Saudi Arabia and Iran. If our speculations are correct—that the effects of mining are basically just effects of oil—then we expect that once these two countries are excluded from the analysis, the effects of mining should disappear.

Table 12.1, then, presents the same two sets of equations as in table 12.1, except that the two oil countries are excluded from the sample. Inspection of these results confirms our speculations. Looking at the bottom set of equations, we see that mining, though still positive, is now very small and in no case is significant. Also, the effects of the four measures of dependence do not change when mining is included in the equations.

Inspecting the top four equations in table 12.2, we see that export-partner concentration continues to have significant negative effects on government revenue. The effect of external public debt, which had previously been weak and negative, is now negative and statistically significant. These two measures of dependence conform to the hypothesis. The effects of both trade and debits are now positive, but so small that they are essentially zero. This zero effect of trade was expected, but the zero effect of debits is contrary to the hypothesis.

The absence of any negative effects of debits is striking because previous studies of dependence have shown that this type of dependence has strong negative effects on the rate of economic growth. It is possible, however, that the absence of any effect of debits on government revenues might result from two opposing tendencies: the *negative* effects of the leverage exercised by foreign capital on the state, and a *positive* effect of foreign capital operating within a country having its profits taxed by the country.

TABLE 12.2   Effects of Economic Dependence on Government Revenue, 1955–70, Oil Countries Excluded[a]

Measure of Dependence	Independent Variables						
	Dependence Measure 1955	Gov. Rev. 1955	Popn. 1955	GNP 1955	Mining as % GNP 1955	R^2	Number of Cases
Total Trade	7.83 (0.416)	2.08* (3.73)	-0.10* (1.71)	22.72* (3.24)	...	.53	43
Partner Concentration	-26.18* (1.79)	1.98* (3.90)	-0.13* (2.20)	35.55* (3.56)	...	.56	43
External Public Debt	- 0.01* (1.90)	2.33* (4.04)	-0.04 (0.505)	27.18* (3.30)	...	.56	37
Debits on Invest. Income	7.77 (.270)	2.20* (4.23)	-0.10* (1.60)	22.95* (3.24)	...	.53	42
Total Trade	6.03 (.313)	2.12* (3.73)	-0.09* (1.85)	20.28 (3.06)	0.07 (.510)	.53	43
Partner Concentration	-27.01* (1.80)	1.99* (3.90)	-0.12* (1.99)	32.80* (3.44)	0.09 (0.738)	.57	43
External Public Dept	-0.01* (1.90)	2.35* (4.65)	-0.02 (0.315)	23.65* (3.16)	0.11 (0.819)	.57	37
Debits on Invest. Income	0.72 (0.033)	2.22* (4.22)	-0.09* (1.45)	20.37* (3.08)	0.09 (0.633)	.54	42

*$p < .10$

a. Weighted least–squares estimates (unstandardized coefficients); t–scores in parentheses. Dependent variable in all equations is government revenue in 1970.

This speculation is lent some plausibility when we consider that both export-partner concentration and external public debt have strong negative effects on government revenue. These two forms of dependence represent more external mechanisms of control. Debits represents a form of foreign control whose locus rests *within* the state. Consequently states do seem to have the ability to tax, at least somewhat, the profits on foreign investment, and thus the overall effect of debits on government revenue is zero (see Gilpin 1975 and Moran 1974 for a similar argument).

We now pursue the question of whether these relationship differ in developed and underdeveloped countries. Because there are too few cases to split the sample and run separate analyses for developed and underdeveloped countries, we investigate this question through an analysis of covariance design. Table 12.3 presents these results: The equations in table 12.3 are the same as those in table 12.2 except that an interaction term is included for each type of dependence. This interaction term allows us to test whether the effects of dependence on government revenue are different in developed and underdeveloped countries. This term in the first equation in the table is labeled "Trade (Rich) 1955." This term is constructed by assigning to each of the countries in the richer half of the sample (GNP per capita in 1955 greater than $300) their score on trade, and assigning to each country in the poorer half of the sample (GNP per capita in 1955 is equal to or less than $300) a score of zero. The inclusion of this interaction term *and* the linear term Trade, 1955 allows us to test the hypothesis that the effects of trade differ in developed and underdeveloped countries. The dummy variable representing the main effect of the dichotomized wealth variable was included in the equation but not presented in the tables. If the effect of the interaction term Trade (Rich) 1955 is not significant, then there

TABLE 12.3   Effects of Economic Dependence on Government Revenue, 1955–70, with Interaction Term for Richer and Poorer Countries[a]

Measure of Dependence	Dependence Measure 1955	Gov. Rev. 1955	Popn. 1955	GNP 1955	Interaction Term[b]	R^2	Number of Cases
		Independent Variables					
Total Trade	-9.22 (0.41)	2.04* (3.77)	-0.06 (0.96)	21.85* (3.41)	21.50 (1.25)	.55	43
External Public Debt	-0.012* (2.13)	2.27* (4.70)	-0.05 (0.07)	26.47* (4.56)	0.006 (1.02)	.57	37
Partner Concentration	-30.63* (1.80)	1.91 (3.71)	-0.12* (1.97)	25.08* (4.21)	7.75 (0.519)	.57	43
Debits on Invest.Income	-12.09 (0.35)	2.15* (4.24)	-0.09* (1.51)	22.99* (3.94)	34.90 (0.93)	.54	42

*$p < .10$

a. Weighted least-squares estimates (unstandardized coefficients); t-scores in parentheses. Dependent variable in all equations is government revenue in 1970.

b. Interaction terms are explained in the text; each is based on the dependence measure used for each equation.

TABLE 12.4   Effects of Government Revenue and Economic Dependence
             on GNP, 1955–70[a]

Measure of Dependence	Independent Variables					
	Dependence Measure 1955	GNP 1955	Popn. 1955	Government Revenue 1955	R^2	Number of Cases
Total Trade	−1.27 (1.03)	2.85* (15.13)	−0.002 (0.732)	0.03 (0.742)	.92	43
External Public Debt	−0.005 (1.33)	2.36* (13.46)	−0.002 (0.746)	0.03 (0.137)	.91	37
Partner Concentration	−1.28 (1.32)	3.37* (17.46)	−0.004 (0.972)	0.004 (0.123)	.93	43
Debits on Invest.Income	−1.60 (1.02)	2.76* (15.03)	−0.003 (0.719)	0.01 (0.378)	.92	42

*$p < .10$

a. Weighted least-squares estimates (unstandardized coefficients); t-scores in
   parentheses. Dependent variable in all equations is GNP in 1970.

is no interaction effect, and the hypothesis of differential effect is not
supported.

In table 12.3 and the subsequent tables we no longer include the
mining term, since once we eliminate the oil countries, mining has no
effect. In table 12.3 we see that none of the interaction terms is significant. This indicates that there is no significant difference between the
effects of any of the dependence measures on government revenue in
the richer or poorer half of the sample of countries in this analysis.

To summarize these findings, we have shown that once oil countries
are excluded from the analysis there are significant negative effects of
export-partner concentration and external public debt on government
revenues in the period 1955 to 1970, while there are no effects of the
volume of trade or debits on government revenues. Further, we found
no differences between richer and poorer countries in these relationships.

EFFECTS OF GOVERNMENT REVENUE AND DEPENDENCE ON GNP
We now proceed to test the second part of the general hypothesis: the
effect of government revenue on gross national product during this
period of 1955 to 1970. We also include the dependence measures in
the equations because we know that they affect gross national product

and interact with government revenue. The analysis proceeds as before. The two oil countries continue to be omitted.

Table 12.4 shows that the effects of all the measures of dependence are negative, although only the effects of external public debt and partner concentration are statistically significant. In chapter 8, Chase-Dunn has shown that these effects are larger when a larger sample of countries is used. The absence of a significant effect of debits is most likely due to the inclusion of government revenue in the equation. This is a plausible interpretation since we saw previously the large amount of interaction between debits, government revenue, and mining.

Table 12.4 also shows that there is no effect of government revenue in any of the equations. All effects are in the predicted positive direction, but their size is extremely small and none are significant.

We now proceed by investigating the effects of government revenue in the richer and poorer countries. This analysis proceeds as before. Table 12.5 presents these effects. In this table we see that in each equation the interaction term of Government Revenue (Rich) 1955 is significant, and that the interaction terms are in each case stronger than the straight linear term, Government Revenue 1955. This is evidence that the effects of government revenue on gross national product differ

TABLE 12.5   Effects of Government Revenue and Economic Dependence on GNP, 1955–70, with Interaction Term for Richer and Poorer Countries[a]

Measure of Dependence	Dependence Measure 1955	GNP 1955	Popn. 1955	Government Revenue 1955	Interaction Term 1955[a]	R^2	Number of Cases
			Independent Variables				
Total Trade	-0.50 (0.479)	2.98* (15.56)	-0.006 (1.30)	0.076 (1.31)	-0.047 (1.34)	.95	43
External Public Debt	-0.005 (1.31)	3.21* (16.31)	-0.001 (0.815)	0.055 (1.18)	-0.052 (1.40)	.95	37
Partner Concentration	-1.32 (1.37)	3.52* (17.45)	-0.001* (1.60)	0.042 (0.98)	-0.049 (1.39)	.93	43
Debits on Invest. Income	0.17 (0.22)	2.89* (15.01)	-0.001 (1.36)	0.063 (1.42)	-0.058* (1.60)	.94	42

*$p < .10$

a. Weighted least-squares estimates (unstandardized coefficients); t-scores in parentheses. Interaction term is explained in text.

TABLE 12.6   Regression Estimates of the Effects of Government Revenue on GNP for Richer and Poorer Countries[a]

| | Measure of Dependence Included in the Equation | | | |
Type of Country	Total Trade	External Public Debt	Partner Concentration	Debits on Invest. Income
Richer Countries	0.29	0.033	0.007	0.005
Poorer Countries	0.076	0.055	0.042	0.063

a. Unstandardized coefficients.

significantly for richer and poorer countries. This finding has been discussed above in chapter 7.

The summary table, table 12.6, shows the effects of government revenue in the richer and poorer samples for each different measure of dependence. From this table we see that the effects of government revenue on gross national product are much larger in the poorer than in the richer sample of countries. For example, the effect of government revenue in poor countries in the equation with external public debt is 1.6 times the size of the effect in richer countries. For the equation with partner concentration the difference is 6 times; and for the equation with debits the difference is 12½ times its effect in rich countries.[4]

The consistency of these results across the four equations and the large size of the effects lead us to conclude that this is an important effect. What these results show is that government revenue positively affects gross national product during this period in both rich and poor countries, but that its effect in poorer countries is quite large, while its effect in richer countries is small. Thus, we can conclude that the second part of the hypothesis is also supported, but that its effects are much stronger in poorer than richer countries.

DISCUSSION

The purpose of this chapter was to attempt to specify the negative effects of dependence on economic growth by focusing on the role of state strength, as measured by government revenue. The basic idea investigated was that part of the reason dependence negatively affects gross national product is that dependence lowers government revenue and government revenue positively affects gross national product. Consequently, this study can be viewed as one attempt to isolate one of the mechanisms by which dependence affects development.

In general we can conclude that the hypothesis was borne out. We found that during the period 1955–70 export-partner concentration and external public debt decreased government revenue, but that debits on investment income had no effect. We suggested why debits had no effect, but this issue requires explicit study. We also found that these effects on government revenue of the different types of dependence did not differ significantly by levels of wealth. In addition we found that government revenue did have positive effects on gross national product, and that these effects are significantly related to levels of wealth. That is, while we found no evidence of interaction by level of wealth for the effects of dependence on government revenue, we did find significant interaction effects by level of wealth for the effect of government revenue on gross national product. And this interaction effect showed that the positive effects of government revenue on gross national product are much stronger for poorer than for richer countries. Consequently, we can conclude that for poorer countries, the negative effect of dependence on government revenue is one important mechanism affecting their relative rates of growth; while for richer countries we can conclude that the negative effects of dependence on government revenue do not exert a substantial effect on their relative rates of growth. In sum, then, the effect of government revenue was an important mechanism in accounting for the negative relationship between dependence and gross national product between 1950 and 1970, but this mechanism was more important in poorer than in richer countries.

The finding that government revenue has a much stronger effect on gross national product in poorer than in richer countries is not unexpected. This finding, however, should not be interpreted to mean that state strength has been relatively unimportant to the development of core countries within the world, for there is abundant historical evidence that the relative strength of states has been one of the major mechanisms for determining the relative economic position of countries within the world system. The strength of states in the core countries of the world system has been well established for a long time, and this is because there has developed a coalition of interest between these states and the major economic interests within these countries. Thus, our finding means only that in the 1955–70 period the relative differences of state strength *within* the more developed countries are not that important for economic growth. In peripheral countries, however, state structures have been historically weaker, more unstable, and often less allied with the dominant economic interests within the country. Consequently, relative differences of state strength within these countries were still important for economic development in the period from 1955 to 1970. These results, then, are consistent with the view that one of the necessary conditions for any peripheral country to develop is an aggressive national mobilization, a strategy that requires a strong state.

NOTES

1 The Brazilian model of development since 1964 is one instance in which a high level of economic dependence goes along with a relatively strong state and rapid economic growth (Evans 1972; Furtado 1973).

2 The following countries were included: Argentina, Australia, Belgium, Bolivia, Brazil, Burma, Canada, Chile, Colombia, Costa Rica, Denmark, Dominican Republic, Ecuador, El Salvador, Finland, France, Greece, Guatemala, Haiti, Honduras, India, Indonesia, Iran, Ireland, Israel, Italy, Japan, Mexico, Netherlands, New Zealand, Nicaragua, Norway, Pakistan, Panama, Paraguay, Peru, Philippines, Portugal, Saudi Arabia, South Africa, South Korea, Sri Lanka, Sweden, Thailand, Turkey, United Arab Republic, United Kingdom, United States, West Germany.

3 Throughout this paper we use significance levels of .10 and .20 with a one-tailed test.

4 These differences are computed from table 12.7. For EXT, .055 is 1.6 times larger than .033; for PART, .042 is 6 times larger than .007; and for DEBIT, .063 is 12.6 times larger than .005.

THIRTEEN · The Ideology of Expanding State Authority in National Constitutions, 1870–1970

John Boli-Bennett

Working within what was described in chapter 1 as the institutional view of world-system social change, this chapter examines national constitutions as political ideology. My concern is the ideology of state authority —that is, the images of the power and authority of their states presented to the world system by national societies. I am much less concerned with the actual power or authority of the state, topics explored in most of the other chapters. The chapters dealing with state corporateness (chaps. 5, 11, and 14) most closely resemble this chapter in their concern for the institutionalization of the state in society, but they focus on the degree to which ideology depicts the state as a unitary whole while I investigate the degree to which ideology depicts the state as having jurisdiction and control over society. The chapter also differs from others in this volume in that it is more historical and descriptive, analyzing the 1870–1970 period with cross-sectional data rather than using panel-analysis methods for the 1950–70 period. I report the results of coding all national constitutions at twenty-year intervals over the longer period to generate indices of the extent of state jurisdiction as it is officially represented in constitutions. I describe the changes in these indices and offer a world-system perspective for understanding them.

STATE CONSTITUTIONAL AUTHORITY AS WORLD-SYSTEM IDEOLOGY
Constitutions embody three forms of ideology. First, they describe the formal authority of the state, defining the areas of social life over which the state has jurisdiction, the demands that the state can make on citizens and those that citizens can make on the state, and the types of mechanisms the state may use to carry out its functions. In other words, constitutions reflect the legitimacy of the state, expressing the degree to which prevailing political ideology ascribes authority to the state. For example, if the constitution says the state has authority over education, then prevailing political ideology accepts state action in the educational domain. "Prevailing political ideology" here refers primarily to the political outlook of the major political forces (parties, interest groups,

classes, and so on) whose power struggles result in the complex compromises that eventually comprise a constitution. The ideology of the general citizenry is much less clearly reflected in constitutions.

Second, constitutions are prescriptive. They express not only the already established authority of the state but the authority that the state is obliged to establish in the future. Some of the constitutional compromises that emerge from political negotiating constitute directives to the state concerning hitherto autonomous areas of social life to which it should expand its jurisdiction. For example, if the constitution says the state has jurisdiction over health care, then political forces agree (but not without dissent) that the state should hereafter begin to operate health insurance programs or administer health care itself. The constitution may also prescribe intensification of state activity in areas already under its authority, or it may authorize the development of new mechanisms for implementing state control. Here again, constitutions reflect more the ideology of major political actors than the ideology of the public, whose position is always relatively uncrystallized on future activities of the state.

Third, there is what initially appears to be the more "purely" ideological character of constitutions. Constitutions depict images that dominant political forces wish to project to the world. For reasons explored below, these images must conform to certain generally recognized features of the world system's conception of the state. At any point in history there is a conception of what it means to be a state and what the minimal obligations of the state are—a *definition* of the state, as it were—that is embedded in the prevailing political ideology and practice of the world system. Historically this conception has reflected primarily the nature of the state in the center, or core, of the world system, but important developments outside the core (in particular, the rise of an autonomous bloc of states dominated by communist parties) have had great impact on the conception. Major political actors in both central and peripheral countries are sensitive to this conception and must compromise with it as well as with each other.

This third aspect of constitutions, as externally oriented ideology that must conform to considerable degree to an established world ideology, is not "purely" ideological. I argue that *the third aspect subsumes the other two.* The ideology supporting state authority is a global phenomenon that is largely independent of, and strongly shapes, particular national processes. The degree to which the public and major political forces accept state jurisdiction over various areas of social life is rather uniform throughout the world. The kinds of programs and new areas of jurisdiction prescribed for future state action are rather standard in all types of countries, whether rich or poor, central or peripheral. We observe great uniformity and standardization in these domains because the ideology of state authority develops at a transnational level and "diffuses" throughout the system very rapidly.

The world ideology of state authority, like many other features of the twentieth-century world, is "progressive" in the sense that it calls for continual expansion or growth of state authority. It calls for an augmentation of state jurisdiction over society and citizens that, like economic growth, population, and pollution, appears to follow an upwardly accelerating curve.

The world ideology affects the internal politics of subunits (countries) in the world system by a large number of mechanisms. Consider the following three examples. The world ideology of state authority strongly influences mass ideology and conditions the public to expect more of the state than it can deliver. The public learns of new programs designed to benefit populations in other countries through the world communications network and it generally tends more to desire the supposed benefits than to consider the political and economic details involved in implementation of the programs. Thus, the public everywhere demands more and more aid from the state, implicitly according expanded authority to the state in the process.

Second, at a more concrete level, states and other organizations in core nations often use their loan and investment policies to impose constraints reflecting the world system conception of the state on peripheral states that have wavered from this conception. The International Monetary Fund and the World Bank, for example, frequently demand orthodox financial accounting, more vigorous supervision of development programs, more detailed national plans, and the like, as conditions for the granting of major loans. Third, along this same line, multinational corporations may insist on such things as better state control of labor, more state-initiated development of transportation systems, or state-financed housing for newly urbanized factory workers as conditions on investment. States must behave like states, or at least put on a show of behaving like states, if they are to participate fully in the world system. This principle applies to states in the core as well as to those in the periphery.

Below I present cross-national evidence that constitutions reflect a transnational ideological process. I make three main points: (1) State constitutional authority has greatly expanded in the past hundred years. (2) State constitutional authority is largely independent of state power, which has increased in a fashion parallel to the increase in state constitutional authority. (3) State constitutional authority is largely independent of variations in national social and economic organization. The evidence supporting these points strongly suggests that the ideology supporting state authority does not respond primarily to national characteristics and processes. Instead, it responds to characteristics of the world system as a whole and the demands the world system places on its national subunits.

CODING STATE AUTHORITY FROM CONSTITUTIONS

The format of most national constitutions consists of three sections, usually in the following order, that enumerate (a) rights of citizens, (b) the formal structure of the state as an organization and the areas of social life over which it has jurisdiction, and (c) duties of citizens vis-à-vis the state. Each of these sections provides a meaningful index of state authority. Some discussion of rights is warranted before explaining the coding system applied to constitutions.

The usual view holds that constitutional rights of individuals represent limitations on the state. Rights, we believe, stand as barriers to state action. This view is naive. Constitutional rights are *citizen* rights; they inhere not in persons but in citizens, that is, persons who stand in a particular relation to the state. Following Marshall (1964), Barker (1944), and Duchacek (1973), my view is that individual rights are defined only in accordance with the ideological commitment that the state must protect, guarantee, or satisfy those rights. As Barker (1944) puts it, "Every right and duty implies a corresponding 'service'; and the more the state multiplies rights and duties, the more it multiplies the necessary services of its ministering officials (p. 3)." Emphasis should be placed on the multiplication of rights and duties *by the state*. Rights do not spring spontaneously into being with the creation of the "modern" individual. They develop in political processes centered on the state, and the more "positive" rights of the twentieth century (see below) are more the creations of the state itself than they are limitations placed on the state by other political forces. Citizen duties, on the other hand, more clearly represent areas of state jurisdiction, defining the precise claims that the state may make on citizens in its management of society.

In order that I might capture fully the constitutional information describing state authority, I studied a large number of constitutions written between 1780 and 1970 to compile a list of every item appearing in any constitution in each of the categories (a) through (c) above. This process produced a total of thirty-eight citizen-rights items, including the more negative rights familiar to American readers (rights that restrain the state: association, speech, press freedom, due process) as well as the many positive rights clearly signifying state jurisdiction over citizens: rights to a home, welfare and social security, equal wages for equal work, health care, and so on. There are fifty-six items representing areas of social life over which the state may have jurisdiction, ranging from agriculture and banking to drugs and alcohol, marriage and the family, labor, national resources, tourism, transportation, and so on. Citizen duties comprise ten items, including the duties to raise or educate children, pay taxes, defend the country, and work.

I also coded a fourth category of forty-five items that include all of the technical mechanisms available to the state to implement its programs. Examples are the state budget, censorship, a civil service, emergency powers, eminent domain, nationalization of economic sectors, national planning and taxation. A full list of all of these items is given in the appendix.

Most of the items were coded (1) if present, (0) if absent. For a subset of the state powers items (category b) a more complex scale with a range from 0 to 3 was used. This scale is explained in detail in Boli-Bennett (1976a); it assigns a higher score in proportion to the extensiveness of state control over a social area. Items for which this scale was used are marked by a (3) in the appendix. Similar scales were used for a few other items; the maximum score each item could receive is given in parentheses (for example, elastic clause [2], welfare [4]).

I created three summary indices from these 149 items by summing the scores for subsets of the individual items. The summary indices will be referred to as (a) citizen rights index (the sum of the thirty-eight rights items); (b) state jurisdiction index (the sum of both the fifty-six social area items and the forty-five implementing mechanism items); (c) citizen duties index (the sum of the ten duties items). These three indices of state authority are closely interrelated, with the correlations among them averaging .50 for the 1870–1970 period and ranging from a low of .19 to a high of .69. Most of the correlations fall between .45 and .65.

The coding schedule was applied to the constitutions in force in all independent countries of the world at twenty-year intervals between 1870 and 1970, that is, all of the constitutions in force in 1870; all of the constitutions in force in 1890, taking into account changes since 1870; all of the constitutions in force in 1910; and so on. A total of 419 constitutions were coded.[1] Table 13.1 shows the number of independent countries and the number of constitutions in force for each of the six coding dates.

STATE CONSTITUTIONAL AUTHORITY, 1870–1970:
RESULTS AND INTERPRETATION
Expansion of State Authority in the World as a Whole
Table 13.2 presents the means for all countries at twenty-year intervals between 1870 and 1970 of the constitutional authority indices. In the upper half of the table are the results for several typical individual items. Note that several of the items have a maximum value greater than unity, as indicated in parentheses. In the lower half of the table are the results for the three summary indices. These are reported for both the entire set

of countries and for a panel consisting of only those countries that were independent by 1870 and remained independent through 1970.

Consider the upper half first. Constitutions increasingly expand state authority in these areas: the means for all items rise sharply over the

TABLE 13.1 Number of Independent Countries and Constitutions, 1870–1970[a]

	1870	1890	1910	1930	1950	1970
Independent Countries	47	51	56	68	82	142
Constitutions	39	44	50	64	81	141

a. A full list of sources of constitutions is given in Boli–Bennett (1976).

TABLE 13.2 Means of Selected Individual Items and Summary Indices of State Constitutional Authority, 1870–1970[a]

	1870	1890	1910	1930	1950	1970
Individual Items						
Right to economic pursuits (2)[b]	0.38	0.45	0.46	0.57	1.04	1.16
Right to social security (1)	0.04	0.02	0.02	0.06	0.24	0.37
State control of general economy (3)	0.30	0.24	0.36	0.81	1.35	1.47
State control of culture and sports (3)	0.04	0.02	0.04	0.16	0.60	0.60
State-directed national planning (2)	0	0	0	0.03	0.32	0.59
Duty to receive education (2)	0.21	0.55	0.66	0.89	1.17	1.04
Summary Indices						
Citizen Rights (57)[b]						
All cases	14.0	15.0	15.8	18.9	24.7	28.1
Independent by 1870 only	14.0	15.2	16.8	19.5	26.2	28.8
State Jurisdiction (160)						
All cases	25.6	26.7	29.1	35.8	49.4	46.2
Independent by 1870 only	25.3	27.3	29.1	37.4	48.2	51.3
Citizen Duties (16)						
All cases	1.40	1.92	2.07	2.31	3.92	3.82
Independent by 1870 only	1.36	1.84	1.96	2.44	4.41	4.80
Number of countries, all cases	47	51	56	68	82	142
Number of countries independent by 1870 only	44	44	44	44	44	44

a. For independent countries only.

b. Maximum values given in parentheses.

period, by at least 200%. The increases are rather small until 1930. Between 1930 and 1950, however, they rise sharply, showing the impact of the depression and World War II. Most of the total increase in the means occurs in this interval. We also see that some of the particular rights or state actions were not "invented" until the 1930s; the right to social security and state-directed national planning have means at or near 0 until 1930 and then increase greatly. State control of culture and sports shows the same result.

The same observations apply to the lower half of the table. For all cases at each time the citizen rights index shows only a modest increase between 1870 and 1930, then jumps sharply upward to 1970. The breadth of rights of citizens expands greatly over the entire period, indicating that the ideology supporting state authority to manage the affairs of citizens, as well as the range of claims citizens could in theory make on the state, is much greater in 1970 than a century earlier. I emphasize that this result obtains even though this period is one of very extensive state formation. The number of states tripled, from 47 to 142, over the period, yet constitutions continually expanded state authority.

Both the state jurisdiction and citizen duties indices follow this pattern. While they show a distinct leveling between 1950 and 1970, the plateau they reach is very high compared to state constitutional authority in 1870. By 1970 the typical state has jurisdiction over a much broader range of social areas and it possesses more implementing mechanisms. Citizens have more duties vis-à-vis the state, in correspondence to their increased rights. As the correlations between the rights and duties indicators are generally high, the two appear to be only partly separable.

If we consider only those states independent by 1870 (essentially Western Europe, Latin and North America, and a few ancient empire states elsewhere) we find that the increases in the three indices of state authority closely parallel those for the entire set of states. State constitutional authority expands practically uniformly in both the older, politically more "developed" states and in the expanding set of all states. This result will be amplified later.

Independence of State Constitutional Authority from State Power
Table 13.3 shows that state authority is only weakly, and negatively, related to state power, so that the expansion of state authority is not a simple reflection of the expansion of state power. The table presents zero-order correlations among the three indices of state authority and two measures of state power. These measures, consisting of three-year averages around each date of analysis, are the following:
Government Revenue as a Proportion of National Income (GR/NI).
This is a direct measure of the degree of state control over national

economic resources, and by extension we can interpret it as a more general measure of the degree of state control over society. It reflects not the ideology of state control but the observable effectiveness of efforts to implement that control, and it is the best available measure of this concept (see chap. 12). It is taken from Banks (1971), Clark (1957), and Mulhall (1892, 1903). Data from Mulhall for the 1870–90 period must be considered only very approximate.

Government Revenue per Capita (GRPC). While not conceptually adequate as a measure of state control because it is so highly confounded with the expansion of economic exchange, this very rough measure has the one virtue of being available for nearly all cases over the entire period. Taken from Banks (1971), it is used for illustrative purposes only.

TABLE 13.3 Correlations among Indices of State Constitutional Authority and State Power,[a] and Means for Indicators of State Power, 1870–1970

	Correlation Coefficients					
	1870	1890	1910	1930	1950	1970
State Power: Government Revenue/National Income with:						
Citizen Rights	.28	-.02	-.48**	-.10	-.09	-.15
State Jurisdiction	-.47**	-.34	-.43**	.13	-.14	-.09
Citizen Duties	-.63**	-.19	.20	-.34**	-.04	-.13
Number of Cases	15	18	23	26	56	112
State Power: Government Revenue Per Capita with:						
Citizen Rights	.07	-.18	-.62***	-.18	-.28**	-.29***
State Jurisdiction	-.02	-.04	-.30**	-.14	-.19	-.08
Citizen Duties	-.36**	-.39***	-.49***	-.32***	-.22**	-.19**
Number of Cases	38	42	49	54	65	132

	Means for Indicators of State Power					
Gov. Rev./National Inc. (%)	9.45	10.0	11.5	14.6	17.7	24.3
Number of Cases	16	19	23	26	56	112
Gov. Rev. per Capita[b]	13.50	21.31	26.81	43.57	61.44	106.00
Number of Cases	41	46	51	55	65	132

** p < .05

*** p < .01

a. Pearson zero-order coefficients. Countries without constitutions excluded; data available for GR/NI for less than half the countries, 1870–1930.

b. In constant 1947–49 U.S. dollars.

Means for the two measures are given in the lower half of table 13.3, where we observe substantial increases in both. Government revenue per capita increases by a factor of eight, with the rate of increase fairly uniform for each twenty-year period. Government revenue as a proportion of national income approximately doubles, following a pattern not unlike that of the indices of state authority. The degree of effective state power has expanded considerably.

The upper half of the table shows the key results. The correlations among the indices of state authority and the indicators of state power are generally small throughout the period, and most of them are negative. Only in 1910 are more than two of the six correlations significant. Thus the ideology of state authority, as expressed in constitutions, is clearly *not* positively related to effective state power; if anything, the relationship is weakly negative. We cannot accept the claim that the ideology of state authority simply reflects expanding state power ("might making right"); other processes must operate here.

Independence of State Authority from National Characteristics
Table 13.4 presents zero-order correlations among the three indices of state constitutional authority and a number of measures of national economic and social organization. Details on these measures are given in chapter 6 of this volume, with the exception of the technical development index. This variable is the result of a factor analysis of a number of measures of industrialization and economic wealth, including steel production, miles of railroad line, national income per capita, proportion of children in primary schools, and urbanization. Details of its construction are given in Boli-Bennett (1976a). All of its components have high to very high loadings on the factor, and I interpret it as a rough but meaningful indicator of the general level of technical development.

Table 13.4 shows that state constitutional authority is not closely related to national economic and social characteristics. Most of the statistically significant correlations are negative, not positive, the same pattern seen in table 13.3. That is, wealthier, more highly urbanized, more highly technically developed countries having more pervasive educational systems tend to have *less* expanded constitutional depictions of state authority. For both the citizen rights and state jurisdiction indices, even the significant correlations are substantively too small to account for much of the variation in state constitutional authority. Only the citizen duties index shows fairly consistent significant results, and these are negative and decline in magnitude over the period. The ideology of state authority thus appears to be somewhat more highly developed in the less wealthy, less urbanized, and less industrial countries.

POLITICAL IDEOLOGY IN THE WORLD SYSTEM AND STATE CONSTITUTIONAL AUTHORITY

What, then, gives rise to the widespread expansion of state constitutional authority in the past hundred years? And how can we account for the unexpected finding that state constitutional authority is moderately greater in the periphery of the world system than in the core? In light of the perspective that constitutions are adaptations to the political ideology of the world system and that they reflect the impact of world political ideology on national political forces, I offer the following observations.

TABLE 13.4   Correlations among Indices of State Authority and Indicators of National Economic and Social Organization[a]

	1870	1890	1910	1930	1950	1970
Citizen Rights Index with:						
Urbanization	−.11	−.25	−.36***	−.17	.01	−.14**
	(38)	(42)	(48)	(59)	(74)	(135)
Technical Development Index	−.39***	−.54***	−.52***	−.25**	−.10	−.13
	(37)	(41)	(45)	(48)	(70)	(134)
National Income/Cap	.21	.10	−.03	−.18	−.15	−.24***
	(15)	(18)	(23)	(30)	(61)	(113)
Primary Education Ratio	−.22	−.39***	−.36***	−.06	.01	−.04
	(16)	(41)	(45)	(55)	(75)	(132)
State Jurisdiction Index with:						
Urbanization	.09	.11	.03	.12	−.09	.20***
	(38)	(42)	(48)	(59)	(74)	(135)
Technical Dev. Index	−.30**	−.26**	−.12	.16	.07	.35***
	(37)	(41)	(45)	(48)	(70)	(134)
National Income/Cap	.46**	.52	.24	−.15	−.19	−.03
	(15)	(18)	(23)	(30)	(61)	(113)
Primary Education Ratio	−.17	−.23	−.17	.04	.17	.27***
	(16)	(41)	(45)	(55)	(75)	(132)
Citizens Duties Index with:						
Urbanization	−.44***	−.52***	−.50***	−.28**	−.15	.06
	(38)	(42)	(48)	(59)	(74)	(135)
Tech. Dev. Index	−.43***	−.45***	−.37***	−.28**	−.23**	.11
	(37)	(41)	(45)	(48)	(70)	(134)
Primary Education Ratio	−.25	−.38***	−.28***	−.17	.02	−.01
	(16)	(41)	(45)	(55)	(75)	(132)

** p <.05
*** p <.01

a.   Pearson zero-order coefficients; number of cases in parentheses.

The general expansion of state constitutional authority reflects in large part the competitive nature of the state system. States serve as vehicles for status competition among political and economic elites (see Wallerstein 1960). Status striving is, above all, ideological competition: states gain status for what is believed about what they do, not simply for what they do per se. Elites try to establish convincing ideological images of the power and authority of the state by rewriting constitutions so they conform to world ideological standards. Such ideologically motivated revisions are relatively easy to make, in contrast to the effort required actually to implement the ideology.

The competitive state system is anarchic and multicentered. As chapter 17 discusses at greater length, the absence of an effective world state and the relative decentralization of the world system (Boli-Bennett 1976a) serve to heighten the general level of competition in the system and to intensify the legitimacy of states. As it were, the demand for a higher level of political integration (a world state) to cope with the high levels of economic and institutional integration reinforces the nation-state's legitimacy as the only available, albeit inadequate, substitute.

As part of the state competitive process, national elites generate and circulate the world ideology of state authority primarily through two mechanisms. First, future political elites frequently study abroad, usually in core countries, or they study under local faculties who were trained abroad or are highly involved in world-system ideological developments. Thus their training is highly structured by world ideology, one of whose most universal elements is acceptance of the state as an indispensable problem-solving mechanism. Hence very few future members of elites express, at the end of their studies, a commitment to anarchy; the very word invokes images of chaos in world ideology. Second, elites are highly susceptible to demonstration effects, copying each other's commitment to new social programs or enforcement procedures rather readily. They tend, once again, to express their ideological acceptance of such activities whether or not they lead to state action (see Waterston 1965 on national planning).

The ideology of the modern world system contains two additional, apparently contradictory, elements that further strengthen the authority of the state: individualism and socialism. The collapse of traditional society and weakening of primordial identity sources brought on by technical development creates gaps in people's ability to define themselves in relation to the social world. The gaps are filled by the ideology of individualism, which makes a virtue of the necessity to build self-directed identities consciously (see Riesman, Glazer, and Denny 1950). At the same time, socialism in various Marxist, Maoist, and populist guises has become the dominant political ideology (Aron 1957; Acton 1957). As Ellul (1968) has put it, the right of today is where the left of forty or fifty years ago was. The link between the primacy of the individual (individualism) and the submission of the individual to the common whole (socialism) is provided by the ideology of citizenship (see the discussion above on citizen rights). The stronger the individual, the more claims the citizen can make on the state. Conversely, the state as the new corporate symbol can demand more of the citizen as each individual becomes stronger and better able to cope with modern society. This two-way process adds considerable legitimacy to the state.

In sum, the general expansion of state constitutional authority is due to the competitive state system, the weakness of the world state, circulation of elites and elite ideologies, and the ideology of citizenship as the link between individualism and socialism. On the second issue, the greater expansion of state constitutional authority in the periphery than in the core, three points are relevant. To some extent the periphery overcompensates ideologically for its relatively weak implementation of state power—as chapter 12 shows, at least in recent decades the implemented power of the state is greater in the technically advanced, more central nations. What cannot be done in practice tends to be more expansively described in ideology. The poorer, less industrialized peripheral nations also emphasize the urgency of rapid development more strongly than core nations, for they have farther to go to catch up in the competition. They have fewer and weaker nonstate organizations to call on to mobilize the development process, and many of these organizations are subsidiaries of core-nation corporations that are considered imperialist and untrustworthy. The state therefore becomes the most acceptable vehicle for accomplishing national goals.

Finally, the periphery may expand state constitutional authority more than the core because it is moving toward genuinely stronger states in the future. Ours is a world in continual disequilibrium; the fit between ideology and practice is generally very poor. This fit may improve if peripheral states continue their present trend of increasing their organizational power at a faster rate than core states. We have already seen numerous examples of greatly expanded state power in peripheral states, usually coming on the heels of revolution (the Soviet Union, China, Cuba, Algeria), and this may become a general phenomenon.

Table 13.5 gives a more detailed look at the relative expansion of state constitutional authority in major sectors of the world system. Three sectors are identified, demarcated here in terms of centrality in the world economy: the core countries, those controlling 3% or more of world trade; peripheral countries, those controlling less than 1% of world trade; and semiperipheral countries, those controlling between 1 and 3% of world trade. This demarcation accords well with both intuitive notions of the membership of each sector and demarcations based on other quantitative variables (note the sets of countries in the core and semi-

TABLE 13.5   Means of Indices of State Constitutional Authority for Central,
Semi-peripheral, and Peripheral Countries, 1870–1970

	1870	1890	1910	1930	1950	1970
Citizen Rights Index						
Central Countries[a,b]	11.5	10.0	11.2	18.4	19.0	25.4
	(8)	(8)	(9)	(8)	(8)	(10)
Semi-peripheral Countries[a,c]	14.2	16.6	14.1	17.6	27.4	24.3
	(5)	(8)	(10)	(15)	(16)	(9)
Peripheral Countries[a,d]	19.3	20.4	21.0	21.5	25.7	18.9
	(25)	(26)	(30)	(38)	(52)	(100)
State Jurisdiction Index						
Central	26.4	26.3	28.8	37.5	40.8	44.6
Semi-peripheral	31.0	35.5	35.5	40.5	58.4	56.7
Peripheral	32.4	31.7	33.0	37.3	51.1	46.2
Citizen Duties Index						
Central	0.75	0.63	1.22	1.75	1.00	2.80
Semi-peripheral	1.40	1.50	1.10	1.53	4.19	4.11
Peripheral	1.96	2.89	3.00	3.03	4.35	3.94

a.   Number of cases in parentheses.

b.   Central countries: those controlling over 3% of world trade. In 1970:
     U.S.A., W. Germany, France, Japan, United Kingdom, Italy, U.S.S.R.,
     Netherlands, Canada, Belgium.

c.   Semi-peripheral countries: those controlling 1–3% of world trade. In
     1970: Austria, Australia, Czechoslovakia, Denmark, E. Germany, Poland,
     Spain, Sweden, Switzerland.

d.   Peripheral countries: those controlling less than 1% of world trade.

periphery given at the bottom of the table). The table shows that, in
general, semiperipheral and peripheral countries have had more expanded state constitutional authority than central countries over the past
century. This is especially true of the citizen rights and citizen duties
indices, and the only exceptions to the general trend occur for 1970, the
most recent analysis time. The periphery and semiperiphery thus do
appear to overcompensate ideologically in conforming to world ideology.
Note in particular the very large values in the state jurisdiction index
for semiperipheral countries; as they near the top, these countries try
even harder, at least ideologically. The most important exception to this
pattern relates to the unexpectedly small value for the state jurisdiction
index for peripheral countries in 1970. However, this low value occurs
at precisely the time of greatest increase in the number of peripheral
countries. Also, it should be remembered that the constitutions of most
of these new countries were imposed on them by their former mother
countries, Britain and France. These older core countries tend more to

copy their own ideology of state authority (which does, to be sure, legitimate a highly expanded state) than to react to world-system demands: they are very unlikely to overconform to world ideology. We should therefore expect more highly expanded depictions of state authority in these peripheral countries as they replace colonially imposed constitutions with new versions more reflective of their own situation and ideology.

CONCLUSION

State constitutional authority has expanded sharply in the past hundred years. This ideological phenomenon is weakly negatively related to effective state power (more powerful states operate under somewhat less expanded constitutional authority) and is only weakly, but negatively, related to such national characteristics as economic development, urbanization, or degree of centrality in the world system. The ideology of state authority is, then, a world-system phenomenon in which constitutions represent, beyond their descriptive and prescriptive properties, responses by the national elites to world political ideology. These responses are highly uniform because every national elite faces roughly the same world ideology and has roughly the same goals in the nation-state status competition, a competition that continually intensifies.

The implications of this argument for national political activities are fairly clear and by no means purely ideological. Elites who do not respond thoroughly to world political ideology are likely to lose legitimacy in the eyes of the major political forces and publics in their countries. They also lose legitimacy in the eyes of various "revolution-exporting" forces abroad. They are subject to overthrow by coup d'etat, often sponsored by military leaders imbued with the ideology of the strong state (in recent years Peru, Brazil, Syria, Libya, Nigeria, and so on) or attack from externally supported groups (Cubans, "national liberation forces" in Africa, and so on). To reverse the common formula, ideology has a way of strongly affecting material history.

APPENDIX
ITEMS OF CONSTITUTION CODING SCHEDULE
Citizen Rights Index

Assembly (2)   Education (2)
Association (2)   Equality before law
Belief and conscience (2)   Exile abolished
Capital punishment abolition   Health
Children   Home (2)
Communications inviolable (2)   Invention protection
Due process   Jeopardy only once
Economic pursuits (2)   Labor dispute actions (2)

Legal protection
Leisure or rest
Marriage by choice
Mass media (2)
Motherhood
Movement
Person inviolable
Political channels (4)
Property
Public employment
Punishment not cruel (3)

Redress if injured by state
Religion (2)
Retroactive law abolished
Self-defense, arms
Social security
Speech
Tax by ability to pay
Testimony not against self
Vote (4)
Wages in accordance with work
Women equal (2)

State Jurisdiction Index
Social Areas under State Jurisdiction

Agriculture (3)
Armed forces
Arms and ammunition (3)
Arts and crafts (3)
Associations
Banking and credit (3)
Benefit societies
Cemeteries
Colonies
Conservation
Cooperatives (3)
Cultural heritage
Culture and sports (3)
Disaster recovery
Drugs and alcohol
Economy (3)
Education (3)
Energy (3)
Fishing, hunting
Foundations
Gambling
Health (3)
Hotel, restaurant (3)
Housing (3)
Insurance
Labor disputes
Labor, general
Landlord-tenant relations

Leisure and rest
Marriage and family
Meteorology
Mining (3)
Mother and child
Natural resources (3)
Occupation access
Population growth
Posts and mail
Press and film (3)
Prices
Professions
Radio and television (3)
Religion (3)
Rent control
Savings
Science (3)
Statistics and census
Stocks and commodities (3)
Surveying
Technical standards
Telephone and telegraph (3)
Tourism (3)
Trade, foreign (3)
Transport and ports (3)
Wages (2)
Warmaking
Weights and measures

Implementing Mechanisms

Abuse of economic power,
   curbs on (2)
Administration (2)
Asylum, political

Budget
Censorship
Citizens abroad
Civil rights

Civil service (2)
Constitutional amendment
Currency
Customs duties
Elastic clause (2)
Elections
Emergency powers
Eminent domain
Exchange, foreign
Extradition
Foreign investment
Foreigners' rights
Foreign relations
Honors and decorations
Immigration and emigration
Income redistribution
Incorporation
Land
Law enforcement

Lawmaking
Loans
Monopoly (2)
Movement within borders
Nationalization
Naturalization and citizenship
Nobility
Pardon and amnesty
Paternity determination
Planning, national (2)
Police
Political parties
Public works
Registration of vital statistics
Socialize citizens
Succession to head of state
Tax (2)
Voting qualifications
Welfare programs (4)

Citizen Duties Index

Children, raise and educate
Defend country (3)
Education for self (2)
Identification card, carrying of
Loyalty to state (2)

Participation as citizen (2)
Pay taxes (2)
Public property, respect for, etc.
Respect for others
Work or labor (2)

NOTE

1 There were several independent countries that had no constitution at some of the coding dates, for example, China in 1870, 1890, and 1910. Analyses given below assign scores of zero on each summary index for such cases. I performed the same analyses excluding such cases altogether and observed no significant differences in the results. I prefer assigning scores of zero because this practice is more faithful to my concern for the ideology of state authority as it is officially expressed to the world system, that is, in constitutions.

FOURTEEN · The Political Incorporation of Women

Francisco Ramirez and Jane Weiss

This chapter examines the influence of expanded state authority and power on patterns of female participation in the educational and occupational systems. In the first section we develop some theoretical ideas that imply that the expansion of state organization will increase both the extension of citizenship to women and the participation of women in areas outside the familial domain. This section amplifies the argument presented in chapter 5 and applies its logic to explain cross-national variations in the status of women. The next section analyzes data on the relative number of women in secondary and tertiary education, in the paid labor force, and in upper occupational strata. The final section discusses the relevance of the findings to our argument concerning the political incorporation of women.

THE EXPANSION OF STATE ORGANIZATION

The emergence of the state has been conceptualized as the differentiation of political functions and roles from other societal structures and activities (see, for example, Fallers 1963; Krader 1968). The rise of the state involved intense struggles between state and rival organizations (see the papers in Tilly 1975). In important respects state organizations triumphed the world over, and states attained a level of institutionalized autonomy from their societies (Easton 1959). However, the extent to which the authority and power of the state permeates society varies across nations. The institutionalization of state authority and power takes place through two general mechanisms: (*a*) reclassifying social activities previously labeled as local or even private concerns (educational admissions policies and hiring policies, for example) to make them embody national purposes and fall under state jurisdiction; and (*b*) validating the concentration of authority in a single decision-making agency (Huntington 1968). The political reclassification of social activities increases the sphere of action within which the state may legitimately act; the legitimation of a unitary decision-making structure increases the likelihood that the purposes and interests of this structure will become the taken-for-granted national interests and purposes (Swanson 1971). We expect states with extensive jurisdiction and centralized state power to symbolically affirm the primacy of the collective purposes and common interests of the nation.

We also expect such states to engage in strategies of political incorporation to a greater degree than states with less institutionalized authority and power. Political incorporation creates linkages between state organizations and such status groups as women, that are politically peripheral within the institutional domains of the states. The linkages consist of a network of definitions, rules, and transactions between the states and the status groups. These ties both affirm and extend the authority of the state over the status group and endow individuals in such groups with membership status in the national collectivity. Political incorporation, hence, both legitimates the dominance of states and normalizes the political status of peripheral groups such as women. States transform peripheral groups by granting their members citizenship rights and responsibilities and by reclassifying the activities or functions associated with the groups. Citizenship status increases the probability that a given group will engage in collective action within the framework of established political institutions. Thus, "subversive workers" become "regular citizens" with the acquisition of voting and other political rights (Marshall 1948; Bendix 1964); and "mere students" emerge as "future leaders" in national educational systems infused with political meaning (Weinberg and Walker 1969; Meyer and Rubinson 1975). Through the same process, the extension of citizenship, women may be transformed from "frustrated females" to "activist members" demanding equal standing before the law and equal access to central institutional patterns.

In the contemporary world system, central institutional patterns that bind peripheral groups to state organizations are (a) the franchise, (b) mass schooling, and (c) the labor market. States often control or influence access to these institutional patterns. Peripheral groups, including women, frequently demand greater access. We view the increased participation of members of a peripheral group in electoral, educational, and employment structures as ritual affirmations of their citizenship. That is, we contend that the extension of citizenship to women not only affirms their rights and responsibilities but also locates them within institutions that certify citizenship. The issue is not that participation in one of these settings necessarily generates new adult-like psychological qualities in women, but rather that the social identity "adult citizen" presupposes greater female participation in these citizenship-validating institutions.

Chapter 5 contended that higher levels of state authority and power lead to the national incorporation of the educational system and to the expansion of mass schooling. We view these processes as instances of the national certification of citizenship and the extension of citizenship to greater numbers within the population. We now advance a more general thesis: those states with more institutionalized authority and power are more likely to organize electoral, educational, employment, and other structures around egalitarian and mobilizing myths which emphasize the purposes and interests of the nation and the validation of citizenship within these institutions, and hence these states are more likely to increase the effective access of peripheral groups to the voting booth, the schoolhouse, and the labor market.

Why should higher levels of institutionalized state authority and power lead to the greater political incorporation of peripheral groups? For the following reasons: (1) The greater the power of the state, the greater its organizational capacity for initiating contacts with the periphery and satisfying its demands. (2) The greater the authority of the state, the more it can afford to challenge threats from special interest groups, successfully competing with these other power centers, from extended kin networks to multinational corporations, for the loyalties of peripheral groups. These two reasons stress a common point: state penetration of society increases with an increase in the power and authority of the state relative to other organizations. We add two further arguments: (3) At higher levels of institutionalization, the state is more likely to transmit unifying myths about the national collective order to peripheral status groups; for instance, myths such as the indivisibility of the national interest, the rise of a new society, the imperative of national development, and so on. (4) Higher levels of institutionalized state organization should result in less tolerance for local or subgroup ideologies. These are more likely to be politically defined as subversive dangers (Bergesen 1977). The state copes with these dangers by dramatizing the reality of the national collective and the moral significance of national citizenship. All individuals must be first and foremost members of the national collective. These two reasons also stress a common point: state penetration of society increases to the extent that state organization fosters a unitary conception of societal or national purposes and interests. State penetration of society, whether this involves an increase in state agencies and personnel or state-sponsored moral rectification campaigns, leads to greater symbolic and structural linkages with peripheral status groups. Thus, we expect the more institutionalized states to engage in strategies of political incorporation because they have more power to do so effectively and because these strategies best promote the image of a unified nation with a common interest.[1]

WOMEN AS A STATUS GROUP

The literature on the social position of women is dominated by the sex-role socialization paradigm. Within this perspective research is undertaken on the following issues: (a) sex-linked variations in childhood socialization experiences; (b) sex differences in attitudes and values (often attributed to [a]); and (c) sex differences in the level of participation and achievement in public institutions (often attributed to [a] or [b] or both). The individual histories are the crucial explanatory variables in these studies. While this approach has led to interesting insights, the emphasis on individuals as units of analysis has diverted attention away from societal-level variations in the participation patterns of women.

Much of the earlier comparative literature on women stresses the beneficial effects of modernization. Some researchers emphasize the material advantages that accrue to women as a consequence of economic development. Lenski (1966), for instance, maintains that with the rise of technology women acquire greater freedom and more incentive to pursue formal learning and develop job-related skills. Others give greater weight to the liberating consequences of modern political ideologies. Goode (1963), for example, treats changes in the status of Western women as a function of the extension of ideas about the dignity and rights of individuals to women.

This perspective has been challenged by those who question the explanatory value of modernization theories as well as by those who reject the application of these ideas to changes in the participation patterns of women in the Third World (Boserup 1970), and even in highly industrialized nations (Knudsen 1969).

We proceed from the assumption that women have traditionally been a politically peripheral status group in national societies. The political incorporation perspective leads to two general hypotheses: at higher levels of institutionalized state authority and power countries are more likely to (a) symbolically extend citizenship to women and (b) increase patterns of female participation in citizenship-validating institutions.[2]

Tests of the first hypothesis have been undertaken, focusing on the degree to which national constitutions affirm equality between the sexes. The results of these unpublished analyses strongly support the first hypothesis. The research that follows examines the relationship between institutionalized state organization and the relative level of female participation in citizenship-validating institutions. More specifically, we test whether higher levels of state authority and power lead to the greater relative participation of women in secondary school systems and in the paid labor force. These tests also allow us to examine the effects of both economic development and political modernization on the relative participation of women in mass schooling and in the labor force. A second set of analyses examines the effects of both state authority and power and modernization on the relative level of female participation in higher education and in the more powerful and well-rewarded occupations. These analyses are undertaken to determine whether the structural pro-

cesses that open educational and employment doors for women at lower
levels continue to equally influence female access to upper echelon positions in the educational and occupational hierarchies.

RESEARCH DESIGN AND MEASUREMENT

We employ both cross-sectional and longitudinal designs. This decision
is due to lack of sufficient data over time on female participation in the
labor force for a panel analysis comparable to the one we have done for
the participation of women in educational institutions.

Our theory leads us to choose to study nation-states. While it is clear
that political and economic factors operating at the local level affect
peripheral groups and that inter-state relationships have implications
for internal developments, we believe that the organization of the state
has primary importance. It could well be argued that women exist as a
peripheral group internationally, but there is, nonetheless, a great deal
of variation among countries in the participation patterns of women. We
attempt to account for these sources of variation.

Our analysis of the participation of women in both mass and elite
levels of education employs a time lag of five years, from 1965 to 1970.
The indicators used to measure the relative level of participation of
women in educational systems was constructed from data obtained from
the UNESCO *Statistical Yearbook* (1971), while measures of the relative participation of women in the national labor force were constructed
from data in the International Labour Organization Yearbook (1972).
Female participation in mass (secondary) and elite (tertiary) levels of
education is measured by the total number of women in each educational level relative to the total number of persons (men and women)
at each level (female secondary ratio and female tertiary ratio). The
female labor force ratio is defined as the total number of employed
women relative to the total number of employed persons in a given
nation-state. The indicator of female participation at more powerful and
prestigious levels of the occupational structure is defined as the number
of women employed in the administrative and managerial sector as a
percentage of the total number of persons in that sector (female managerial ratio).[3] The indicators of female occupational participation are
coded for 1965. These indicators measure the degree of female participation relative to the total number of persons in the school systems and
in the labor force.

The indicators of institutionalized state authority and power are the
same ones employed in chapter 5 and described in detail in chapter 3.
These are the index of centralized state power, the size of the national
cabinet, and government revenue. The indicator of economic development employed is gross national product per capita, while the measure
of political modernization is the C. E. Black index of modernity. (See

chaps. 3 and 6 for a description and discussion of these measures.)
Country scores were computed for around 1965 on all the independent
variables.

RESULTS

We have analyzed data on the relative level of participation of women
in secondary educational systems and in the labor force, and in tertiary
systems and in administrative and managerial positions within nation-
states for sixty-six countries; the number of cases included in any equation varies from thirty-eight to fifty-seven, as data are not available for
all countries for each of the independent variables. Restricting the analysis to the same set of countries in each equation, a data quality control
check, does not substantially alter the findings (see Weiss and Ramirez
1976).

In each analysis, we focus on the following effects to test several
hypotheses: (1) In each question we include an indicator of state authority and power hypothesized to have positive effects. These effects
are implied by the political incorporation perspective. (2) We also include a measure of economic development and an indicator of political
modernization; the modernization perspective implies that the effects of
these variables should be strongly positive. (3) In our analysis of female
participation in the occupational structure, we control for the relative
number of women in higher education (female tertiary enrollment ratio), having demonstrated and discussed the strong role this variable
plays in previous analyses (Weiss and Ramirez 1976). (4) In analyses
of female participation in the educational system we include the lagged
dependent variable.

Analysis of the Participation of Women in Systems of Mass
Schooling and in the Labor Force

Table 14.1 presents the result of six analyses. The dependent variable
in the first three equations is the female secondary ratio; the female labor
force ratio is the dependent variable in the next three equations. The
main findings are as follows: (a) In five out of six equations the indicator of state authority shows the predicted positive effect. The coefficient is statistically significant in all of these five analyses, including all
three analyses of the relative number of women in the labor force. (b)
The level of economic development is unrelated to the proportion of
women in secondary education, but positively influences the relative
level of female participation in the labor force. (c) In equation (6) the
C. E. Black index of political modernity shows a statistically significant
negative effect. However, in all the other equations this measure fails to
have a significant association with either dependent variable. Moreover,
the direction of its influence is inconsistent. (d) In the first three equa-

TABLE 14.1   Effects of State Authority on the Proportion of Women in
Secondary Education and the Proportion of Women in the
Labor Force[a]

		Independent Variables						
Dependent Variable	State Authority Measure	Political Modernization	GNP per Capita	Fem.Pri. Ratio	Fem.Sec. Ratio	Fem.Ter. Ratio	R^2	No.of Cases
Proportion of Women in Secondary Education								
Equation (1)	Political Participation							
	0.0072	0.0016	−0.00019	0.41***	0.68***	...	.92	43
	(0.0041)	(0.0052)	(0.0011)	(0.17)	(0.063)			
	.10	.03	−.01	.22	.81			
Equation (2)	Cabinet Ministers							
	0.0011*	−0.00064	−0.00013	0.35***	0.67***	...	.94	61
	(0.00072)	(0.0036)	(0.00069)	(0.082)	(0.056)			
	.06	−.01	−.01	.26	.75			
Equation (3)	Gov. Rev./GDP							
	−0.00016	0.0023	0.00011	0.20**	0.70***	...	.95	57
	(0.00063)	(0.0030)	(0.00092)	(0.088)	(0.058)			
	−.01	.03	.01	.14	.82			
Proportion of Women in Labor Force								
Equation (1)	Political Participation							
	0.059**	0.010	0.0020**	...	...	0.30**	.22	45
	(0.035)	(0.0092)	(0.00093)			(0.14)		
	.25	.16	.31			.30		
Equation (2)	Cabinet Ministers							
	0.0095***	−0.0021	0.0030	...	...	0.29**	.44	48
	(0.0025)	(0.013)	(0.0028)			(0.14)		
	.48	−.03	.17			.27		
Equation (3)	Gov. Rev./GDP							
	0.0048**	−0.024**	0.0046*	...	...	0.00044	.29	43
	(0.0021)	(0.0097)	(0.0027)			(0.095)		
	.49	−.51	.37			.00		

*p < .10
**p < .05
***p < .01

a.   Dependant variables measured in 1970; independent variables measured in 1965. Entries are
     unstandardized slope, standard error in parentheses, and beta.

tions, as is to be expected, the 1965 levels of relative female participation in primary and secondary school systems are strongly associated
with subsequent 1970 levels of the female secondary ratio. This implies
simply that the proportion of women in secondary school systems is
contingent upon there having been a pool of women enrolled at the
previous level from which the secondary level participants can be drawn.
(See chaps. 3 and 4 for a discussion of this point with respect to total

educational enrollments.) (e) Lastly, in equations (4) through (6), the female tertiary enrollment ratio shows a positive effect on the relative number of women in the labor force. This finding is not altered when we add to the equation the female primary and female secondary enrollment ratios. That this is true even though it is known that the great majority of employed women do not have college degrees (or even high-school degrees in many countries) is an intriguing finding we have discussed elsewhere.[4]

Analysis of the Participation of Women in Tertiary Education
Systems and in Administrative and Managerial Positions
Table 14.2 presents the results of six additional analyses. The dependent variable in equations (7) through (9) is the relative number of women in tertiary education systems; the proportion of women in administrative and managerial positions is the dependent variable in equations (10) through (12). The basic issue we address in this section is whether the structural factors that positively influenced female participation at the lower levels continue to show favorable effects at elite levels. For theoretical reasons and because they positively influenced female participation in mass schooling and in the labor force, we are especially interested in the consequences of state authority. We will, however, follow the same format used in the previous analyses and inspect the effects of the modernization indicators and the measure of female participation in higher education. None of the six equations found in table 14.2 (eqs. [7] through [12]) shows any support for an overall positive effect of state authority.[5] The decline in the efficacy of state authority is especially evident when comparing its influence on the participation of women in the more powerful and well-rewarded positions (eqs. [10] through [12]) with its impact on female participation in the labor force (eqs. [4] through [6]). High levels of state authority clearly open doors for women to the labor force as a whole, but the doors to the elite occupations seem more difficult to penetrate. In the analysis of female participation in tertiary education systems (eqs. [7] through [9]) the size of the beta coefficients varies only slightly from those in the equations examining the effects of state corporateness on the participation of women in secondary schooling systems, but in none of the equations in table 14.2 are the findings significant.

Next consider the effects of economic development and political modernization. Economic development fails to have a positive effect in any of the analyses. In fact, in three equations its effects are statistically significant but negative. The evidence suggests that there is some factual basis for the growing skepticism regarding the blessings to women of economic development. The effects of the C. E. Black index of political modernity are curious; this measure has a strong positive impact in all three analyses of the expansion of the level of female participation in tertiary education, but its effects on female access to administrative and managerial positions, albeit positive, never attain statistical significance. Note that the relative level of female tertiary enrollment is the only variable that strongly influences female access to elite occupations. Perhaps one should think of political modernity as having a direct positive effect

TABLE 14.2   Effects of State Authority on the Proportion of Women in Tertiary Education and the Proportion of Women in Administrative and Managerial Positions[a]

Dependent Variable	State Authority Measure	Independent Variables				R^2	No.of Cases
		Political Modernization	GNP per Capita	Fem. Sec. Ratio	Fem. Ter. Ratio		
Proportion of Women in Tertiary Ed.							
Equation (7)	Political Participation						
	−0.00090	0.024***	−0.0044**	−0.072	0.99***	.83	38
	(0.0084)	(0.0083)	(0.0021)	(0.12)	(0.099)		
	−.01	31	−.24	−.06	.83		
Equation (8)	Cabinet Ministers						
	0.00099	0.19***	−0.0035**	0.025	0.91**	.85	57
	(0.0012)	(0.0072)	(0.0016)	(0.088)	(0.083)		
	.05	.23	−.16	.02	.84		
Equation (9)	Gov. Rev./ GDP						
	0.0010	0.018***	−0.0047***	0.15*	0.80***	.88	52
	(0.00095)	(0.0061)	(0.0018)	(0.088)	(0.080)		
	.07	.23	−.23	.15	.78		
Proportion of Women in Admin./ Managerial Positions							
Equation (10)	Political Participation						
	−0.040	0.0044	0.00010	...	0.25**	.27	38
	(0.029)	(0.0064)	(0.00063)		(0.10)		
	−.22	.11	0.25		.38		
Equation (11)	Cabinet Ministers						
	0.00031	0.0096	−0.00046	...	0.32***	.34	40
	(0.0019)	(0.010)	(0.0021)		(0.10)		
	.02	.22	−.05		.37		
Equation (12)	Gov. Rev./ GDP						
	0.0020	0.0029	−0.0018	...	0.31***	.30	39
	(0.0021)	(0.0098)	(0.0025)		(0.089)		
	.23	.07	− .17		.51		

*p < .10
**p < .05
***p < .01

a. Dependent variables measured in 1970; independent variables measured in 1965. Entries are unstandardized slope, standard error in parentheses, and beta.

on female entry into higher education and through this variable an indirect positive influence on female entry into the better rewarded occupations. Note, however, that since the economic and political indicators are highly and positively intercorrelated with one another in these equations, the size of the positive effects of political modernization and/or the size of the negative effects of economic development may be somewhat inflated. This methodological caveat should caution readers against drawing hasty inferences.

Summary of Results

These analyses were undertaken primarily to test the proposition that higher levels of state authority and power would lead to greater female participation in citizenship-validating institutions such as mass schooling and the labor force. The evidence supports this proposition. In table 14.1, the positive influence of state authority on female participation is significant at the .10 level in five out of six equations. Higher levels of state authority, however, do not appear to increase the admission of women to tertiary education systems or to the more powerful and prestigious levels of the occupational hierarchy (table 14.2).

The thesis that economic and political modernization positively influence the participation of women finds little support in our analysis. The effects of both variables vary in direction from one equation to another. Expanded female participation in tertiary education positively influences female participation at all levels of the labor force. While we find that the presence of women in primary educational settings positively affects the subsequent participation levels of women in secondary schools, we do not observe the same degree of influence from secondary participation to later inclusion in tertiary systems of education. This suggests that linkages between access to primary and access to secondary schools are greater than between access to secondary and access to tertiary.

FURTHER RESEARCH DIRECTIONS

The political incorporation perspective suggests that higher levels of state authority lead to greater affirmations of citizenship for women and their greater participation in citizenship-validating institutions. Further research directions include the following:

1 We propose to examine the impact of state authority on the extent to which marriage diminishes the citizenship status of women. More specifically, do higher levels of state authority lead to (a) greater legal equality between husbands and wives, for example, with respect to parental authority over children, and (b) less difference between the labor-force participation rates of married and single women? Measures of both (a) and (b) have been constructed and analyses are under way.

2 We propose to examine the relationship between the degree to which women are constitutionally defined as equal citizens and their relative participation in mass schooling and in the labor force. If the symbolic affirmation of equality between the sexes involves more than political rhetoric, then one should expect to find a positive relationship between level of egalitarian ideology and degree of egalitarian participation. Analyses of this relationship are also under way.

3 We can study the relationships among state organization, egalitarian ideology, and egalitarian participation over a much longer time frame —between 1870 and 1970, for instance—to determine the extent to which the findings reported in this paper are specific to the historical period for which the data are available.

4 We can study the extent to which expanded state authority and egalitarian ideology affect male participation in familial institutions, especially in child-rearing activities; that is, does the political incorporation of women imply changes in the division of labor between the sexes in the household? Some data on Eastern and Western European male participation rates in child-rearing activities has been compiled. Much more work needs to be done to assess whether the political incorporation of women implies role-sharing between the sexes or the exploitation of women via role inflation.

NOTES

1 An underlying assumption of this perspective is that the individual is the unit that needs to be certified citizen—not the individual as a representative of the clan or town but the individual qua individual. Obviously this assumption has not always been acceptable, but increasingly all nation-states act as if all individuals were important or at least redeemable. One manifestation of this belief is the compulsory schooling requirement, a right and obligation that pertains to all individuals.

2 For an excellent historical illustration of how a nation-state may accelerate participation patterns both via a constitutional affirmation of equality between the sexes and through mobilizational strategies, see Kristeva (1975).

3 We have chosen the category of administrators and managers as more representative of the powerful and well-rewarded positions women hold in a society than the often-used category of professionals. The professions most often filled by women can hardly be construed as powerful and well rewarded, but may best be viewed as quasi-elite semiprofessions. In addition, we find that the mean relative participation level for women in the professions cross-nationally is .41, nearly double that of the mean relative level of participation of women in the labor force as a whole (.27). We have chosen administrators and managers as more clearly representing positions of greater power and income. Note that the mean relative level of participation for this category (0.10) also reflects its elite character.

4 We have previously sought to explain this process in terms of "institutional demystification," that is, the generalization of the acceptance of a peripheral group in one citizenship-validation institutional setting to other such institutional settings (Weiss and Ramirez 1976).

5 We have also tested for the effects of increasing participation of women in the labor force on their participation in administrative and managerial positions and in tertiary education systems. This was done to assess (a) the possibility of a "trickle-up" effect—that is, the argument that as women fill positions in the labor force they will gradually come to fill the more elite positions proportionately; and (b) the further possibility that as women enter the labor force in greater numbers, the same processes that operate to move women into the labor force will necessitate an expansion of the number of women in colleges and universities in order that they may be appropriately trained to fill necessary positions. In neither case did we find any effects of increasing participation in the labor force on subsequent expansion in the proportion of women in the administrative and managerial positions or in tertiary education systems.

VI THEORETICAL DIRECTIONS FOR FURTHER INQUIRY

FIFTEEN · The Dynamics of Ethnic Boundaries in Modern States

Michael T. Hannan

Much of the theoretical and empirical work reported in this book concerns the effects of state power and legitimacy on national development. In this chapter I wish to argue that if we are to go beyond these preliminary results, we must employ more complex models of power and legitimacy. Both power and legitimacy are relative concepts. They refer to the relative concentration of the means of control and of authority, respectively. The state is powerful when its capacity to amass resources and its organization for applying them surpass those of other organizations in the same society. Similarly, the state is legitimated to the extent that authority resides in it rather than in other institutions such as the church, clan, and so on. In the language we have used elsewhere, the power and legitimacy of the state refer to the relative positions within nations of the center and the periphery. Actions of the center to increase control and authority over persons and activities in the periphery ordinarily give rise to counteractions in the periphery. Therefore the power of the center in any period reflects a dynamic balance of forces. This balance depends on the levels of resources and capacities to organize of the center and periphery.

Our research uses only point-in-time measures of the balance of power between the central state and other institutions. The static, point-in-time, perspective captures only part of the processes of interest. The various types of modernization that we consider affect both center and periphery. In doing so, they presumably set off chains of competitive interactions between the center and periphery. These sequences of competitive interactions undoubtedly affect both the course and the speed of national development. Moreover, these dynamics are important and interesting in their own right. Thus it is important to move beyond static representations of the power and legitimacy of the state and to attempt to model the dynamics of the interactions between center and periphery.

Rather than argue this point generally, I consider one particularly interesting instance of the problem: the rise of ethnic and linguistic resistance to expansion of the central state. In earlier chapters we treated ethnolinguistic fractionalization as an indicator of state effectiveness.

State formation and expansion involves attempts at eliminating subnational differences that might serve as counterloyalties to the state. Given two or more states that were initially equally diverse in language and ethnicity, the point-in-time levels of current ethnolinguistic diversity ought to measure the relative power of the state as contrasted with that of ethnic political organization. This would be true, however, only if ethnicity were completely primordial and passive.

Recent events in both metropolitan and developing nations belie the contention that ethnicity is wholly a cultural remnant of previous social and political arrangements. We see numerous instances in which ethnic organization and ethnic political activity arise with renewed vigor in advanced stages of the modernization processes (see the papers in Glazer and Moynihan 1975a for many examples). These ethnic movements are shaped by the nature of the relations between centers and peripheries. To the extent that the maintenance of linguistic and other cultural distinctions within a nation become a focus of reactive political movements, the relationship between what we have taken as an indicator, ethnolinguistic fractionalization, and the concept we intended to measure, state power, is both complex and dynamic.

My purpose in this paper is to sketch a theoretical perspective that permits analysis of dynamic relationships between various types of modernization and the activation, creation, and defense of ethnic boundaries. The major thrust of this proposal is to subsume within one theory the two main facts that characterize the modern fate of ethnicity and ethnic movements: (1) The spread of modern economic and political structures causes a decline in ethnic diversity. (2) High levels of economic and political modernization may under certain conditions impart a renewed social and political importance to ethnic boundaries.

The two observations are often seen as contradictory. It is certainly the case that the observations are most often discussed in contexts which make radically different assumptions about the nature of ethnic group structure. The first and more conventional perspective is that ethnic distinctions within modern societies are vestiges of former geographical and social isolation. The process of modernization is assumed to subordinate such local loyalties to modern national and larger cultural identities.[1] The second observation is usually made in the context of the argument that modernization *creates* ethnic distinctions. In this view, ethnicity is primarily reactive. Further, ethnic identities are viewed not primarily as local loyalties to which individuals are socialized, but as reflections of institutional arrangements, particularly power arrangements, in society. The two positions imply vastly different long-run outcomes. The primordial identity view suggests that ethnic distinctions will disappear as processes of modernization increase in scope and intensity. The reactive identity view suggests that this will not be the case as long as power or other institutional differences persist.

Though the two positions differ in important respects, the mechanisms involved in each have not been explicated precisely enough for one to judge whether they are contradictory. Further, given the quite different conceptions of ethnicity involved, it is not surprising that no attempts have been made to develop a more general formulation which subsumes the two processes as special cases.

The need for such a general formulation is clear. Both processes appear to characterize the modern world. There does appear to be a secular trend toward lowered ethnic diversity. At the same time ethnic distinctions frequently regain importance in advanced modern states. Important instances include Quebec in Canada, Wales, Scotland and Northern Ireland in the United Kingdom, Brittany in France, the Basque provinces in Spain and France, and Flanders in Belgium. More important, the two trends appear to be interrelated.

The theory I propose is ecological. I build on Barth's (1956, 1969) brilliant analysis of the cultural ecology of ethnic boundaries in premodern societies. Applying Barth's style of analysis to the modern context requires a number of modifications. My strategy is to use the formal apparatus of population ecology theory to formalize the model of competition that underlies Barth's analysis, and to use this formal structure to derive implications for the modern situation. The reasoning is most straightforward for the first part of the process, the decline of ethnic diversity. Analysis of the second and more interesting part of the process, the reemergence of ethnic boundaries as important political and social facts, is looser and more speculative.

The main outlines of the theory are as follows. Ethnic distinctions are often hierarchically organized in the sense that one ordinarily has multiple identities (as a member of a family, clan, language group, and so on) that relate him or her to successively larger populations. Whether ethnic organization becomes an enduring element of social organization depends on which of the identities are activated in collective action, and consequently which cultural boundaries are defended. The smallest scale identities are impediments to organization on the basis of widely shared identities. As long as the smallest scale identities remain strong and salient to collective action, the likelihood of effective and sustained action on the basis of widely shared ethnic identities is low. However, any process that lowers the salience of small-scale identities will weaken this impediment to large-scale collective action. I argue that economic and political modernization commonly have such effects. When modern centers penetrate the local community, they undermine the salience of small-scale identities. This happens for a number of reasons. I place primary emphasis on the disparity in power between the center and any particular locality in the periphery. Sustained mobilization in opposition to further penetration by the center must be on a scale commensurate with that of the center. Therefore, successful penetration by the center alters the condition of competition among the various bases of collective action in a direction that favors large-scale identities. Whether or not the basis of large-scale collective action is ethnic or some other, for example class, depends on the pattern of cultural identities and on the manner in which the expansion of the center eliminates subsystem boundaries.

The most important feature of the proposed theory is that it relates the reemergence of ethnicity to the process that typically destroys ethnicity.[2] It implies that the center can be so successful in breaking down subsystem boundaries that it creates the conditions for successful ethnic collective action in opposition.

ETHNIC ORGANIZATION

Discussions of ethnic organization and collective action are plagued by a lack of clarity in definitions. Thus the initial problem is to provide a satisfactory definition of ethnicity and ethnic organization. At a minimum, an ethnic group is a socially distinct population. Although individuals may be assigned ethnic characteristics, the stable properties of ethnic groups attach to populations.[3] Barth (1969) suggests that membership in an ethnic group tends to be ascriptive, that is, membership is socially inherited on the basis of social origins; ethnicity is also exclusive in the sense that an ethnic classification of a population is a partition; and it is imperative, meaning that members do not have a choice of whether or not to invoke the ethnic identity in cross-ethnic interaction. In all three senses, ethnicity is an *organizing principle* of populations. That is, when interaction in some system is organized around distinctions which are ascriptive, exclusive, and imperative, the population is fractionated into ethnic groups.

Barth's own research suggests that even this rather minimal definition may be too restrictive. Ethnicities are not necessarily rigidly ascribed; there is frequently a good deal of movement of persons across certain stable ethnic boundaries (see references in Horowitz 1975). These findings imply that ethnic identities are attributed to individuals on the basis of some combination of social origins and current behavior. When current behavior is heavily weighted, individuals have some choice over ethnic identity to the extent that they can make choices among alternative behaviors. But, once the course of action is taken, attribution of ethnicity follows.

So for what follows, I use the following minimal definitions: an *ethnic identity* is an attributed and imperative social identity that partitions a population; an *ethnic group* is a population that is organized with reference to an ethnic identity. For the moment, I do not specify what it means for a population to be organized with reference to some identity. Let it suffice to note that the term includes use of the identity as a criterion of membership and of shared interest.

The various definitions of ethnicity proposed in the social science literature differ in the extent to which anything is added to the above minimal definition. The primordial identity view typically includes the stipulation that ethnic groups possess distinctive and integrated cultural content as well as a relatively closed field of social interaction (see Naroll 1964). Barth (1969) argues convincingly that it is a mistake to include these elements as defining properties of ethnic organization. To do so involves the implicit assumption that ethnic boundaries are unproblematic. When ethnic boundaries are strong and persistent in time, cultural and social solidarity will ordinarily result. However, ethnic groups which are either emerging or being selected against need not exhibit such solidarity.

The proposed theory attempts to account for both loss of ethnic diversity and the revival of ethnicity. In this context it would be a mistake to add the additional stipulations to the definition of ethnicity. Rather, social and cultural solidarity will be viewed as *consequences* of particularly impenetrable ethnic organization.[4]

My emphasis is on the fact that the identity is socially organized rather than on the social and cultural content of the ethnic identity. A purely ecological theory cannot be expected to account for the emergence of specific cultural content. It is the fact that the identity is organized which gives large-scale social importance to the cultural content. Ecological theory addresses the *form* in which the content is organized.[5]

The Ecology of Ethnic Boundaries

The restriction that an ethnic group is exhaustive and thus has a delimited social organization implies the existence of a *boundary*. Barth contends that the social functioning of ethnic organization can be best understood by examining the processes that maintain ethnic boundaries. His research and that of his students has put these processes in very clear light. Consider, for example, the ethnic boundaries in Swat, North Pakistan. The territory contains three broad geophysical zones: a broad alluvial plain with a climate that supports two crops a year; upland valleys that support one crop per year; and highlands that will not support any crop raising. Three distinct ethnic groups inhabit the territory in such a manner that the ethnic boundaries coincide with the geophysical or habitat boundaries. Most important, these boundaries remain fixed in space despite relatively high rates of movement across the ethnic boundaries. Why should the ethnic boundaries coincide with those of the productive niches?

Barth (1956, 1969) sees two processes as determining ethnic boundaries in this system. The first involves competition and power relations among ethnic groups. The region was originally occupied by only two ethnic groups, the Gujars, engaged in full-time nomadic herding, and the Kohistanis, practicing mixed herding and agriculture. Given that both populations herd, they compete for grazing territory. The mixed herder-agriculturalist Kohistanis prevailed in such competition due to their superior military and organizational capabilities. So in this first phase the Gujars occupied only that portion of the region remote enough from the crop-producing region that it could not be herded by the Kohistanis.

In the second stage, the two-crop agriculturalist Pathan ethnic group invaded the territory and pushed the Kohistanis out of the most favorable farming land. The superior military and organizational abilities of the invading population continually prevailed in the competition for land. Since the Pathan do not herd, they do not compete for resources with the Gujars. Eventually the Gujars came to inhabit those portions of the Pathan territory (steep slopes) where farming was not feasible. This land was not previously available to the herders as it was occupied by Kohistanis.

In the new equilibrium, the boundaries around each ethnic group remain quite fixed in space. This is quite remarkable given the observed large-scale movement of people across the boundaries. Why do the boundaries remain fixed while the ethnic identities of the migrants change?

Barth argues that ethnic identities change in response to local niche conditions in a manner that maintains the equivalence of niche and ethnic boundaries. Productive systems exert constraints on social organizational features such that for each productive system there is a most appropriate form of social organization. Further, value systems tend to develop which are consistent with these constraints. That is, action which is feasible under the productive and organizational constraints facing the population tends to become valued. Ethnic identities tend to employ as cultural content those values which exist in the population; consequently, ethnic group identities crystallize around distinctive properties of the niche.

To the extent that a set of niches and associated productive and organizational systems differ, the content of the associated ethnicities will tend to diverge. Moreover, action which is consistent with a particular ethnic identity will be most feasible within the niche in which the ethnicity developed. So migrants across ethnic boundaries are faced with a choice. They may engage in action which is suboptimal or deviant from their original ethnic perspective. Alternatively, when possible, they may change ethnic identity. If migrants tend to choose the latter option, ethnic boundaries ought to remain stable in space even in the face of relatively high rates of migration across the boundaries.

Consider a particularly clear instance. Haaland (1969), in conducting field work among the horticulturalist Fur in Western Sudan, found a 1% per year shift in ethnic identity to Baggara ethnicity. The Fur and Baggara, although in contact for centuries, have remained culturally distinct. They differ in overt cultural features including language and social organization. In fact, the only significant sociocultural feature they share is religion. Nonetheless, when limitations on investment possibilities in the Fur settlements force some Fur to become full-time nomadic herders they eventually cross the ethnic boundary and become Baggara in the eyes of both ethnic groups. Haaland suggests that the change process occurs as follows:

> When does a Fur become a Baggara? . . . If a Fur . . .
> succeeds in accumulating cattle, he will sooner or later realize
> that the optimal way of maintaining this form of value is to
> establish himself as a nomad. This choice implies that he puts
> himself into a position where he will not have access to other
> values current among the Fur. According to Fur standards of
> evaluation, the consumption of pattern of the nomad is a poor
> substitute for the consumption pattern of a villager. . . .
>
> . . . The Fur value husband-wife autonomy in economic life. . . .
> As long as the family subsists by millet cultivation there
> is no great economic advantage gained by pooling resources;
> it makes no difference for the result of production if husband
> and wife work separately.
>
> When a Fur establishes himself as a nomad, he bases his
> subsistence on a more complex pattern of production.
> Great economic advantages are obtained if the spouses agree
> on a division of labor within a joint economic enterprise.
> [Haaland 1969; pp. 59–67].

The process which applies to consumption patterns and form of household organization extends to most areas of life. This example is particularly dramatic since the constraints facing the nomads are quite different from those facing the horticulturalists. As a result, the cultural content associated with the respective niches is quite different. Yet, as Barth's model suggests, the ethnic boundary remains coincident with the niche boundary even in the face of continual mobility across the boundary.

While Barth and his students formulate the process in terms of individual choices of ethnic identity, it is not difficult to reformulate the argument in less voluntaristic terms. When ethnic identities are ascribed to persons on the basis of their economic and social behavior, any environmental influence that leads to such adaptive behavior will subject the individual to risk of ethnic change. That is, shifts in niche location will tend to bring forth behavioral adaptations that will lead others to assign or attribute an altered ethnic identity to the individual.[6]

Whether the ethnic identity change is voluntaristic does not alter the basic proposition. The major orienting perspective is that *in equilibrium, ethnic group boundaries coincide with niche boundaries.*

NICHE THEORY

The concept of niche has played a central role in almost all ecological theory since it was introduced by Elton and Grinnell. Elton's conception of the niche as the *role* a species plays is familiar to social scientists. Grinnell used the same term to refer to climatic and geological features of the environment facing populations. While the empirical referent for each usage was very different, both conceptions emphasized the dependence of species on characteristics of the environment. For Elton, the environment was primarily composed of other species, for example, the food chain, and Grinnell emphasized the physical environment.

In the first modern statement, Hutchinson (1957) combined both emphases in a more abstract focus. The environment faced by a population may be characterized as consisting of N properties such as number of predators of a certain type, abundance of given resources, temperature, rainfall, and so on. These N dimensions taken together define an N-dimensional space. Within this space are combinations of environmental states within which the population can survive, that is, reproduce itself. All of these points taken together constitute a volume which Hutchinson labels the *fundamental niche.*

The fundamental niche of an ethnic group is the set consisting of the totality (union) of all points in some space, to be specified below, in which survival probability exceeds some minimal quantity. The Swat situation studied by Barth is particularly instructive. Consider the situation depicted in figure 15.1. The fundamental niche of the pure herders consists of the entire space—that of the mixed agriculturalist-herders is A and B and that of the two-crop agriculturists is only A.

In general, ethnic identities that are realized in social organization and behavior that are very specialized to a particular habitat and type of production will have low survival values in regions in which the type of production is not feasible. In this sense, geophysical factors limit the fundamental niches of many types of ethnic organizations, particularly premodern varieties. However, Gujar herders, for example, are not found in all of the three regions that constitute their fundamental niche. This discrepancy motivates the distinction between fundamental and realized niches. The realized niche of any organization, for example a species, consists of that portion of the fundamental niche which is inhabited in the face of competition for the resource(s) supporting the niche.

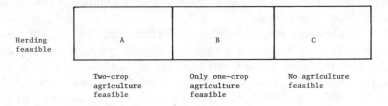

Fig. 15.1   Fundamental Niches of Different Production Modes in Swat

Our focus is on realized rather than fundamental niches. That is, we recognize that the fitness of any specified organization will fall below the critical minimal level in points in its fundamental niche in which it is inferior to its competitors. Thus when I refer to niches, it is more properly to *realized* niches.

Consider the fitness function (Levins 1968) depicted in figure 15.2, where W denotes fitness; θ, the value of W below which the organization cannot survive; and E, a single environmental variable. Then the area between A and B is the niche of this particular organization on this environmental dimension.

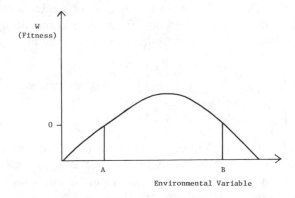

Fig. 15.2   Fitness Function on a Single Environmental Variable

Barth found the realized niche of the two-crop agriculturalists to consist of points in A in figure 15.1, that of the mixed agriculturalist-herders to consist only of points in B, and that of the pure herders to consist only of points in C. Thus only for the dominant two-crop agriculturalists do the fundamental and realized niches coincide.

While it is interesting to recast Barth's processes in the language of fundamental and realized niches, it is more important to extend the power and scope of the model. To do so we must add specific competition mechanisms to the model.[7] I turn first to a general discussion of competition theory and then to a discussion of the nature of competition among ethnic organizations.

The link between Barth's model and formal competition theory is the finding that in no case does more than one ethnic group occupy the same niche. This appears to be an instance of the famous *principle of competitive exclusion* (Volterra 1931; Gause 1934). The usual formulation (see Slobodkin 1961) is that no two species or populations can continuously occupy the same niche. But a number of objections have been leveled at this formulation, and a more precise statement is needed.

The natural starting point is with the Lotka-Volterra growth equations for two competing species. Let X_1 denote the population of species 1 and X_2 species 2. The usual logistic growth curves are

$$\frac{dX_1}{dt} = r_1 X_1 \left(\frac{K_1 - X_1}{K_1} \right); \quad \frac{dX_2}{dt} = r_2 X_2 \left(\frac{K_2 - X_2}{K_2} \right), \tag{1}$$

where r_1 and r_2 are the intrinsic rates of increase of the two populations and K_1 and K_2 are the carrying capacities of the environment for the two species, respectively; i.e., K_1 is the maximum population of X_1 that the environment can sustain. Equations (1) do not allow for any competition. Two species are said to compete when an increase in numbers of either population tends to decrease the number of the second. The simplest possible formulation is that the presence of competitiors reduces the carrying capacity of the environment for a population:

$$\frac{dX}{dt} = r_1 X_2 \left[\frac{(K_1 - \alpha_{12}X_2) - X_1}{K_1} \right],$$

$$\frac{dX_2}{dt} = r_2 X_2 \left[\frac{(K_2 - \alpha_{21}X_1) - X_2}{K_2} \right]. \tag{2}$$

Analysis of the Lotka-Volterra equations (2) leads to interesting qualitative results. First, it can easily be demonstrated that under general conditions the competitive exclusion "principle" is not a logical consequence of the model. That is, there are stable two-component equilibria even in the face of competition. More precisely, for the case modeled in equation (2), a stable equilibrium will be attained if

$$\frac{1}{\alpha_{21}} > \frac{K_1}{K_2} > \alpha_{12}. \tag{3}$$

But the condition stated in equation (3) supports the generality of the principle. Note first that if the two species occupy identically the same niche ($\alpha_{12} = \alpha_{21} = 1$), no stable equilibrium is possible. Further, the greater the level of competition, the narrower the range of stable two-component equilibria. Thus we can conclude that the greater the niche similarity of two resource-limited competitors, the less feasible it is that a single environment or habitat can support both of them in equilibrium.

This appears to be the case, for example, for the competition of the ethnic organizations attached to herding and mixed herding-horticulture in the region of niche overlap (area B in fig. 15.1). It is easy to imagine that in some preequilibrium state both types of ethnic organizations and both types of economies existed in this region. But the niches were similar enough that competitive processes led to the exclusion of the population of herders from this region.

It is more interesting to consider cases in which the community contains more than two components. The Lotka-Volterra system may be expanded to include m competitors:

$$\frac{dX_i}{dt} = r_i X_i (K_i - \Sigma \alpha_{ij} X_j)/K_i \quad (i,j = 1, \ldots, m). \tag{4}$$

The general system (4) has a community equilibrium:

$$K_i = X_i + \Sigma \alpha_{ij} X_j \quad (i = 1, \ldots, m). \tag{5}$$

These equations can be expressed in matrix form:

$$k = Ax, \tag{6}$$

where x and k are $(m \times 1)$ column vectors and A is the $(m \times m)$ *community matrix*:

$$A = \begin{array}{l} 1 \; \alpha_{12} \; . \; . \; . \; . \; \alpha_{1m} \\ \alpha_{21} 1 \qquad\qquad\quad . \\ . \qquad\qquad\qquad\quad . \\ . \qquad\qquad\qquad\quad . \\ \alpha_{m1} \qquad\qquad\qquad 1 \end{array}$$

whose elements are the competition coefficients.

The so-called theory of community structure is the analysis of the equilibrium behavior of the system of equations (6) from the perspective of postulated competition processes. The following results depend upon this system and thus on the applicability of this general competition model to ethnic organization relations.

The Lotka-Volterra model serves as a good approximation not so much to the growth paths of competing populations but to the equilibrium characteristics of communities. The question for present purposes is whether or not the approximation remains a good one when the application is to human social organization. We have made an argument to this effect in general terms elsewhere (Hannan and Freeman 1977). The key issue is the applicability of this notion of competition. Lieberson (1971, pp. 9–10) argues persuasively for a competition perspective on ethnic relations: "Competition is inherent between languages in contact because the optimal conditions for their native speakers are normally incompatible. . . . Since the gains that one language makes are to the detriment of the other, there is competition." In those cases in which the viability of the ethnic organization can be meaningfully assessed by analysis of changes in its numbers relative to those of other ethnic groups in the same system, the competition model appears to be appropriate.[8] In any suitably short time interval the population of the entire system is approximately a constant and thus ethnic groups gain and lose members at the expense of each other.[9] In short, the model developed here holds only under conditions of competition among ethnic group organizations.

MODERNIZATION AND THE LOSS OF ETHNIC DIVERSITY
The first empirical assertion for which this theory is constructed is the observation that economic and political modernization decrease ethnic diversity measured in terms of numbers of distinct ethnic organizations. Community structure theory suggests two parallel approaches. One focuses on the effects of modernization on the structure of constraints in the system; the second considers the effects of modernization on connectedness in the system.

Considerable attention has been devoted to analysis of extensions and modifications of the principle of competitive exclusion. One promising line of attack has focused on the effects of changes in the number of constraints which are the dimensions of fundamental niches. The main results take the following form. Under conditions of resource competition, community species diversity is limited by the number of distinctive resources and other constraints on growth. More precisely, no stable equilibrium can be attained by a community with m components (for example species) and less than m distinct resources and other constraints on growth (Levin 1970). In the long run, then, the diversity of resources and other constraints sets an upper bound to community diversity.

It is extremely difficult to apply this result directly to calculate the upper bound on community diversity even in the nonhuman context. The chief difficulty is that of identifying distinct constraints. A good deal of empirical work is required if one is to judge how different two constraints must be to have distinct consequences from the perspective of community equilibria. Yet, the theorems do imply useful qualitative results: environmental changes which add (eliminate) constraints from a system, increase (decrease) the upper bound of diversity.

Since this result holds generally for systems where competition follows equation (6), it applies as well to Barth's model. In particular, the model implies that *under conditions of competition, any increase (decrease) in the number of constraints on the expansion of ethnic groups will increase (decrease) the upper bound on ethnic diversity.*

The next step in the argument is to connect this implication with modernization. Economic modernization involves at least three processes: (1) increasing application of nonhuman energy to production, i.e. industrialization; (2) the freeing of labor and capital and the establishment of markets; and (3) increasing scale and complexity of production organization and the bureaucratization of production. In discussions of consequences of economic modernization, the most usual focus is on the presumed increase in social diversity. It is commonplace to point to the explosive growth of occupational titles over the past hundred years as evidence of the positive effect of modernization on diversity. This evidence suggests that economic modernization increases the number of resources and other constraints.

I am persuaded that economic modernization has the opposite effect, at least in the long run. The expansion of a modern economic center by the three processes referred to above has the consequence of breaking down local economic boundaries and incorporating labor and capital in larger and larger exchange networks. As modernization proceeds, individuals and firms whose fates were weakly connected in the premodern economy come to stand in many of the same relations to events in the center and to events characterizing the entire economy. Disturbances created in one sector of a modern economy have consequences throughout the economy to a much greater extent than was the case in earlier economies. Consequently, modern economic units are adapted less to local conditions and more to center events.

One can imagine cases in which the emerging center introduces a great diversity of adaptation constraints into peripheries that were previously subject to a few, common constraints. In such a situation modernization would increase the number of constraints in the total economic system. The literature on economic modernization suggests that this is not the usual pattern, however. Local contingencies in the periphery typically vary considerably from locality to locality while the emerging modern center poses many fewer contingencies. For example, individuals adapt by membership in large labor unions as the effective labor market becomes coincident with, say, nation-state boundaries. If it is true that most labor unions adapt to the economy in similar ways, it makes little difference that one individual is a machinist and another a teacher. In short, I argue that in the long run *economic modernization tends to simplify the structure of constraints and to reduce the number of distinct economic constraints within systems.*

Next we consider the implications of political modernization on ethnic diversity. There is little agreement on either the usefulness or the meaning of the term political modernization. At best two images dominate the literature. The first concerns the process of state-building by which potential centers of power eliminate rival forms of control over resources and events. The process of state-building is usually seen to involve a series of stages (see for example Rokkan 1975). My reading is that these stages refer to the establishment of control over successively smaller scale organizations, resources, and actions in the society. In the initial stages the emerging center must eliminate other large-scale pretenders to political control, for example the church in the case of the development of the modern nation-state in Europe. Once such large-scale control is established, state-building orients toward controlling specific resources and actions, for example the state may attempt land reform or to gain control over markets, education, and so on. Finally, the state attempts to incorporate individuals as agents of the state. This stage in the process is often called nation-building (see Bendix 1964). Rather than invoke different labels for different phases (which may be simply the same process worked out at different levels of social organization), I refer to the global process as state-building. I think of it as the construction of a hierarchical structure of political controls at successively lower levels of action, from control over the means to violence in a national territory to incorporation of the individual as an agent of the state.

The second image that dominates the literature concerns the representativeness of political organizations, the extent to which organizational mechanisms exist to bring the interests of members to bear on the formulation and adjudication of political issues. Only one aspect of this image is obviously relevant to the present discussion: that concerns the units that are represented. If the members are individuals (citizens), the structure of relationships of individuals to political events is simplified and so too is the analysis of the effects of state-building. Members may be corporate, however. In fact, ethnic groups may be directly represented in the state. From the perspective adopted here, the incorporation of an ethnic population as a corporate unit in the state organization is best treated as a particular outcome of the competitive relationship between state structures and other forms of political organization. The classic state attempts to eliminate all sources of counterloyalty. When it succeeds, it incorporates individuals as citizens. When it succeeds only partially, it may compromise and incorporate groups or populations. In either case, I prefer to focus on the underlying competitive process. Thus my interest is in the first broad image, state-building, and in the organizational response of populations being brought under the control of the state.

The argument concerning the effects of state modernization on the structure of social organizational constraints is fairly transparent. Effective state-building eliminates local political boundaries and replaces them with a unitary set of relations between the various peripheries and the center. It is difficult to imagine how this process could not simplify the constraint structure.

These assumptions, when taken together with the earlier statements, yield the desired relationships between modernization and ethnic diversity: (1) Economic modernization tends to lower the upper bound for ethnic diversity within economic systems. (2) Effective state-building tends to lower the upper bound for ethnic diversity within states. Each proposition may be restated in terms of the increasing connectedness of modern systems. The foregoing discussion depends strongly on such imagery. The overall thrust of modernization, as I define it, is to join the fates of previously unconnected populations. The community structure representation of competition provides a simple framework within which to model this sort of process. Increasing connectedness implies increases in the magnitudes of the coefficients of the community matrix. Rather than repeat all of the reasoning involved in the previous propositions, I will simply assert that both economic modernization and effective state-building tend to increase the connectedness of social systems, that is, to increase the coefficients of A in equation (6).

To pursue the implications of changes in connectedness, we make reference to an emerging theory on the stability of multicomponent systems. Although it seems intuitively pleasing that more complex systems ought to be more stable, it is now believed that more connected systems are more vulnerable to environmental interference (since a disturbance at any point is propagated widely through the system). Simon (1973), for example, has argued convincingly that nature (that is, natural selection) "loves hierarchy" because hierarchies are less connected than other structures. May (1973a) and Levins (1973) advanced a number of mathematical and empirical arguments that less connected structures with the same number of components are more likely to attain a stable equilibrium. More precisely, let C denote connectance or the average probability that two populations will interact (compete), and s, the strength of interaction or the average magnitudes of the competition coefficients; continue to assume m components in the system. May's (1973) simulations indicate that the stability of the system is a function, $P(m, C, s)$; holding m constant, increases in either C or s will lower the probability of attaining a stable equilibrium. Alternatively, increases in either C or s will tend to lower the equilibrium diversity of the community.

I believe that economic and political modernization increase both connectance and strength of interaction. At some stage in the construction of the theory it may be profitable to model each effect separately. For the present I use the term connectivity to encompass both effects. Increases in the connectivity of a system with competition characterized by equation (6) will tend to lower the equilibrium diversity. The two results on the effect of modernization on ethnic diversity follow from these arguments as well.

MODERNIZATION AND THE RISE OF ETHNIC POLITICAL ACTIVITY

The second empirical observation to be explained is a tendency for ethnic activity, particularly political activity, to increase in scale and intensity in fairly advanced stages of the various modernization processes. Much of this activity appears to be oriented toward firming and defending boundaries around ethnic groups. I use the term ethnic political activity to refer to this type of action. That is, by ethnic political activity I mean collective action, either institutional or noninstitutional, that is directed at maintaining, strengthening, or extending ethnic boundaries. A good deal of historical evidence suggests that this sort of activity is fairly frequent and intense in the early contact phase among the different ethnic groups that make up polyethnic nations, that is, primarily during the early conquest phase. It tends to decline once political and military control are established. In at least some cases the rather extended period of ethnic quiescence is followed by a renewed intensity of creating and defending of ethnic boundaries. This pattern seems to have occurred both in the British Isles (Hechter 1974a, b) and in Belgium (Ruys 1973). Horowitz (1975) argues that this pattern also characterizes the history of many newly independent states.

The focus on political activity implies a limited scope to the argument. To model variations in ethnic political activity it is not enough to consider the stability of ethnic boundaries. It is conceivable that ethnic boundaries will not become politicized even though they are enduring features of the social organization. However, Lieberson (1970, p. 10) argues that language seldom remains neutral:

> Language . . . enters into other forms of competition as a
> potential asset in the market place, the political order, or the
> social realm. In the same way that trading stamps are used by
> merchants to obtain a competitive edge, so too will language
> play a role in these normal forms of competition in multilingual
> communities.

If Lieberson's conjecture is correct regarding ethnicity, my arguments ought to hold quite generally.[10] If ethnicity is more rarely used politically, the scope is correspondingly more limited.

It seems safe to assume that the elimination of ethnic boundaries always leads to a certain amount of reactive political activity. In my view, the problem is not to explain variations across situations in the likelihood that loss of an ethnic boundary will produce a political reaction. Rather, the central question concerns conditions under which such a protopolitical tendency becomes activated in an organized fashion. After all, it is only when the political action by those on the periphery is organized and the response from the center is organized that a boundary becomes reactively organized. The problem is to formulate a model which specifies the conditions under which the modernization processes which eliminate ethnic boundaries will tend to encounter or produce *organized* resistance.[11]

It is helpful at the outset to distinguish two cases. In the first and simpler case modernization expands from more than one center, each of which has a distinct associated ethnic identity. The second case concerns modernization from a single ethnically homogeneous center into a poly-ethnic periphery. Ethnic political action in the first case does not differ substantially from ordinary intercommunity or interorganizational conflict. Ethnic diversity on the periphery in the second case, usually termed reactive ethnic activity, requires a somewhat more unusual treatment. My concern is primarily with the latter case. Before moving to that discussion, I will make some brief comments on the former.

Consider a closed system containing m ethnic populations and $j < m$ expanding ethnically homogeneous centers. If each center controls a hinterland, that is, if the larger system is decomposable into j subsystems, arguments from the previous section imply that, if modernization proceeds unhampered in each sector, ethnic diversity will tend toward zero in each system. At some stage in the process it is very likely that the system will be characterized by j ethnic populations in competition and conflict with each other. Since these j ethnic populations will be larger than those in the original set, and since activities of the center are more widely noticed and more systematically recorded than those of the periphery, it seems quite likely that historians and other observers will conclude that the amount of ethnic activity has greatly increased. At least some of the increase might be spurious due to the inability of the observers to make ethnic distinctions among the initial periphery populations. There may as well be a genuine increase in the importance of ethnic political activity to the system. Ethnic loyalties are likely to become activated in a greater proportion of political contests when the system is composed of a small number of relatively large ethnic groups since any outcome is likely to similarly affect very large numbers of persons with the same ethnic identity.

More usual, as well as more interesting, is the case in which a system is penetrated by a single ethnically homogeneous center. To deal with this case, additional assumptions must be added to the general competition argument. I assume that sustained competition and conflict requires some minimal power parity among the participants in the competition. The power of a population is a function of its size, its resource levels, its technology, and its organizational capacity (see Lenski and Lenski 1978). The very fact of expansion of the modern sector implies that the center surpasses the periphery in resources, technology and organizational capacity. Organizations on the periphery must then be relatively large if they are to sustain competition and conflict. My strategy is to search for general conditions under which organizations on the periphery will acquire a scale sufficient to contest the expansion of the center.

Systems undergoing modernization are typically initially composed of many partially decomposable subsystems. The collection of subsystems contains many distinctive niches and associated ethnic identities and organizations. Most important, the average size and power of the ethnic populations is small relative to the emerging system. As long as the emerging center is able to contest with each peripheral ethnic organization singly, each contest will be brief and in favor of the center.

If an ethnic stand is to be made against the center, it must be on the basis of some identity larger than that of the premodern ethnic identities. We need not assume that individuals have a single social identity. Quite the contrary; individuals possess multiple social or cultural identities. For example, an individual may simultaneously be socially located as a member of a clan or lineage, a local culturally bounded community, a religious community, a linguistic community, and so on. Each such cultural partition of a population forms the basis of potential ethnic organization. In some circumstances we notice organization around smaller scale distinctions, for example lineages or local communities, and in other circumstances around larger scale distinctions, for example major language divisions. Because an individual's time and commitment are limited, increasing commitment to ethnic collective activity at one level implies a reduced commitment at other levels. In other words, ethnic identities at different levels compete for the time and intensity of commitment of their potential members.[12] This is the same notion of competition used earlier, since the sum of time and commitment available are constant and some types of organizations grow only at the expense of other organizations.

Recall that Barth proposed that success in organizing an ethnic boundary around some set of cultural criteria depends on two factors: (1) the appropriateness of the cultural content to the behavioral contingencies of the local niche structure; and (2) the power mobilized by the ethnic organization relative to the larger system. In situations in which the larger system exercises weak and infrequent constraints on the local systems, the first criterion ought to dominate. When the first criterion dominates, very small-scale and specialized ethnic organizations ought to be more successful at attracting members.

Modernization upsets the premodern equilibrium. We have already argued that modernization results in increases in the connectivity of the system so that each subsystem's fate becomes more closely tied to those of the whole and of other subsystems. Although the impact of this change may not directly alter the fit between cultural content and local conditions, it certainly affects the second component in the success function, power relative to the system. As the system becomes more connected, the size of the interacting population increases and the size of the largest competitor increases for all but the largest unit. As a result, the conditions of organization (more precisely, of selection among forms of organization at different scale levels) are altered. Attempts at organizing around larger scale cultural identities, even if no less frequent or intense, ought to be more successful. Given the fixed time available for organization and participation, attempts at organizing or maintaining ethnic organizations premised on smaller scale, more local identities ought to be correspondingly less successful.

The argument can be taken a step further. When boundaries around small-scale ethnic organizations are actively and successfully defended, any sort of large-scale collective action by sectors of the periphery is unlikely. As long as the line of contest is drawn at the local level, populations that stand in the same relation to the center will be unlikely to act collectively in opposition to the center. If the effect of modernization in reducing ethnic diversity results in the elimination of smaller scale ethnic boundaries, the organizational potential of larger scale ethnic organizations is increased.

All of these effects require that large-scale cultural identities be available.[13] The situations of interest vary in the availability of such identities. One extreme is the segmental pattern in which each identity includes the same-sized population. In a premodern equilibrium each individual has presumably aligned himself with the ethnic organization that maximizes the fit between cultural identities and current life circumstances. When modernization increases connectivity in the system, the gains of switching to an ethnic organization based on other available cultural identities are negative since all possible ethnic organizations have the same size and there are costs to ethnic change. Under these conditions, the center ought to be able to contest separately with each ethnic competition and to eliminate each ethnic boundary in the system, with little or no resistance.

On the other hand, when cultural identities form hierarchies (see Simon 1973) with respect to size of included populations, the processes I described will lead to selection in favor of organizations based on the largest scale identities. *Selection against boundaries at low levels in the hierarchy increases the size of the population that can be actively mobilized by those organizing on the basis of larger scale identities.*

DISCUSSION

In passing I have indicated ways in which ecological theories of ethnic boundary dynamics depart from sociological convention. These include use of a definition of ethnicity that focuses on boundaries rather than content, and the conception of competition. To sharpen some distinctions, it is useful to contrast the argument made above with two recent and important sociological treatments of ethnic conflict: Hechter's analysis of the "cultural division of labor" and Bonacich's use of "split labor market theory."

Hechter (1974a, b) counterposes two models of ethnic change. The functionalist theory argues that increasing social differentiation eliminates ethnic diversity. The so-called reactive theories argue that ethnicity is not threatened by contact with other populations; rather, ethnic boundaries are strengthened as a consequence of intense interaction with other populations. Hechter's specific reactive theory focuses on the role of ethnicity in the stratification system. He argues that ethnic solidarity arises from a cultural division of labor. Labor can be said to be culturally divided "when individuals are assigned to specific types of occupations and other social roles on the basis of observable cultural traits . . ." (Hechter 1974b, p. 1154). In other words, ethnic solidarity is assumed to be most intense when culturally distinguishable populations occupy nonoverlapping segments of the occupational distribution.

Bonacich (1972, 1975) makes the opposite argument. She argues that ethnic antagonism is most intense when two or more ethnic populations interact in a split labor market. According to Bonacich (1975, p. 603), "The central tenet of split labor market theory is that, when the price of labor for the same work differs by ethnic group, a three-way conflict develops among business, higher priced labor, and cheaper labor which may result in extreme ethnic antagonism." Note that the concept refers to differences in wage rates *for the same occupations*. So according to this theory, ethnic antagonism and ethnic solidarity will be most extreme when a cultural division of labor has been broken down. When the different ethnic populations enter the same occupations, the competition is most intense.[14]

My argument agrees with the split labor market theory. It holds that competition is a function of niche overlap. The more alike are the occupational distributions of two groups, the greater the competition between them. Bonacich's argument has a second desirable feature: it concerns a three-way competitive relationship. One cannot understand the dynamics of the competition between two ethnically distinct populations of laborers without considering the role of ownership. More important, the competition between any two elements in this system would be fundamentally altered by the elimination of the third from the system.

The ecological theory of ethnic boundary dynamics is consistent with the view that competition processes are complex. In fact, the formal theory provides a convenient representation of the dynamics of N-party competitive processes. But there is a sense in which my argument demands a more comprehensive model of competition.

Virtually all sociological treatments of ethnic competition treat ethnicity as primordial. Most deal only with the case in which an ethnic population is infused by immigration into a system. In such cases the boundaries around ethnic populations may be unambiguous and the actors in the competitive play clearly defined. But the case I am considering is quite different. I have argued that multiple levels of ethnic boundaries characterize many systems, and the operative question is which boundaries will be defended. Thus I argue that one should consider simultaneously two types of competition: (1) competition among ethnically organized populations; and (2) competition among organizational foci for members. While populations organized along the prevailing lines are competing with each other for power and scarce resources, within each population there is competition among forms of organization for the time and commitment of potential members.[15] In short, I argue that we consider competition both among actual social organizations and also among actual and potential forms of organization. The two types of competition cannot be isolated from each other; the results of one type greatly affect the other. Indeed, the main thrust of the foregoing argument is that the likely outcome of competition between an emerging center and various concrete peripheral communities greatly affects the competitive balance between organization on the basis of local identities and organization on the basis of very widely shared cultural identities.

It may help reinforce this theme to consider briefly another example of this type of process that is very close to the theme of this book. As a number of chapters make clear, the operation of the world economy has resulted in a dense web of economic relationships between metropolitan nations and specific production sectors of peripheral nations. The multinational corporations have not by and large invested in national economies. Rather, they have invested in specific plants and industries in many nations. One consequence of this dense web of economic relations is to regularize, within and between nations, the conditions of production and of political action in a great many localities. In the language used earlier, the dominance of a world economy greatly simplifies the structure of constraints within nations by breaking down regional and subregional economies and polities and replacing a diverse set of dependencies with a unitary form of dependence. If the argument made concerning ethnic mobilization within nations is applicable to this situation, the implications are the same as those outlined earlier. Simplification of the constraint structures within nations and increases in connectedness within nations will lower the gains from political organization formulated in terms of local issues and identities and increase the gains from organization on the basis of more inclusive identities. In the present political climate, one higher level is particularly likely to be chosen: the nation-state. There are an increasing number of institutional and structural supports for action on the nation-state level that make it quite likely that national boundaries will come to be the boundaries that are defended in such circumstances. This should be true even when the national boundaries were established on culturally arbitrary lines, for example the colonial boundaries used to demarcate nations in much of Africa.

Such a development has consequences for the levels of ethnic action within nations as well. If the operation of the world economy leads to the defense of national boundaries, the power of national centers will likely increase. An increase in the power of such centers may then set off the dialectical process to which this paper was addressed. That is, expansion of the powers of the national center will tend to alter the conditions of political competition within states in such a way as to increase the salience of large-scale ethnic identities. Working out the joint dynamics of the process within and between states should lead to a richer understanding of the dynamics of these sorts of competitive processes.

NOTES

1 There are at least two widely known versions of this argument. In the functional theory of change, it is asserted that local normative structures become subordinated to those of the center by processes of differentiation and adaptive upgrading. Alternatively, the state-building model asserts that emerging state centers strive to eliminate all sources of loyalty alternative to the state.

2 Most recent work on reactive ethnicity such as the papers in Glazer and Moynihan (1975) attempt special theories for the rise of ethnic organization in the modern state (Horowitz 1975 is a notable exception).

3 This assertion is elaborated below in the discussion of the possibilities for high ethnic turnover at the individual level in conjunction with stable ethnic boundaries.

4 Nothing is presumed either about the physical characteristics of members (as in the study of racial groups) or about the relative size and/or power of the ethnic group vis-à-vis the rest of the system (as in the study of minority groups).

5 It is quite interesting that such a strong exponent of normative determinism as Parsons would now argue, following David Schneider, that modern ethnic organizations are all form and no content (Parsons 1975, p. 65).

6 The argument continues to assume that passing is possible. Obviously, polyethnic situations differ in this respect. My impression is that the existence of a state bureaucracy impedes such movement across ethnic boundaries. Horowitz (1975) provides numerous examples of the fluidity of ethnic boundaries.

7 As we will see, niche theory is a special case of general competition theory. In this case, it is more useful to formulate the argument in competition terms.

8 For other statements on competitive theories of ethnic relations, see Park (1950), Lieberson (1961, 1970), Harris (1964), Blalock (1967), and Bonacich (1972).

9 This claim follows from the definition of an ethnicity as a partition, and from the closed-system assumption.

10 Bell (1975) and Glazer and Moynihan (1975) argue that the success of ethnic revivals in the contemporary period is best explained by some affinity between ethnicity and politics. But this is merely an assertion, not an explanation.

11 This is the perspective that Tilly has used so fruitfully to analyze French collective political violence. In Lodhi and Tilly (1973, p. 315) he argues, "We find two broad types of action behind most instances of collective violence. In the one, an agent of authority lays claim to some valued resource . . . and members of the affected population forcibly resist that claim. . . . In the other . . . a group of people visibly lays claim to certain objects or actions, and some other group—most frequently agents of the government—forcibly resist. . . . given the initial action, the presence or absence of violence depends on the availability of organized groups prepared to challenge the claims being made."

12 The individual decision-making involved is likely to be similar to that described by Coleman (1973) in discussing the reasons for the increasing tendency for individuals to delegate their decision-making rights to very large-scale corporate actors.

13 It is also important to consider the conditions under which new identities are formed. I assume that the costs of aligning with some new identity are greater than those of shifting allegiance from one to another of a set of identities already possessed or attributed. So the likelihood of ethnic political activity is more likely when larger scale identities exist because the costs of switching to the center ethnicity are greater in this case than when large-scale ethnicities counter to the center must be created de novo.

14 Hechter (1974a) clouds the issue somewhat by later measuring the degree to which labor is culturally divided in terms of income gaps between regions. Incomes, of course, depend on wage rates, which depend both on ethnicity and occupation.

15 This distinction parallels Marx's distinction between competition within classes and class conflict.

SIXTEEN · Cycles, Trends, and New Departures in World-System Development

Christopher Chase-Dunn and Richard Rubinson

Previous chapters have considered the effects of the world system on national development from the perspective of individual nations (considered jointly) and over short time periods. While this focus addresses many important issues, it does not address some that are crucial to understanding how the world system operates. The purpose of this chapter is to sketch the main structural features of the world system *taken as a whole* and to identify the processes that maintain and change this system.

The first section defines some of the main concepts used to describe the structure of the modern world system and briefly outlines a descriptive schema of the structural processes, cycles, and trends operating in the system. The second section applies the schema to the patterns of development during the period from 1950 to 1970. We ask whether or not the patterns of development in this period are cyclical repetitions due to the normal operation of the laws of capitalist development, or are symptoms of the transition to a new type of system based on different developmental tendencies.

Following Immanuel Wallerstein (1974a), we conceive of the modern world system as an "effective division of labor," a world economy, in which fundamental commodities are produced and exchanged. The social structures, political regimes, and class alliances within this hierarchical division of labor are affected by it and in turn act upon it to determine which regions will occupy the main structural positions which compose the larger system. The main structural distinction in this system is that between core and peripheral areas. Particular regions may be upwardly or downwardly mobile, and this change in relative position is what is usually referred to as national development. For example, the United States emerged from a peripheral position in the eighteenth century to a semiperipheral position until the Civil War and Reconstruction, when it entered the core of the system. As a core power it eventually succeeded the United Kingdom as *the* hegemonic core power and now is beginning to experience a decline in relative position similar to Britain's loss of hegemony in the late nineteenth century (Rubinson 1978).

But the success of some countries is often at the expense of others, so that the stratification of the world economy into core, semiperipheral, and peripheral areas is a constant feature of the system. Since its emergence in the long sixteenth century this system, which is "capitalist" in the sense that most production is for profit on the market, has expanded such that it is now global in scope.

The key political institution of the modern world system is the state system (or "international system") composed of many competing states, none of which has been able to dominate the entire economic division of labor. This political structure is very different from that found in earlier world systems (world empires), in which a single state apparatus eventually emerged to centralize the accumulation of economic surplus. The modern world system is politically multicentered, a characteristic which both allows capital accumulation to proceed without the costly overhead which develops in political empires, and forces political opposition to the system to be localized within state structures which do not have the ability to affect the whole system. Some of the stronger states in core areas of the modern world system have occasionally created colonial empires, but these are partial empires which do not extend over the entire arena of economic competition.

CORE, PERIPHERY, AND SEMIPERIPHERY

In the core of the system states are relatively strong in the sense that they have the ability to mobilize great resources when necessary. The economies in core areas tend to be diversified and well-integrated relative to those in peripheral areas. They tend to have an infrastructure which connects different parts of the home market, a complex internal division of labor, and a high level of productivity in both manufacturing and agriculture. Labor is skilled and receives relatively high wages.

In peripheral areas of the world system the economic structure is typically composed of a "modern" sector (mines, plantations, ports) and a "traditional" sector (villages, tribal reserves, the bush, the mountains, and so on), with the latter serving as a labor reserve both for the modern sector and for core areas. The modern sector has historically been specialized in the production of one or two raw materials for export. Peripheral countries tend to have a transport and communications infrastructure which is relatively unintegrated and "externally" oriented such that regions are linked with the larger world economy rather than with one another. The home market is small and dependent on industrial imports from the core, although in this century many peripheral areas have begun to develop an industrial sector producing for the home market. Labor is relatively unskilled and wages are very low, even lower than would be expected from the differences between labor productivity between the core and the periphery (Emmanuel 1972). This wage differential is due to the political forms of coercion (both national and international) which keep wages low in the periphery.

The semiperiphery is intermediate in terms of its type of labor control and its exchanges with the core and periphery. Semiperipheral states are those which combine both core and peripheral characteristics. They tend to have within their boundaries a mix of core and peripheral activities, and to trade both "up" and "down" in the world division of labor.

The basic structure of the modern world system has been reproduced as it has moved through a series of geographical expansions to encompass the whole globe. Wallerstein suggests that there have been four epochs since the birth of the system: its emergence out of European feudalism, from 1450 to 1640; its consolidation, between 1640 and 1815; its expansion to the whole globe, between 1815 and 1917; and its further consolidation and "revolutionary" tensions, from 1917 to the present.

DESCRIPTIVE SCHEMA OF WORLD SYSTEM DEVELOPMENT

These four epochs can be analytically understood in terms of three kinds of elements: (1) those underlying institutional features and developmental laws that are basic to capitalism as a system; (2) cyclical processes which repeat themselves in each of the epochs; and (3) secular trends which increase at a varying rate across all of the epochs. An analytical schema which specifies these elements and some of their interrelations has been elaborated elsewhere (Chase-Dunn and Rubinson 1977; see also Hopkins and Wallerstein 1977). Here we will briefly describe the schema and then apply it to the post–World War II period which has been the focus of the previous chapters.

The institutional constants of the world-system are as follows:

1 The capitalist mode of production. The main motor of the system is production for profit on the market (commodity production) in the context of the core-periphery division of labor.

2 The core-periphery division of labor and forms of labor control. Core labor is relatively "free" wage labor and peripheral labor is subjected to a variety of political forms of coercion (for example slavery, serfdom). This differentiation of core-periphery forms of labor control creates a wage differential in which returns to labor are less in the periphery than in the core, even holding constant the productivity of labor. This allows core areas to continually appropriate a portion of the surplus product produced in peripheral areas. These forms of labor control are articulated through the world market, which is not a "perfect" market because the terms of exchange are continually influenced by the operation of the state system. The core-periphery division of labor is reproduced by a number of mechanisms which are described and analyzed in Chase-Dunn and Rubinson (1977).

3 The state system. This is a political system in which class struggle is largely contained within territorial states. Core states are stronger than are peripheral states, both in relation to their own populations and in relation to other states, and no single state exercises control over the whole arena of economic competition. It is at the world-system level, and not at the national level, that capitalism exhibits a fundamental differentiation between economic and political structures.[1]

The cycles which repeat themselves in each of the epochs are the following:

1 The long wave. This is a cycle in which the relative rate of capital accumulation and overall economic activity increases and then decreases toward stagnation. This cycle has often been called the long wave or Kondratiev cycle (Schumpeter 1939; Mandel 1975).

2 Core competition. This refers to a cycle of unicentricity vs. multicentricity in the distribution of power and competitive advantage among core states. Unicentric periods are those in which power and competitive advantages are relatively concentrated in a single hegemonic core state. Multicentric periods are those in which there is a more equal distribution of power and competitive advantage among core states. There have been three hegemonic core states since the sixteenth century: the United Provinces, the United Kingdom, and the United States.

3 The structure of core-periphery trade and control. A periodic change in the pattern of control and exchange between the core and the periphery has also characterized the world system. Periods of relatively free-market multilateral exchange are followed by periods in which trade is politically controlled and tends to be contained within colonial empires. The causal relations between the cycle of core competition and the structure of core-periphery trade and control are specified in Chase-Dunn (1978).

The secular trends which have increased over the whole period of capitalist development are the following:

1 The integration of new populations and territories into the world division of labor. The system has expanded to take in formerly external arenas (albeit at an uneven rate) since the first expansion of Europe in the long sixteenth century. The limits of this type of expansion were reached in the late nineteenth century when the whole globe became integrated into the world division of labor. The consequences of this "ceiling effect" are discussed in the second section of this chapter.

2 The intensification and deepening of commodity relations. Land, labor, and wealth have been increasingly made commodities in both the core and the periphery. More spheres of life have taken the commodity form in the core than in the periphery, but all areas have experienced a secular increase in every epoch.

3 State formation. The power of states over their populations has increased in every period in both the core and the periphery but, as above, the relative gap between the core and the periphery has been maintained. States have increasingly expropriated the authority of other actors and organizations. For most epochs parts of the periphery were stateless in the sense that they were subject to direct political domination (colonialism) by core states. "Sovereign" states which have emerged in most of the periphery with decolonization remain weak vis-à-vis their citizens compared to core states, but the process of state formation has begun in almost all areas of the contemporary periphery.

4 Increased size of economic enterprises. The average size in terms of amount of capital and number of workers controlled by economic enterprises has increased in every epoch, although again at a varying rate which tends to correspond to the cyclical rate of accumulation. All four secular trends are caused by struggles within and between classes to appropriate shares of the economic surplus product.

We now apply this framework to the contemporary period to help interpret the patterns of development revealed in the research reported in earlier chapters. The basic question we want to answer is, Which of these findings indicate truly new departures and which are repetitions of cyclical or secular processes which have operated in earlier periods of world-system development?

We contend that, at the level of the basic processes of development, not much is really new in the contemporary period. This flies in the face of most interpretations of the changes which have occurred in the twentieth century. The shift in power among states, the emergence of a separate socialist bloc, the growth of transnational institutions, and the growing scarcity of natural resources, are often seen as indications that modern society is undergoing a fundamental transformation. Often the very rate and scale of change itself is seen as a qualitatively new feature. We contend that many of the patterns of change in the contemporary period can be seen in the earlier epochs of world-system development, and that there has not yet been a fundamental reorganization at the systemic level. Many of the signs that, according to analysts, indicate a new era are simply cyclical repetitions of processes which have been characteristic of the world system since its emergence.

But we do not want to argue that the world system will never undergo basic transformation. We contend that the present period may be best understood as a period of transition, much as the long sixteenth century was a period of transition between feudalism and capitalism. Now, as then, this transition is not a feature of individual nation-states, but rather of the larger system itself.

We contend that the fundamental changes which are occurring or will occur are the result of the operation of processes endogenous to the system itself. The secular trends which we outlined above result from the class conflict which capitalist development creates.[2] These secular trends have begun to reach natural and social upper limits, and these "ceiling effects," in combination with the continued operation of the cyclical processes, are intensifying the contradictory tendencies within the system, and will eventually lead to its transformation to a very different kind of system.

We shall now discuss the structural constants, cycles, and secular trends as they apply to the post–World War II period in order to answer the question raised above: Which of the observed patterns of change are due to repetitions of processes which are the normal operations of the system, and which indicate truly new and fundamental changes?[3]

STRUCTURAL CONSTANTS: CAPITALISM, CORE-PERIPHERY DIVISION OF LABOR, AND THE STATE SYSTEM
Capitalism and Socialism

One claim often made is that the contemporary socialist bloc is in itself a fundamentally new development. In terms of our definition of the capitalist mode of production (commodity production for profit on the world market), the "socialist" states remain part of the capitalist world economy. The long-run significance of the emergence of new forms of property in these states for the transformation of the larger system is not yet understood (Chavance 1977), but the emergence of these forms has not led to the restructuring of the mode of production at the level of the whole system. Socialist movements have succeeded in taking state power in areas within the world economy but they have not been able to create a socialist mode of production.

The breakup of the socialist bloc indicates that many of the processes which affect relations among other states in the system also affect relationships among the socialist states. Further evidence of this is the re-emergence of trade between the socialist states and the West. After a period of controlled mercantilist withdrawal and internal mobilization of capital accumulation, these countries have resumed commodity production for the world market. The use of the state apparatus to protect internal markets and to mobilize accumulation is not an exception, but rather has been the most frequent form of development in the capitalist world economy. Thus the socialist states do not represent a new departure in this regard.

We also note several other significant indications that socialist states are part of the capitalist world economy. First, as Frank (1977) has shown, no socialist state has been able to develop a "socialist" theory or practice of international trade. These countries trade very much in the same way that nonsocialist states trade. Second, socialist states have incurred high costs in maintaining their isolation from core capital and culture. These costs have had important consequences for their internal development and have created incentives for their reentry into the world market as commodity producers. Third, socialist states have been subjected to both military threat and tremendous economic inducements to open their markets to the core powers. The scramble among the United States, Germany, and Japan for access to the markets of the Soviet bloc and China have produced clear internal splits within these regimes over the question of how and when to open up. In all of these respects socialist states act like nonsocialist ones. They operate within the formula of production for profit on a market, and their calculations (both economic and political) are capitalist calculations (Bettelheim 1975).

The Core-Periphery Division of Labor

The core-periphery division of labor is based on a difference in levels of exploitation and political coercion between core labor and periphery labor. Both areas have developed less coercive forms of labor control over the history of the world system, but the relative gap between them has been reproduced. The question we want to ask about the post–World War II period is whether or not there is any evidence that this difference has been reduced, and, if it has, is this a temporary reduction or a trend toward the elimination of the core-periphery division of labor.

Both the core and the periphery have experienced major reorganizations in the systems of labor control. In the periphery, serfdom and slavery were first expanded and then were replaced by various relatively coercive forms of wage labor, indenture, and tenantry (Mintz 1977). In the core, "precapitalist" forms of labor control were replaced by yeomanry (kulaks, free farmers) and relatively "freer" wage labor in cottage industry and the factory system. The wage system has become the most usual juridical form of labor control across the system, but there remain differences between the core and the periphery. Peripheral workers are still much more likely to be part-time wage workers with at least some part of their lifetime means of sustenance coming from subsistence production (village communities, home production, and so on). Proletarianization is much more complete in the core in the sense that most labor is wage labor. But this has not had the consequences which Marx expected to follow from the separation of the workers from the means of production. Core workers do not control the means of production, but they have developed organizations (labor unions, professional associations) which protect them from market forces to a certain extent.

In arguing that there has been a reorganization of the "international division of labor" in the postwar period, Fröbel, Heinrichs, and Kreye (1977) focus on the increased industrial production for the world market which is occurring in the periphery. Industrial production has indeed shifted toward the periphery, and the labor force of most core states has become increasingly specialized in tertiary services (Bairoch 1975), and this has had important consequences for the quality of life in both core and periphery. But the structural nature of the core-periphery division of labor is relative, not absolute. Textile production, the key core industry of the early nineteenth century, has become a peripheral industry in the twentieth. Now that peripheral areas are producing textiles, core areas are producing computers and aircraft. The gap in terms of capital intensity and wages has been reproduced and possibly even increased.

There is little doubt that the core-periphery gap continues to exist, but has the magnitude of it changed? This is a hard question to answer with any precision because it involves a comparison between both the political rights of labor and the level of wages and other benefits. The postwar period has seen an expansion of the formal citizenship rights and state services in the periphery (chaps. 3, 5, and 13), but whether the actual content of these has been greater than the gains made in welfare rights and benefits by labor in the core is difficult to say. Similarly, data on the wages and overall income of workers in the core and the periphery has not been analyzed in a way which would answer the question we are asking. Emmanuel's (1972) rough comparisons indicate that the wage gap holding constant technical productivity, has increased greatly since the 1870s, but more complete data would be necessary to see if this trend has continued, slowed, or been reversed. Aggregate data on the level of GNP per capita indicate that there was not a significant reduction in the gap between nations during the 1950 to 1970 period, but this does not directly address the question of the gap between returns to core and periphery labor.

Research on the effects of national dependence on foreign investment has shown that this mechanism by which the core exploits the periphery continues to have negative effects on national economic growth in the period under consideration (chap. 8). This mechanism reproduces the gap in levels of economic development between the core and the periphery, but the cross-national evidence does not directly bear on possible changes in the magnitude of the gap.

The answer to the question posed awaits further research. We can only surmise that the gap has not decreased in the contemporary period.

The State System

An important change has occurred in the state system with the decolonization of most of the remaining colonies in the periphery. For the first time this system of formally sovereign states encompasses *the entire* economic division of labor. The absence of formal colonies may constitute an important change in the balance of power between the core and the periphery. It has been argued that core exploitation of the periphery can be accomplished with fewer overhead costs in a neocolonial than in

a colonial relationship. It is true that the expenses of colonial administration were a constant complaint of the "bearers of civilization," but it
may be that these expenses are exceeded by the need to circumvent and
to accept the national policies of peripheral states, whose intent is to
capture an increasing share of world surplus. One thing is clear: formal
sovereignty brings at least the possibility of effective resistance to core
exploitation, and this means an increase in the costs of exploitation.[4]

We note, importantly, that the ability of states to distort the market
to the advantage of certain groups is one of the most basic processes of
the capitalist world economy, and one which has allowed capitalism to
expand (Tardanico 1978). But this expansion of the state system to the
entire globe has the long-term effect of creating more constraints on
capital by raising the costs of exploitation. So, while the fundamental
nature of the state system has not changed, it continues to provide more
constraints on capital and hence, in the long run, to weaken the system.

The argument has been made by observers of the rapid growth of
multinational corporations that nation-states are no longer capable of
controlling these giant firms (Vernon 1971). The state system, it is
argued, must be replaced by some form of international sovereignty
which will be able to coordinate policy in order to control the multinationals. The coming of the world economic contraction and the rise
of economic nationalism has shown that the multinationals are very
susceptible indeed to state regulation. This turn of events has cast into
doubt the notion that some form of world state is about to emerge.[5]

In the most fundamental sense, the nature of the state system and its
function in the world economy has not changed. The increase in the
number of states encompassing the globe represents a long-term secular
trend in the world system. That this trend has now reached its limit will,
we argue later, cause changes in the world system. This represents not
a new departure, but a consequence of the operation of the world system. States now, as always, have been the major organizational mechanisms for distorting the market in the interests of those groups which
control the state. The recent phenomena of states or groups of states
taking action to affect commodity prices, to control the flows of capital
and labor, and so on do not represent any new departure. This has
always been the role of the state within the world economy.

CYCLES: ACCUMULATION, CORE COMPETITION, AND THE
STRUCTURE OF CORE-PERIPHERY TRADE
The Long Wave
The period of worldwide economic growth between the end of World
War II and 1967 was the last part of the expansion phase of a long wave
which reached its peak and has begun to turn down. We should expect
relatively slower and more uneven growth for the next twenty years or

so. Is there anything new about this economic cycle in the contemporary period which might indicate that the world system is in transition or crisis? Earlier cycles have produced political and technological reorganizations of production without changing the basic nature of the system.

Amin (1976) has argued that postwar Keynesian "fine economic tuning" has flattened out the shorter business cycles. The implementation of economic policy has regulated money supply and affected wages and prices within national economies. But state action, especially in a period of worldwide economic contraction, is itself competitive, and there are only weak international mechanisms for preventing the intensification of competition and conflict between national economies. As states attempt to interfere with the operation of the world market they intensify the anarchy of investment decisions and exacerbate the economic contradictions which cause stagnation in the world economy. In periods of contraction core states tighten their controls over trade with each other and with peripheral areas in order to protect revenues and the incomes of their dominant classes. This creates a more mercantilist world economy of trade wars and, potentially, military conflicts between core powers. The fall of the Breton Woods international monetary agreement in 1971, the rising protectionism of recent years, the increasing levels of unemployment, and the generally slower and more uneven rates of growth are indicators of the downturn. All these symptoms, however, are nothing new to the capitalist world economy.

Thus, the increasing anarchy in the international financial system which has characterized the last several years of economic contraction was preceded by a period of stability built around the hegemony of the US dollar (Block 1977). But this cycle is essentially like that of the period of financial peace in the first two-thirds of the nineteenth century described by Polanyi (1944) and Hobsbawm (1968), followed by a period of international financial anarchy during the downturn of 1873–96. Thus, we also now find an ambivalence in the United States between a "new internationalism" and a "new protectionism" which is quite similar to that which Hobsbawm described for England during the contraction which followed its hegemony.

Core Competition

The rise and fall of hegemonic core states appears to occur over shorter and shorter intervals if we may generalize from the three hegemonies which have occurred since the formation of the modern world system. The period between the Dutch hegemony of the seventeenth century and the British hegemony of the nineteenth century was much longer than that between the British and that of the United States. The three hegemonies also suggest that there is an approximate correspondence between the size of the hegemonic core power and the size of the whole world economy, although, as we shall see, the relatively large size of the US home market and internal natural resources may be consequential for the contemporary period.

The period from World War II to 1970 may be regarded as the golden age of the hegemony of the United States. Politically the United States was as supreme as any nation has ever been in the history of the modern world system. But there is also evidence that throughout this period the United States was losing its economic superiority to other core powers. The percentage of total world product produced by the United States declined from 42% in 1950 to 30% in 1970 (Meyer, Boli-Bennett, and Chase-Dunn 1975, table 2). The appropriate comparison is to Britain in 1875—still dominant in the world economy and in international diplomacy, but increasingly challenged by other core powers. It has been observed of the Dutch and British hegemonies that they matured through three stages. The first stage was based on a competitive advantage in the production of consumer goods which were able to invade national markets in the core and the periphery and to create new markets because of their low prices. For the Dutch the key commodity was salted herring, and for the British it was cotton textile manufactures. The second stage of the hegemony was based on the export of capital goods: Dutch shipbuilding and British machinery, railroad equipment, and steamships. The third stage is based on the export of investment capital and the performance of services which take advantage of the centrality of financial and commodity circulation which the earlier economic superiority has established. Both Amsterdam and London became world financial centers and maintained their centrality long after the national advantage in production had declined.

Let us consider the United States hegemony in this light. The first point is that, due to its extraordinarily large size and potential for internal expansion, the United States was less dependent on exports than either of its predecessors. The US hegemony was not based on key commodity exports, although the general pattern of success in terms of exporting first less-processed and later more-processed goods and investment capital was repeated. Agricultural exports were first supplemented by the export of iron and steel toward the end of the nineteenth century. The historically high cost of labor in the United States created an early competitive advantage in capital goods, and exports of machinery were important from the 1880s onward. Later automobiles and electrical equipment (both consumer durables and capital goods) became important. The early export of investment capital in large amounts seems to contradict the British pattern in some ways. Large amounts flowed abroad even prior to World War I. This may have been due to the generally mercantilist character of the international economy after 1873. Tariff barriers were never as low as during the Pax Britannica, even after World War II when the United States became the purveyor of the free-trade ideology. This heightened level of obstacles to international trade was a consequence of the secular increase in the number and strength of states in the system.

Thus the Pax Americana was quite short. The fall of the Breton Woods agreement signaled the end of the use of the US dollar as *the* world currency. The postwar recovery of the national economies of the other core powers, especially West Germany and Japan, created stiff competition for US industry. The flow of US investment capital abroad during the postwar period has been both the cause and the consequence of the shift in competitive advantage to other areas. The internal economic relocation toward the "sunbelt" may provide a partial respite from this loss of competitive advantage. Also, attempts to form a super-core community of world capital (the Trilateral Commission), while almost certain to fail, may prolong the financial (but not productive) centrality of the United States in the world system.

A simple extrapolation from the core competition cycles would predict that a period of disorganization and conflict will ensue, and eventually a new hegemonic core state should emerge. If the pattern holds, there should be economic stagnation until the 1990s, a new boom until the 2010s, then a period of war and depression ending with the emergence of a new hegemony. The question of cyclical repetition or transformation of the nature of the system may be clearly posed in these terms: What kind of international or world-level state could emerge that would alter the economic processes which produce and maintain core states? If this does not occur and the cycle continues, which state or bloc of states will constitute the new hegemonic core power?[6] What would be the essential difference between a world state and new hegemonic core state? It would be foolish to attempt prophecy beyond the prediction that the cycle will continue once more, and it will be the last one. The forces creating political organization and coordination at the level of the whole system will, barring some regressive catastrophe, eventually result in a socialist world government.

The Core-Periphery Structure of Trade and Control

We have observed that the structure of core-periphery relations cycles between a relatively multilateral trade pattern and a relatively bilateral one in which each core power trades only with its "own" periphery and political controls over exchange are predominant. The rise and fall of hegemonic core powers and the cycles of expansion and contraction of world economic growth have been systematically related to these shifts in core-periphery relations. An emerging hegemonic core state seeks to trade with colonies or peripheral markets of other core powers. Thus Britain after the Napoleonic Wars aided the Latin American independence movements in order to obtain freer access to this peripheral area. Also, a period of economic expansion in which growth is occurring everywhere reduces the pressures for political monopolization and protectionism as more groups of both producers and consumers come to have an interest in freeing up trade. These factors tend to make the structure of trade between core countries and peripheral areas more multilateral (Quinlan 1978).

The emergence of core powers which compete successfully in production with the formerly hegemonic core power increases the demand for raw materials and the competition for markets. This encourages the use of political power to protect markets and sources of raw materials, and results in a more bilateral and protectionist world economy of colonial empires. The late nineteenth-century rush for new colonies (the "new imperialism") and the tightening of controls over trade with older colonies resulted from such increasing competition in the core.

During the post–World War II period the matrix of world trade has become increasingly more multilateral. The average percentage of a nation's exports which went to its largest export partner declined from 39% in 1950 to 29% in 1969.[7] This was a period of relatively few political controls on core-periphery trade.[8] The decolonization of the most of the remaining colonies and the invasion by the United States and the Soviet Union of many of the former colonial markets of other core countries contributed to this multilateralization. Thus this period conforms to the cyclical pattern with respect to the relationship between economic expansion and multilateralization. The US was in the late stage of its hegemony, so that its role in creating the free-trade pattern was more a consequence of its international policies than of the low price of its export commodities.

If this cycle were to continue, we would predict a reversal in the multilateralization of the world trade matrix, the tightening of colonial controls over peripheral areas, and a rush of the core states to colonize new peripheral areas. Because of the "ceiling effects" to be discussed in the next section, further extension of the capitalist world economy to new territories and populations is impossible, and the recolonization of the formally sovereign peripheral states also seems unlikely. But what may be possible is movement toward a more bilateral exchange structure based on political trade agreements that core powers make with particular peripheral states. Due to the increased competition for raw materials and markets, peripheral areas may be able to obtain more favorable terms of trade by making bilateral trade agreements with those core states that can afford them. International trade syndicates such as OPEC may check this bilateralization to a certain extent and force core powers to compete with one another on a more equal basis. This would be an advantage to the smaller core powers and the less well-endowed peripheral areas, and would tend to produce a new alignment of political forces in the world economy along core-periphery lines. But the ability of OPEC and the periphery to maintain solidarity may succumb to the pressure on the better-endowed peripheral states to take advantage of the offers being made to them by individual core states.

SECULAR TRENDS AND CEILING EFFECTS

We postulated the existence of four systemic secular trends in our schema: extension to new populations and territories, intensification of the commodity form, increases in the power of states vis-à-vis their citizens, and increases in the size of firms. These four trends have increased in every epoch, although some have reached natural and systemic limits with consequences for the question of reproduction or transformation of the system.

Expansion to New Population and Territory

It has been argued that capitalism must expand in order to survive.[9] The capitalist world economy has geographically expanded to the point where it now includes virtually all the territory and population of the globe. By the end of the nineteenth century this extensive expansion had come close to its limit. Every formerly external arena had been incorporated in the capitalist world economy, either as periphery or as semiperiphery. There still remained some few territories and populations that were merely surrounded by a colonial boundary, and clearly some areas and peoples were relatively marginal, but the possibility of extensive expansion had begun to reach its limit.

In order to understand the consequences of this limit on extensive expansion we must explore its causes. To simplify a large corpus of theoretical discussion, we may say that the immediate cause of expansion has been the competition for raw materials, markets, cheap labor, and generally profitable investment opportunities. Often the political events surrounding a period of expansion reveal that it is not the vulgar demand for immediate economic return, but rather the competition between core states which creates the anticipatory nature of colonial expansion. Trade both precedes and follows the flag, depending upon the position of the colonizing state in the larger system and its success in obtaining an exploitable piece of the periphery. Data on the establishment of new colonial administrations indicate that both Britain and France established colonies throughout the nineteenth century, and it was only the newcomers (United States, Germany, Japan, Belgium, and Italy) that accounted for the "new imperialism" after 1885. Britain and France had been imperialist all along (Bergesen 1979).

But what are the underlying causes of this competition for new markets, raw materials, cheap labor, and investment opportunities? Successful capital accumulation creates working-class organizations which can contend with capital for a larger share of the surplus product. Also, the concentration of productive advantage in a particular hegemonic core state is usually followed by the spread of the new types of production to other core states. Thus both the price of labor and the power of labor rise in the core at the same time that core states begin competing with one another for resources in unexploited areas. Both the struggle between labor and capital and the competition between capitalists in different core states drive the expansion to previously unexploited territories and populations. What are the effects of limits on this type of expansion? Clearly, the effect is to force these needs to be met within the existing system itself. This leads to increased pressures to "commodify" areas of life not yet subjected to the accumulation process, and it also increases the costs of exploitation and the density of political opposition across the system.

Intensive Expansion: Further Commodification of Realms of Life
Polanyi (1944) described the great transformation to capitalism in terms of the reorganization of land, labor, and wealth into transferable "free" commodities subjected to a price-setting market. This process has proceeded apace in every epoch of the development of the modern world system, although some "traditional" uncommodified relations have been reproduced, and new limitations on commodification have emerged in some areas of life. In both the core and the periphery, however, the trend toward the commodification of labor has continued during the contemporary period. In the periphery the dependence of workers on wage labor has continued to increase. There remain a large number of "semiproletarians" whose wage labor income is supplemented by subsistence production. But the continued commercialization of agriculture, rural-urban migration, and the expansion of the urban service sector (including the labor-absorptive "informal sector")[10] indicates the growing influence of market forces over the labor process.

In core countries production for use in the home has decreased as the percentage of women in the wage labor force has risen (chap. 14). Uncommodified labor within the family has been transferred to the market economy. The commodity form has also extended to aspects of life which were but recently held to be transcendental. Marriage has become a rational exchange between individuals rather than a merging of interests. Children have become "consumer durables" in the eyes of economists eager to complete the commodification of life.

What are the causes of this further expansion of the commodity form? We would suggest that the intensification of the commodity form, the drawing of ever more spheres of life into the capital accumulation process, is partly a result of the same forces which caused extensive expansion. The competitive nature of capitalist production creates the need for expanded markets, more raw materials, lower cost labor, and expanded opportunities for profitable investment. The ceiling effect limiting extensive expansion discussed above causes the commodification of realms within the system not yet fully brought into the accumulation process.

Does this intensification have limits similar to those of extensive expansion? Certainly the world labor force may one day be fully dependent on commodity production. But, as old forms of resistance to market forces crumble, new forms appear. In the periphery the creation of the decolonized states limits to some extent the determination of the price of labor by world market forces. In the core, labor unions, the welfare state, and educational certification are new rational institutions which come to influence the price of labor. But these forms have not yet altered the overall commodification of labor in the system as a whole. Imperfect commodities are still commodities, and imperfect markets tend to determine the distribution of rewards over the long run. It has been pointed out that states have interfered with market forces throughout the history of the capitalist world economy, and yet competition at the level of the whole system has, in the long run, tended to subject both core and peripheral labor to world market forces. The contemporary period is no exception.

The Power of States vis-à-vis Their Citizens

Although there has always been a gap between the core and the periphery, the amount of power, authority, and resources of states has increased in every epoch of world-system development, including the present one (chaps. 11 and 13; Boli-Bennett 1976a, b). Class struggle within the core and between the core and the periphery causes the amount of resources necessary for maintaining the institutional conditions for capital accumulation to increase, and the organization which performs this function is the nation-state. In the core the struggle between capital and labor leads not only to wage increases but also to the expansion of the welfare state. In the periphery, the growth of a class of indigenous Westernized bureaucrats with nationalist interests results in national independence movements and the expansion of the state as a defensive organization against core economic and political power. State power is increased across the system as classes seek to have their interests institutionalized and protected.

The authority of traditional solidary groups, the community, the church, the family, the tribe, the clan, and so on over individuals has been usurped by the nation-state. Parents are no longer allowed to beat their "own" children. The percentage of national income which is appropriated or directly produced by the state has risen. The number of collective goods provided directly or indirectly by the state has expanded, and one or another form of national economic and physical planning has been adopted by almost every modern state.

A related process is nation-building, or the extent to which the national society itself becomes a new solidarity, a culturally integrated community. This too is more advanced in the core than in the periphery, but has continued to develop in both (chaps. 3–5). The rise of subnational or ethnic movements in which earlier solidarities become revitalized as mechanisms of political organization occurs in both the core and the periphery (chap. 15). Peripheral areas have always been subjected to political forces which have limited and disrupted the nation-building process. Colonial policy often intentionally created antagonisms between traditional groups, or imported culturally alien groups to serve as a buffer between the indigenous peoples and their colonial masters. In the contemporary period peripheral states have often attempted nation-building by excluding or discriminating against former colonial elites or buffer groups.

Subnational movements in the periphery in the contemporary period have almost always been encouraged by one or another core power seeking to gain advantage relative to other core powers. On the other hand subnational, or ethnic, movements in the core have generally been similar to nationalism in the periphery—a form of reactive resistance to a core state which uses a revitalized "primordial" solidarity as basis for political mobilization. The rash of subnational movements in core states in the contemporary period may have been encouraged by the reactive nationalism of the periphery in this period.

The trend toward ever greater state power over the lives of citizens seems to not have reached its limits. For one thing there remain sources of nonstate authority in national societies, and for another thing new realms of life are created by the process of development which may or may not be subjected to the control of national states. But let us do a mental experiment and imagine that *all* authority within national societies became subject to the state. All property would be owned and controlled by the nation-state. All primordial groups would be subject to it. No guilds, labor unions, professional associations, private enterprises, community groups, and so on could be organized outside of the authority of the national state. Would even this degree of nation-state authority fundamentally alter the nature of the capitalist world system? Clearly, the answer depends on the relationship among the states. If they acted as 140 capitalist firms producing commodities for the world market, very little would be different at the systemic level. Only the organization of coordination and cooperation at the world level would alter the underlying processes which presently determine the development of the system.

Size of Enterprises

We have observed that the average size of capitalist firms has increased in every epoch, and this trend has certainly continued in the post–World War II period. Since the end of the nineteenth century the economies of core states have been described as "monopoly capitalist" because the size of firms reached the point that *national markets* for some types of commodities were subjected to oligopoly pricing. The size of firms relative to the size of states and national markets has continued to increase such that the biggest capitalist corporations are now larger in terms of the assets than are a large number of the world's nation-states. The growth of "multinational" corporations has stirred the recent discovery of transnationalism and the claim that this new development in the world economy will transform the present state system into a more coordinated "international" political order (Keohane and Nye 1970).

The world-system perspective implies two observations about the size of firms in the present period. First, the world system has always been transnational in the sense that crucial economic and political relationships and exchanges have crossed national boundaries. Second, the size of the largest firms has definitely increased, but the size of the system in terms of total product and population has also increased. Thus, when comparing the Dutch East India Company of the seventeenth century with General Motors in the twentieth century we must take into account the size of the whole system at these two times. If this comparison could be accurately made it would probably show that the average firm size relative to system size has increased, though not to the extent indicated by simply comparing the firms to one another.

One thing is clear. The size of firms relative to the size of states has definitely increased. This would seem to imply a change in the relationship between purely economic and political power in the system. This was the observation which caused the transnational theorists to suppose that the unbridled multinational corporations would create the necessity for world-level political organization (Vernon 1971). These suppositions appear to have been false, at least in the short run. The world economic contraction has caused the reassertion of economic nationalism, and the multinational corporations, rather than the nation-states, seem to be the ones at bay. But if the long-run cycles continue we can expect another expansion of global firms during the next upswing of the world economy. It is then that the political consequences of production on a global scale should become apparent. The question of effects of the size of firms on the state system must also take into account the extent to which states themselves have begun to act as firms in the world economy. As we have pointed out, states have always involved themselves in the accumulation process, but most would agree that this involvement has increased in the twentieth century. This has not sub-stantially altered the competitive nature of the world economy, however.

CONCLUSIONS

In applying our structural schema of world-system development to the post–World War II period we have concluded that most of the patterns of development observed in this period are repetitions of earlier features or cycles of the larger system. Capitalism is still the dominant mode of production. The core-periphery division of labor remains a feature of the system, although the question of changes in the magnitude of the gap between core and periphery needs further research. The state system shows no signs of dissolution, although its extension to the whole pe-riphery is surely a significant development affecting the costs of core-periphery exploitation. The long cycles of economic growth and stagna-tion appear to be continuing. The cyclical pattern of competition among core states and the circulation which results in the rise and fall of hege-monic core states seems to be continuing. The cycle in which core-pe-riphery trade becomes alternatively more multilateral and then bilateral is being repeated. The political restrictions on core-periphery trade seem to be more to the advantage of peripheral states than was the case during previous periods in which colonial empires subjected peripheral areas to direct political domination. This also increases the cost of core-periphery exploitation. The limit to extensive expansion to new popula-tions and territories has been reached but the other secular trends—commodification, increasing power of states, and increasing size of firms —have not reached any insuperable limits.

What can be concluded from these observations about the significance of the changes noted above for the continued operation of the system? The limits on further expansion of the capitalist accumulation process to new territories and populations imply that the contradictions inherent in this process must be resolved within the system itself. Similarly, the increasing costs of core-periphery exploitation, while they have not yet begun to eliminate this dimension of the accumulation process, increase the necessity for capital to accommodate itself to the classes and interest groups which make claims upon it in the core. If these trends continue, the two major forms of class struggle in the system—the struggle be-tween capital and labor and the struggle between the core and the pe-riphery—will reinforce each other and reduce the profitability of private capital accumulation in the system as a whole.

In the near future, however, we do not see any fundamental alteration in the basic nature of the world economy. Rather, we see the present economic contraction ending, as have previous ones, with a somewhat greater share of surplus product expropriated by the semiperipheral areas, a greater concentration of capital within all three zones, and consequently a greater amount of political resistance to the system as a whole. At the end of the present contraction, we see another cycle of expansion and contraction, but whether the expansionary phase will result in the creation of a fourth hegemonic power is problematic. The long-run view, however, is that this last cycle is likely to be the final one; for as the secular trends continue to increase, political resistance will also. When capitalists no longer have fresh room for profitable investment, they will not invest, and this will bring about a political crisis which will change the fundamental nature of the world system.

NOTES

1 In Marxist terminology the institutional constants of the modern world system are capitalist commodity production with expanded reproduction in the core, and primitive accumulation in the periphery in the context of the core-periphery division of labor and the state system. This is a departure from Marx's own understanding of the fully developed capitalist mode of production which, focusing on the core of the system, defined capitalism as synonymous with the wage system of labor exploitation.

2 Marx's contention that class struggle is the motor of capitalist development and the source of the transformation of capitalism is extended by the world-system perspective (Wallerstein 1976a). Objective classes are understood to exist in relation to the world economy, whereas conscious classes are organized in relation to territorial nation-states. The political structure of the system cuts across the struggle between world capital and world labor, as does the core-periphery dimension of exploitation. But, even though class alliances between labor and capital are characteristic of political regimes in both the core and the periphery, the struggle between capital and labor, as well as intraclass struggles, creates the dynamic which alternately concentrates and expands capitalist production.

3 The timing of and relationship between different cycles varies somewhat in the different epochs. We do not yet understand the causal structure which produces these cycles, but some of the discrepancies are undoubtedly due to the influence of exogenous variables such as climatological changes, epidemics, and so on which delay or alter the developmental processes. This problem exists in the twentieth century as well. A great natural disaster or war might still disrupt the system, although increasing human control over nature and the technical ability to regenerate social production probably reduces the importance of exogenous factors over time. For this reason we will assume that deviations from the cycles in this century are due to systemic contradictions rather than exogenous influences.

4 Not all classes in the periphery benefit from this to the same degree, however. It has been shown that peripheral states which are relatively strong have higher levels of economic growth (chaps. 6 and 7) and are less negatively affected by dependence on foreign investment (chap. 12). This does not constitute direct evidence that the aggregate effect for the periphery as a whole is to increase its bargaining power, although this seems most likely.

Chirot (1977) overemphasizes the importance of this increase by claiming that the whole periphery has become semiperipheral. While this may be only a semantic difference, it is important to emphasize that the core-periphery division of labor is at least as important to the dynamics of postwar development as it was in earlier periods.

5 Formation of a world state would indeed constitute a fundamental change in the nature of the world system, and we expect this process to eventually make headway, but the immediate future seems more likely to be characterized by increased conflict between core states and disorganization of political relations at the world level.

6 For a discussion of one possible outcome see Wallerstein (1976c).

7 This has been calculated from data taken from the United Nations International Trade Statistics Yearbook for the sixty-nine countries for which data were available in 1950.

8 Krasner (1976) has shown that this is also true of trade between core countries.

9 Rosa Luxemburg (1968) explained this in terms of overproduction relative to effective demand, which made penetration of precapitalist markets a necessity. Others have stressed the need for raw materials, cheap labor, and profitable investment opportunities. Whichever of these is thought to be most important as an explanation, the contradiction between the social nature of production and the "private" appropriation of profit can be partially resolved in the short run by periodic crises which reorganize the accumulation process, but do not necessarily transform the basic nature of the system.

10 The informal sector includes petty traders, domestic service, and small businesses which employ family labor (Portes, forthcoming).

SEVENTEEN · Issues for Further Comparative Research

John W. Meyer and Michael T. Hannan

The studies reported in this book examine the effects of modern social institutions on each other—political and social effects on economic development, on educational expansion, and so on. We began with a conception of national societies as relatively independent units which developed endogenously. And many of our findings can be understood from this perspective: Richer countries expand education more rapidly (chaps. 3 and 4), and stronger states control and expand public education (chap. 5). Economic growth is affected by secondary educational expansion (chap. 6) and by state power (chaps. 6, 7, and 12). Poorer countries are likely to end up with weaker (chap. 12), but one-party (chap. 11) regimes. Stronger states produce various sorts of internal equalization (chaps. 8 and 14).

But findings like these, important as they may be, cannot explain the consistent changes in national social organization around the world in recent decades. Education expands more universally and unidirectionally than can easily be explained by political and economic factors within countries (chaps. 3 and 4). State power rises consistently and the system of nation-states expands to cover the whole world (chaps. 11 and 12; Meyer, Boli-Bennett, and Chase-Dunn 1975). It would be a mistake to see these worldwide changes as simply reflecting processes internal to particular national societies. The emergence, in the most unlikely parts of the world, of formally independent nation-states, each controlling a newly elaborated educational system, and each institutionalizing the modern principles of citizenship and formal equality, requires another level of explanation. The world system itself has been changing—and changes in national societies must be seen as closely interrelated with this transformation.

The studies reported in this book attempt to deal with this underlying situation through a number of devices:

Interpretive Adaptations
When we repeatedly find that state strength affects subsequent modernization, we do not pretend that we have found some universal process relating political centralization to social modernization. In another era,

when political centralization took on the trappings of empire, enclosing economic and social space within its boundaries, centralized power could contain and suppress economic and social changes that we call modernization (Wallerstein 1974a). In our world—one with a relatively unified cultural system and a densely linked economy, but without a centralized political system—centralized states have great advantages.

Describing and Modeling Change

Faced with essentially universal changes, we sometimes attempt to model the processes involved. In this spirit, we model the rapid educational expansions in national societies around the world (chaps. 3 and 4). And we describe the expanding ideology of state authority and responsibility (chap. 13) and the system of unitary or one-party regimes (chap. 11). If we cannot, within the confines of our data, explain the expansion of the state system and the modern educational system around the world, at least we can describe *how* these institutions diffuse around the world.

Incorporating World-System Linkage as an Explicit Variable

Since most structural features of the world system do not vary over the period we study (chap. 16), we cannot use structural variations in the world system as explanatory variables in empirical analysis. However, we can characterize the relation of each country to this larger system, to see what effects these relations have on national development. Many of our most important findings take this form: More dependent (or less powerful) nations experience smaller gains in economic growth (chap. 8), but this does not result from specialization in primary production (chap. 9). They are likely to maintain weaker states (chap. 12) with one-party regimes (chap. 11). And countries with stronger internal information systems are likely to reduce their dependence (chap. 10). Dependence, however, does not seem to slow social modernization, if educational expansion can be taken as a measure (chap. 3).

Our efforts to use features of the world system as explanatory factors take us some of the way toward understanding the evolution of world society during the present period. They do not take us far enough.

THE PROBLEM

We need to understand (*a*) the processes maintaining and changing the contemporary world system; (*b*) the effects of this system on the construction of national societies; and (*c*) the effects of systematic changes in the structure of national societies on the evolution of the world system. These problems call for research designs which follow changes in the world system itself over longer periods of time. The data in chapter

13 on the ideology of state authority move in this direction. So do the theoretical ideas in chapters 15 and 16.

The core problem in considering the recent past concerns explaining how modern, rationalized institutions have penetrated so universally and consistently. The question applies with special force to peripheral countries. Not long ago it was feared that these countries might become balkanized, and might regress (or become pastoralized) with the breakdown of the colonial system. This has not happened; and these countries too have moved in directions that are generally called modern.

Economic Growth and the Shift to the Tertiary Sector

Most countries have expanded economic production since World War II (chap. 6). This growth has cut across all economic sectors. Growth in both agricultural and industrial production has outstripped population growth, which is itself rapid. But the most rapid growth in recent decades has occurred in the tertiary (or service, or "postindustrial") sector. This pattern applies both in developed and in peripheral societies (Kuznets 1971).

Thus, much economic growth has more of a *social* quality than the usual images (drawn from considerations of commodity production) convey. Tertiary-sector growth involves the expansion of governments, educational systems, professional activity, military organizations, or exchange activities ("penny capitalism"). Many traditional activities have been recast in modern terms, and new organizations and services created. The newly organized activities take on modern value, and contribute to national product. In this sense much of the new economic growth is socially and politically constructed and defined.

The links among national economies are becoming stronger as well. Data on imports (or exports) as proportions of gross national product do not show this increase clearly because reductions in international transport costs lower these ratios. But commodity flows across national boundaries show great increases. International flows involving tertiary sectors show few increases, but this too is misleading, since national account statistics ignore pure information flows (for example scientific ideas, organizational and political forms, and so on).

The State System

The world political structure now mainly contains formally independent states. State boundaries seem relatively fixed; and great tensions are created by what might otherwise seem to be minor boundary conflicts. The critical issues arise over which regimes will operate given states. Thus the recent independence of Angola was accompanied by the worldwide assumption that this set of social groups would be controlled by a single state; conflicts arose only over which regime would dominate the state.

The system of states, especially in peripheral areas, seems as much maintained by powerful world political forces as by forces internal to national societies. Dominant states use military and financial resources to maintain the power of peripheral states over their populations. For example, social forces internal to Angola would likely not have been sufficient to maintain a unified state in control of the population and territory without external aid.

The contemporary world system does more than support an almost complete network of states. It appears to induce these states to increase their control over their societies, incorporating more areas of social life (chap. 13). More government seems to be required (Huntington 1968), and internal and external forces lead to the replacement of limited state forms by more comprehensive ones. The modern state assumes economic responsibilities, regardless of its economic resources. It extends citizenship statuses (for instance, universal education; see chap. 5), welfare rights, and so on. More than could have been imagined three decades ago, even peripheral states are forced—at least symbolically—to assume responsibility for social and economic progress.

These pressures create political problems, as responsibilities for creating progress can seldom be met. A current resolution of such pressures, particularly in peripheral societies, is the unitary—one-party or military—regime (chap. 11). The population is mobilized under restrictive conditions of participation and representation, and state authority is located in organs several steps removed from society. The organization of the state system, in defining new and urgent social and political problems, seems to favor strong states and to undercut the representative functions of political systems.

To a striking extent, particularly in view of the centralization of the world economy, the world system continues to lack a political *center*. International political organizations lack strength. The state system continues—in an intensified form—the peculiar features that Wallerstein (1974a) treats as a central aspect of the Western world system of recent centuries. The world system, though economically and culturally integrated, differs from previous systems in lacking a political center that can control economic and social life.

Social Modernization

Modern institutional and organizational forms have sprung up and expanded almost everywhere during this period. We have paid particular attention to the expansion of modern forms of educational organization. Similar growth can be documented for modern forms of health care organization, state bureaucracy, and so on. And we have argued that the strength of the state system has at least partly accounted for the success of these forms.

Culture and Stratification System

Common definitions of the (technical) nature of reality, of value, of the nature of man, and of equity, seem dominant in the modern system. The world system has moved toward a single stratification system, in which all nations compare their progress on the same scales. Differences among societies are seen more as inequalities and distributional inequities within a single system, rather than as the result of independent evolution of discrete units. This understanding serves as an engine of mobilization, modernization, and state power in peripheral societies. States in the periphery adopt progress in the world system as a purposive national goal.

POSSIBLE EXPLANATIONS

We now turn to a discussion of some arguments about the nature of the interrelations among these trends.

Technical and Environmental Factors

The period we studied is one of unparalleled rates of technological innovation and energy utilization. The rapid integration of the world economy and cultural system was made possible largely by revolutions in communications and transportation technology. The widespread application of modern information-processing technology (for example, computers) to the management of complex webs of economic and social transactions has also had a major impact. Perhaps even more important in retrospect, the 1950–70 period witnessed the rapid consumption of cheap fossil fuels. Much of the economic growth of the period can be viewed as the returns on a technically facilitated harvest of stored solar energy.

Technological innovation and increased energy consumption undoubtedly affected each of the processes we studied. They permitted massive population growth that altered age distributions. Perhaps more aged populations would have proceeded more cautiously in state expansion, social modernization, and so on. Clearly the rise of enormous cohorts of young persons altered the conditions of political competition within states to favor mobilizing regimes. Also, real incomes rose so that states could allocate larger national products. The rapid rise in real incomes, though apparently temporary, produced waves of optimism that fueled the expansion of modern institutions.

Integration, World Pluralism, and the Rise of the State System

Expansion and integration of the world cultural and economic systems create pressures for expanded political organization and control at higher levels (see chap. 15). First, as the system integrates, growth and modernization become rulelike collective purposes. What organization will take jurisdiction over these purposes? Second, inequalities both internal and external to given social groups come to be seen as inequities (class-consciousness on a world scale). What organization will provide justice? Third, the organization of an explicit system of expanded competition—on modern terms—erodes the traditional controls of village, community, and kinship. What organization can command loyalty on a scale large enough to compete?

One answer is a world state. And indeed, the ideologies of West and East and the Third World all refer to some world state as an ideal locus of authority. But there is no world state. In this situation, resources and legitimacy flow to the rationalized nation-state elements of the state-system. *These* organizations adopt the pursuit of growth, justice, and power in the world system as collective ends.

The development of the state system has been enhanced by a shift *away* from a centralized world political system in the twentieth century (paralleling similar shifts in earlier cycles of the world system). When the European imperial system fell at the end of World War II, world political power lay in the hands of two states (organized primarily as nation-states in reaction to the older European system) that were in sharp conflict. This situation produced normative pressures and political opportunities for the formation of independent states throughout the Third World.

Just as the rise of capitalism and the competitive market economy located legitimate authority and social power in the individual, the rise of the contemporary world economy and culture legitimates and empowers nation-states as organs of collective action.

The State-System and National Mobilization

The processes just discussed make the nation-state an extraordinary center of mobilization—driven to reorganize its population and to penetrate society with national and modern institutions. National integration in a competitive world economy and stratification system both causes and results from development, in contrast to static control over domestic life. Societies with strong states, in fact, maintain higher rates of development (chaps. 6, 7, and 12). Further, this drive for development covers many aspects of modernization.

Societies tend less than might be expected to specialize in particular types of development. This can be seen as resulting from a general drive for state and national autonomy. But in a politically uncontrolled world, it makes sense from the perspective of a given society and state. Specialization is rational in a world in which markets, relationships, and interdependencies are characterized by stability and certainty. In a more uncertain world, it may be more rational to attempt to modernize in a relatively complete fashion—producing the whole range of commodities and services autonomously—in order to maximize certainty (Williamson 1975).

The world cultural system authorizes states to control national societies and to implement modern institutional forms. These authorizations are not simply airy cultural ideals; they are standards in terms of which internal populations, alternative elites, and external political forces will react, replacing laggard states with stronger ones. Consequently, states which do not engage in aggressive nation-building risk internal fragmentation. New nations, particularly, experience crises of boundary formation and maintenance, and many of their political characteristics follow from this problem.

But the functional need for states to mobilize their populations does not really explain how it happens that they can do so. Here the state system plays an important role, especially in peripheral areas. External forces provide military and economic resources, and social legitimacy, to states. These resources drive states to overcome the potential alternative allegiances of their populations, and to impose national institutions. The ability of states to control their populations is their most important social and economic resource in competition in the wider world system. The world economy maintains power over the allocation of most resources. Capital, technology, and commodities flow relatively freely in world markets, and their values are set in large part by these markets. States can attempt to control flows of capital, commodities, and technology, but with uncertain legitimacy and success. Thus most states— especially in the periphery—have little control over world markets. But with respect to allocations of labor, states have much more control. The state system and world cultural rules give states autonomous control over population movement. As a consequence, despite flows of capital, commodities, and technology at high levels, labor flows are relatively, and perhaps absolutely, restricted. Nothing in recent history compares with the gigantic labor flows which populated the Americas and redistributed populations in other parts of the world (for instance, Africa) in previous centuries. In our world system tiny labor flows (like "brain drains") or minor ones (like the shifts of Mediterranean workers to northern Europe) seem only marginally legitimate. They are considered anomalies and social problems.[1]

This situation confers on national economics, societies, and states their greatest resource. Obtaining growth through capital accumulation and commodity imports is time-consuming and uncertain. Obtaining growth by mobilizing and redirecting the labor force—in particular, around modern social and material technologies, which also flow rather freely—is easier. Given national control over labor flows, labor costs are set mainly by local conditions rather than by world market price. Labor in peripheral areas is thus inexpensive. Peripheral states can compete most effectively in the race for modernization by redirecting labor into labor-intensive service activities, especially of modern technical kinds. We suspect that this is a major reason why so much economic growth in the world takes the form of service activity. Labor flows can easily be directed into government service, education, military activity, and so on, contributing heavily to national modernization and national economic progress (by present national accounting systems). Measured economic growth occurs, thus, through the redirection of activity into arenas socially *defined* as necessary and valuable.

One can look askance at the progress so created—expansion of tertiary activities in impoverished societies may create economic value without much affecting the capacity to generate goods and services. This phenomenon perhaps accounts for some of the peculiar features of the recent social change in peripheral societies.

SPECULATIONS ON FUTURE PATTERNS

We do not recommend an extrapolation of this analysis to the future. While the processes we discuss may be general, several important features of the situation are changing in ways that may alter trends. For instance, the era of cheap fossil fuels has ended and rates of economic growth have slowed. Rates of population growth have also declined, in many cases precipitously. Western nations already face new and potentially far-reaching structural changes due to the coming demographic dominance of the aged. And the early optimism that technology could solve the problems of underdevelopment has been replaced by an increased awareness that technological solutions create their own problems. Each of these factors makes it more difficult to mobilize populations and also hampers the ability of states to deliver on their promises. Consequently, the system we describe is probably unstable.

But technical, material, and demographic factors are not the only sources of instability in these patterns. The processes we described above may create "contradictions" that undermine structures. Nations adapt to world-system contingencies by relying on the centralized state form of organization, but this form of adaptation involves quasi-dialectical processes that produce maladaptation.

Many of the mobilizationally oriented centralized states we study are new states. And new states have a number of advantages in the modern state system. They have high levels of internal and external legitimacy and resources from the outset. So new states in the current period avoid most of the perils that generally befall new organizations. And they do enjoy the advantages of newness. They can institute structures and internal rules that are well adapted to current circumstances. The state structures the older center nations evolved over long periods contain features that are not well adapted to the present. In concrete terms this means that new states have an opportunity to eliminate many structures restricting state action in older states. Similarly, new states can avoid established commitments to groups they represent and employ, and recruit employees from a narrow base so as to ensure homogeneity in terms of values and interests. Consequently, new structures may perform certain tasks, for example social modernization, more effectively than structures that survive from an earlier era.

But the normal processes of organizational change erode these advantages over time. By the process that Michels (1959) labeled the "iron law of oligarchy," structures become adapted to serve the narrow interests of their elites as the elites become cut off from the populations they represent initially. Thus flows of information, essential to effective adaptation and collective response, are diminished. At the same time the ceremonial activities that organizational elites generate to validate and legitimate organizations rebuild inefficiency in organizational structures.

Moreover, state structures face a special problem. Successful state- and nation-building greatly increases the scale of the state apparatus. As scale increases, the charismatic flavor that pervades successful new organizations is strained. The organization may flounder at precisely the point that it becomes too large and complex, so that a single leader or leading coalition cannot effectively supervise the work of key personnel (Hannan and Freeman 1977). Further, as more diverse interests and social groupings are incorporated into the state, it comes to reflect the diversity of interests of the society. The political struggles that formerly would have occurred between communities, say, now occur within and among the bureaus of the state.

Similar contradictions may accompany the other strategies that we attribute to mobilizing societies. We suggested that the combination of cheap labor in the periphery and national boundaries around labor markets leads to heavy investments in service industries such as education. But what are the long-run costs of this strategy? In order to construct a modern educational system expeditiously, low-wage teachers are made state employees. Eventually these teachers may combine with other civil servants to extract high wages from the state, turning themselves into expensive labor. Moreover, the students and their parents may use international standards to evaluate the performance of schools and demand continually higher levels of investment in upgrading the system. Before long the once cheap investment consumes a sizable fraction of the national product, diverting resources from other uses.

Processes of organizational change may thus trap mobilizing states. Centralization and mobilization may enable new states to compete well in the short term. But in the long run, bureaucratization and the associated rise of the tertiary sector build more and more rigidity into the structure of the state, constraining response to changes in the environment. In particular, centralized states may have little capacity to manage economic action in a period of world economic decline or stagnation, or to adapt to restrictions on further modernization created by large increases in the cost of energy.

We need to study these processes and to separate the effects of newness from the effects of pure mobilization or centralization. This is an important argument for analyzing the processes over longer periods, particularly including data for the 1970–80 period as soon as it becomes available.

In the absence of such evidence, we speculate about some of the consequences of the instability for societies and states created by the current larger structures. One outcome may be the high rate of regime turnover (political instability) that can be observed. As the costs of maintaining rigid and specialized state structures mounts, pressures for fundamental reform increase. The most plausible strategy for such reform in centralized states is to oust the regime and replace it with another. But, for all the reasons we have discussed, each new set of regimes tends to adopt highly mobilizational policies.

On the other hand, if the state system were sufficiently autonomous and stable, states might become insulated from the demands of their populations. Their success could come to be defined on the terms of the state system, independent of pressures from society. One could imagine a world of highly bureaucratic unitary states, each maintaining itself through its own power and the power of the system in which it was embedded. This outcome seems unlikely for two reasons. First, the state system does not seem likely to acquire effective control over the world economy. Individual states may attempt such controls, but they cannot control the system, which continues to undercut the autonomy of its state components. Second, aside from its weak capacity to control the world economy, the state system is politically unstable. Relations and coalitions among states change, undercut by both political and economic changes, and continually threaten relations between states and their populations.

We might also conceive of a breakdown in state controls over internal labor forces and citizenries—an integrated free-market world—as a possibility, although the authority of states over their populations and labor forces is one of the verities of the present system. Any such breakdown would undercut the current modernization of peripheral societies, and the rise of urban tertiary economic sectors in these societies. State power in peripheral societies—which rests in some part on control of labor— would be greatly weakened, and both states and societies would be pastoralized. Elite social and economic activities would flow to centers which would have dramatically lowered wage rates, and peripheral hinterlands would, following the models of peripheral societies in the nineteenth-century world of a freer labor market, have weak states, low urbanization, and specialization in primary economic activities (although, possibly, at higher wage rates than at present).

This kind of free-market world—a Western ideological notion whose implications are not often spelled out—seems very unlikely. In the present densely integrated world economic and cultural system, the levels at which explicit political controls are formulated are much more likely to shift upward in scale rather than downward into world individualism.

The explicitness of the contemporary world system, and the rise to dominance of ideologies of collective (usually state or national) jurisdiction over social and economic life, invite the rise of a more centralized world political system. Such a system, achieving partial control over all aspects of the world economy, could produce widely varying effects, depending on its structure. Clearly, the power of individual nation-states would be lowered. So might the pressures on each national society to build its own nation in standardized forms, as might the contemporary pressures to incorporate populations (with welfare rights) and dragoon them (with citizenship obligations) into modernity. For better or worse, some of the kinds of social change we have studied might proceed more slowly. Further, if distributional rules in a world system were organized politically rather than economically, social and economic specialization might increase. A world state, even a weak one, might thus have some of the trappings of a world empire, exerting less modernizing pressure, and enabling (and encouraging) local reactive diversity and specialization.

A more explicitly organized world political system in fact has developed, though we often do not recognize it because its forms differ from those of the nation-state. The close integration of a set of competing societies of great structural similarity produces (and has produced over recent centuries) very high levels of conflict, and has also produced very high legitimacy for conflict-reducing mechanisms. International agencies, perhaps, have gained little power. But the network of relations among states slowly increases its control over world social life, and slowly takes on more and more aspects of a partially centralized system. Increasingly, flows of communications, commodities, labor, technologies, and capital investments occur through the explicit intermediation of state organizations and their agents. Describing this slow process—for instance, the increasing proportions of world commodity flows that are explicitly managed and regulated by nation-states and international agencies—is an important research task.

The expanding and uncontrolled world economy which Wallerstein and others see as a central force in recent centuries has few new domains in which to expand. We may be entering into a long slow process through which a world political system gains control in the name of peace, development, and equity. The prospect is not an entirely attractive one. A more highly organized world political system may do less to accomplish the ends that justify it than to weaken the legitimacy of demands for these ends.

NOTES

1 Of course, large labor flows still occur. In both Europe and the United States, substantial proportions of the employed populations have emigrated across national boundaries. Especially large movements accompanied the political conflicts during and after World War II. Our point there is that the ratios of labor flow to capital and commodity flows are low, probably much lower than in the past.

References

Acton, H. B. 1957. *The illusion of the epoch.* Boston: Beacon.

Adelman, Irma, and Morris, Cynthia T. 1967. *Society, politics and economic development.* Baltimore: Johns Hopkins Press.

————. 1971. *Anatomy of patterns of income distribution in developing countries.* Final research report, U.S. Agency for International Development, CSD–2236.

————. 1973. *Economic growth and social equity in developing countries.* Stanford, Ca.: Stanford University Press.

Aitken, Hugh G. J., ed. 1959. *The state and economic growth.* New York: Social Science Research Council.

Almond, Gabriel, and Verba, Sidney. 1963. *The civic culture.* Princeton: Princeton University Press.

Amin, Samir. 1973. *Le développement inégal: essai sur les formations sociales du capitalisme périphérique.* Paris: Editions de Minuit.

————. 1974. *Accumulation on a world scale.* New York: Monthly Review Press.

————. 1976. *Unequal development.* New York: Monthly Review Press.

Anderson, C. Arnold, and Bowman, Mary Jean, eds. 1966. *Education and economic development.* Chicago: Aldine.

Apter, David E. 1963. *Ghana in transition.* New York: Atheneum.

Arnove, R. F. 1975. Sociopolitical implications of educational television. *Journal of Communications* 25: 144–56.

Aron, Raymond. 1957. *The opium of the intellectuals.* Trans. T. Kilmartin. London: Secher and Warburg.

Arrighi, Giovanni. 1970. International corporations, labour aristocracies, and economic development in tropical Africa. In *Imperialism and underdevelopment,* ed. R. Rhodes, pp. 220–67. New York: Monthly Review Press.

Baer, Werner. 1961. The economics of Prebisch and ECLA. *Economic Development and Cultural Change* 10–11: 169–82.

Baldwin, K. E. 1966. *Economic development and export growth: A study of Northern Rhodesia: 1920–1960.* Berkeley: University of California Press.

Banks, Arthur S. 1971. *Cross polity time series data.* Cambridge: MIT Press.

————, ed. 1976. *Political handbook of the world.* New York: McGraw-Hill.

Banks, Arthur S., and Textor, Robert. 1963. *A cross-polity survey.* Cambridge: MIT Press.

Baran, P. 1957. *The political economy of growth.* New York: Monthly Review Press.

Barker, Ernest. 1944. *The development of public services in Western Europe, 1660–1930.* London: Oxford University Press.

Barrat-Brown, Michael. 1974. *Economics of Imperialism.* Baltimore: Penguin.

Barth, Fredrik. 1956. Ecologic relationships of ethnic groups in Swat, North Pakistan. *American Anthropologist* 58: 1079–89.

———. 1969. Introduction. In *Ethnic groups and boundaries,* ed. F. Barth, pp. 9–38. Boston: Little, Brown.

Baumgartner, Tom; Buckley, Walter; and Burns, Tom R. 1975. Toward a systems theory of unequal exchange, uneven development and dependency relations. Paper prepared for the Third International Congress of Cybernetics and Systems, Bucharest.

Beckford, George. 1971. *Persistent poverty: underdevelopment in plantation regions of the world.* New York: Oxford University Press.

Bell, Daniel. 1975. Ethnicity and social change. In *Ethnicity: theory and experience,* ed. N. Glazer and D. P. Moynihan, pp. 141–74. Cambridge: Harvard University Press.

Bellah, Robert N., ed. 1965. *Religion and progress in modern Asia.* New York: Free Press.

Ben-David, Joseph, and Zloczower, Abraham. 1962. Universities and academic systems in modern societies. *European Journal of Sociology* 3: 45–85.

Bendix, Reinhard. 1956. *Work and authority in industry: ideologies of management in the course of industrialization.* New York: Wiley.

———. 1964. *Nation-building and citizenship.* New York: Wiley.

———. 1967. Tradition and modernity reconsidered. *Comparative Studies in Society and History* 9: 292–346.

———. 1968. *State and society.* Berkeley, Ca.: University of California Press.

Benedict, Ruth. 1938. Continuities and discontinuities in cultural conditioning. *Psychiatry* 1: 161–67.

Benot, Y. 1973. *Qu'est-ce que le développement?* Paris: Maspero.

Berg, Ivar. 1971. *Education and jobs: The great training robbery.* Boston: Beacon Press.

Bergesen, Albert. 1977. Political witch hunts: the sacred and the subversive in cross-national perspective. *American Sociological Review* 42: 220–33.

———. 1979. Global cycles: the expansion and contraction of colonialism from 1500 to 1970. To appear in *Sociological studies of the modern world-system,* ed. Albert James Bergesen. New York: Academic Press.

Berman, B. J. 1974. Clientelism and neo-colonialism: center-periphery relations and political development in African states. *Studies in Comparative International Development* 9: 3–25.

Bettelheim, Charles. 1975. *Economic calculation and forms of property.* New York: Monthly Review Press.

Bienen, Henry, and Morell, David, eds. 1976. *Political participation under military regimes.* Beverly Hills, Ca.: Sage.

Black, C. E. 1967. *The dynamics of modernization.* New York: Harper and Row.

Blalock, Hubert M., Jr. 1967. *Toward a theory of minority-group relations.* New York: Capricorn.

———. 1969. *Theory construction.* Englewood Cliffs, N.J.: Prentice-Hall.

Blau, Peter M., and Duncan, O. D. 1967. *The American occupational structure.* New York: Wiley.

Blaug, M., ed. 1968, 1969. *Economics of education* vols. 1 and 2. Baltimore: Penguin.

Block, Fred. 1977. *The origins of international economic disorder.* Berkeley, Ca.: University of California Press.

Boli-Bennett, John. 1975. The expansion of the state: causes and consequences in the modern historical period. Stanford, Ca.: Stanford University Dept. of Sociology.

———. 1976a. The expansion of nation-states, 1870–1970. Ph.D. dissertation, Stanford University.

———. 1976b. Global integration and the rise of the universal omnivorous state. To appear in *Sociological studies of the modern world-system,* ed. A. J. Bergesen. New York: Academic Press.

Bonacich, Edna. 1972. A theory of ethnic antagonism: the split labor market. *American Sociological Review* 37: 547–59.

———. 1975. Abolition, the extension of slavery and the position of free blacks: a study of split labor markets in the United States, 1830–1863. *American Journal of Sociology* 81: 601–28.

Bornschier, Volker. 1975. Abhaengige industrialisierung und einkommensentwicklung. *Schwiezerische Zeitschrift für Sociologie* 1: 67–105.

———. 1978. *Multinational corporations in the world economy and national development.* Zürich: Bulletin of the Sociological Institute of the University of Zürich, No. 32.

Bornschier, Volker; Chase-Dunn, Christopher; and Rubinson, Richard. 1978. Cross-national evidence of the effects of foreign investment and aid on economic growth and inequality: a survey of findings and reanalysis. *American Journal of Sociology,* 84: 651–83.

Boserup, Ester. 1970. *Women's role in economic development.* New York: St. Martin's.

Boudon, Raymond. 1974. *Education, opportunity, and social inequality: changing prospects in western society.* New York: Wiley.

Boulding, Kenneth E. 1953. *The organizational revolution—a study in the ethics of economics of organization.* New York: Harper Brothers.

———. 1966. The economics of the coming Spaceship Earth. In *Environmental quality in a growing economy,* ed. H. Jarrett, pp. 3–14. Baltimore: Johns Hopkins University Press.

———. 1970. *A primer on social dynamics—history as dialectics and development.* New York: Free Press.

Bourricaud, F. 1966. Structure and function of the Peruvian oligarchy. *Studies in Comparative International Development* 2: 17–31.

Bowles, Samuel, and Gintis, Herbert. 1976. *Schooling in capitalist America.* New York: Basic Books.

Bowman, Mary Jean, and Anderson, C. Arnold. 1963. Concerning the role of education in development. In *Old societies and new states,* ed. C. Geertz, pp. 249–79. New York: Free Press.

Braudel, Fernand, and Spooner, Frank. 1967. Prices in Europe from 1450 to 1750. In *The economy of expanding Europe in the sixteenth and seventeenth centuries. Cambridge economic history of Europe,* vol. 4, ed. E. E. Rich, pp. 374–486. Cambridge: Cambridge University Press.

Breen, M. P. 1975. Severing the American connection: down under. *Journal of Communications* 25: 183–86.

Briggs, F. E. A. 1962. The influence of error on the correlation of ratios. *Econometrica* 30: 162–77.

Brim, Orville, and Wheeler, Stanton. 1967. *Socialization after childhood: two essays.* New York: Wiley.

Campbell, Donald T., and Stanley, Julian S. 1963. *Experimental and quasi-experimental design for research.* Chicago: Rand McNally.

Chafe, William H. 1972. *The American woman.* London: Oxford University Press.

Chase-Dunn, Christopher. 1975. International economic dependence in the world-system. Ph.D. dissertation, Stanford University.

———. 1978. Core-periphery relations: the effects of core competition. In *Social change in the capitalist world economy,* ed. Barbara H. Kaplan, pp. 159–76. Beverly Hills, Ca.: Sage.

Chase-Dunn, Christopher, and Rubinson, Richard, 1977. Toward a structural perspective on the world-system. *Politics and Society* 7: 453–76.

Chavance, Bernard. 1977. Production relations in the USSR. *Monthly Review* 29: 1–13.

Chenery, H. B., and Strout, A. M. 1966. Foreign assistance and economic development. *American Economic Review* 56: 144–51.

Cherry, C. 1961. *On human communication.* New York: Science Editions.

Chirot, Daniel. 1977. *Social change in the twentieth century.* New York: Harcourt Brace Jovanovich.

Clark, Colin. 1957. *The conditions of economic progress.* 3d ed. London: Macmillan.

Cohen, Yehudi. 1964. *The transition from childhood to adolescence.* Chicago: Aldine.

Coleman, J. S., ed. 1965. *Education and political development.* Princeton: Princeton University Press.

Coleman, James S. 1968. The mathematical study of change. In *Methodology in social research,* ed. H. M. Blalock, Jr. and A. Blalock, pp. 428–78. New York: McGraw-Hill.

———. 1973. Loss of power. *American Sociological Review* 38: 1–17.

Collins, Randall. 1971. Functional and conflict theories of educational stratification. *American Sociological Review* 36: 1002–19.

Coombs, Philip. 1968. *The world educational crisis: a systems analysis.* Oxford: Oxford University Press.

Coppock, J. D. 1962. *International economic instability.* New York: McGraw-Hill.

Currie, Janice. 1977. Family background, academic achievement and occupational status in Uganda. *Comparative Educational Review* 21: 14–28.

Cutright, Phillips. 1963. National political development: measurement and analysis. *American Sociological Review* 28: 253–64.

Cutright, Phillips, and Wiley, James A. 1969–70. Modernization and political representation: 1927–1966. *Studies in Comparative International Development* 5: 23–44.

Daalder, Hans. 1966. Parties, elites and political developments in western Europe. In *Political parties and political development*, ed. J. La Palombara and M. Weiner, pp. 43–77. Princeton: Princeton University Press.

Davis, Kingsley. 1969. *World urbanization, 1950–1970*, vol. 1. Population Monograph Series No. 4. Berkeley: University of California Press.

Day, Richard. 1976. The theory of long waves: Kondratiev, Trotsky, Mandel. *New Left Review* 99: 67–82.

Dean, H. 1971. Scarce resources: the dynamics of American imperialism. In *Readings in U.S. Imperialism*, ed. K. T. Fann and D. C. Hodges, pp. 139–54. Boston: Porter Sargent.

Delacroix, J. 1974. Information processes and economic development: a longitudinal study of dominance-dependence relationships in the world ecosystem. Ph.D. dissertation, Stanford University.

Denison, E. 1962. *The sources of economic growth in the United States and the alternatives before us.* New York: Committee for Economic Development.

Deutsch, K. 1966. *Nationalism and social communication: an inquiry into the foundations of nationality.* Cambridge: MIT Press.

Doreian, Patrick, and Hummon, Norman P. 1976. *Modeling social processes.* Amsterdam: Elsevier.

Dos Santos, Teotonio. 1970. The structure of dependence. Papers and proceedings. *American Economic Review* 60: 231–6.

Dreeben, Robert. 1968. *On what is learned in school.* Reading, Ma.: Addison-Wesley.

Duchacek, Ivo K. 1973. *Rights and liberties in the world today: constitutional promise and reality.* Santa Barbara, Ca.: ABC–CLIO.

Duncan, O. D. 1964. Social organization and the ecosystem. In *Handbook of modern sociology*, ed. R. E. Faris, pp. 36–82. Chicago: Rand McNally.

———. 1969. Some linear models for two-variable panel analysis. *Psychological Bulletin* 72: 177–82.

————. 1972. Unmeasured variables in linear models for panel analysis. In *Sociological methodology 1972*, ed. H. Costner, pp. 36–82. San Francisco: Jossey-Bass.

————. 1975. *Introduction to structural equation models.* New York: Academic Press.

Durkheim, Emile. 1912. *The elementary forms of the religious life.* London: George Allen and Unwin.

Easterlin, R. A. 1967. Effects of population growth on the economic development of developing countries. *Annals of the American Academy of Political and Social Science* 369: 98–108.

Easton, David. 1959. Political anthropology. In *Biennial review of anthropology.* ed. B. Siegel, pp. 210–62. Stanford, Ca.: Stanford University Press.

Ehrensaft, Philip. 1971. Semi-industrial capitalism in the third world. *Africa Today* 18: 40–57.

Eisenstadt, S. N. 1956. *From generation to generation.* Glencoe, Ill.: Free Press.

————. 1966. Modernization: protest and change. Englewood Cliffs, N.J.: Prentice-Hall.

————. 1971. *Political sociology.* New York: Basic Books.

————. 1973. *Tradition, change, and modernity.* New York: Wiley.

Ellul, Jacques. 1968. *A critique of the new commonplaces.* Trans. Helen Weaver. New York: Knopf.

Emerson, Rupert. 1963. *Political modernization: the single-party system.* Denver: University of Denver Press.

Emmanuel, Arghiri. 1972. *Unequal exchange: a study of the imperialism of trade.* New York: Monthly Review Press.

Evans, Peter. 1971. National autonomy and economic development: critical perspectives on multinational corporations in poor countries. *International Organization* 25: 675–92.

————. 1972. The developmental effects of direct investment. Paper presented at the annual meeting of the American Sociological Association, New Orleans.

Fallers, Lloyd. 1963. Political sociology and the anthropological study of African politics. *European Journal of Sociology* 4: 311–25.

Finsterbusch, K. 1973. Recent rank ordering of nations in terms of level and rate of development. *Studies in Comparative International Development* 8: 52–70.

Frank, André Gunder. 1965. *Capitalism and underdevelopment in Latin America.* New York: Monthly Review Press.

————. 1966. The development of underdevelopment. *Monthly Review* 18: 17–31.

————. 1969. *Latin America: underdevelopment or revolution.* New York: Monthly Review Press.

————. 1971. On the mechanisms of imperialism: the case of Brazil. In *Readings in U.S. Imperialism*, ed. K. T. Fann and D. C. Hodges, pp. 237–56. Boston: Porter Sargent.

————. 1972. The development of underdevelopment. In *Dependence and underdevelopment*, ed. J. D. Cockcroft, A. G. Frank, and D. Johnson, pp. 3–17. New York: Doubleday.

————. 1977. Long live transideological enterprise. *Review* 1 (summer): 91–140.

Freeman, John, and Hannan, Michael T. 1975. Growth and decline processes in organizations. *American Sociological Review* 40: 215–28.

Freeman, John, and Kronenfeld, Jerold. 1973. Problems of definitional dependency. *Social Forces* 52: 108–21.

Fröbel Folker; Heinrichs, Jürgen; and Kreye, Otto. 1977. The tendency towards a new international division of labor. *Review* 1 (summer): 73–90.

Fuguitt, Glen, and Lieberson, Stanley. 1974. Correlation of ratios of difference scores having common terms. In *Sociological methodology 1973–4*, ed. H. Costner, pp. 128–44. San Francisco: Jossey-Bass.

Furtado, Celso. 1965. Development and stagnation in Latin America: a structuralist approach. *Studies in Comparative International Development* 1: 159–75.

————. 1973. The post-1964 Brazilian "model" of development. *Studies in Comparative International Development* 8: 115–127.

Galeano, E. 1971. Latin America and the theory of imperialism. In *Readings in U.S. imperialism*, ed. K. T. Fann and D. C. Hodges, pp. 205–24. Boston: Porter Sargent.

Galtung, Johan. 1971. A structural theory of imperialism. *Journal of Peace Research* 8: 81–117.

Gause, G. F. 1934. *The struggle for existence*. Baltimore: Williams and Wilkins.

Geertz, Clifford. 1973. *The interpretation of cultures*. New York: Basic Books.

Gilpin, Robert, 1975. *U.S. power and the multinational corporation: the political economy of direct foreign investment*. New York: Basic Books.

Girling, Robert. 1973. Dependency and persistent income inequality. In *Structures of dependency in Latin America*, ed. Frank Bonilla and Robert Girling, pp. 46–62. Stanford, Ca.: Institute for Political Studies.

Girvan, Norman. 1973. The development of dependency economics in the Caribbean and Latin America. *Social and Economic Studies* 22: 1–33.

Glazer, Nathan, and Moynihan, Daniel P. 1975a. *Ethnicity: theory and experience*. Cambridge: Harvard University Press.

————. 1975b. Introduction. In *Ethnicity: theory and experience*, ed. N. Glazer and D. P. Moynihan, pp. 1–26. Cambridge: Harvard University Press.

Glezakos, C. 1973. Export instability and economic growth—a statistical verification. *Economic Development and Cultural Change* 31: 670–78.

Gobalet, Jeanne G., and Diamond, Larry J. 1977. Effects of investment dependence on economic growth: the role of internal structural characteristics. Stanford, Ca.: Stanford University Dept. of Sociology.

Godwin, R. Kenneth. 1974. Two thorny theoretical tangles: the relationship between personality variables and modernization. *Journal of Developing Areas* 8: 181–98.

Goldberger, Arthur S. 1971. Econometrics and psychometrics: a survey of communalities. *Psychometrika* 36: 83–108.

Goode, William. 1963. *World revolution and family patterns.* New York: Free Press.

Gray, Clive S. 1969. *Resource flows to less-developed countries.* New York: Praeger.

Griffin, Keith B., and Enos, J. L. 1970. Foreign assistance: objectives and consequences. *Economic Development and Cultural Change* 18: 313–27.

Haaland, Gunnar. 1969. Economic determinants in ethnic processes. In *Ethnic groups and boundaries,* ed. F. Barth, pp. 58–73.

Hannan, Michael T. 1971. *Aggregation and disaggregation in sociology.* Lexington, Ma.: Heath-Lexington.

————. 1976. Methodological problems in analyzing the effects of educational organizations on social structure. Paper presented at the conference on youth, higher education, and social change, Warsaw.

Hannan, Michael T., and Freeman, John. 1974. Environment and the structure of organizations. Paper presented at the annual meeting of the American Sociological Association, Montreal.

————. 1977. The population ecology of organizations. *American Journal of Sociology* 82: 929–64.

————. 1978. Internal processes of growth and decline. In *Environment and organization,* ed. M. Meyer et al., pp. 177–99. San Francisco: Jossey-Bass.

Hannan, Michael T., and Meyer, John W. 1973. Education and economic development: some baseline models. Stanford, Ca.: Stanford University Dept. of Sociology.

Hannan, Michael T.; Rubinson, Richard; and Warren, Jean. 1974. The causal approach to measurement error in panel analysis: some further contingencies. In *Measurement in the social sciences,* ed. H. M. Blalock, Jr., pp. 293–324. Chicago: Aldine.

Hannan, Michael T., and Young, Alice A. 1977. Estimation in panel models: results on pooling cross-sections and time series. In *Sociological methodology,* ed. D. Heise, pp. 52–83. San Francisco: Jossey-Bass.

Hansen, David, and Haller, Archibald. 1973. Status attainment of Costa Rican males: a cross-cultural test of a model. *Rural Sociology* 38: 266–67.

Harbison, Frederick. 1973. *Human resources as the wealth of nations.* New York: Oxford University Press.

Harbison, Frederick, and Myers, Charles. 1964. *Education, manpower, and economic growth.* New York: McGraw-Hill.

Harris, Marvin. 1964. *Patterns of race in the Americas*. New York: Walker.

Hart, C. W. M. 1963. Contrasts between prepubertal and postpubertal education. In *Education and culture*, ed. George Spindler, pp. 400–425. New York: Holt, Rinehart.

Hayter, Teresa. 1971. *Aid as imperialism*. Baltimore: Penguin.

Hechter, Michael. 1974*a*. *Internal colonialism: the Celtic fringe in British national development 1536–1966*. Berkeley: University of California Press.

―――. 1974*b*. The political economy of ethnic change. *American Journal of Sociology* 79: 1151–78.

―――. 1975. Review of I. Wallerstein, *The modern world-system*. *Contemporary Sociology* 4: 217–22.

Heilbroner, Robert L. 1972. *The making of economic growth*. 4th ed. Englewood Cliffs, N.J.: Prentice-Hall.

Heise, David R. 1970. Causal inference from panel data. In *Sociological methodology 1970*, ed. E. Borgatta and G. Borhnstedt, pp. 3–27. San Francisco: Jossey-Bass.

Henderson, C. R. 1952. Specific and general combining ability. In *Heterosis*, ed. J. W. Gowens, pp. 352–70. Ames: Iowa State College Press.

―――. 1963. Selection index and expected genetic advance. In *Statistical genetics and plant breeding*, Publication No. 982, pp. 141–62. Washington: National Academy of Sciences.

Henderson, C. R., Jr. 1971. Comment on 'The use of error components models in combining cross-section with time-series data'. *Econometrica* 39: 397–401.

Heyneman, Stephen. 1976. Influences on academic achievement: a comparison of results from Uganda and more industrialized societies. *Sociology of Education* 49: 200–11.

Hirschman, Albert. 1958. *The strategy of economic development*. New Haven: Yale University Press.

Hobsbawm, Eric. 1968. *Industry and empire*. Harmondsworth, Middlesex, England: Penguin.

Holsinger, Donald. 1975. Education and the occupational attainment process in Brazil. *Comparative Education Review* 19: 267–75.

Hoogvelt, A., and Child, D. 1973. Rhodesia: economic blockade and development. *Monthly Review* 25: 41–50.

Hopkins, Terence K. 1969. Third world modernization in transnational perspective. *Annals of the American Academy of Political and Social Sciences* 386: 126–36.

Hopkins, Terence K., and Wallerstein, Immanuel. 1977. Patterns of development in the modern world-system. *Review* 1 (fall): 111–45.

Horowitz, Donald L. 1975. Ethnic identity. In *Ethnicity: theory and experience*, ed. N. Glazer and D. P. Moynihan, pp. 111–40. Cambridge: Harvard University Press.

Horowitz, Irving Louis. 1972. *Three worlds of development*. New York: Oxford University Press.

318   REFERENCES

Horowitz, Irving Louis, and Trimberger, Ellen Kay. 1976. State power and military nationalism in Latin America. *Comparative Politics* 8: 223–44.

Hoselitz, Bert. F. 1960. Social structure and economic growth. In *Sociological aspects of economic growth*, ed. B. F. Hoselitz, pp. 23–51. Glencoe, Ill.: Free Press.

Hummon, Norman P.; Doreian, Patrick; and Teuter, Klaus. 1975. A structural control model of organizational change. *American Sociological Review* 40: 691–700.

Huntington, Samuel P. 1968. *Political order in changing societies*. New Haven: Yale University Press.

Hurley, N. P. 1975. University satellite for Latin America. *Journal of Communications* 25: 157–64.

Hutchinson, G. E. 1957. Concluding remarks. *Cold Spring Harbor symposium on quantitative biology* 22: 415–27.

Illich, Ivan. 1970. *Deschooling society*. New York: Harper and Row.

Inkeles, Alex. 1971. Continuity and change: the interaction of the personal and the sociocultural systems. In *Stability and social change*, ed. B. Barber and A. Inkeles, pp. 265–81. Boston: Little, Brown.

Inkeles, Alex, and Smith, D. 1974. *Becoming modern: individual change in six developing countries*. Cambridge: Harvard University Press.

International Bank for Reconstruction and Development. 1971. *World tables*. Washington: IBRD.

———. 1973. *World economic atlas*. Washington: IBRD.

International Labor Organization. 1972. *Yearbook of labor statistics*. Geneva: ILO.

International Labour Organization. 1971. *Labour force projections*. Parts 1–5. Geneva: ILO.

International Monetary Fund. 1957. *Supplement to balance of payments yearbook, 1950–1964*, Vol. 8. Washington: IMF.

———. 1950–1955. *Balance of payments yearbook*, Vols. 1–5. Washington: IMF.

———. 1966. *Supplement to balance of payments yearbook, 1960–1964*, Vol. 17. Washington: IMF.

———. 1972. *International financial statistics supplement, 1972*. Washington: IMF.

International motion picture almanac. n.d. Various editions. New York: Quigley.

Jalée, P. 1965. *The pillage of the third world*. New York: Monthly Review Press.

Jencks, Christopher. 1972. *Inequality: a reassessment of the effects of family and schooling in America*. New York: Basic Books.

Johnson, Dale L. 1972. Dependence and the international system. In *Dependence and underdevelopment*, ed. J. D. Cockcroft, A. G. Frank, and D. L. Johnson, pp. 71–111. New York: Doubleday, Anchor Books.

Johnson, John J., ed. 1962. *The role of the military in underdeveloped countries*. Princeton: Princeton University Press.

Johnston, J. 1972. *Econometric methods.* 2d ed. New York: McGraw-Hill.

Jöreskog, Karl G. 1969. A general approach to confirmatory maximum likelihood factor analysis. *Psychometrika* 38: 183–202.

———. 1970. A general method for analysis of covariance structures. *Biometrika* 57: 239–51.

———. 1973. A general method for estimating a linear structural equation system. In *Structural equation models in the social sciences*, ed. A. S. Goldberger and O. D. Duncan, pp. 88–112. New York: Academic Press.

Jöreskog, Karl E.; Gruvaeus, G. T.; and van Thillo, M. 1971. ACOVS: a general computer program for analysis of covariance structures. Research Bulletin. Princeton: Educational Testing Service.

Kahl, Joseph. 1968. *The measurement of modernism.* Austin: University of Texas Press.

Kaufman, Robert L. 1976. The solution and interpretation of differential equation models. *American Sociological Review* 41: 746–47.

Kaufman, Robert R.; Geller, Daniel S.; and Chernotsky, Harry I. 1975. A preliminary test of the theory of dependency. *Comparative Politics* 7: 303–31.

Kenny, David A. 1973. Cross-lagged and synchronous common factors in panel data. In *Structural equation models in the social sciences*, ed. A. S. Goldberger and O. D. Duncan, pp. 153–67. New York: Seminar Press.

Keohane, Robert, and Nye, Joseph S. 1970. *Transnational relations and world politics.* Cambridge: Harvard University Press.

Kim, C. I. Eugene. 1976. Transition from military rule: the case of South Korea. In *Political participation under military regimes*, ed. Henry Bienen and David Morell, pp. 24–38. Beverly Hills, Ca.: Sage.

Klapp, Orrin. 1969. Collective search for identity. New York: Holt, Rinehart and Winston.

Knudsen, Dean D. 1969. The declining status of women: popular myths and the failure of functionalist thought. *Social Forces* 48: 183–93.

Krader, Lawrence. 1968. *Formation of the state.* Englewood Cliffs, N.J.: Prentice-Hall.

Krasner, Stephen. 1976. State power and the structure of international trade. *World Politics* 28: 317–347.

Kristeva, Julie. 1975. On the women of China. *Signs: Journal of Women in Culture and Society* 1: 57–91.

Kuh, Edward, and Meyer, John R. 1955. Correlation and regression estimates when the data are ratios. *Econometrica* 23: 400–16.

Kuznets, Simon. 1971. *Economic growth of nations.* Cambridge: Harvard University Press.

LaPalombara, J., and Weiner, M. 1966. *Political parties and political development.* Princeton: Princeton University Press.

Lazarsfeld, Paul; Pasanella, Ann K.; and Rosenberg, Morris. 1972. *Continuities in the language of social research.* New York: Free Press.

Leff, N. H. 1968. The exportable surplus approach to foreign trade in under-developed countries. *Economic Development and Cultural Change* 17: 346–55.

Lenin, V. I. 1965 (1916). *Imperialism: the highest stage of capitalism.* Peking: Foreign Language Press.

Lenski, Gerhard. 1966. *Power and privilege.* New York: McGraw-Hill.

———. 1976. History and social change. *American Journal of Sociology* 82: 548–64.

Lenski, Gerhard, and Lenski, Jean. 1978. *Human societies: an introduction to macrosociology.* 3d ed. New York: McGraw-Hill.

Lent, J. A. 1975. The price of modernity. *Journal of Communications* 25: 128–35.

Levin, J. L. 1966. *The export economies.* Cambridge: Harvard University Press.

Levin, S. A. 1970. Community equilibria and stability, and an extension of the competitive exclusion principle. *American Naturalist* 104: 413–23.

Levins, Richard. 1968. *Evolution in changing environments.* Princeton: Princeton University Press.

———. 1973. The limits of complexity. In *Hierarchy theory: the challenge of complex systems,* ed. H. Pattee, pp. 109–27. New York: George Braziller.

Lieberson, Stanley. 1961. A societal theory of race relations. *American Sociological Review* 26: 902–08.

———. 1970. *Language and ethnic relations in Canada.* New York: Wiley.

Lieberson, Stanley, and Hansen, Lynn K. 1974. National development, mother tongue diversity, and the comparative study of nations. *American Sociological Review* 39: 523–541.

Lipset, Seymour Martin. 1960. *Political man: the social bases of politics.* Garden City, N.Y.: Doubleday, Anchor Books.

———. 1963. *The first new nation.* Garden City, N.Y.: Doubleday.

Lodhi, Abdul Q., and Tilly, Charles. 1973. Urbanization, crime and collective violence in 19th century France. *American Journal of Sociology* 79: 296–318.

Lundgren, Peter. 1976. Educational expansion and economic growth in nineteenth-century Germany: a quantitative study. In *Schooling and Society,* ed. Lawrence Stone, pp. 20–66. Baltimore: Johns Hopkins University Press.

Luxemburg, Rosa. 1968 (1913). *The accumulation of capital.* New York: Monthly Review Press.

MacArthur, Robert H. 1972. *Geographical ecology: patterns in the distribution of species.* Princeton: Princeton University Press.

MacArthur, Robert H., and Levins, Richard. 1964. Competition, habitat selection and character displacement in a patchy environment. *Proceedings of the National Academy of Sciences* 51: 1207–10.

McBean, A. 1966. *Export instability and economic development.* Cambridge: Harvard University Press.

McClelland, David C. 1966. Does education accelerate economic growth? *Economic Development and Cultural Change* 14: 257–78.

Machlup, Fritz. 1970. *Education and economic growth*. Lincoln: University of Nebraska Press.

Magdoff, Harry. 1969. *The age of imperialism—the economics of U.S. foreign policy*. New York: Monthly Review Press.

Maizel, A. 1968. *Export and economic growth of developing countries*. Cambridge: Cambridge University Press.

Malinowski, Bronislaw. 1930. Parenthood—the basis of social structure. In *The new generation*, ed. V. P. Calverton and S. D. Schmalhausen, pp. 113–68. New York: Macauley.

Malinvaud, E. 1970. *Statistical methods in econometrics*. Amsterdam: North-Holland.

Mandel, Ernest. 1975. *Late capitalism*. London: New Left Books.

Marshall, T. H. 1948. *Citizenship and social class*. New York: Doubleday.

————. 1964. *Class, citizenship, and social development*. New York: Doubleday.

Marx, Karl. 1853. The future results of British rule in India. *New York Tribune—Selected Works* 2: 657–64.

————. 1967 (1867). *Capital*, vol. 1. New York: International Publishers.

May, Robert M. 1973a. *Stability and complexity in model ecosystems*. Princeton: Princeton University Press.

————. 1973b. Ecological systems in randomly fluctuating environments. In *Progress in theoretical biology*, ed. R. Rosen and F. Snell, pp. 1–50. New York: Academic Press.

Mazrui, Ali. 1971. Pluralism and national integration. In *Pluralism in Africa*, ed. Leo Kuper and M. G. Smith, pp. 333–50. Berkeley: University of California Press.

Meier, Gerald M. 1976. *Leading issues in economic development*. New York: Oxford University Press.

Merriam, Charles. 1931. *The making of citizens*. Chicago: University of Chicago Press.

Meyer, John W. 1970. The charter: conditions of diffuse socialization in schools. In *Social processes and social structures*, ed. W. R. Scott, pp. 564–78. New York: Holt, Rinehart and Winston.

————. 1971. Comparative research on the relationships between political and educational institutions. In *Politics and education*, ed. M. Kirst and F. Wirt, pp. 564–78. Lexington, Ma.: Heath.

————. 1977. The effects of education as an institution. *American Journal of Sociology* 83: 55–77.

Meyer, John W.; Boli-Bennett, John; and Chase-Dunn, Christopher. 1975. Convergence and divergence in development. *Annual Review of Sociology* 1: 223–46.

Meyer, John W.; Hannan, Michael T.; and Rubinson, Richard. 1973. National economic growth, 1950–1965; educational and political factors. Presented at the SEADAG Seminar on Education and National Development, Singapore.

Meyer, John W., and Rubinson, Richard. 1975. Education and political development. *Review of research in education* 3: 134–62.

Michels, Robert. 1959 (1915). *Political parties: a sociological study of the oligarchical tendencies of modern democracy*. Trans. Eden Paul and Cedar Paul. New York: Dover Publications.

Mintz, Sydney W. 1977. The so-called world system: local initiative and local response. *Dialectical Anthropology* 2: 253–70.

Moore, Barrington. 1966. *Social origins of dictatorship and democracy: lord and peasant in the making of the modern world*. Boston: Beacon Press.

Moore, Wilbert, and Feldman, David. 1960. *Labor commitment and social change in developing areas*. New York: Social Science Research Council.

Moran, Theodore. 1974. *Multinational corporations and the politics of dependence: copper in Chile*. Princeton: Princeton University Press.

———. 1973. Transnational strategies of protection and defense by multinational corporations. *International Organization* 27: 273–301.

Morley, Samuel A.. 1975. What to do about foreign direct investment: a host country perspective. *Studies in Comparative International Development* 10: 45–56.

Mulhall, Michael G. 1892. *The dictionary of statistics*. London: G. Routledge and Sons.

———. 1903. *The dictionary of statistics*. 4th ed. London: G. Routledge and Sons.

Myrdal, Gunnar. 1957. *Rich nations and poor*. New York: Harper and Row.

Narroll, Raoul. 1964. Ethnic unit classification. *Current Anthropology* 5: 283–312.

Naya, S. 1973. Fluctuation of export earnings and economic patterns in Asian countries. *Economic Development and Cultural Change* 21: 69–41.

Nerlove, Marc. 1971. Further evidence of the estimation of dynamic economic relations from a time-series of cross-sections. *Econometrica* 39: 341–58.

Ness, Gayl, and Ness, Jeannine. 1972. Metropolitan power and the demise of the overseas empires. Paper presented at the annual meetings of the American Sociological Association, New Orleans.

Nielsen, François. 1974. The interrelationship of educational and economic institutions: pooling of cross-sections and heteroscedasticity. Stanford, Ca.: Stanford University Dept. of Sociology.

Nkrumah, K. 1967. Neo-colonialism: the last stage of imperialism. *Science and Society* 31: 78–81.

O'Connor, J. 1970. International corporations and economic underdevelopment. *Science and Society* 34: 42–59.

———. 1971. The meaning of economic imperialism. In *Readings in U.S. imperialism*, ed. K. T. Fann and D. C. Hodges, pp. 23–68. Boston: Porter Sargent.

O'Laughlin, Carleen. 1971. *National economic accounting*. Oxford: Pergamon.

Park, Robert E. 1950. *Race and culture*. Glencoe. Ill.: Free Press.

Parsons, Talcott. 1958. The school class as a social system. *Harvard Educational Review* 29: 297–318.

———. 1971. *The system of modern societies*. Englewood Cliffs, N.J.: Prentice-Hall.

———. 1975. Some theoretical considerations on the nature and trends of change in ethnic identity. In *Ethnicity: theory and experience*, ed. N. Glazer and D. P. Moynihan, pp. 53–83. Cambridge: Harvard University Press.

Paukert, Felix. 1973. Income distribution at different levels of development. *International Labor Review* 108: 97–125.

Payer, Cheryl. 1971. The perpetuation of dependence: the IMF and the third world. *New York Monthly Review* 23: 37–50.

———. 1974. *The debt trap*. Harmondsworth, Middlesex, England: Penguin.

Pearson, Lester. 1969. *Partners in development*. New York: Praeger.

Pelz, D. C., and Andrews, F. M. 1964. Causal priorities in panel study data. *American Sociological Review* 29: 836–48.

Petras, J. 1968. U.S.–Latin American studies: a critical assessment. *Science and Society* 23: 148–68.

———. 1974. The U.S.–Cuban policy debate. *Monthly Review* 26: 22–33.

Pinto, Anibal, and Knakal, Jan. 1973. The centre-periphery system 20 years later. *Social and Economic Studies* 22: 34–89.

Polanyi, Karl. 1944. *The great transformation*. Boston: Beacon.

Portes, A. 1973a. Modernity and development: a critique. *Studies in Comparative International Development* 8: 247–79.

———. 1973b. Factorial structure of modernity. *American Journal of Sociology* 79: 15–44.

———. Forthcoming. The informal sector and the world-economy. *Institute for Development Studies Bulletin*. Sussex: University of Sussex.

Prebisch, R. 1950. *The economic development of Latin America and its principal problems*. New York: United Nations.

Przeworski, Adam, and Teune, Henry. 1970. *Logic of comparative social inquiry*. New York: Wiley.

Quinlan, Daniel. 1978. World economic position and national development. Ph.D. dissertation, Johns Hopkins University.

Ramirez, Francisco. 1974. Societal corporateness and status conferral: a comparative analysis of the national incorporation and expansion of educational systems. Ph.D. dissertation, Stanford University.

Ramirez, Francisco O.; Rubinson, Richard; and Meyer, John. 1973. National educational expansion and political development: causal interrelationships, 1950–1970. Presented at the SEADAG Seminar on Education and National Development, Singapore.

Rapkin, David P. 1976. Trade, dependence and development: a longitudinal analysis. Paper presented at the annual meeting of the Southern Political Science Association, Atlanta.

Resiner, E. H. 1927. *Nationalism and education since 1789*. New York: Macmillan.

Ricardo, David. 1933 (1817). *Principles of political economy and taxation*. London: Dent.

Riesman, D.; Glazer, N.; and Denney, R. 1950. *The lonely crowd*. New Haven: Yale University Press.

Rogers, Everett. 1963. *Diffusion of innovations*. Glencoe, Ill.: Free Press.

———. 1969. *Modernization among peasants: the impact of communication*. New York: Holt, Rinehart and Winston.

Rokkan, Stein. 1970. *Citizens, elections and parties*. New York: David McKay.

———. 1975. Dimensions of state-formation and nation-building: a possible paradigm for research on variations within Europe. In *The formation of national states in western Europe*, ed. Charles Tilly, pp. 562–600. Princeton: Princeton University Press.

Rollins, C. E. 1956. Mineral development and economic growth. *Social Research* 23: 253–80.

Rostow, W. W. 1962. *The process of economic growth*. New York: W. W. Norton.

Routh, Guy. 1965. *Occupation and pay in Great Britain, 1906–1960*. Cambridge: Cambridge University Press.

Rubinson, Richard. 1974. The political construction of education. Ph.D. dissertation, Stanford University.

———. 1976. The world-economy and the distribution of income within states: a cross-national study. *American Sociological Review* 41: 638–59.

———. 1978. Political transformation in Germany and the United States. In *Social change in the capitalist world economy*, ed. Barbara H. Kaplan, pp. 39–74. Beverly Hills, Ca.: Sage.

Ruys, Manu. 1973. *The Flemings: a people on the move, a nation in being*. Tielt, Belgium: Lannoo.

Samuelson, Paul A. 1970. *Foundations of economic analysis*. New York: Atheneum.

Samuelsson, K. 1961. *Religion and economic action*. New York: Basic Books.

Schelling, Thomas C. 1958. *International economics*. Boston: Allyn and Bacon.

Schuessler, Karl. 1973. Ratio variables and path models. In *Structural equation models in social science*, ed. A. S. Goldberger and O. D. Duncan, pp. 201–28. New York: Seminar Press.

———. 1974. Analysis of ratio variables: opportunities and pitfalls. *American Journal of Sociology* 80: 379–96.

Schultz, T. W. 1963. *The economic value of education*. New York: Columbia University Press.

Schumpeter, Joseph. 1939. *Business cycles*. New York: McGraw-Hill.

Seidman, A., and Green, R. H. 1970. Old motives, new methods: foreign enterprises in Africa today. In *African perspectives: papers in the history, politics and economics of Africa,* ed. C. Allen and R. W. Johnson, pp. 251–72. London: Cambridge University Press.

Selsam, H.; Golday, D.; and Martel, H. 1970. *Dynamics of social change: a reader in Marxist social science.* New York: International Publishers.

Shils, Edward. 1971. No salvation outside higher education. *Minerva* 6: 313–21.

Shorter, Edward, and Tilly, Charles. 1974. *Strikes in France.* Cambridge: Cambridge University Press.

Sideri, Sandro. 1970. *Trade and power: informal colonialism in Anglo-Portuguese relations.* Rotterdam: Rotterdam University Press.

Simon, Herbert A. 1973. The organization of complex systems. In *Hierarchy theory,* ed. H. Patee, pp. 1–28. New York: George Braziller.

Singer, Hans. 1950. The distribution of gains between investing and borrowing countries. *American Economic Review* 40: 473–85.

Slobodkin, L. B. 1961. *Growth and regulation of animal populations.* New York: Holt, Rinehart and Winston.

Smelser, Neil J. 1959. *Social change in the industrial revolution.* Chicago: University of Chicago Press.

———. 1963. Mechanisms of change and adjustment to change. In *Industrialization and society,* ed. B. F. Hoselitz and W. E. Moore, pp. 32–54. Paris: UNESCO/Mouton.

Smith, A .D. 1973. *The concept of social change: a critique of the functionalist theory of social change.* London: Routledge and Kegan Paul.

Smith, E. S. 1971. *Religion, politics and social change in the third world.* New York: Free Press.

Snyder, David, and Tilly, Charles. 1972. Hardship and collective violence in France, 1830–1960. *American Sociological Review* 37: 520–32.

Solow, R. 1957. Technical progress and the aggregate production function. *Review of Economics and Statistics* 39: 312–20.

Spence, Michael. 1973. Job market signalling. *Quarterly Journal of Economics* 87: 355–375.

Stanley, Manfred. 1972. *Social development.* New York: Basic Books.

Steadman, Henry J. 1970. Some causal priorities in the development of national education systems and economic growth. Paper presented at the annual meeting of the American Sociological Association.

Stein, Stanley, and Stein, Barbara. 1970. *The colonial heritage of Latin America.* New York: Oxford.

Stephenson, J. B. 1968. Is everyone going modern? A critique and a suggestion for measuring modernism. *American Journal of Sociology* 74: 265–75.

Stinchcombe, Arthur L. 1965. Social structure and organizations. In *The handbook of organizations,* ed. James G. March, pp. 153–93. Chicago: Rand McNally.

———. 1968. *Constructing social theories.* New York: Harcourt, Brace and World.

Stoneman, Colin. 1975. Foreign capital and economic growth. *World Development* 3: 11–26.

Sunkel, Osvaldo. 1973. Transnational capitalism and national disintegration in Latin America. *Social and Economic Studies* 22: 132–76.

Swanson, Guy. 1958. *Birth of the gods.* Ann Arbor: University of Michigan Press.

———. 1976. *Religion and regime.* Ann Arbor: University of Michigan Press.

———. 1971. An organizational analysis of collectivities. *American Sociological Review* 36: 607–23.

Szymanski, Albert. 1972. Dependence, exploitation and development. Eugene: University of Oregon Dept. of Sociology.

———. 1973. Military spending and economic stagnation. *American Journal of Sociology* 79: 1–14.

Tanzer, Michael. 1969. *The political economy of international oil and the underdeveloped countries.* Boston: Beacon.

Tardanico, Richard. 1978. A structural perspective on state power in the capitalist world-system. Paper presented at the annual meeting of the American Sociological Association, San Francisco.

Taylor, Charles L., and Hudson, M. C. 1971. *World handbook of political and social indicators,* vol. 2. Ann Arbor, Michigan: Interuniversity Consortium for Political Research, University of Michigan.

Thompson, James D. 1967. *Organizations in action.* New York: McGraw-Hill.

Thompson, Kenneth. 1971. Universities and the developing world. In *The task of universities in a changing world,* ed. S. Kertesz. South Bend, Ind.: University of Notre Dame Press.

Thurow, Lester. 1975. *Generating inequality.* New York: Basic Books.

Tilly, Charles. 1964. *The Vendée.* Cambridge: Harvard University Press.

———. 1973. Do communities act? *Sociological Inquiry* 43: 209–240.

Tilly, Charles, ed. 1975. *The formation of national states in Western Europe.* Princeton: Princeton University Press.

Trimberger, Ellen. 1972. A theory of elite revolutions. *Studies in Comparative International Development* 7: 191–207.

———. 1976. *Revolution from above.* New Brunswick, N.J.: Transaction Press.

Tugwell, F. 1974. Petroleum policy in Venezuela: lessons in the politics of dependence management. *Studies in Comparative International Development* 9: 184–220.

Tyack, David. 1966. Forming the national character. *Harvard Educational Review* 36: 29–41.

United Nations. 1951. *Yearbook of international trade statistics, 1950.* New York: United Nations.

———. 1963. *Yearbook of international trade statistics, 1961.* New York: United Nations.

United Nations Conference on Trade and Development. 1969. *Handbook of international trade and development statistics.* New York: United Nations.

United Nations Educational, Scientific, and Cultural Organization. 1955. World survey of education. Vol. 1, *Handbook of Educational organization and statistics.* Geneva: United Nations.

————. 1958. *World survey of education.* Vol. 2, *Primary education.* Geneva: United Nations.

————. 1961. *World survey of education.* Vol. 3, *Secondary education.* Geneva: United Nations.

————. 1966. *World survey of education.* Vol. 4, *Higher education.* Geneva: United Nations.

————. 1950–1971. *Statistical yearbook.* Vols. 2–23. Louvain, Belgium: Belgium: UNESCO.

————. 1958. Book production 1937–1954 and translations 1950–1954. In *UNESCO statistical report,* Statistical Division, Doc. ST/S/21.

Van Gennep, Arnold. 1960. *The rites of passage.* Chicago: University of Chicago Press.

Vernon, Raymond. 1971. *Sovereignty at bay: the multinational spread of U.S. enterprises.* New York: Basic Books.

Viner, Jacob. 1952. America's aims and the progress of underdeveloped areas. In *The progress of underdeveloped areas,* ed. B. F. Hoselitz, pp. 175–202. Chicago: University of Chicago Press.

Volterra, V. 1931. Variations and fluctuations of the number of individuals in animal species living together. *Animal ecology,* ed. R. Chapman, pp. 412–14, 423–33. New York: McGraw-Hill.

von der Mehden, Fred. 1964. *The politics of developing nations.* Englewood Cliffs, N.J.: Prentice-Hall.

Von Eschen, D. 1975. Three structural theories of economic development. Paper presented at the annual meeting of the American Sociological Association, San Francisco.

Walleri, R. Dan. 1976. The political economy of international inequality: a test of dependency theory. Ph.D. dissertation, University of Hawaii.

Wallerstein, Immanuel. 1960. Ethnicity and national integration in West Africa. *Cahiers d'études Africaines* 1: 129–39.

————. 1969. *Africa: the politics of unity.* New York: Random House.

————. 1972. Three paths of national development in sixteenth century Europe. *Studies in Comparative International Development* 7: 95–101.

————. 1974a. *The modern world-system.* New York: Academic Press.

————. 1974b. The rise and future demise of the world capitalist system: concepts for comparative analysis. *Comparative Studies in Society and History* 16: 387–415.

————. 1974c. Dependence in an interdependent world: the limited possibilities of transformation within the capitalist world economy. *African Studies Review* 17: 1–26.

————. 1976a. Class conflict in the capitalist world-economy. Binghamton, N.Y.: Fernand Braudel Center.

————. 1976b. American slavery and the capitalist world-economy. American Journal of Sociology 81: 1199–1213.

————. 1976c. Semi-peripheral countries and the contemporary world crisis. Theory and Society 3: 461–83.

Warren, Jean 1973. An ecological analysis of the expansion of national education systems. Ph.D. dissertation, Stanford University.

Waterston, A. 1965. Development planning: lessons of experience. Baltimore: Johns Hopkins University Press.

Weber, M. 1958. The protestant ethic and the spirit of capitalism. Trans. Talcott Parsons. New York: Scribner's.

Weinberg, Ian, and Walker, Kenneth, 1969. Student politics and political systems. American Journal of Sociology: 75: 77–96.

Weiss, Jane A.; Ramirez, Francisco O.; and Tracy, Terry. 1976. Female participation in the occupational system: a comparative institutional analysis. Social Problems 23: 593–608.

Werts, Charles E.; Jöreskog, K. G.; and Linn, R. L. 1973. Indentification and estimation in path analysis with unmeasured variables. American Journal of Sociology 78: 1469–84.

White, Leslie. 1959. The evolution of culture: the development of civilization to the fall of Rome. New York: McGraw-Hill.

————. 1960. Foreword. In Evolution and Culture, ed. M. D. Sahlins and E. K. Service, pp. v–xii. Ann Arbor: University of Michigan Press.

Williamson, Oliver E. 1975. Markets and hierarchies: analysis and anti-trust implications. New York: Free Press.

Young, Frank W. 1965. Initiation ceremonies: a cross-cultural study of status dramatization. New York: Bobbs-Merrill.

Young, R. 1970. The plantation economy and industrial development. Economic Development and Cultural Change 18: 343–60.

Index

Adelman, I., 141, 204
Amin, S., 134, 285
Analysis of covariance structures (ACOVS), 120
Andean Pact, 149
Anderson, C., 88

Baggara, 259
Banks, A., 120
Baran, P., 119, 133, 136
Barker, E., 225
Barrat-Brown, M., 150 n.3
Barth, F., 255–62, 265, 270
Beckford, G., 135, 142, 148–49
Bell, D., 275 n.10
Bendix, R., 5, 79, 138
Bergesen, A., 188
Blaug, M., 82 n.3
Boli-Bennett, J., 226
Bonacich, E., 272
Book translations, 171–74, 179–81
Bornschier, V., 207
Boulding, K., 158
Bowman, M., 88
Breton Woods, 285, 287

Capital flows, 137–38, 139, 303
Capital formation: and economic dependence, 141, 144–45, 147; and economic development, 92, 99
Capitalism: causes and contradictions of, 289–90; decline and fall of, 287, 294–95; and Marx's concept of class struggle, 295 n.2; as the structure of the world economy, 52, 277–78, 281–82
Chase-Dunn, C., 140, 207, 212, 218
Chirot, D., 296 n.4
Citizenship: as a factor in political incorporation, 239; as the link between individualism and socialism, 232–33; and marriage, 247; rights and duties of, 225, 235–37, 283; role of education in, 79–80

Coercion, 123, 209
Coleman, J., 275 n.12
Colonization and decolonization, 190–91, 280, 283–84, 288, 292. *See also* Independence
Commodification, 279, 290–91
Commodities trade dependence. *See* Dependence
Communist nations: economic growth in, 114 n.7, 115 n.22; state power and authority in, 90, 114 n.7
Compulsory education, 79, 82 n.3
Confirmatory factor analysis, 119–20
Constitutions: coding format (provisions) of, 225–26, 235–37; as world-system ideology, 222–25, 231–35
Coppock, J., 156
Core nations: competition between, 279, 285–87; economic description of, 277; expansion of state constitutional authority in, 228, 233–35; exploitation of peripheral nations by, 131–37, 139, 148, 150 n.4, 210–11, 283–84; state strength in, 220; trade with periphery by, 279, 287–89. *See also* Informational and value imports; National development and wealth; Raw materials export
Cross-lag effect, 23, 33 n.2
Cutright, P., 204

Debt dependence. *See* Dependence
Delacroix, J., 150 n.3, 207
Democratic regimes, 203–5
Dependence: alternatives to, 149, 177, 184 n.4; definition of, 131–32; as a factor in the centralization of state power, 195, 197–99; as a factor in economic development, 132–39, 142–46, 148–50, 207–8, 217–20; as a factor in educational expansion, 39, 46, 48–49, 54; as a factor in ethnic dynamism, 273–74; as a factor in government revenues, 212–17, 220; as a

329